THE FIGHT AGAINST BIG TOBACCO

The Movement, the State, and the Public's Health

SOCIAL PROBLEMS AND SOCIAL ISSUES

An Aldine de Gruyter Series of Texts and Monographs

SERIES EDITOR

Joel Best, *University of Delaware*

THE FIGHT
AGAINST
BIG TOBACCO

The Movement, the State, and the Public's Health

Mark Wolfson

ALDINE DE GRUYTER

New York

About the Author

Mark Wolfson is Associate Professor and Director for Community Research, Department of Public Health Sciences, the Wake Forest University School of Medicine. His research has been funded by both governmental and private research grants.

ALDINE DE GRUYTER
A division of Walter de Gruyter, Inc.
200 Saw Mill River Road
Hawthorne, New York 10532

This publication is printed on acid free paper ⊗

Library of Congress Cataloging-in-Publication Data

Wolfson, Mark, 1953–
  The fight against big tobacco : the movement, the state, and the public's health / Mark Wolfson.
        p. cm. – (Social problems and social issues)
Includes bibliographical references and index.
  ISBN 0-202-30597-X (cloth : acid-free paper) – ISBN 0-202-30598-8 (Paper : acid-free paper)
  1. Antismoking movement – Minnesota.   2. Antismoking movement – United States.   I. Title.   II. Series.
  HV5767.M6 W65   2001
    362.29'67'0973–dc21   00-012616
Manufactured in the United States of America

10 9 8 7 6 5 4 3 2 1

To my father and the memory of my mother

Contents

Preface

The genesis of this book begins in an unusual place: Gate 20 of the old University of Minnesota football stadium, since demolished to make room for the scarcest resource on the campus of an urban university (parking). In the fall of 1990, I had begun my first faculty position in the Division of Epidemiology in the University of Minnesota School of Public Health (UMSPH). The division at the time was spread across a couple of buildings on the East Bank campus of the UM, including a couple of suites of offices that had been built in the innards of the old football stadium, where my office was located. Despite its unprepossessing outward and inward appearance, Gate 20 and Gate 27 of the old stadium had an impressive history and present, including being the location at which Dr. Ancel Keys did the pioneering research that resulted in the development of the K-ration.

I had trained as a sociologist at the Catholic University of America. My areas of focus were organizations and social movements, and I had the great fortune of having the opportunity to work as a research assistant for a top sociologist of social movements, and wonderful mentor, John McCarthy, who has since moved on to Penn State. When I began working with him in 1984, John had just received the first of two National Science Foundation grants to study the citizens' movement against drinking and driving. John, Debra Harvey, Teresa Ankney, and I (John Crist joined the project at a later stage) surveyed over four hundred local anti-drinking-and-driving citizens' groups throughout the country, with an eye to understanding the interaction of organizational and environmental factors in explaining the emergence, growth, development, and impact of these groups.

After a California stint (postdoctoral fellowships at Stanford and the Alcohol Research Group in Berkeley), I accepted a faculty position in public health at the University of Minnesota. My work on collective action on drinking and driving was timely, in that public health, as a field of research and practice, was increasingly interested in community organizing and advocacy as means of achieving changes in the social environment that would be beneficial to public health. I quickly became involved in what is called in the parlance of public health an "observational" study of enforcement of alcohol age-of-sale and purchase/possession laws and an "intervention" study testing the effectiveness of a community-organizing model to reduce youth access to alcohol, both with Alex Wagenaar. This was interesting work, and built in many ways on my sociological interests in organizations and social movements as well as my recent evolution into a public health "expert" on adolescent alcohol use.

Meanwhile, I was hearing a lot about the growing tobacco control movement in Minnesota from two of my colleagues at Minnesota, Jean Forster and Mary Hourigan. Jean and Mary had done some pioneering work on youth access to tobacco in several Minneapolis-St. Paul metropolitan area communities, and had developed close ties with the two key movement organizations—the Association for Nonsmokers-Minnesota (ANSR) and the Minnesota Coalition for a Smoke Free Society-2000. Mary had worked at the coalition for a time, and Jean was on the board of both ANSR and the coalition. They both had worked closely with activists and staff from both organizations.

I was intrigued by this public health movement. I had of course read newspaper accounts of the movement over the years, and had used Troyer and Markle's (1983) book, *Cigarettes: The Battle over Smoking* in a Social Problems course I taught in graduate school. Proposition 99 was passed in California while I was a postdoc in the Bay Area, and I had followed the debates and mobilization efforts that surrounded its passage. It seemed apparent to me that tobacco control was a growing social movement in a critical area of public health. And I knew, through the help of my colleagues, that I could gain access to the movement. Mary and Jean were both excited about the idea of an analysis of tobacco control in Minnesota as a social movement, and gave me lots of encouragement, as well as "sponsorship" with movement activists. Coming from the University of Minnesota School of Public Health also gave me credibility with the activists.

I succeeded in obtaining a couple of small grants from the UM and entered the field. I quickly discovered that tobacco control leaders were extremely proud of the movement's accomplishments in the state, and wanted to share their perspectives and experiences with me as a way of making sure that the story would get told. My training in social movements had left in me an appreciation of the importance of understanding the "social infrastructure" on which movements build, and I knew going in that Minnesota had built heavily on the infrastructure of health care and public health. What I had not fully appreciated at the outset was the close, collaborative relationship between government (or "state") actors and the leaders of tobacco control movement organizations. I remember vividly attending my first meeting of the Smoke Free Coalition's public policy committee, which was mapping out strategy for the upcoming 1992 legislative session. I was struck by the fact that, here at one table, strategizing together, were members of single-issue social movement organizations (the Coalition and ANSR, the latter of which is considered the "radical flank" of the movement), two of the three health voluntaries [American Cancer Society (ACS) and American Lung Association (ALA)], representatives of medical societies, and government officials and staff—primarily from the Minnesota Department of Health. The more interviews I conducted, meetings I attended, and archival materials I read, the more I was struck by this integral relationship between movement and state actors—a relationship I came to characterize as "state/movement interpenetration."

In this book, I develop these two themes—building on the infrastructure of health, and state-movement interpenetration, to try to understand the emergence, growth, and outcomes of the tobacco control movement in Minnesota. I focus on both the advantages and constraints associated with these two themes. And I attempt to assess the generalizability of the pattern I observed in Minnesota to the movement in other states and other countries and to other social movements.

It was difficulty to decide on a starting and ending point for my assessment of the movement. In the early part of my research on the movement, I glanced up at the Sierra Club Wilderness Calendar in my study and saw this quote from Emerson, which brought home my dilemma: "The method of nature: who could ever analyze it? That rushing stream will not stop to be observed. We can never surprise nature in a corner; never find the end of a thread; never tell where to set the first stone." Ultimately, I decided on the Surgeon General's 1964 (USDHEW 1964) report as a starting point for the movement as a whole; I picked up the Minnesota narrative in the early 1970s with the effort to pass the Minnesota Clean Indoor Air Act. I kept trying to "leave the field" and focus only on writing (and my other professional and personal responsibilities), but this proved difficult, because things kept changing and important and significant events kept happening, in Minnesota and nationally. For all intents and purposes, I completed my field work around 1995-1996, although I have made an effort to reflect the incredibly important developments in the tobacco control movement, in Minnesota and nationally, in the late 1990s.

I am deeply indebted to many individuals who contributed, in a variety of ways, to the completion of this book. Several former colleagues from the University of Minnesota were instrumental in helping me conceptualize the book, introducing me to the tobacco control movement in Minnesota, and providing ongoing support and encouragement for the project. In the earliest phases of this project, while she was at the School of Public Health, Mary Hourigan helped me obtain initial funding for the project, helped link me to the movement, and served as a combination advisor/informant (in the anthropological sense)/motivator/visionary. Jean Forster also provided me with enormous insights and support all along the way. I also benefited greatly from early discussions with Harry Lando of the

UMSPH. John McCarthy (then at Catholic University) and Ron Troyer (at Drake University) also provided me with encouragement and advice at an early stage of this project.

I enjoyed the assistance of a long succession of talented, insightful, and industrious staff over the course of this project. I want to thank the research assistants whose efforts contributed to this book, including Jill Elnicki, Anne Edwards, Kevin Sitter, Doreen Kloehn, Johanna Rosenthal, Francie Mantak, April Pickrel, David Grosvenor, Dan Stewart, Abbey Sidebottom, Nina Alesci, and Anita Hege. I also want to thank the secretarial staff who helped with transcribing interviews and preparing the manuscript. They include Anne Edwards, Jan Gangelhoff, Lee Kubiak Brown, Monica Brownrigg, Stefani Conyers, Margie Konopliv, and especially Debbie Allen, who provided many hours of assistance in checking references and preparing the final manuscript. Thanks to all.

I want to thank several people who reviewed drafts of the book and made insightful suggestions at various points along the way, including Brian Powers, John McCarthy, David Altman, Tracy Enright Patterson, and Dan Zaccaro. Richard Koffler at Aldine and Joel Best provided excellent input on both content and form. Thanks especially to Richard for his encouragement, support, and patience.

I want to thank the many movement activists, who were incredibly generous in taking the time to share their experiences and insights with me. I want to especially thank the president of ANSR, Jeanne Weigum, who willingly submitted to not one but two marathon interviews, allowed me to poke around in ANSR's files, and invited me to attend board meetings. Similarly, staff, board members, and volunteers from ANSR, the Minnesota Smoke-Free Coalition-2000, the American Cancer Society, the American Lung Association, and other organizations were incredibly cooperative and helpful. Thanks, too, to over one thousand activists and members of tobacco control organizations who took the time to fill out and return my survey. There is a great deal of sophistication among participants of this movement. Several of the main themes of the book have been articulated in one form or another by activists in the movement. I acknowledge my debt to theorizing and conceptualization that has taken place within the movement.

I would like to acknowledge the contributions of several funders for their direct or indirect support for this project. A National Institutes of Health Biomedical Research Support Grant, awarded to me by the University of Minnesota School of Public Health, and a grant from the Graduate School of the University of Minnesota provided support for the first stages of this research. This support enabled me to conduct a first round of in-depth interviews with movement activists and a survey of rank and file members and affiliates of movement organizations. A grant from the Nonprofit Sector Research Fund of the Aspen Institute provided funding for a survey of organizations involved in tobacco control efforts at the state and local level throughout the country. The Substance Abuse Policy Research Program of the Robert Wood Johnson Foundation funded a related study on enforcement of tobacco age-of-sale laws, which I draw on at times in the book.

The grant from the Robert Wood Johnson Foundation raises an important issue. I have received research grants and consultation fees from a number of organizations that play a role in the tobacco control movement and, as a consequence, are discussed in this book. They are the Robert Wood Johnson Foundation, from which I have received research funding for a study of enforcement of tobacco age-of-sale laws and consultation fees or honoraria for reviewing grant proposals and other work for the foundation. Similarly, I have served as a coinvestigator on a research study funded by the National Cancer Institute, and have received consultant fees for participating in NCI grant review panels. I have also provided pro bono consultation services to many of the tobacco control organizations that I discuss in the book, including the Association of Nonsmokers-Minnesota and the Minnesota Division of the American Cancer Society. I at times write about colleagues and friends, including several former colleagues from the University of Minnesota School of Public Health, where I was on the faculty in the early and mid-1990s. I have tried to maintain "critical distance" in thinking and writing about these actors with whom I have had, and in some cases continue to have, relationships of various kinds. Needless to say, it is up to the reader to decide whether I have been successful in maintaining this distance.

Finally, I want to thank my family—Clara, Lily, and Adam—for their support and forbearance over the long course of this project. I look forward to reclaiming our weekends and evenings together.

1

Social Movement Theory and Tobacco Control

INTRODUCTION

Tobacco use—smoking and use of smokeless tobacco—is the leading preventable cause of death in the United States. The Centers for Disease Control and Prevention estimated that cigarette smoking was responsible for over four hundred thousand deaths in 1990, including 30% of all cancer deaths and 21% of all cardiovascular disease deaths (Centers for Disease Control and Prevention, 1993a).[1] A telling statistic, often cited by tobacco control advocates, is that the number of deaths from tobacco use in the United States is greater than the number of deaths from alcohol use, motor vehicle accidents, suicides, AIDS, homicides, illegal drugs, and fires combined (Lynch and Bonnie, 1994).

Tobacco's toll is not limited to the United States. According to estimates by the World Health Organization and the World Bank, in 1990 over three million deaths throughout the globe—six percent of all deaths—were attributable to tobacco use (Murray and Lopez, 1996). Only malnutrition accounted for more deaths.

Over the past twenty-five years, a formidable social movement has emerged in response to this vital public health problem. A number of organizations play key roles in this movement. These include nonprofit advocacy organizations, such as Action on Smoking and Health (ASH), Americans for Nonsmokers Rights (ANR), Doctors Ought to Care (DOC), Stop Teenage Access to Tobacco (STAT), the Group Against Smokers' Pollution (GASP), and the Campaign for Tobacco-Free Kids. The "health voluntaries"—the American Cancer Society, American Heart Association, and American Lung Association—are also key actors in the movement. Associations of health professionals—such as the American Medical Association and state medical societies—have demonstrated active involvement in tobacco control advocacy. Finally, federal, state, and local government agencies have played central roles in the tobacco control movement.[2]

Over the course of the second half of the twentieth century, the tobacco control movement has become an important agent of social change. The movement has succeeded in educating the public about the health risks of tobacco use, changing social norms concerning tobacco use, reducing smoking rates, and encouraging the adoption of federal, state, local, and private-sector policies discouraging tobacco use. While the movement has not succeeded in a number of important areas—most notably, reducing smoking rates among adolescents and eliminating disparities in smoking by socioeconomic status—it has grown to be a major force in contemporary U.S. society, and has significantly altered how many of us lead our lives.

How has this movement become such a large and pervasive force? This book develops two central arguments to answer this question. First, the tobacco control movement was able to grow rapidly by building on a rich "infrastructure" of health organizations and health professionals. Ironically, the movement's base in these institutions has in some ways constrained the issues it has pursued and the strategies and tactics it has used to pursue them. Second, the movement has an integral relationship with government, a relationship that I characterize as state-movement "interpenetration." This relationship has also contributed to the movement's rapid growth and its widespread influence. And again, the relationship has imposed important constraints on the tactics and strategies employed in the movement. As explained in the following section, this relationship also presents a challenge to our theoretical understandings of state-movement relations.[3]

THEORY AND RESEARCH ON SOCIAL MOVEMENTS

It is reasonable to ask whether tobacco control efforts fall within the domain of social movement theory. Efforts to control the use of tobacco—especially those that use political means to achieve policy changes—are widely considered to be a social movement. For example, proponents of tobacco control often refer to these efforts as a "movement" (e.g., Pertschuk and Erickson, 1987). Moreover, tobacco control advocates seek social changes that go beyond individual changes in behavior. In the past twenty years—especially in the past ten—a key distinction has been made between persuading people to change their behavior (e.g., smoking) and changing the social and legal environment that enables and supports tobacco use. In the words of longtime nonsmokers' rights activist and scientist, Stanton Glantz, "the health community [historically] viewed the problem of smoking in a medical rather than a social and environmental context, in which the focus should be on the smoker (the patient) rather than on the environment, which moves into politics" (Glantz, 1987:746).

This approach is embodied in enactment of laws that prohibit smoking in restaurants and other public places; restrictions on the availability of tobacco to youth through commercial sources such as convenience stores, grocery stores, and vending machines; and increases in state and federal taxes on cigarettes and smokeless tobacco products.[4]

Finally, advocacy organizations have played a central role in efforts to achieve these changes. In both the area of clean indoor air and youth access to tobacco, local, grassroots activism has played a key role, especially in the earlier years in the development of these two areas, before government agencies became heavily involved in advocacy efforts [see Glantz 1987 on clean indoor air and Sylvester 1989 on youth access to tobacco].[5] Thus, common usage, a focus on structural change, and involvement in advocacy support the application of the term "social movement" to tobacco control efforts, and the use of social movement theory to understand them, and to further develop this body of theory.

The analysis presented in this book is informed by theory and research on social movements over the past twenty-five years. Work on social movements during this period has been guided by several theoretical perspectives. Resource mobilization theory (McCarthy and Zald, 1977) developed in response to earlier perspectives on social movements, which emphasized the irrational or expressive aspects of social movements (e.g., Turner and Killian, 1972; Kornhauser, 1959; Gurr, 1970; Davies, 1962). Resource mobilization theory, as developed and articulated by Zald and Ash (1966), Oberschall (1973), McCarthy and Zald (1973, 1977), Gamson (1990), and Jenkins (1983), emphasizes the central role that resources—including money, volunteer labor, legitimacy, and expertise—play in social movements. Analysts drawing on this perspective have assessed the ways in which the amount and types of resources available to groups affect the emergence, form, and impact of collective action (McCarthy and Zald, 1973; Staggenborg, 1986; Gamson, 1990; Wolfson, 1995a; Jenkins and Eckert, 1986).

A second set of analysts, whose perspective has sometimes been characterized as "political process" theory, emphasize the role that "political opportunity" plays in explaining the emergence and trajectory of social movements (Jenkins and Perrow, 1977; McAdam, 1982; Tarrow, 1994; Tilly, 1978).[6] According to McAdam, these writers "saw the timing and fate of movements as largely dependent upon the opportunities afforded insurgents by the shifting institutional structure and ideological disposition of those in power" (1996:23). Based on the work of Tarrow (1994) and other analysts, McAdam (1996:27) and colleagues (1996:10) have developed a list of the dimensions of political opportunity:

1. The relative openness or closure of the institutionalized political system.

2. The stability or instability of that broad set of elite alignments that typically undergird a polity.
3. The presence or absence of elite allies.
4. The state's capacity and propensity for repression.

A third theoretical perspective that has informed recent social movement research is concerned with "framing" processes (Snow et al., 1986; Snow and Benford, 1992; Gamson and Meyer, 1996; Benford and Snow, 2000). Work on framing represents a deliberate attempt to bring a concern with culture and meaning back into the study of social movements (Benford and Snow, 2000). Specifically, this work is concerned with the ways in which activists and other participants in movements actively create common understandings underlying collective action. "Framing work" seeks to define a particular state of affairs as being in need of redress. For example, tobacco control advocates have worked to define children's access to cigarettes through vending machines and stores as an unacceptable threat to children's health (see Chapter 2). Similarly, activists have argued that exposure of nonsmokers to secondhand smoke at work, in public transportation, restaurants, and stores is an unacceptable infringement on the rights of nonsmokers (see Chapters 2, 3, and 4). Activists also work to create "frames" for responding to an unacceptable shared grievance. For example, the idea that people should band together to lobby their city council or state legislature to enact laws restricting youth access to tobacco, or to enact laws prohibiting smoking in certain work and public settings, is—usually—not a matter of a lightbulb going off in someone's head. Rather, activists work hard to define these or other concrete activities as appropriate responses to a state of affairs defined as in need of action. Framing is contentious work, since government agencies and other authorities, scientists, industries whose products or behavior are the target of regulatory efforts, countermovements, and factions within a social movement may actively promote alternative definitions of (1) whether a particular state of affairs constitutes a problem, and (2) appropriate responses to the problem (Meyer and Staggenborg, 1996; Benford and Snow, 2000).

Finally, new social movement (NSM) theory is concerned with explaining the emergence and dynamics of contemporary social movements (Melucci, 1980; Touraine, 1981; Laraña et al., 1994; Kriesi et al., 1995; Pichardo, 1997). It distinguishes these "new" social movements—such as environmental movements, peace movements and movements opposing the deployment of nuclear weapons, and gay rights movements, from past movements—in particular, from working-class movements of the past (Pichardo, 1997). It is argued that the emergence of these movements is tied to the shift in Western countries from an industrialized to a postindustrial economy. These movements tend to be concerned with quality of life issues associated with the new economy, rather than issues of resource allocation. These movements, it is argued, are largely rooted in the middle class, and issues of self-identity are said to play a central role in explaining movement participation (Pichardo, 1997; Buechler, 1995).

In a recent review and synthesis of work on social movements, McAdam and colleagues (1996) argued that work by analysts from each of these perspectives on or theories of social movements has converged on a core set of factors used to explain the emergence and development of social movements. One of these factors is "mobilizing structures," which are defined as "those collective vehicles, informal as well as formal, through which people mobilize and engage in collective action" (McAdam et al., 1996:3). This concept of mobilizing structures includes informal and formal social groups that movements may build on, including friendship networks, neighborhoods, work networks, churches, unions, and professional associations (McCarthy, 1996:145). It also includes formal and informal groups that are "dedicated" to (i.e., are singularly meant to be used to) advance the goals of the movement. Examples include informal activist networks as well as formally organized social movement organizations (SMOs), among others (McCarthy, 1996:145).

A second category of factors is political opportunities. As explained above, the concept of political opportunity is meant to describe the political environment in which a movement operates and with which it interacts. It includes the degree of openness of the formal political structure to advocacy efforts, the nature of alignments between powerful "elites," actual alliances between movements and these elites, and the state's ability and inclination to repress a movement (McAdam, 1996:27; McAdam et al., 1996:10).

The third set of factors identified in the review and synthesis by McAdam and colleagues (1996) falls under the rubric of "framing processes." As discussed above, this term is meant to capture the efforts of movement participants to create and promote interpretations or "meanings" of events and situations in such as way as to catalyze collective action.

This book will draw on previous theoretical and empirical work on social movements—especially the emerging synthesis, described above—to help understand the tobacco control movement. In particular, two streams of the literature that are part of this synthesis are especially germane to this study. The first stream follows from the concern with "mobilizing structures." Specifically, I will draw from theory and research concerned with the ways in which movements are built on preexisting patterns of social relations (or social "infrastructure"), and the consequences of this for the ways in which a movement is structured and its goals are framed, the tactics and strategies it employs, its growth trajectory, and its impact.

The second stream of social movement theory and research deals with the relationships between "the state" and movements. Clearly, this work falls squarely within the focus on political opportunity. Although I will draw from the insights of past work on this topic, I will argue that existing theory and research on states and social movements is inadequate to the task of understanding the tobacco control movement. In fact, the pattern in the tobacco control movement does not seem to "fit" any of the existing conceptualizations of state-movement relations. Thus, one aim of this book is to develop a new model of this relationship, one that I term state-movement "interpenetration."

THE SOCIAL INFRASTRUCTURE OF MOVEMENTS

A spate of recent scholarship on social movements has explored the ways in which movements emerge from and are shaped by existing associational "infrastructures," such as churches, block clubs and other networks based in neighborhoods, friendship networks, fraternal organizations, and unions (Morris, 1984; McAdam, 1982; Oberschall, 1973; Snow et al., 1980; Rosenthal et al., 1985; McCarthy, 1987; Gould, 1993). Although he drops the term in later work, and subsumes infrastructure into the concept of "mobilizing structures," McCarthyprovides this definition and examples:

> [T]he range of everyday life micromobilization structural social locations that are not aimed primarily at movement mobilization, but where mobilization may be generated: these include family units, friendship networks, voluntary associations, work units, and elements of the state structure itself. . . . I mean to include all of the institutions commonly included within the boundaries of the concept "civil society" as well as institutional structures of the state and the economy that serve as relational contexts for insurgent mobilization. (1996:141, 364)

A classic example of this is the way that the 1960s civil rights movement built on existing structures in the South, including historically black colleges and universities, black churches, and local chapters of the NAACP (Morris, 1984). The extent to which a movement can build on existing sets of organizations and relationships depends on a number of factors. The first such factor is the degree to which the problem that a movement addresses, and the strategies and tactics it uses to address them, can be articulated—or, in the language of recent analyses of social movements, "framed"—in a way that is consistent with the belief systems, aspirations, life experiences, and interests of these organizations and associations and the people in them (Benford and Snow, 2000; Jenkins and Wallace, 1996; McCarthy and Wolfson, 1992) In addition, the amount and quality of resources in organizations and networks will affect the ability of a movement to build organizations, recruit members and other adherents, and engage in collective action.[7]

The analysis presented in this book represents, in part, an attempt to identify the kinds of infrastructures from which the tobacco control movement emerged and gained support—including money, labor, space, equipment, expertise, and goodwill. It also represents an attempt to understand how these bases of support have shaped the movement's development. For example, many individuals trained in various medical specialties, nursing, and public health have played important leadership and activist roles in the movement. In addition, many of the key organizational actors in the movement are health organizations. While building on the "infrastructure" of health organizations and professions has facilitated the rapid growth and development of the movement, it has also constrained it in important ways—for example, in selection of issues, strategies, and tactics, and in the characteristics of the adherents it attracts, as we shall see in subsequent chapters.

STATES AND SOCIAL MOVEMENTS

The state plays a prominent role in many recent accounts of social movements. Analysts operating from a variety of theoretical perspectives—resource mobilization, political process, new social movements, framing—have emphasized the important role of the state in shaping the emergence, growth, and decline of movements (McCarthy and Zald, 1977; McAdam, 1982; Jenkins and Klandermans, 1995).

How has the relationship between the state and movements been theorized? I argue that writing on this subject has been dominated by three images of the state's role in these relationships: (1) as a target, (2) as a provider of constraints and opportunities, and (3) as a facilitator or sponsor. Throughout the book, and especially in Chapters 7 and 10, I use case materials from the tobacco control movement to see how well the case conforms to existing conceptualizations. I argue that existing approaches do not do a good job of characterizing or explaining the empirical pattern found in the tobacco control movement. A new model of the state/movement relationship is suggested by my analysis of this movement. This model describes the "interpenetration" of state and movements.

Conceptualizations of State-Movement Relations

The most pervasive image of the relationship of states and movements is the state as target of the movement. For example, social movement organizations often seek formal recognition of their claims to a voice on policy issues within a particular issue arena (Tilly, 1978; Gamson, 1990). Tilly has termed the achievement of formal access "polity entry" and Gamson "acceptance" by authorities. It is argued that entry into the polity, and consequent access to institutionalized means of influence, represents a qualitative change in the potential influence of groups on government decision-making (Tilly, 1978).

In addition to formal recognition, social movement activists and organizations seek "concessions" from government and other authorities (Gamson, 1990). These concessions are as varied as social movement demands. Some of the more commonly noted concessions are passage of legislation, appropriations, court decisions, and policy changes by administrative agencies. There is a growing literature on the effects of social movement organization, tactics, strategies, and ideology on state decisions to grant such concessions (Amenta et al., 1994; Gamson, 1990; Burstein, 1985; Freeman, 1975; Broadbent, 1989; Wolfson, 1995a; Giugni, 1998). Regardless of whether a movement seeks formal recognition or concessions, the image is one of movement actors applying pressure on the state, using a variety of strategies and tactics, to meet its demands.

A second conceptualization is that states represent or create a system or systems of constraints and opportunities faced by movements. This view is embodied in the concept of "political opportunity," which was introduced above. The focus is on structural features of political systems that are related to the relative degree of openness or permeability of the system [what Eisinger has termed the "structure of political opportunities" (1973:11)], such as the openness of the formal political system, the stability of elite alignments, and the presence of elite allies (McAdam, 1996:27; also see Kitschelt, 1986; McAdam et al., 1996:10; Jenkins and Perrow, 1977; McAdam, 1982; Tarrow, 1994; and Tilly, 1978).

Several authors have used the idea of political opportunity to explain the comparative development, trajectory, and outcomes of social movements. For example, Kitschelt (1986) applied a conceptual scheme depicting political opportunity to the antinuclear power movements in Sweden, the United States, France, and West Germany.[8] He found that the level of mobilization and extent of the impact of the movement in each nation could be explained in large measure by the political opportunity structure. Similarly, the political system of the Unites States, lacking such features of European democracies as proportional representation and parliamentary government, has been used to explain the failure of socialism to take root [Howe (1985); see also Lipset (1950) for a similar analysis of socialism in the Canadian provinces] and the prevalence of single-issue, nonpartisan social movements in the United States (Jenkins, 1983). Finally, at the level of local government in the United States, the reformed government structure, consisting of "non-partisan elections, at-large constituencies and manager governments [has been] associated with a lessened responsiveness of cities to the enduring conflicts of political life" (Lineberry and Fowler, 1967:715).

A third image of the relationship of states and social movements affords a more active role for the state than in the first two conceptualizations, described above. It focuses on active efforts by the state to either facilitate or repress a social movement. The actions of government authorities to repress collective action and destroy or incapacitate social movement organizations have received considerable attention (Tilly, 1978; Barkan, 1984; Gamson, 1990; Marx, 1979; della Porta, 1995, 1996). This work underscores the importance of decisions by authorities whether to permit or prohibit different forms or organizational sponsors of collective action. In addition, recent work has begun to examine subtler means of social control of social movements, such as the enforcement of Internal Revenue Service regulations concerning the tax-exempt status of nonprofit organizations in the United States (Mitchell, 1979; McCarthy et al., 1991).

Government authorities may also facilitate the efforts of social movements. For example, some authors have argued that foundation and federal government support for the U.S. civil rights movement was an important factor in the successes achieved by that movement (McCarthy and Zald, 1973, 1977). Others have argued that apparent facilitation by authorities often results in the co-optation or channeling of movements into adopting moderate goals and tactics (McAdam, 1982; Jenkins and Eckert, 1986; Helfgot, 1974; Piven and Cloward, 1977).

These themes—state as target, as provider of constraints and opportunities, and as facilitator or sponsor—are apt characterizations of many examples of state/movement relations. However, in the course of my study of the tobacco control activism in Minnesota, I was struck by the lack of fit of these conceptions with the pattern observed in that movement. In this book, I will present case material on the tobacco control movement and develop an alternative conception based on that movement.

METHODS

The book uses an extended case study approach, focusing on the early emergence and widespread growth of the tobacco control movement in Minnesota, but also drawing on secondary sources analyzing the movement in other states and nationally.

The study on which this book is based involved collection of both qualitative and quantitative data. Qualitative data are from fieldwork, including attending meetings of movement organizations, events sponsored by movement organizations, and city council and state legislative hearings. In addition, archival data from newspaper stories and organizational records were compiled, and in-depth interviews were conducted with movement leaders and activists and government officials in Minnesota. Quantitative data are from a survey of a 1992 stratified random survey of 1196 individuals affiliated with organizations involved in organized tobacco control efforts in Minnesota (see Wolfson, 1995b). In addition, a national survey of organizations involved in tobacco control advocacy efforts was conducted in 1996-1997. This survey is used in Chapter 10 to place the Minnesota experience in national context [see Wolfson (1997) for a detailed description of the methods used in this survey].

PLAN OF THE BOOK

This book develops two central arguments to understand how the tobacco control movement became a large and pervasive force for social change in the second half of the twentieth century. First, the tobacco control movement was able to grow rapidly by building on a rich "infrastructure" of health organizations and health professionals. Ironically, the movement's base in these institutions has to some extent constrained the issues it has pursued and the strategies and tactics it has used to pursue them. Second, the movement has an integral relationship with government, a relationship that I characterize as state-movement "interpenetration." This relationship has also contributed to the movement's rapid growth and to its widespread influence. And again, the relationship has constrained the tactics and strategies employed in the movement.

The book is divided into three parts. In this chapter (Chapter 1 of Part 1), I have introduced the topic of interest and the two streams of social movement theory and research that will be useful for the task at hand—the ways in which movements build on social infrastructure and state-movement relations. In Chapter 2, I present a capsule history of the tobacco control movement in the United States. I describe the social construction of the health consequences of smoking and smokeless tobacco use, which laid the intellectual groundwork for the movement. I then present the main policy strategies that government and movement organizations have pursued: smoking cessation programs, education and information campaigns, increased tobacco taxes, indoor air policy, youth access to tobacco, and limits on advertising. I then describe the structure of the movement in the United States: national, state, and local advocacy organizations; government and foundation-supported coalitions; health voluntary organizations; and organizations of health professionals. The chapter concludes with an overview of the history of the movement in Minnesota, which has led the nation in tobacco control policy and activism, in many cases serving as a model for efforts in other states.

Part 2 examines the constituent parts of the movement in Minnesota. As in most social movements, single-issue advocacy organizations have played a key role in the tobacco control movement. In Minnesota, two advocacy organizations have played a central role: the Association of Nonsmokers-Minnesota (ANSR) and the Minnesota Coalition for a Smoke-Free Society 2000 (Smoke-Free Coalition). Chapter 3 recounts the origins and early histories of both of these groups, including their involvement in passage of the 1985 Omnibus Bill on Nonsmoking and Health. Both of the major themes of this book—the way the movement has been built on a preexisting infrastructure of health organizations and health professionals, and the integral relationship between the state and the movement—are evident in this chapter. We also begin to see both the strengths and limitations of these two aspects of the tobacco control movement. Chapter 4 continues with a discussion of the more recent history of ANSR and the Smoke-Free Coalition.

Chapter 5 examines the role the "health voluntaries"—the American Lung Association, the American Heart Association, and the American Cancer Society have—have played in the movement in Minnesota—an important role, but one that is clearly secondary to that of the single-issue groups described in Chapters 3 and 4. The twin themes of the book reemerge in this chapter. The health voluntaries represented an organizational "infrastructure" on which the emerging movement could build in its early years. For example, ANSR, which is one of the two key single-issue organizations in the movement, began as a project of the American Lung Association. The other single-issue organization, the Smoke-Free Coalition, formed around a nucleus of health voluntaries along with a handful of other health organizations. These preexisting organizations, with considerable stores of resources, such as money, staff, volunteers, expertise, and legitimacy, facilitated the growth of the movement. In particular, the legitimacy of these organizations has helped legitimate both the movement as a whole and particular legislative initiatives. But, once again, the use of this infrastructure, and the resources associated with it, comes at a price. The voluntaries vigilantly protect their image as mainstream, highly legitimate organization, thus constraining choices of issues and tactics.

Chapter 6 examines the role of health care professionals and health care organizations in the movement. Health professionals—physicians, nurses, respiratory therapists, health educators, and others—play a key role in this movement, both individually and collectively. Individually, health professionals represent the largest occupational group active in the movement. They represent a key reservoir of potential volunteers who can be easily recruited into activism. In many ways, tobacco control activism may be viewed as a natural outgrowth or expansion of the traditional roles of health care providers, who come to move their efforts "upstream" to actively prevent, rather than just provide medical treatment for, emphysema, lung cancer, heart disease, and other medical conditions related to tobacco use. Organizations consisting of health professionals have also played an important role in the movement. In particular, state and local medical societies have made important contributions. As described in Chapter 3, the Smoke-Free Coalition grew out of the Hennepin County Medical Society and the Minnesota Medical Association in the mid-1980s. Moreover, the state medical society, its auxiliary (consisting of members' spouses—almost entirely wives), and local medical societies have been active members of the Smoke-Free Coalition, and major players in the medical society have played key leadership roles in the Smoke-Free Coalition.

Health care organizations—especially managed care organizations and health insurance companies—have also played an important role in the tobacco control movement in Minnesota. Blue Cross and Blue Shield of Minnesota, MedCenters Health Plan, and the Park Nicollet Medical Center were early sponsoring members of the Smoke-Free Coalition, but on the whole, did not play a very active role in the coalition or in the movement at large. In recent years, Blue Cross/Blue Shield and several of the large managed care organizations have come to play a more prominent role. For example, Blue Cross/Blue Shield was the prime mover behind the formation of the Tobacco Tax Coalition for a Healthy Minnesota in 1993, and jointly filed suit with the Minnesota Attorney General against the tobacco industry in 1994. In addition to becoming more prominent in the Smoke-Free Coalition and the Tobacco Tax Coalition, in the last few years managed care organizations have been increasingly visible on the issue of youth access to tobacco. I argue that this increase in involvement coincided with discovery of "population health" initiatives by health care organizations—particularly managed care organizations. In closing, this chapter returns to a recurring theme: the involvement of health care organizations has helped the movement grow, and has contributed considerable legitimacy, especially in the last few years. The entry of these organizations into the fray is significant, in that they devote considerable resources to lobbying, and they appear to be less constrained then the voluntaries.

Chapter 7 examines the role of the state in the tobacco control movement. Federal involvement in the tobacco control movement has primarily taken three forms: direct regulatory action (by rule or statute), sponsorship and publication of research and other materials, and attempts to catalyze state- and local-level collective action by providing technical assistance and funding.

In Minnesota, the Minnesota Department of Health (MDH) has been a central player in the movement. MDH's involvement in the movement can be traced back at least a decade and a half, to the publication of the Minnesota Plan for Nonsmoking and Health in 1984, which led to the creation of the Section for Nonsmoking and Health within MDH in 1985. In the late 1980s and early 1990s, MDH administered the state's nonsmoking and health program and participated in the Smoke-Free Coalition. However, MDH came to take on a much more prominent role in the movement with the advent of the NCI ASSIST Project in 1991. Minnesota is one of seventeen states that participated in ASSIST. ASSIST provided MDH with the resources to actively promote tobacco control efforts in a large number of local communities throughout the state. The Minnesota Attorney General (AG) is a second state agency that is heavily involved, in a proactive way, in tobacco control advocacy in the state and beyond. For example, the AG, in conjunction with a number of other state attorneys general, has worked to publicize the issue of children's exposure to secondhand smoke, and to encourage fast food restaurants and other businesses commonly patronized by youth to adopt voluntary smoke-free policies. In addition, the AG jointly filed a ground-breaking lawsuit with Blue Cross/Blue Shield against the seven largest tobacco companies and two trade organizations. This was the first such suit in the nation to allege antitrust conspiracy and consumer fraud. This chapter concludes with a discussion of the extent to which conventional images of state-movement relationships fit the pattern observed in the tobacco control movement. I argue that the conventional images of the state-movement relationship present an incomplete picture, and that the idea of state-movement "interpenetration" better characterizes the present case. In tobacco control, it is hard to know where the movement ends and the state begins. Although much of the movement is rooted in civil society—professional groups, the health voluntaries, health care organizations—it is next to impossible to think about the movement without thinking about the state. The state is not limited to being an external force that acts on, or is acted upon by, the movement, but is in fact an integral part of the movement.

Chapter 8 examines the opposition to the tobacco control movement. The main source of opposition to the tobacco control movement is economic interests that benefit from the agricultural production of tobacco and manufacture and sale of cigarettes and other tobacco products. First and foremost among these interests are a small number of cigarette manufacturers responsible for the vast majority of cigarettes sold and consumed in the United States and their trade associations. The tobacco industry has been quite successful in heading off meaningful federal-level controls on tobacco over the past twenty-five years—although the 1996 rules on tobacco and youth promulgated by the Food and Drug Administration (which have since been overturned in federal court) are a major exception. With a few exceptions, the industry has also enjoyed considerable influence in most state legislatures. However, the industry often lacks the manpower and credibility to consistently head off local legislation that it perceives to be harmful to its interests. This national pattern is reflected in Minnesota's experience.

The landmark Minnesota Clean Indoor Air Act, enacted in 1975, was the first comprehensive state clean indoor air act in the nation. It required the creation of separate smoking and nonsmoking areas in public buildings. The act, which has served as a model for other states, represented an important victory for the tobacco control movement. The industry, which had ignored the bill, awakened to the threat posed by the movement after its passage. The industry mobilized effectively to fight state tobacco control legislation in Minnesota and other state legislatures. Because Minnesota, along with a handful of other states, has led the nation in tobacco control advocacy and policy, the industry has devoted considerable resources to its political agenda in the state. The strategies the industry has employed in Minnesota are similar to those it has used in other states. It has sought passage of relatively weak restrictions at the state level that would preempt stronger measures at the local level. Another successful tactic of the industry at the state level has been to target key committee chairs to kill legislation. At the local level, representatives of the tobacco industry work closely with state and local retailing interests, most notably the Minnesota Grocers Association and the Minnesota Retail Merchants Association. This strategy is important because it projects an image of local interests, not just outside interests, acting in opposition to local ordinances regarding clean indoor air and youth access to tobacco. Finally, in Minnesota, as in a number of other states, smokers' rights groups have evolved (the Minnesota Smokers' Rights Coalition). These groups rely heavily on tobacco industry funding and technical assistance. While the groups are generally dismissed as tobacco industry front organizations by state and local policymakers, group leaders do have some visibility, and work hard to portray tobacco control efforts in a negative light.

Part 3 of the book begins (in Chapter 9) by examining the ways in which the organizations surveyed in Part 2 come together in "Arenas of Contention," such as the state legislature and city councils. Since the Smoke-Free Coalition's founding in 1984, the movement's legislative effort has been led by the Coalition's Public Policy Committee. With respect to state legislative efforts, ANSR works mainly as a member of the coalition, but sometimes takes the lead responsibility for lobbying under its own banner, especially in the area of clean indoor air legislation. ANSR also works separately from the coalition at times because it wishes to take a more aggressive position or use more aggressive tactics on a legislative issue.

Since passage of the Minnesota Clean Indoor Air Act in 1975, the movement has had something of a checkered record at the state legislature, due in large part to the tobacco industry's mobilization to opposed tobacco control measures at the state level. One of the most important victories was passage of the Omnibus Nonsmoking and Disease Prevention Act in 1985, which provided for staffing at MDH to implement the Minnesota Clean Indoor Act, raised the state cigarette tax, and earmarked a portion of this increase to support tobacco use prevention programs to be conducted by the Minnesota Department of Health and the Minnesota Department of Education. Since 1990, the movement's state legislative agenda has focused on three issues: additional restrictions on where smoking is allowed, youth access to tobacco, and increases in the state tobacco tax. Efforts to tighten up the Minnesota Clean Indoor Act—for example, to extend the coverage to factories, warehouses, and common areas of apartment buildings and condominiums—have encountered considerable tobacco industry opposition, and have not been successful. Similarly, post-1991 efforts to achieve meaningful increases in the state cigarette tax—increases that would actually reduce smoking rates, especially among adolescents—have also encountered substantial opposition, both from the tobacco industry and an avowedly antitax governor—and have met with defeat. Even an effort to broaden the coalition pursuing the tax in 1993, by earmarking part of the proposed increase to social service and health programs, did not succeed in obtaining the large increases being sought.

The movement was stymied for a number of years in the early and mid-1990s in trying to enact measures to increase restrictions on youth access to tobacco. In 1992, a bill passed that increased the penalties for tobacco retailers who sold to minors—but also penalized youth for purchase or possession of tobacco products by minors, a provision that was opposed by most in the tobacco control movement. In the 1996 session, the only victory that was achieved on youth access was not gaining passage of a movement-supported bill, but in narrowly blocking passage of a industry bill with weak statewide restrictions that would preempt stronger local actions. Finally, in 1997, the movement forces achieved a major victory in the area of youth access. Given the favorable national developments on youth access, and the string of defeats on the issue at the Minnesota legislature, there was a strong feeling among the Minnesota tobacco control forces that they needed a "win" in the 1997 session. Movement forces mobilized heavily and repeatedly throughout the legislative session, and, after a long and convoluted legislative battle, the Reducing Youth Access to Tobacco bill was enacted. The new law required licensing of all retail outlets selling tobacco products, mandatory once-a-year compliance checks by local authorities, and a ban on self-service sales of single packs of cigarettes. In addition to the restrictions on youth access to tobacco, the new law included new penalties—suspension of driver's license—for minors who purchase or attempt purchase tobacco products and for adults who lend their identification to minors to enable them to purchase tobacco products, and a requirement that manufacturers of cigarettes and smokeless tobacco submit an annual report to MDH disclosing the presence of ammonia, arsenic, cadmium, formaldehyde, and lead in their products.

In contrast to its uneven record at the state level, the movement has achieved a number of significant victories at the local level, where the industry often lacks the manpower and the legitimacy to prevail. Starting in the late 1970s, local tobacco control ordinances have passed in many Minnesota communities. For example, Minneapolis passed one of the first ordinances in the country restricting free distribution of cigarettes in 1979. In 1989, White Bear Lake, a Saint Paul suburb, became the first city in the nation to ban the sale of cigarettes through vending machines. Early on, passage of local ordinances was often the result of local advocacy, carried out largely by ANSR, the University of Minnesota School of Public Health, and, in recent years, local ASSIST coalitions. However, a natural diffusion process appears to have taken hold for at least some of these local policies. By 1993, 94% of Minnesota cities with populations greater than two thousand required licenses for tobacco retailers and 25% restricted vending machine sales in some way. Local-level tobacco control activism and policy innovation in Minnesota has drawn the attention of movement and government organizations throughout the nation.

Chapter 10 summarizes the findings of the book and their implications for understanding the tobacco control movement and for social movement theory and research. I begin by discussing the impact of the movement, including both intended and unintended consequences. I then summarize the findings of the book, including the ways in which the movement has built on the social infrastructure of health professionals and organizations, and the "interpenetration" of the movement and the state. I argue that the pattern of state-movement interpenetration has some generalizability beyond the tobacco control movement, and that it calls for an new or expanded model of the relationship between states and movements. I also argue that this relationship points to some important questions for social movement theory and research. These include strategic questions, such as the nature of the trade-offs inherent in state-movement interpenetration and the ways in which social movement organizations and state agencies negotiate the constraints associated with such relationships. They also include questions asking how and why interpenetration occurs. Finally, I offer some comments on the future of the tobacco control movement, focusing on the explosion of litigation in recent years, the development and growth of state tobacco control programs, and the issue of tobacco control in developing nations.

NOTES

1. Updated estimates by the CDC indicate that from 1990 through 1994, an average of 430,700 deaths each year were attributable to smoking (Malarcher et al., 1997).

2. The choice of the term "tobacco control movement" is deliberate, and I believe it reflects the predominant terminology within the movement itself (see Davis, 1995). This "framing" emphasizes the focus on regulating a harmful product—such as the way it is produced, taxed, marketed, and sold. In addition, the term is broad enough to apply to efforts to regulate products that are smoked (cigarettes, tobacco in pipes, and cigars) as well as smokeless (or "spit") tobacco products (chewing tobacco and snuff). Thus, the term "tobacco control movement" is preferred over "antismoking movement," "antismoker movement," and "anticigarette movement."

3. While I primarily focus in this book on the role of social infrastructure and the state, many factors are likely to have contributed to the rapid growth, and substantial impact, of the movement. These include the presence of an easily defined enemy that engaged in illegal activity and the success of efforts to galvanize support for tobacco control measures by framing the issue in terms of public health, protecting youth, and protecting the rights of nonsmokers. While I touch on all of these issues, several other accounts of the tobacco control movement feature them more prominently (see Troyer and Markle, 1983; Troyer, 1989; Glantz and Balbach, 2000; Nathanson, 1999; Kluger, 1996).

4. Thus, characterizing tobacco control efforts as a social movement is consistent with the classic definition of McCarthy and Zald: "A social movement is a set of opinions and beliefs in a population representing preferences for changing some elements of the social structure or reward distribution, or both, of a society" (1977:20).

5. Some may argue that the term "social movement" should be reserved for arenas of conflict in which noninstitutionalized strategies of social change predominate. I prefer to view the selection of tactics as contingent: organizations pursuing social change are continually making tactical decisions, sometimes using institutionalized methods, such as engaging in electoral politics, and other times using noninstitutionalized methods, such as protest. In the words of Tarrow "[m]ovements are not limited to particular types of action but have access to a variety of forms, either alone or in combination. It is their flexibility that allows them to combine the demands and the participation of broad coalitions of actors in the same campaigns of collective action" (1994:115).

6. In the interest of brevity, I strive here to characterize constellations of theoretical and empirical work by one or two overarching themes, such as resources or political opportunity. Of course, the actual picture is much more complicated. For example, "resource mobilization" theorists, such as McCarthy and Zald (1973, 1977), emphasized political opportunity as well as resources. Similarly, "political process" theorists often emphasized the importance of indigenous resources, such as the central role of black churches, black colleges, and local chapters of the

NAACP in the southern civil rights movement (McAdam, 1982; Morris, 1984). As argued below, work guided by each of the theoretical traditions discussed here (resource mobilization, political process, framing, and new social movements) has converged on a common set of factors to explain the emergence and course of social movements.

7. McCarthy (1987) has written of the richness and density of the infrastructures available to some movements, and the "infrastructural deficits" of other movements (or countermovements) as an explanation for differences in the growth trajectories of different movements. In addition, he argues that characteristics of social infrastructures across societies may help explain differences in the kinds of infrastructures that are utilized by movements in different societies. For example, church-based mobilization is more common in the United States than in other Western democracies because of higher rates of church affiliation.

8. Kitschelt identified four structural factors that influence the receptivity of systems to outside influence during the policy formulation stage:

"[1] The number of political parties, factions, and groups that effectively articulate different demands in electoral politics. . . .

"[2] [T]he capacity of legislatures to develop and control policies independently of the executive.

"[3] Patterns of intermediation between interest groups and the executive branch. . . .

"[4] [N]ew demands must find their way into the process of forming policy compromises and consensus. . . . There must be mechanisms that aggregate demands" (1986:63).

Similarly, Kitschelt offered three determinants of the capacity of states to implement their policies, which mitigate against influence by social movements during the implementation phase:

"[1] National policies are implemented more effectively when the state apparatus is centralized."

"[2] [G]overnment control over market participants is a key variable for government effectiveness in many policy areas."

"[3] Policy effectiveness is also determined by the relative independence and authority the judiciary enjoys in the resolution of political conflict." (1986:63–64).

2

Tobacco Use and Tobacco Control
in the United States

Tobacco, which is indigenous to the New World, was introduced in Europe in the early 1500s (Best, 1979; Harrison, 1986). Interest in its medicinal properties spread, and it rapidly became known as something of a panacea, used topically to treat a variety of skin conditions as well as gunshot wounds, and internally to treat a variety of maladies, including gonorrhea and the plague (Best, 1979; Harrison, 1986; Kluger, 1996). By the late sixteenth century, tobacco—usually smoked in pipes, but also chewed and taken as snuff—had also become popular as a "recreational" drug (Best, 1979; Harrison, 1986; Kluger, 1996; Tate, 1999).

In England and the other northern European countries, efforts were launched in the early seventeenth century to define smoking as deviant and regulate or prevent it. Tracts were issued—including one anonymously authored by King James I of England—that argued that tobacco use is (1) immoral and irresponsible (like drunkenness), (2) has negative health effects, (3) is "religiously offensive," (4) is "a habit of low prestige," and (5) contributes to an unfavorable balance of trade (since the "finest smoking tobacco" was imported from Spain's colonies) (Best, 1979; Harrison, 1986). In addition, heavy taxes were levied on tobacco imports in England, and laws prohibiting trading and smoking tobacco were enacted in many of the other Northern European nations (Best, 1979). However, the English authorities soon came to recognize the economic value of tobacco. Taxes on imports produced needed revenues, and the English colonies were heavily dependent on the tobacco crop. By the end of the seventeenth century, tobacco had been "vindicated" in England, which had come to treat tobacco production and trade as a protected industry and worked to influence other European countries to repeal their antitobacco laws (Best, 1979; Harrison, 1986; Kluger, 1996).

Tobacco control activism in the United States has occurred in two long waves. During the first wave, in the late nineteenth and early twentieth centuries, educators, physicians, and reformers, many of whom were involved in other movements (including the abolition, suffrage, and temperance movements), lobbied for restrictions on smoking (Gottsegen, 1940; Wagner, 1971; Sobel, 1978; Troyer and Markle, 1983; Tate, 1999).[1] While pipe smoking and snuff had been popular since colonial times, and chewing tobacco and cigar smoking grew over the course of the nineteenth century, it was the dramatic growth of cigarette smoking in the late 1800s and early 1900s that fueled the indignation, concern, and energies of the reformers (Gottsegen, 1940; Troyer and Markle, 1983; Kluger, 1996; Tate, 1999).[2]

The reformers largely viewed smoking as a moral issue. While some attention was paid to the health effects of smoking, the behavior was largely viewed in moral terms. Smoking by youth—boys—was an important part of the concern. In fact, one experiences a sense of *deja vu* in reading some of the literature of the movement from this era. For example, a pamphlet put out by the No-Tobacco League of America, based in Indianapolis, foreshadows contemporary concerns about marketing to youth in its title, "Billboards Angle for Boy Smokers."

Organizationally, the anticigarette movement drew heavily on the model of the Temperance movement.[3] Lucy Page Gaston, whose parents were active in both the abolition and temperance movement and who herself had been a member of the Women's Christian Temperance Union (WCTU), founded the Chicago Anti-Cigarette League in 1899 (Sobel, 1978; Tate, 1999). Gaston traveled the country giving speeches, and similar organizations started in other cities. These organizations coalesced into the National Anti-Cigarette League in 1901 (Sobel, 1978). The new organization had chapters throughout the United States and Canada and claimed 300,000 members (Tate, 1999). By the second decade of the twentieth century, several additional organizations were involved in anticigarette and antitobacco advocacy, including the No-Tobacco League (mentioned above), the Non-Smokers' Protective League, and the Anti-Cigarette Smoking League. In addition the WCTU and the YMCA were active in efforts to prevent cigarette smoking (Tate, 1999).

The movement culminated in the passage of cigarette prohibition laws in fourteen states in the late 1800s and early 1900s, mainly in the South and Midwest. However, by the mid-1920s, the movement was on the wane. By 1928, all of these laws had been repealed (Gottsegen, 1940; Gusfield, 1993). Minnesota, which enacted cigarette prohibition in 1909, repealed the law in 1913. The most remarkable reversal was Idaho, which passed and repealed cigarette prohibition in the same 1921 legislative session.

The tobacco control movement went through a quiescent period between the activity in the earlier part of the century and the 1950s and 1960s.[4] While there was some ordinance activity at the local level—such as a dramatic upswing beginning in the 1940s in the number of ordinances requiring local licensing of tobacco vendors in Minnesota (Forster, Komro, and Wolfson, 1996)—this appeared to stem from a general devolution of responsibility from the state to local governments rather than a desire to control tobacco use.

Scientific research, which began to produce consistent evidence of the links between smoking and lung cancer and other harmful outcomes in the 1950s, set the stage for a growing tide of activism from the 1960s on—a tide that is increasing to this day. In the second—and current—wave of tobacco control activism in the United States, claims-making is based heavily on evidence of the health effects of tobacco use as well as protection of the rights of nonsmokers. In the following sections, I present an overview of the production of scientific knowledge on the health effects of tobacco use, summarize what is known about the prevalence of tobacco use in the United States, followed by a discussion of the health consequences of tobacco use. Following this, I describe the main policy strategies that government and movement organizations have pursued, followed by an overview of tobacco control efforts in Minnesota, which has been a leader in tobacco control activism and policy.

SOCIAL CONSTRUCTION OF THE HEALTH AND ECONOMIC CONSEQUENCES OF TOBACCO USE

The production of scientific knowledge about the health effects of tobacco use is closely intertwined with the development of modern epidemiological methods. Prior to the 1950s, the studies on smoking and lung cancer that had appeared in the scientific literature had reported conflicting results (Susser, 1985). Mervyn Susser, a prominent epidemiologist who was editor of the *American Journal of Public Health* for many years, characterized four studies published in 1950 on smoking and lung cancer (Schreck et al., 1950; Wynder and Graham, 1950; Levin, Goldstein, and Gerhardt, 1950; Doll and Hill, 1950) as "the prototypes that initiated the present upsurge in case-control studies" (Susser, 1985:162). According to Susser (ibid.:163), "The hypothesis of the association between smoking and lung cancer was not well known and hitherto undocumented"—so much so, that the editor of the journal that published two of the papers—the *Journal of the American Medical Association*—was initially reluctant to publish them. These studies not only provided compelling evidence of the relationship between smoking and lung cancer. They—the Doll and Hill (1950) study in particular—"set a new standard for the case-control study. This work— together with Doll and Hill's national cohort study of British doctors that followed [Doll and Hill, 1956]—provided the second major intellectual lever in shifting the paradigm of chronic disease from an intrinsic to an environmental causal model. It stands as a classic exemplar for the investigation of a given outcome and an array of exposures" (Susser, 1985:163).

The American Heart Association, the American Cancer Society, the National Tuberculosis Association (now the American Lung Association), and the American Public Health Association played an important role in persuading the Kennedy administration to name an expert study committee to advise the Surgeon General on the health effects of smoking, which eventually led to the influential 1964 *Surgeon General's Report on Smoking and Health* (Cohn, 1965). Based on its review of existing scientific evidence, the report concluded "Cigarette smoking is causally related to lung cancer; the magnitude of the effect of cigarette smoking far outweighs all other factors. In comparison with nonsmokers, average male smokers of cigarettes have approximately a nine to ten fold risk of developing lung cancer and heavy smokers at least a twenty fold risk" (USDHEW, 1964).

The 1964 Surgeon General's report had far-reaching consequences. It was an important catalyst for the adoption of new public policy, such as the 1965 passage of the Cigarette Labeling and Advertising Act and the Federal Communication Commission's issuance of rules requiring airing of cigarette counteradvertisements. It also led to an upsurge in activism by consumer protection groups and the founding of a single-issue tobacco control organization—Action on Smoking and Health (ASH)—by John Banzhaf in 1967 (Troyer and Markle, 1983; see Chapter 3 for a description of ASH and other organizations involved in tobacco control advocacy). The report served as something of a "wake up call" to the tobacco industry— leading to an aggressive response on the part of the cigarette companies' public relations and legal departments (Glantz et al., 1996). And, it marked the beginning of the long-term decline in adult per capita cigarette consumption [Centers for Disease Control and Prevention(CDC), 1999a].

In the thirty-seven years since the first report, the Surgeon General has issued an additional twenty-six reports documenting the evidence on the health consequences of tobacco use and, especially in recent years, strategies for tobacco use prevention and cessation. The reports have focused on smoking by women (1980), the changing cigarette (1981), cancer (1982), cardiovascular disease (1983), chronic obstructive lung disease (1984), involuntary smoking (1986), nicotine addiction (1988), smoking cessation (1990), youth (1994), and minority groups (1998).[5]

PREVALENCE OF TOBACCO USE IN THE UNITED STATES

Despite dramatic declines in tobacco use since the publication of the first surgeon general's report on smoking and health in 1964, tobacco is still widely used in the United States. The CDC estimated that 48 million adults (age 18 and older)—one-quarter (24.7%) of the U.S. adult population— were current smokers in 1997 (CDC, 1999b).[6] Smoking is strongly socially patterned, by race/ethnicity (current smoking rates range from 16.9% among Asian/Pacific Islanders to 34.1% among American Indian/Alaska Natives), gender (22.1% of women and 27.6% of men), education (ranging from 11.6% of those with 16 or more years of education to 35.4% of those with 9–11 years of education), and age (ranging, among adults, from 12% of those 65 and older to 28.7% of those 18–24) (CDC, 1999b). The fifty states vary in adult cigarette smoking rates, ranging from 14.2% in Utah to 30.8% in Kentucky (1998 data, reported in CDC, 1999c).

National surveys suggest that rates of use of smokeless tobacco—chewing tobacco and snuff—are relatively low. For example, the National Household Survey of Drug Abuse (NHSDA) reported that 3.1% of the U.S. population aged 12 and older reported past-30-day smokeless tobacco use in 1998 (USDHHS, 1999). However, data from national surveys tend to obscure the fact that there is considerable regional and gender-based variation in smokeless tobacco use. In the seventeen states in which a question about current smokeless tobacco was included in the CDC's 1997 Behavioral Risk Factor Surveillance System (BRFSS), the prevalence of current smokeless tobacco use among adult males (18 or over) ranged from 2.6% in Arizona to 14.7% in Wyoming and 18.4% in West Virginia (CDC, 1998).

The CDC defines current tobacco use among youth as use of a tobacco product "on one or more of the 30 days preceding the survey" (CDC, 2000). Using this standard, over one-third (34.8%) of high school students were current tobacco users in 1999 (ibid.). Cigarette smoking was the most common form of tobacco use: 28.4% of high school students smoked cigarettes. Cigar smoking was the second most common form of tobacco use: 15.3% of high school students were current cigar users. Cigar use is followed in prevalence among high school students by smokeless tobacco use (6.6%), smoking "kreteks" (5.8%; kreteks are clove-flavored cigarettes) and "bidis" (5.0%; bidis are small, flavored cigarettes made from tobacco wrapped in a tendu or temburni leaf; CDC, 1999d), and pipes (2.8%; CDC, 2000). Among middle school students in 1999, 12.8% reported any current tobacco use, with the most common forms of tobacco use again being smoking cigarettes (9.2%) and cigars (6.1%).

HEALTH CONSEQUENCES OF TOBACCO USE

Researchers have linked smoking and smokeless tobacco use with an astonishing array of ailments. These include a wide range of ailments—some life threatening and some minor—affecting the smoker. But tobacco use—

in particular smoking—has negative health consequences for others as well. The production of a vast reservoir of knowledge about the health consequences of smoking has provided individuals and organizations involved in tobacco control efforts with extensive ammunition in their advocacy efforts. In this section, I briefly review the array of health consequences with which smoking, smokeless (or "spit") tobacco use, and exposure to secondhand smoke have been linked.

Health Consequences for the User of Tobacco Products

The strong link between smoking and *lung cancer* is widely known. Cigarette smoking is estimated to account for 85% of lung cancer cases (USDHHS, 1989). The Centers for Disease Control and Prevention (CDC) estimated that in 1990, 120,000 lung cancer deaths were attributable to smoking (CDC, 1993a). This represents 79% of the cancer deaths, and 29% of all deaths, from smoking in that year.

Smoking also plays a major role in respiratory diseases—especially chronic obstructive pulmonary disease, which includes both emphysema and chronic bronchitis (USDHHS, 1984, 1998a) The CDC estimated that there were almost 85,000 smoking-attributable deaths from respiratory diseases in 1990, or 20% of all the deaths associated with smoking in that year.

In addition to its role in causing lung cancer, smoking has been found to be associated with cancer in a number of additional sites, including the mouth, larynx, esophagus, stomach, bladder, pancreas, kidney, liver, colon, cervix, penis, breast, and skin (Ambrosone et al., 1996; Grodstein, Speizer, and Hunter, 1995; Harish and Ravi, 1995; Mizoue et al., 2000; Potter, 1999; USDHHS, 1998a).

It still comes as a surprise to many in the United States that the largest number of deaths from smoking are not from lung cancer, not from emphysema, but from cardiovascular diseases, such as coronary heart disease and stroke (USDHHS, 1983; Malarcher et al., 1997). Cardiovascular diseases are the leading cause of death in the United States (McGinnis and Foege, 1993), and, in the words of the 1983 Surgeon General's report, "Cigarette smoking should be considered the most important of the known modifiable risk factors for coronary heart disease in the United States" (USDHHS, 1983:iv). The CDC estimated that 180,00 deaths—or 43% of all smoking-related deaths—resulted from cardiovascular disease in 1990 (CDC, 1993a; also see Malarcher et al., 1997).

In addition to its role in causing cancer, COPD, and cardiovascular disease, smoking has been implicated in interfering with development of normal lung function in adolescents (Gold et al., 1996), absenteeism, industrial accidents, occupational injuries, and discipline (Ryan, Zwerling, and Orav, 1992), diabetes (in women; Rimm et al., 1993), facial wrinkling (Ernster et al., 1995), impotence (Rosen et al., 1991), reduced fecundity and fertility among women (Zenzes, Wang, and Casper, 1995), miscarriage (DiFranza and Lew, 1995), earlier menopause (Zenzes et al., 1995), adult (myeloid) leukemia, macular degeneration (the leading cause of blindness in the elderly; Seddon, Willett, Speizer, and Hankinson, 1996), gum disease (periodontitis; Haber, 1994), graves' disease (Prummel and Wiersinga, 1993), sleep disturbances (Wetter and Young, 1994), and depression (Breslau, Kilbey, and Andreski, 1993).[7] Finally, smokeless tobacco use causes recession of the gums, leukoplakia (oral lesions), and oral cancer (USDHHS, 1992).

Health Consequences Affecting Others

Research has identified a number of ailments affecting people exposed to secondhand smoke, which has bolstered the arguments of tobacco control activists seeking controls to protect nonsmokers from exposure to secondhand smoke. Among children, these ailments include respiratory symptoms and illnesses (Mannino et al., 1996; Ferris et al., 1985). Relative to children of nonsmoking parents, children of parents who smoke have a greater incidence of acute lower-respiratory-tract infections (Ware and Fischer, 1984; Chen, Li, Yu, and Qian, 1988; EPA, 1993). The 1993 EPA report estimated that, each year, exposure to environmental tobacco smoke (ETS) contributes to up to 300,000 cases of lower-respiratory-tract infections among infants and young children, which result in between 7,500 and 15,000 hospitalizations (EPA, 1993). Relative to children of nonsmoking parents, children of parents who smoke also have a greater incidence of upper-respiratory-tract illnesses (sore throats) (Willatt, 1986; Fleming, Cochi, Hightower, and Broome, 1987). Children exposed to secondhand smoke are more likely than other children to experience restricted activity, bed confinement, and school absence (Mannino et al., 1996). In addition, several studies have reported increased frequency of middle-ear infections (Strachan, Jarvis, and Feyerabend, 1989; EPA, 1993).

Some studies have reported increased frequency of onset or aggravation of asthma among children of smoking parents (Gortmaker, Walker, Jacobs, and Ruch-Ross, 1982). The EPA report reported that exposure to ETS results in more frequent and severe symptoms among children with asthma (EPA, 1993). It goes on to report that the data "strongly suggest" an association between exposure to ETS and onset of asthma (ibid.).

Long-term respiratory effects may include increased risk of chronic air flow obstruction as an adult (USDHHS, 1984), as well as other consequences of pulmonary function deficits (Ferris et al., 1985). Moreover, children of smokers show slightly lower rates of increase of lung function as the lung matures (Tager et al., 1987; Kauffmann, Tager, Munoz, and Speizer, 1989).

Sudden Infant Death Syndrome (SIDS) is the most common cause of death among infants between the ages of one month and one year, accounting for 5,000 deaths in the United States annually (EPA, 1993). The EPA report found that "there is strong evidence that infants whose mothers smoke are at increased risk of dying suddenly and unexpectedly during the first year of life. . . . [However,] in view of the fact that the cause of SIDS is still unknown . . . at this time this report is unable to assert whether or not passive smoking is a risk factor for SIDS" (ibid.:253). More recent research categorizes exposure to cigarette smoke as a "major risk factor" for SIDS (Raza et al., 1999).

A number of studies have found a significant relationship between parental smoking and risk of cancer in children or adults. These studies have focused on both fetal and childhood exposure. Maternal smoking during pregnancy has been found to raise the overall risk of cancer (Neutel and Buck, 1971; Stjernfeldt, Berglund, Lindsten, and Ludvigsson, 1986; Golding, Paterson, and Kinlen, 1990), including lung cancer (Correa et al., 1983).

Among adults, exposure to secondhand smoke has been linked to lung cancer, respiratory health, and heart disease. The Environmental Protection Agency (EPA) report, *Respiratory Health Effects of Passive Smoking: Lung Cancer and Other Disorders*, published in 1993, classified ETS as "a human lung carcinogen, responsible for approximately 3,000 lung cancer deaths annually in U.S. nonsmokers" (EPA, 1993:v).

With regard to respiratory symptoms, the EPA report stated that "new evidence . . . has emerged suggesting that exposure to ETS may increase the frequency of respiratory symptoms in adults" (ibid.:263). These symptoms may include wheezing, chronic cough, and shortness of breath (dyspnea) (ibid.).

Although the EPA report did not focus on the effects of ETS on heart disease, it has become apparent in recent years that the health burden from it far exceeds the burden stemming from cancer caused by ETS exposure. Compared to the 3,000 to 3,700 annual estimated deaths from lung cancer as a result of passive smoking (EPA, 1993; Wells, 1988; Glantz and Parmley, 1991), estimates of the number of deaths from heart disease as a result of passive smoking have ranged from 32,000 deaths a year (Wells, 1988) to 37,000 deaths a year (Glantz and Parmley, 1991) to 35,000–40,000 deaths a year (Steenland, 1992) to 62,000 deaths a year (Wells, 1994).

In addition, researchers have identified a number of ailments of children born to mothers who smoked during pregnancy. These include a number of pregnancy outcomes, such as reduced birth weight, preterm birth, and increased risk of perinatal death (Källén, 1997). Maternal smoking has been estimated to contribute to 17 to 26% of low birth weight in the United States (Lightwood, Phibbs, and Glantz, 1999; USDHHS, 1990). In addition, smoking has been implicated in a number of birth defects, including limb reduction malformations (Källén, 1997) and congenital urinary tract anomalies (Li et al., 1996). In addition, mothers' smoking has been implicated in their offsprings' problem behavior in later life: controlling for postnatal smoking, maternal smoking during pregnancy was associated with an increased probability that female adolescents would smoke (Kandel, Wu, and Davie, 1994). Recently, researchers have discovered ailments of children born to fathers who smoked during pregnancy, including lower birth weight (Martinez, Wright, Taussig, and the Group Health Medical Associates, 1994).[8]

Finally, smoking is the leading cause of fire deaths in the United States (United States Fire Administration, 1999; Ballard, Koepsell, and Rivara, 1992). Based on data from the National Fire Protection Association, the CDC estimated that 1,362 burn deaths were attributable to smoking in 1990 (CDC, 1993a).

It is clear from the preceding discussion that tobacco use has been implicated in a wide variety of negative health outcomes.[9] What does all of this amount to? How significant is the burden that tobacco use imposes on the public's health in the United States? Dr. J. Michael McGinnis (who at the time was the Deputy Assistant Secretary for Health, Disease Prevention and Health Promotion at the U.S. Department of Health and Human Services) and Dr. William H. Foege (of the Carter Presidential Center and Emory University) reviewed and synthesized data on the role of external (i.e., nongenetic) factors in the 2.15 million deaths of U.S. residents in 1990 (McGinnis and Foege, 1993). This effort was a dramatic departure from the traditional approach of classifying deaths by underlying diseases (such as heart disease, cancer, stroke, and accidents) rather than the factors—many of which are potentially modifiable—that caused these diseases. The results, published in the *Journal of the American Medical Association,* underscored the huge role tobacco plays in mortality in the United States. Of the nine top "actual causes of death" discussed by McGinnis and Foege, tobacco was far and away the leading contributor to deaths in the United States in 1990, accounting for an estimated 400,000 deaths, or 19% of all deaths in that year. This surpassed by a wide margin the estimated deaths from diet and activity patterns (300,000 deaths, or 14%), alcohol (100,000 deaths, or 5%), microbial agents (90,000 deaths, or 4%), and the other five causes. The estimate of 400,000 deaths resulting from tobacco is consistent with the CDC's estimate of 418,690 deaths in the United States in 1990 (CDC, 1993a). If tobacco's toll is calculated by years of potential life lost (YPLL), an estimated 1.15 million years before age 65, or 5.05 million years to life expectancy, were lost as a result of cigarette smoking in 1990 (ibid.). Using the YPLL-65 method, this translates into 9.4% of all lost years of potential life before age 65 in the United States in 1990 [calculated from data reported in CDC (1993a, 1993b)].[10]

The burden of tobacco use cannot be measured by deaths, or potential years of life lost, alone. In addition to being a leading cause of mortality, tobacco use results in widespread morbidity as well. Heart disease, cancer, and respiratory diseases resulting from tobacco use are associated with discomfort, pain, and diminished quality of life.

Moreover, illnesses related to tobacco use impose a significant economic burden. The CDC estimated that $21.9 billion, or 7.1% of all medical-care expenditures in the United States in 1987, was attributable to cigarette smoking (CDC, 1994a). This included $11.4 billion in hospital charges, $6.6 billion in physician charges, $2.2 billion in nursing-home care, $1.2 billion in home health care, and $527 million in prescription drug costs. When the smoking-attributable percentages from this study are applied to more recent (1993) health care expenditure data, the estimated smoking-attributable costs for medical care increase to $50 billion (CDC, 1994a). The U.S. Office of Technology Assessment added estimates of the economic costs of health care, lost productivity due to smoking-related disability, and lost productivity due to smoking-related premature deaths, to generate an overall estimate of the social cost of smoking of $68 billion in 1990 (Herdman, Hewitt, and Laschover, 1993).

EXPOSURE TO ENVIRONMENTAL TOBACCO SMOKE

Recent research has documented that a substantial percentage of children are exposed to secondhand smoke in their homes. Mannino and colleagues (1996) used data from the 1991 National Health Interview Survey to estimate the prevalence of exposure among youth. On the basis of parents' self-reports about smoking in the home, Mannino and colleagues estimated that 31% of children between the ages of 1 and 10 in the United States were exposed to ETS on a daily basis. Children from families of lower socioeconomic status (classified on the basis of the family being below the poverty level or the responding family member having a twelfth-grade education or less) had especially high rates of daily exposure: 41%, compared to 21% of children from higher SES homes. The CDC, using data from the Current Population Surveys and the Behavioral Risk Factor Surveillance System, also generated estimates of the number of children exposed to ETS in the home (CDC, 1997a). The CDC estimated that in 1996, 15 million children and adolescents under the age of 18 (21.9% of children in the United States) were exposed to ETS in their homes. In more than 70% of households in which a child lived with a current adult cigarette smoker, smoking was permitted in some or all areas of the home.

The CDC used data from the Third National Health and Nutrition Examination Survey, conducted from 1988 to 1991, to generate estimates of the prevalence of exposure of the U.S. adult population (age 17 and older) to ETS (Pirkle et al., 1996). Thirty-eight percent of this nationally representative sample of adults reported that they currently used tobacco, 39% reported that they did not use tobacco and were not exposed to ETS at home or in the workplace, and 23% reported that they did not use tobacco but were exposed to ETS either in the home, at work, or in both locations (ibid.). Where did this exposure take place? Among these non–tobacco using respondents who were exposed to ETC, over two-thirds (67%) reported being exposed to ETS at work, and almost half (47%) reported being exposed in the home (calculated from ibid.:Table 1). However, the self-report data indicating that one-quarter of nonsmokers are exposed to ETS may be a gross underestimate. As part of the NHANES examination, blood samples were taken from each subject and the level of cotinine was assessed. Cotinine is a major metabolite of nicotine that is commonly used as a measure of exposure to nicotine in the past one to two days (ibid.). An astonishing 88% of non–tobacco users in the NHANES sample showed detectable levels of cotinine. It is possible that this number slightly overestimates the percentage of persons exposed, because some smokers may have reported that they did not use tobacco, and because a small number of people may not be exposed to ETS but have measurable levels of cotinine in their blood from eating foods that contain small amounts of nicotine, such as potatoes, tomatoes, eggplant, cauliflower, and green peppers (ibid.). Nevertheless, these data suggest that exposure to ETS, through exposure at home, work, social settings, vehicles, and other settings, was nearly ubiquitous during the period covered by the 1988–1991 period covered by NHANES.

STRATEGIES OF THE MOVEMENT

The contemporary tobacco control movement has two overarching goals: (1) to prevent people from suffering the health hazards associated with tobacco use, and (2) to protect people from experiencing the discomfort and health hazards associated with exposure to secondhand smoke. In order to achieve these goals, actors in the movement—both within and outside government—have developed a variety of strategies. The main strategies that government and movement organizations have pursued include education and information campaigns, taxes and other "economic incentives," indoor air policy, strategies to reduce youth access to tobacco, limits on advertising, and litigation. These strategies are described briefly below; and are woven throughout the discussion of movement organizations (in Part 2) and arenas of contention (in Part 3).

Smoking Cessation Programs

Most smokers in the United States want to quit. The CDC estimated that, of 47 million adults who were current smokers in 1995, 32 million (68%) wanted to quit smoking completely (CDC, 1997b). Most people who successfully quit (i.e., no relapse for six months after the quit attempt) do so on their own—without the aid of any formal program (Shiffman, Mason, and Henningfield, 1998). This is largely a function of the large number of people who attempt to quit—for example, 46% of daily smokers stopped smoking for at least one day in the twelve months preceding the 1995 National Health Interview Survey (CDC, 1997b). Unfortunately, self-quitters have very high rates of relapse (Shiffman et al., 1998). Other methods, such as behavioral counseling, Nicotine Replacement Therapy (NRT) (e.g., nicotine gum and the nicotine patch), and other prescription drugs (such as bupropion, known commercially as Zyban), have demonstrated much higher success rates (Shiffman et al., 1998; Hurt et al., 1997). Efforts to encourage people to quit, educate them about successful methods, and make effective cessation therapies available to greater numbers of smokers are all important aspects of contemporary tobacco control efforts (USDHHS, 1991). However, these efforts may be seen as somewhat peripheral to the movement (see CDC, 1999e:996), for several reasons. First, they have for the most part not generated political action (although efforts in the past few years to obtain insurance coverage for smoking cessation therapies may be an exception). Second, the organizations that have been most concerned with cessation efforts have been government agencies [such as the National Cancer Institute and the Agency for Health Care Policy and Research (e.g., Fiore et al., 1996. The latter agency is now known as the Agency for Healthcare Research and Quality)] and some of the health voluntary organizations, such as the American Lung Association. The single-issue groups, both at the national level and in Minnesota, have not made cessation a major focus of their efforts.

Education and Information Campaigns

From the time of publication of the first Surgeon General's report on smoking and health in 1964, there have been widespread efforts to education the public about the health risks of smoking and to discourage them from doing so. Has the publication of research and media campaigns focused on discouraging tobacco use translated into widespread changes in opinions about health consequences of smoking? The first Gallup poll to include a question on this—"Do you think cigarette smoking is harmful, or not?"—was conducted in 1949. Already, 60% of respondents believed that smoking was harmful. This increased to 70% in 1954, 90% in 1977, and 95% in 1999 (Moore, 1999). The 1989 Surgeon General's Report (USDHHS,

1989) reviews tobacco control efforts over a 25-year period. The report documents increases in the percentage of people who believe that smoking is harmful to health (from 81% of all adults in 1964 to 90% in 1975), that any amount of smoking is hazardous to health (from 47% in 1970 to 72% in 1986), that cigarette smoking causes lung cancer (from 41% in 1954 to 89% in 1987), that cigarette smoking causes heart disease (from 40% in 1964 to 77% in 1987), emphysema and chronic bronchitis [from 50% in 1964 to 84% (emphysema) and 77% (chronic bronchitis) in 1987; ibid.].Similarly, the report compiles data from a number of national surveys showing increases in the percentage of the adult population who believed that smoking is hazardous to nonsmoker's health (from 46% in 1974 to 81% in 1987; ibid.). Among youth, the percentage of high school seniors who believed that smoking entails a great risk to health rose from 51% in 1975 to 69% in 1991 (USDHHS, 1989, 1994).

Overall, there are high levels of awareness that smoking poses significant health risks. However, debate continues on whether there is still room for upward movement in the public's perceptions of these risks (Weinstein, 1998; Schoenbaum, 1997; Viscusi, 1992). For example, there is evidence that current smokers—especially heavy smokers—significantly underestimate the risks of becoming ill and dying from smoking (Brownson et al., 1992; Chapman et al., 1993; Schoenbaum, 1997, Weinstein, 1998). Moreover, the role of smoking in producing heart disease is not as widely understood as are the relationships between smoking and lung cancer and emphysema (Brownson et al., 1992). Segments of the general population, such as older individuals, people with less education, and people with limited proficiency in English, may lack comprehensive knowledge of the health consequences of smoking (Brownson et al., 1992; USDHHS, 1998b). The hazards of secondhand smoke are not as widely known as the health consequences of smoking (USDHHS, 1998b). There is evidence that youth tend to underestimate the risks inherent in smoking. In a 1991 survey, 31% of high-school seniors did not believe that smoking one or more packs of cigarettes a day posed a great risk to health; 14% believed that the health effects of smoking had been exaggerated (USDHHS, 1994). While the vast majority of youth are aware that use of smokeless tobacco can cause cancer (Allen et al., 1993), a minority believe that the risk of harm is great (USDHHS, 1994).

Mass media coverage of the health risks of smoking, along with educational campaigns sponsored by the U.S. government and other organizations, have been a mainstay of tobacco control efforts during the second half of the twentieth century. A National Cancer Institute monograph (USDHHS, 1991) argues that each of three major "informational events" resulted in downturns (which were in some cases short-lived) in per capita consumption of cigarettes in the United States. The first of these was the media's reporting of the emerging scientific evidence on the health risks of smoking, beginning in the 1950s. Troyer and Markle (1983) show dramatic increases in counts of stories on smoking and health in the *Index Medicus*, the *New York Times*, and the *Reader's Guide to Periodical Literature*, beginning in the early 1950s. The second major "informational event" was the publication of the *1964 Surgeon General's Report on Smoking and Health* (USD-HEW, 1964). The third major informational stimulus was the mandated cigarette counteradvertisements, which ran on television from 1967 until the television cigarette ads ban took effect in 1970.

In addition to the three efforts described above, there have been a wide variety of information and education campaigns, including mandated health warnings on cigarette advertising and cigarette packages and information and education campaigns sponsored by the federal government, state governments, and the health voluntaries (the American Cancer Society, the American Lung Association, and the American Heart Association). To a large extent, the single-issue organizations—such as Action on Smoking and Health at the national level and the Association of Nonsmokers-Minnesota and the Minnesota Smoke Free Coalition in the Minnesota case study—have left educational efforts about the health effects of smoking to government organizations and the health voluntaries. Because of their interest in the secondhand smoke issue, they have striven to educate their members, policymakers, and others about the health consequences of exposure to secondhand smoke. And educational efforts that publicize the mendacity and unethical and illegal behavior of the tobacco industry have been an important educational "niche" of the single-issue movement organizations, as well as, more recently, state government tobacco control programs in some states.

Increases in Taxes on Tobacco Products

There is a large body of literature indicating that increasing the price of cigarettes—which can be accomplished by increasing federal or state taxes—results in significant reductions in the prevalence of smoking, especially among adolescents (Grossman, Sindelar, Mullahy, and Anderson, 1993; Peterson, Zeger, Remington, and Anderson, 1992; Wasserman, 1992; Wasserman, Manning, Newhouse, and Winkler, 1991; Hu, Sung, and Keeler, 1995; Emont, Choi, Novotny, and Giovino, 1993). Tobacco tax increases have received support and legitimation as a tobacco control strategy from many quarters, including the Institute of Medicine (Lynch and Bonnie, 1994) and the National Cancer Institute (increasing tobacco taxes was one of the interventions called for in the American Stop Smoking Intervention Study, which is described in Chapter 7; Stillman et al., 1999; USDHHS, 1991). In addition to direct effects on consumption of tobacco products as a result of price increases, some states have allocated a portion of the revenue from increased tobacco taxes to fund tobacco control programs.

Indoor Air Policy

Beginning in the 1970s, the issue of secondhand smoke, or ETS, became a key area of activists' focus. It also was the issue around which a resurgence in grassroots activity at the state and local levels occurred. For example, the Association of Nonsmokers Minnesota (ANSR), begun in 1973 as an offshoot of the state American Lung Association, was instrumental in the introduction and passage of the first comprehensive state clean indoor air act in the nation, requiring the creation of separate smoking and nonsmoking areas in public buildings (Kahn, 1983). Other organizations, such as local groups affiliated with Group Against Smokers' Pollution (GASP), advocated for state and local clean air laws (Troyer and Markle, 1983; Troyer, 1989). More recently, the 1993 Environmental Protection Agency report on the health effects of passive smoking (Environmental Protection Agency, 1993) appears to have contributed additional momentum to organizations focusing on restrictions on smoking in public places and reducing exposure to secondhand smoke.

Examples of clean indoor air or no-smoking policies that have been pursued include restrictions or bans on smoking in restaurants, work sites, apartment buildings, day care facilities, shopping centers, recreational facilities, and hospitals. For example, standards on smoking in hospitals established by the Joint Commission on Accreditation of Healthcare Organizations required accredited hospitals (which represent about 80% of hospitals in the United States) to ban smoking in hospitals by December of 1993 (exceptions are allowed for individual patients based on physicians' orders; Longo, Brownson, and Kruse 1995).

Youth Access to Tobacco

Until the late 1980s, research and programmatic efforts on youth focused almost exclusively on educational messages—usually delivered in school or using mass media—that attempted to discourage youth from smoking. As described below, a new understanding of the issue—one that focuses on the availability of tobacco products to young people—emerged in the late 1980s and early 1990s, and has become institutionalized as a major focus of activists, researchers, and government agencies. This shift, or expansion in the way the issue of youth tobacco use is framed—from changing the "hearts and minds" of young people to persuade them that tobacco use is unhealthy, or uncool—to reducing the availability of tobacco products—has been characterized as a "sea change" in research and intervention on tobacco use by young people (Forster and Wolfson, 1998).

Research on youth access to tobacco products, which began to be published in the late 1980s and early 1990s, helped reshape the definition of the problem of adolescent tobacco use. First, several studies documented the ease with which youth can obtain tobacco products. A majority of teenagers responding to surveys reported that it would be easy to obtain cigarettes (Johnston, O'Malley, and Bachman, 1992; Forster, Klepp, and Jeffrey, 1989). Teenagers who smoke reported that commercial outlets were an important source of cigarettes (Forster et al., 1989; Cummings et al., 1992; CDC, 1996). And a number of studies found that a majority of retail outlets sampled would sell cigarettes to minors (DiFranza, Norwood, Garner, and Tye, 1987; DiFranza and Brown, 1992; Altman, Foster, Rasenick-Douss, and Tye, 1989; Forster, Hourigan, and McGovern, 1992; Hoppock and Houston, 1990; Nelson, Marson, and Roby, 1989; Thomson and Toffler, 1990; USDHHS, 1994) (the use of tobacco "purchase attempts," as in this last group of studies, is described in greater detail below). Cummings and colleagues (1994) estimated that 255 million packs of cigarettes were sold to minors in 1991, generating sales revenues of close to $500 million. DiFranza and Tye (1990) estimated that 3% of tobacco industry profits derived directly from sales of cigarettes to children in 1988.

In addition to research documenting the availability of tobacco products through commercial sources, a series of studies was published demonstrating the key role of youth smoking in the development of long-term, addicted smokers. The vast majority of smokers begin the habit in childhood or adolescence. For example, data from the 1991 NHSDA indicated that 82% of persons aged 30–39 who smoked or in the past had smoked daily first tried a cigarette before reaching the age of 18; 53% became daily smokers before reaching that age (USDHHS, 1994). People who start smoking earlier in life are less likely to quit than people who take up the habit later (Breslau and Peterson, 1996). Pierce and Gilpin (1996) estimated that half of the people in the 1975–1979 birth cohort who take up smoking as adolescents will continue for 16 years (males) or 20 years (females). The CDC estimated that five million people who were between the ages of 0 and 17 in 1995 will die prematurely from smoking-related illnesses if current patterns of smoking (i.e., uptake and cessation) continue (CDC, 1996).

Based on this new understanding of the problem of youth tobacco use, a variety of strategies has been developed to reduce youth access to tobacco. Advocacy efforts to reduce youth access, on the part of single-issue organizations, the health voluntaries, health care organizations and organizations of health professionals, and government agencies, have proliferated.

Several approaches to limiting access have been developed. First, there is an emphasis on documenting the availability of tobacco products to children in the local community. A common "tactic"—first developed by university researchers working with activists (Altman, 1989; DiFranza et al., 1987; Forster et al., 1992), and then picked up on a widespread basis by researchers, activists, and government agencies—is to enlist children to attempt to purchase tobacco products (usually cigarettes, but smokeless tobacco products have been the focus of some efforts—see Boyle, Stedman, and Forster, 1995). These purchase attempts (also known as "compliance checks," "stings," and "confederate buys") are used by activists, researchers, and government agencies to document and publicize the level of the problem of commercial availability of cigarettes and smokeless tobacco products to youth. They are also used by law enforcement officials to enforce laws prohibiting the sale of tobacco products to persons under the legal age (which is 19 in Alabama, Alaska, and Utah and 18 in the remaining 47 states). This tactic, which began with a handful of researchers in the late 1980s and early 1990s, has spread to a degree barely imaginable ten years ago. It has spawned a substantial research literature (reviewed in Forster and Wolfson, 1998).[11] The approach has spread to many other countries, including Canada (Quebec; Nguyen et al., 1995), Australia (Wakefield, Carrangis, Wilson, Reynolds, 1992), New Zealand (Ford, Scragg, and Weir, 1997), and Mexico (CDC, 1997c). Finally, purchase attempts have been or are being implemented on a massive scale by a number of state and federal government agencies. For example, the California Tobacco Retailer Youth Purchase Survey, conducted in 1994, involved 1,775 over-the-counter cigarette purchase attempts (Roeseler, Capra, and Quinn, 1994). The Synar Amendment, enacted in 1992, requires states to enforce tobacco age-of-sale laws "using both random and targeted unannounced inspections of both over-the-counter and vending machine outlets" (USDHHS, 1993a). States are also required by Synar to demonstrate increasing levels of compliance with the law on the part of retailers over several years. Synar has resulted in "virtually institutionalizing the use of sting operations" (Jacobson and Wasserman, 1997). Finally, the Food and Drug Administration, in its efforts to enforce its 1996 rule, "Regulations Restricting the Sale and Distribution of Cigarettes and Smokeless Tobacco to Protect Children and Adolescents" (USDHHS, 1996), entered into contracts with state and local agencies to conduct compliance checks in a subset of the estimated 500,000 tobacco vendors in the United States (Marwick, 1997). However, the Supreme Court overturned these regulations in March 2000, ruling that the FDA lacks the authority to regulate tobacco products (Gottlieb, 2000).

As a result of this new "framing" of the problem of tobacco use, and the activism it has engendered, state laws and local ordinances concerning youth access, such as vending machine bans, self-service merchandising bans, age-of-seller restrictions, licensing fees sufficient to cover enforcement costs, mandatory compliance checks, and graduated civil penalties, have proliferated (USDHHS, 1994; Forster et al., 1996). In addition, pressure is being applied to vigorously enforce existing laws and ordinances concerning access to tobacco by youth (USDHHS, 1993a). In our 1996–1997 national survey of 642 state and local government and nonprofit organizations involved in tobacco control advocacy efforts, 79% reported heavy involvement in addressing youth access to tobacco and 68% reported having participated in compliance checks in the year preceding the survey.

The development of framings of the problem, and strategies for its solution, that focus on youth access to tobacco was an important accomplishment for the movement. Measures to regulate youth access to tobacco products enjoy high levels of public support (see Ashley, Bull, and Pederson, 1995; Bailey and Crowe, 1994 ; CDC, 1991a, 1994b; Marcus et al., 1994). Despite this public support, a focus on youth access to tobacco is not without its critics in the movement. For example, Stanton Glantz, a leading researcher and activist, argues that a focus on youth access diverts energy and attention away from what he considers to be more effective strategies (e.g., clean air policies / smoking bans), and that "the Youth Access Trap"— tends to divert attention from tobacco industry practices, and glamorizes smoking by characterizing it as a "forbidden fruit" for youth (Glantz, 1996).

Advertising to Youth

Advertising to youth is an important focus of the tobacco control movement. Movement actors argue that cigarette and smokeless tobacco manufacturers deliberately target youth with their advertising, and that youth are influenced by these ads. Movement organizations have worked for a number of years to first of all publicize the advertising practices of the tobacco industry, and to impose restrictions on advertising that targets, or exposes, youth to protobacco use messages.

Six billion dollars was spent on advertising and promotion of tobacco products in 1993 (Altman et al., 1996a). The largest component of this was $2.6 billion (43.3%) spent on coupons and "retail value added promotions at the point of purchase" (Altman et al., 1996a). Another $756 million (29.1%) was spent on specialty item distribution (e.g., free samples of tobacco, T-shirts, lighters, hats, and product catalog, including catalogs for "cigarette continuity" or "frequent smoker" programs; Sumner and Dillman, 1995). Expenditures for tobacco advertising on billboards have grown dramatically since enactment of the ban on tobacco advertising on television in 1970. According to the Federal Trade Commission, these expenditures grew from $7.3 million (2% of tobacco advertising and promotion expenditures) in 1970 to $319 million (9.7% of expenditures) in 1988 (Altman, Schooler, and Basil, 1991).

Are youth exposed to these advertising efforts? In fact, most youth in the United States are heavily exposed to advertising for cigarettes and smokeless tobacco products. For example, a 1994 survey of 13-year-olds in San Jose, California found that 88% reported exposure to cigarette marketing, either through ads in magazines, on billboards, at stores, or at events (Schooler, Feighery, and Flora, 1996). And the popularity of the Joe Camel character, even among very young children, has been well documented (DiFranza et al., 1991; Pierce and Choi et al., 1998)

Tobacco control advocates argue that promotion campaigns in which promotional items such as clothing or equipment are either offered at the time of purchase or in exchange for coupons obtained through the purchase of tobacco products, are inducements for children to buy or otherwise obtain tobacco products (Coeytaux, Altman, and Slade, 1995). In the previously mentioned 1994 survey of 13-year-olds in San Jose, California, one-quarter of these young adolescents owned cigarette promotional items (Schooler et al., 1996). In a national survey conducted in 1993, 35% of minors (12–17 years old) participated in tobacco promotion campaigns. Over 10% of minors reported owning or once having owned one or more tobacco promotional items (Coeytaux, 1995). Extrapolating to the U.S. population, the authors estimate that 7.4 million minors have participated in such campaigns and 2.2 million have owned tobacco promotional items (ibid.). In a 1992 survey of a high school in New Mexico and another in Massachusetts, 39% of students had heard of Camel Cash and 8.6% had collected Camel Cash (Richards, DiFranza, Fletcher, and Fischer, 1995). Five percent of students under 18 reported that they had purchased Camel cigarettes in order to obtain Camel Cash.

The evidence reviewed above indicates that (1) advertising of tobacco products is pervasive, (2) many of the messages may appeal to youth, and (3) youth are heavily exposed to these messages. But does exposure to advertising actually contribute to smoking by youth? Several studies have documented an association of exposure to advertising and smoking. For example, in a study of 13-year-olds, exposure was associated with higher rates of smoking (Schooler et al., 1996). In a national sample of adolescents, a strong association was found between awareness of involvement in tobacco product promotions and susceptibility to use and actual use of tobacco products (Altman et al., 1996a). A relationship between receptivity to advertising and susceptibility to smoke among never smokers has also been demonstrated (Evans et al., 1995). In a large, longitudinal study of California adolescents, Pierce, Choi, and colleagues (1998) found that receptivity to tobacco advertising—measured by having a favorite tobacco advertisement or possession or willingness to use a tobacco promotional item—was associated with "progress in the smoking uptake process."[12] On the basis of these associations, the researchers estimated that, between

1993 and 1996, over a third of all experimentation by California adolescents could be attributed to tobacco advertising and promotion.

Activists and movement organizations have developed a number of strategies to reduce or eliminate advertising of tobacco products to youth. First, they have worked hard to identify tobacco industry efforts to market tobacco products to youth, and to bring these to the attention of policy-makers and the public at large. In addition, a number of strategies have been developed to restrict advertising. Legal restrictions that have been developed include restrictions on placement of billboards, such as bans on locating them near schools and near hospitals.[13] In addition, outright bans of billboards have been proposed in some communities (see Garner, 1996).

The 1998 Master Settlement Agreement between the tobacco industry and 46 states (which I discuss in Chapter 10) imposed a number of restrictions on tobacco marketing, including bans on:

- brand name sponsorships of concerts, team sporting events, or events with significant youth audiences;
- sponsorship of events involving paid underage participants;
- the use of tobacco brand names in stadiums and arenas;
- the use of cartoon characters in advertising, packaging, and promotions;
- payments for promotion of tobacco products in movies and other entertainment settings;
- the distribution and sale of merchandise with tobacco brand name logos;
- transit and outdoor advertising;

and a requirement that existing tobacco billboards and transit ads be removed.

Litigation

Tobacco litigation has come into its own in the last few years. It has been known for some time that suits against the tobacco companies—like other product liability suits (for example, those involving dangerous products such as asbestos) have tremendous potential to impact the public's health (Daynard, 1988). First of all, successful suits could transfer costs associated with health care and lost productivity from tobacco use from families and third-party payers to tobacco companies, forcing increases in the prices of tobacco products and consequent declines in consumption, especially among children and adolescents. Second, the suits, if well publicized, may help educate potential and actual tobacco users about the negative health consequences of tobacco use. Third, successful suits could have a kind of regulatory function, by forcing the industry to curtail deceptive advertising and promotion practices. Fourth, information revealed in the discovery process concerning tobacco company disinformation campaign could embarrass the companies and reduce their political clout in Congress, state legislatures, and town halls, and among regulatory bodies (Daynard, 1988).

For a litigation strategy to control tobacco to work, the litigation must be successful. And, for years, that was the rub. During what analysts of tobacco litigation have come to call the "first wave" (from about 1954 to 1973) and the "second wave" (from 1983 to 1992) of litigation (Daynard, 1988; Kelder and Daynard, 1996), tobacco companies won every case, using one or a combination of three arguments: smoking is a free choice, there is no definitive proof that smoking causes disease, and the industry itself sponsors research on smoking and health (see Chapter 8 for a discussion of this last topic; Annas, 1997). However, the record in the "third wave"—which began with the Castano case, filed in 1994 in Louisiana—is looking much more promising (Annas, 1997; Kelder and Daynard, 1996). According to Kelder and Daynard, five factors are making the difference:

> (1) the expenditure of time, money, and resources on behalf of millions of plaintiffs (as opposed to a single plaintiff) in the class action lawsuits; (2) an array of well-financed and well-organized plaintiffs' attorneys sharing resources and information in both classes of cases; (3) the absence of blameworthy plaintiffs in both classes of cases and the absolute unavailability to the industry of its two favorite affirmative defenses—assumption of the risk and contributory negligence—in the state medical cost reimbursement actions; (4) an abundance of evidence of industry wrongdoing garnered from former industry researchers and internal documents that make the claims put forward much easier to prove; and (5) a new set of facts concerning tobacco industry knowledge of the addictive and pharmacologic properties of nicotine and of tobacco industry efforts to manipulate nicotine levels so as to addict smokers. (1996:58)

These developments—and new litigation "tactics"—are reflected in the settlements and awards over the last few years. Until 1997, the industry had never paid damages, either as part of a settlement or a court verdict, in a product liability case. Then, in 1997 the state of Florida's suit against the tobacco industry was settled for $11 billion, Minnesota's suit was settled for $6 billion, Mississippi's suit was settled for $3.4 billion, the class of 60,000 flight attendants settled their class action suit for $300 million, and the 46-state, $206-billion-dollar Master Settlement Agreement was reached. These recent developments in the movement are discussed in Chapter 10.

TOBACCO CONTROL IN MINNESOTA

The state of Minnesota has become a major center of antitobacco activism and policy in the United States. According to Michael Cummings of the Roswell Park Cancer Institute (1993:270), "For the past decade, tobacco control advocates throughout the world have looked with envy and admiration at the accomplishments of the Minnesota campaign against tobacco." It has been a leader in activism—led by such groups as the Association for Nonsmokers-Minnesota and the Minnesota Coalition for a Smoke-Free Society 2000.[14] It boasts a string of firsts in public policy. In 1975, the state enacted the first comprehensive Clean Indoor Air Act, requiring the creation of separate smoking and nonsmoking areas in public buildings (Kahn, 1983). The Minnesota Department of Health (MDH) developed the first widely used model for estimating the impact of smoking on health care expenditures (SAMMEC II; see Lynch and Hopkins, 1996). Minnesota was the first state to prohibit distribution of free tobacco samples (Associated Press, 1995). State legislation in 1985 (the Omnibus Nonsmoking and Disease Prevention Act) increased the tobacco excise tax by 5 cents, earmarking a small amount (under a penny) to support MDH smoking prevention programs, becoming the first state to dedicate tobacco tax revenues to tobacco use prevention and control programs (Phelps, 1996a). In 1997, state legislation was enacted that required licensing of all retail outlets selling tobacco products, mandatory once-a-year compliance checks by local authorities, a ban on self-service sales of single packs of cigarettes, and a requirement that manufacturers of cigarettes and smokeless tobacco submit an annual report to the state disclosing the presence of ammonia, arsenic, cadmium, formaldehyde, and lead in their products.

Minnesota has also been an innovator and leader in the development and implementation of local tobacco control policies. In 1979, the Minneapolis City Council passed one of the first ordinances restricting the free distribution of cigarettes (Minnesota Department of Health, 1984). The ordinance subsequently became a model for other local jurisdictions. In October 1989, White Bear Lake, a city of 25,000 in the Minneapolis-St. Paul Metropolitan Area, became the first city in the United States to ban the sale of cigarettes through vending machines (Forster, Hourigan, and J. Weigum, 1990; Minnesota Department of Health, 1991). Within a year, 19 additional communities in Minnesota enacted similar bans (Forster et al., 1990), as did a number of other communities across the United States. Roseville, a suburb of St. Paul, "is recognized as the first city to ban self-service single pack sales" (Associated Press, 1995). The small town of Chanhassen, a few miles west of Minneapolis, is the first city to ban self-service sales of all tobacco products (ibid.). Finally, the city of Preston (population 1530) passed an ordinance in 1994 that limited point-of-sale advertisements of tobacco products to two small signs per store, the first such local restriction on point-of-sale tobacco advertising in the nation (Association for Nonsmokers-Minnesota, 1994b).

Assessments by the tobacco industry reinforce the understanding of Minnesota's pivotal role in the history of the Tobacco Control Movement. For example, documents filed in Ramsey County District Court included this 1984 assessment written by an executive of Brown and Williamson Tobacco Corporation: "As we look forward, one of our tasks is to blunt in every possible way the march of the antismokers in Minnesota, where a special movement is underway, using legislation and propaganda to put the state in the forefront of the drive for a smoke-free society" (quoted in Phelps, 1996a:D1). A 1985 memo written by the Tobacco Institute's vice president for state activities stated, "If in the unfortunate circumstances we suffer heavy losses in Minnesota, it would give real impetus for the surgeon general to carry his crusade, utilizing Minnesota's example, to other state legislatures nationwide" (quoted in Phelps, 1996b:D1). A regional official of the Tobacco Institute, in another memorandum, wrote: "Every possible legislative, political, social and theoretical angle is being utilized in our efforts to get out of this session unscathed. Since Minnesota has seen fit to designate itself, as Surgeon General Koop states, 'a model for the country' with regard to antismoking legislation, our only choice in this matter is a complete victory. Anything less could be used against us in other states. We will employ all means to secure that victory" (quoted in ibid.:D3).

In Part 2 of this book, I will examine the development of tobacco control efforts in Minnesota, focusing in particular on the way the movement has built on a rich "infrastructure" of health organizations and health professionals, and on the "interpenetration" of the movement and the state.

NOTES

1. A parallel movement occurred in Britain during the same period (see Hilton, 1995; Walker, 1980).

2. In 1870, 13.9 million cigarettes were sold in the United States. This number increased to 2,233.3 million in 1890 and 7,863.2 million in 1910 (Gottsegen, 1940; Troyer and Markle, 1983). Improved technology that allowed the mass production of cheap cigarettes, the development of safe and reliable matches, and the use of mass marketing methods contributed to the tremendous growth in cigarette consumption (Troyer and Markle, 1983; Kluger, 1996; Tate, 1999).

3. Temperance movement organizations often included tobacco use in their efforts to fight intemperance (see Gordon, 1924). For example, Bessie Lathe Scovell (1939), the president of the Minnesota Woman's Christian Temperance Union, writes that "the Tobacco Habit" was added to the Minnesota WCTU's "Departments of Work" in 1885.

4.   Curiously, the nation that had the strongest antismoking movement during the 1930s and early 1940s was Nazi Germany (Proctor, 1996). According to Proctor (ibid.:1450), the movement was strongly supported by "Nazi medical and military leaders worried that tobacco might prove a hazard to the race." Proctor reassures us that this "does not mean, however, that antismoking movements are inherently fascist" (ibid.:1453).

5.   In addition to the Surgeon General reports, reports on the health effects of exposure to secondhand smoke have been issued by the National Research Council (1986) and the Environmental Protection Agency (1993).

6.   Current smokers were defined as individuals who reported that they had smoked 100 or more cigarettes in their lifetime and that they smoke either "every day" or "some days" (USDHHS, 1998a).

7.   Several of these studies acknowledge that it is unclear whether the observed associations between tobacco use and the health problem in question are causal in nature.

8.   The authors of this report surmise that the mechanism at work here is in utero exposure resulting from the mother's exposure to secondhand smoke from the father.

9.   A few positive aspects of smoking have been suggested in the literature. As noted by Schelling (1992), some people find smoking to be pleasurable. Moreover, there appear to be a few potential therapeutic uses of tobacco. For example, nicotine (administered using a patch in this experiment) was found to be associated with improvements in the symptoms of ulcerative colitis (Sandborn et al., 1997). Findings on cognitive function appear to be somewhat mixed. According to Launer, Feskens, Kalmijn, and Kromhout, (1996:219), "Cigarette smoking has been inversely correlated with the risk for Alzheimer's disease" (Graves et al., 1991), and "Nicotine delivery may improve performance on selected cognitive tests" (Levin, 1992). However, according to Launer and colleagues (1996:219), "these findings do not support the hypothesis of a protective effect of smoking on cognitive function."

10.   There have been debates within the movement about the utility of continuing to spend money on research on the health effects of tobacco use, when it is widely known that tobacco use contributes to a number of serious illnesses. Davis (1992) observed that new research findings may provide a vehicle for recruiting new allies. For example, recent evidence on the association between smoking and cataracts may provide a basis for recruiting some of the nation's 15,500 ophthalmologists involved in patient care in efforts to promote smoking cessation and tobacco control.

11.   This literature has examined such methodological questions as the effects of using "consummated" versus "unconsummated" buys (Cummings, Saunders-Martin, Clarke, and Perla, 1996) on the purchase rates obtained. The propensity of different kinds of outlets to sell tobacco products to youth—vending machines, gas stations, convenience stores, grocery stores, liquor stores—has been investigated (reviewed in Forster and Wolfson, 1998). Variation in purchase success by personal characteristics—such as age, gender, race/ethnicity—has been explored (ibid.). Ethical questions—such as whether participation by nonsmoking youth in compliance checks results in increased probability of smoking or intentions to smoke—

have been explored (in fact, participation may result in reduced intentions to smoke—see Alcaraz, Klonoff, and Landrine, 1997).

12. "Progress in the smoking uptake process" was defined as upward movement between the following categories: would not consider experimenting, would consider experimenting (smoked between 1 and 99 cigarettes), and established smoking (smoked 100 or more cigarettes).

13. There is evidence that low-income and minority neighborhoods are saturated with billboards advertising cigarettes and alcohol (Altman et al., 1991).

14. Both the Coalition and ANSR have been recognized as exemplary coalitions and grassroots organizations, respectively. The coalition, for example, received the 1993 State Coalition Award from the Association of State and Territorial Directors of Public Health Education and the U.S. Centers for Disease Control and Prevention. According to one participant with a long history in Minnesota tobacco control efforts, "It's very interesting to see ASSIST—it's really kind of modeled after what we did in the [Smoke-Free] Coalition, but NCI won't, or the NIH, or Cancer Society for that matter, won't say it's modeled after Minnesota. . . . It's kind of gratifying to see that, but you'd like to see them get recognition, which isn't going to be forthcoming. And partly, if you accept that, and I understand why the national organization like the NCI can't say we modeled this after Minnesota, because it wouldn't sell in the rest of the country. . . . There's strange people here in Minnesota, it's a small state, they've got all these social activists. . . . Minnesota's got all those social activists, and they're the only ones who went for McGovern and Mondale."

3

The Single-Issue Groups—1

This chapter and the subsequent chapters in Part 2 of this book examine the "mobilizing structures" used in the tobacco control movement, first by broadly sketching the organizational structure of the movement at the national level, and then focusing in greater detail on single-issue tobacco control groups in Minnesota. In the first of two chapters on the single-issue organizations, I focus on the origins of the Association of Nonsmokers-Minnesota (ANSR) and its activities in the 1970s and early 1980s, including its involvement in two key pieces of state legislation—the 1975 Minnesota Clean Indoor Air Act (MCIAA) and the 1985 Omnibus Bill on Nonsmoking and Health. The two central themes of the book—the way in which the movement has build on a preexisting "infrastructure" of health organizations and professionals, and the close, collaborative relationship between movement organizations and state agencies—will be evident in this discussion.

As in most social movements, single-issue groups play a key role in the tobacco control movement. In the modern movement (post-1964), many of the first single-interest groups to become active focused their efforts on what was often a personal, directly experienced grievance: exposure to secondhand smoke. Action on Smoking and Health (ASH)—founded by John Banzhaf in 1967 (Troyer and Markle, 1983)—has actually had a fairly broad focus that was consistent with the consumerist perspective that had been popularized by the work of Ralph Nader and others. Its first issue was the "defense and enforcement" of the 1967 FCC decision (which itself was the result of a petition filed by Banzhaf) requiring the airing of antismoking commercials (Troyer and Markle, 1983). ASH subsequently was involved as a proponent of many of the key tobacco control policies of the early 1970s, including new restrictions on smoking on airplanes (issued by the Civil Aeronautics Bureau in 1973), buses (issued by the Interstate Commerce Commission in 1974), and railroads (issued by the Interstate Commerce Commission in 1976). Over the years, ASH has maintained this national-level, policy focus, although it has a large mailing list of adherents (primarily financial contributors) throughout the fifty states.

ASH had a clear national focus. Beginning in the 1970s, local and state-level groups—such as Group Against Smokers' Pollution (GASP) groups—have advocated for clean air polices at the state and local level in many states. GASP is a kind of loose—in fact, a very loose—network of organizations. According to one veteran activist in Minnesota speaking in the early 1990s:

> GASP is ... just a bunch of little organizations. The GASP organizations aren't associated with each other at all. One GASP has nothing to do with any other GASP.... The only thing they share is the name, and most of their organizations are really small. I think you can put all of the other organizations that have paid staff that are in the nonsmokers movement on one hand—and probably one hand of a butcher, if you know what I mean.[1]

A few of these GASP organizations have become especially prominent with respect to national visibility in the movement. In the mid-1990s, five national tobacco control activists and experts were asked to list the five or six most effective "grassroots tobacco control groups" (Hyman, 1997). Two of the three groups mentioned most often were GASP organizations—New Jersey GASP and Massachusetts GASP (the Minnesota grassroots tobacco control organization, ANSR, was also among these three).

People concerned with nonsmokers' rights in California, as well as Florida, had organized during the late 1970s to support ballot initiatives to enact clean indoor air laws along the lines of the Minnesota Clean Indoor Air Act of 1975 (the legislative battle for the Minnesota law is described later in this chapter). However, the tobacco industry—stung by its defeat in Minnesota—mobilized multimillion dollar advertising campaigns against these initiatives, which were defeated (Glantz, 1987). Several of the key players who supported the two California initiatives—including Stanton Glantz, a professor at the University of California at San Francisco—formed a new organization in 1980, which they named Californians for Nonsmokers' Rights (ibid.). The new organization adopted a strategy of focusing on local nonsmoking measures, since it is harder for the tobacco industry to mobilize against local policy proposals compared to state legislation (Glantz, 1987; Sylvester, 1989; see also Chapter 9 for a more extended discussion of this theme).[2] The organization changed its name to Americans for Nonsmokers Rights (ANR, and took on an explicit national focus, in 1984 (Kluger, 1996). According to a key actor in the Minnesota movement, who has had considerable contact with ANR:

> They felt they had a message to carry outside of the state of California. But I think they felt there was a need for a national organization which was not be-

ing met by ASH. And I think that's a feeling shared by a lot of people. I don't think very many people think that ASH really has as strong a national approach as they would like to see. ASH really is very . . . has a real limited agenda. And they do a good job at what they do [such as filing the suit that got tobacco out of the airways] . . . and they were the heroes and the stars on that. . . . I guess they see themselves as playing a real role in national legislation. But they certainly don't coordinate anybody else. . . . You know, we've got to have a constituency and in the case of national legislation, a constituency, there's other organizations. And we need to be able to call somebody in Nebraska and say we need to get you on so and so's case. We need organization. Go talk to senator whoever. And ASH never has played that well.

ANR has advocated for, and served as an information resource for advocates working for the development of state and local nonsmoking ordinances. With support from the Smoking, Tobacco, and Cancer Program of the National Cancer Institute, it has tracked the adoption of local smoking ordinances in cities throughout the United States (e.g., Pertshuck and Shopland, 1989).

Meanwhile, a number of organizations focusing on youth tobacco use had been started. Doctors Ought to Care (DOC) was founded in 1977, and by 1993 counted 8,000 members and 40 state chapters (Blum, Vidstrand, and Solberg, 1995; Morain, 1993). DOC focuses on tobacco and alcohol marketing to youth, and uses paid satirical counteradvertising to lampoon and counteract the marketing efforts of these industries (Blum, 1994; Blum et al., 1995; Morain, 1993)

Stop Teenage Addiction to Tobacco (STAT) was founded by Joe B. Tye III in 1985 (Kluger, 1996). The president of ANSR, Jeanne Weigum, characterizes STAT, and its value to ANSR, as follows:

STAT has a little different role, too. Their mission appears to be much more kids and educational. And that's a relatively recent development, and they're trying to be national kind of clearinghouse on youth information. I think their publications have been marvelous. . . . Their newsletter is really worth seeing. Their cartoons we borrow, snitch, steal, use their cartoons. You know those are things . . . I think that that kind of pollinization really helps all of the organizations when people come up with good stuff. . . . We're on everybody's newsletter. I mean . . . we exchange newsletters with everybody.

More recently, the National Center for Tobacco Free Kids began in 1996, supported by generous funding from the Robert Wood Johnson Foundation (RWJF) as well as contributions from the American Cancer Society, the American Medical Association, and the American Heart Association (Robert Wood Johnson Foundation, 1996).[3] From its inception in 1996, the

National Center for Tobacco-Free Kids established a high-visibility role in advocating for FDA regulation of tobacco sales and promotion to youth. The center sponsored a national television campaign meant to build popular and congressional support for FDA regulation, a public opinion poll that demonstrated widespread support for the rule proposed by the FDA, and a variety of other advocacy efforts (Campaign for Tobacco-Free Kids, 1996; Forster and Wolfson, 1998). The Campaign for Tobacco-Free kids was also central to efforts to ensure adequate implementation of the FDA regulations. For instance, lobbying by the campaign and other tobacco control groups appears to have played an important role in 1997 approval of the Clinton administration's request for funding of FDA-sponsored efforts to enforce the new regulations. The Senate initially approved only $4.9 million for the effort, which would have been sufficient to fund enforcement efforts in only ten states. However, an intense lobbying campaign took place during the summer recess, and in September the Senate approved an increase in funding to the amount requested by the administration, ($34 million; Forster and Wolfson, 1998). However, in a significant setback, the Supreme Court overturned the FDA regulations in March 2000, ruling that the FDA lacks the authority to regulate tobacco products (Gottlieb, 2000).

In addition to these single-issue groups, a number of multiple issue groups, such as consumer organizations, have had substantial involvement in tobacco control efforts. Ralph Nader in 1970 unsuccessfully petitioned the Federal Highway Commission to prohibit smoking on buses. In 1971, a federal court refused Nader's request to ban smoking on commercial air carriers. Public Citizen, a consumer organization founded by Nader in 1971, prepared and submitted to the FDA a lengthy and detailed legal analysis supporting FDA's authority to regulate tobacco products during the comment period on the proposed legislation (Zieve and Morrison, 1996). From 1990 to 2000 the Advocacy Institute sponsored SCARCNet, an Internet-based tobacco control news service and strategy exchange, which played a key role in the exchange of information on implementation of tobacco control efforts.[4]

RWJF's SmokeLess States program, which began in 1994, is the largest nongovernmental tobacco control effort in the United States. The national program office at the American Medical Association provides grants to "statewide coalitions working in partnership with community groups" "[to] reduce tobacco use among Americans, particularly children and youth" (Robert Wood Johnson Foundation, 1993, 1996). Each project must include four elements: mobilizing state coalitions, a public education campaign, enhanced prevention and treatment capacity, and tobacco policy development. The latter includes "promotion of ordinances and other policy actions to inhibit access to tobacco products—including illegal sales— among children and youth" (Robert Wood Johnson Foundation, 1993). As of mid-1996, RWJF had provided a total of over $8 million to a nonprofit or government organization in each of nine states for implementation grants and close to $2 million to similar organizations in ten additional states for capacity-building grants (Robert Wood Johnson Foundation, 1996). RWJF announced plans in May 1996 to fund up to twenty-one additional statewide coalitions aimed at reducing tobacco use, particularly among children and youth.

SINGLE-ISSUE GROUPS AND TOBACCO CONTROL IN MINNESOTA

In Minnesota, two advocacy organizations have played a central role in the movement: the Association of Nonsmokers-Minnesota (ANSR—the initials are from the original name of the organization, Association for Nonsmokers Rights), and the Minnesota Coalition for a Smoke-Free Society 2000. In addition to being the twin hubs of the movement in Minnesota, both groups have garnered national attention and recognition.

ANSR was the first single-issue tobacco control organization in Minnesota, and one of the first such groups in the United States. It began as a program of the Hennepin County office of the American Lung Association in 1973, when a staff person and a group of volunteers began working on the issue secondhand smoke.

At the outset, and throughout its history, ANSR—members and staff alike—has been motivated by grievances related to exposure to secondhand smoke. For example, one leader of ANSR said:

> I was really bothered tremendously by smoke, and I had graduated from the university, and I remember classes at the "U" that were so smoky that you could virtually not breathe. There were times when we would vote in a class not to allow smoking and at some point during the class, somebody would say it's so bad in here I can't breathe. Sometimes this was even initiated by smokers. . . . Half the people in a relatively small room, including the professor, would be smoking and windows would be closed. Even if you opened them, you know how bad that is. It would be so bad you absolutely would gag.

Later, after this person began working in a suburban Minneapolis school system, she experienced similar problems:

> I remember being in a faculty meeting where a number of people were smoking and I became particularly sensitized and started sneezing and could not quit sneezing. I just . . . I sneezed and I sneezed and I sneezed, and virtually everybody was aware that what was the problem was the smoke, and they

didn't stop smoking. It was just absolutely appalling. I just . . . I could not . . . I mean the meeting virtually couldn't go on, and yet the smoker didn't quit smoking. . . . I was sneezing, and everybody else was sort of looking around, and sort of looking at the smoker and he continued to smoke until the cigarette was gone. And somebody got up and opened a window. And that wasn't uncommon. You know, it was . . . there was no sense that there was sort of an obligation of the community to not allow this to happen at that point. . . . There was just a really limited sense of nonsmokers having any rights at all at that point.

One of the first projects the group took on was an effort to identify what restrictions, if any, governed smoking in public places:

They did some early things like they tried to catalog what laws and ordinances related to smoking and clean indoor air in communities. They tried to do a survey of what are the laws that related to clean indoor air in St. Paul, Minneapolis, Bloomington, Plymouth, etc. They discovered there were different ordinances. Every time you crossed a city line, there was a different ordinance. They were primarily health and safety ordinances so there were some elevator ordinances, there were some smoking around food preparation areas [ordinances], there were some around fire, inflammables [ordinances]—that kind of thing. But even those kind of fairly simple health and safety regulations really varied tremendously from one city to another. I think they did some kind of a restaurant survey, and I think we did kind of a grocery store survey. I think they were trying to deal with pretty obvious kinds of problem areas initially and then it was kind of as an outgrowth of that activity that they tried to do the first Clean Indoor Act and all they got the first time through was a resolution.

The fledgling organization's second attempt to persuade the Minnesota legislature to enact the nation's first, comprehensive clean indoor air legislation—in 1975—was successful.[5] ANSR members linked up with Phyllis Kahn, a Democratic-Farmer-Labor (DFL) representative from Minneapolis who trained as a biophysicist at Yale (Minnesota Secretary of State, 1991) and had been elected to the Minnesota House in 1972. Several factors contributed to the passage of this bill: it was supported by the ALA, the ACS, and other health organizations in Minnesota, former Surgeon General Jesse Steinfeld and other physicians testified in support of the bill (Steinfeld testified when it was first introduced in 1974; Kahn, 1983), and, most importantly, the tobacco industry did not mobilize against it on anywhere near the scale they did on subsequent legislative battles in Minnesota and in other states (see Chapters 8 and 9). However, Kahn (ibid.:1300) makes ANSR's role plain: "The reason [the bill passed] was the work of a persistent and devoted (although small and new) organization, the Association for Non-Smoker's Rights (ANSR). Its activities included helping to write the bill, getting witnesses before committees, writing letters, and maintaining visibility in the legislative process at every stage."

One of the distinguishing features of ANSR is that—unlike any of the other organizations involved in the movement in Minnesota—it has—and has had, since early in its existence—a large membership base. Members are recruited in a variety of ways. Early in the organization's history, it advertised in local newspapers. For example, Jeanne Weigum, recalled her own entree into the organization:

> I saw a small personal ad in the personals as I recall. It was in the classifieds or else it was just a very tiny article, like a filler piece at the bottom of a page, and I cut that and I left it by the telephone for a long time, and one day I just called and said I wanted to be a card-carrying member. At that time the dues were one dollar.

Many people responded to this and similar advertisements that ran when ANSR, and the issue of secondhand smoke, was receiving press coverage because of the 1975 MCIAA:

> Ed [Brandt, one of the early ANSR activists] tells a story of new memberships coming on in, just flowing in. Sounds as he tells it like there were buckets of memberships coming in, and I suspect that that was the time that our membership was at its highest.

At the time, there were few mechanisms by which somebody aggrieved about their exposure to secondhand smoke could identify others with similar grievances. This is illustrated by Jeanne Weigum's recollection of the first ANSR meeting she attended:

> I went to a meeting that was at St. Thomas [the University of St. Thomas, in St. Paul]. They had meetings about twice a year at that point. I went to a meeting that was like an all-day Saturday meeting . . . more kind of a workshop kind of thing, and discovered that my neighbor was there too. I was shocked. . . . I was very surprised to see him there.

Because of the novelty of the issue at the time, the press found it interesting. Jeanne Weigum continues:

> The style of ANSR meetings back then, and until we left the lung association, was an all-day Saturday meeting, and we had one or two of those a year. They tended to be incredibly time-consuming in terms of planning and that kind of thing. Lots of speakers, lots of effort. And the press always came. It was a big deal. I mean, we got press coverage because then it was new and often different enough that the press found an annual meeting to be interesting. And I mean, try and get the press interested in an annual meeting today.

Later in the 1970s, ANSR expanded its organizational involvement to include part-time donated staff from the Minnesota, Ramsey County, and Hennepin County Lung Associations. According to one observer,

> It was a program activity of the lung associations that cut across all three lines so it didn't make sense for Hennepin to do alone. It wasn't smoking cessation, it wasn't this study. It was a separate program area which the lung association had the foresight to see was important.

However, this structure led to some problems:

> They were supposed to be handling different facets, but there never was very good coordination. There became increased friction between the three organizations. . . . There seemed to be a lot of griping about who was going to do something.

ANSR at the time had a large and active board of directors. One participant said that "it was a working board, and the majority of things that got done were done by board members, so if you came onto that board, you were coming on to do the job." Moreover, "It was a big board. It seems to me it was about a 25 person board. . . . Too big. It was not manageable." The board had some very solid members, and

> then there were this other half of the board who were really committee [members], and would have been just delighted to be on a committee. [They] were kind of out of their water. When we became an independent organization [in 1981], one of the first things we had to do was get rid of those people. Yeah, we needed to. And, unfortunately, most of them really did leave the organization at that point. They felt kind of left out, unwanted, that kind of thing. That's very hard.

Each of the three lung associations had a representative on the board. However, the ANSR board, and some of the programmatic efforts of the organization—particularly its interest in advocacy efforts—created tensions within the lung associations:

> I think it always made them uncomfortable. I think they were always uncomfortable with the activist kind of things that the ANSR board wanted to do, and sometimes the ANSR board wanted to do things that they shouldn't do. I mean there's also that. I think that there is a real service provided by the lung association in terms of preventing the board [from doing things that would have been] much more aggressive than would have been helpful.

One example of the radical instincts of some of the members of the board involved a litigious-minded member:

I can remember one guy that wanted us to sue the state of Minnesota. And every meeting he came and wanted us to sue the state of Minnesota for lack of enforcement of the Clean Indoor Air Act. Well, it was a stupid thing to do. And I don't know if the board really ever had gone along with it, but the Lung Association wouldn't—not the board head. . . . The more mature, go slow approach of the Lung Association did provide a service of keeping things from spinning out of control at times.

ANSR experienced quite a bit of turnover in leadership in its early years. There were early presidents who alienated other board members or the membership in a variety of ways. And board members themselves came and went:

There were a lot of people who came and went, you know. And it tended to be that people who were involved in the original passing of the Clean Indoor Act did not stick with the organization. . . . There were the types of people who worked to pass the law did not seem to be the kind of people who stuck around to make sure it got enforced. . . . This had to do with again the wrong kind of people being on the board.

In the early years ANSR had an open, participatory decision-making style that sometimes led to problems:

We used to have meeting once a year to establish the program of work for the coming year, and this would be an open meeting. So it would be members of the board and anybody else who wanted to come. It's an odd way of doing it, because you get people coming to establish the programs for the following year who don't really have that much history.

Jeanne Weigum, who was to become the longtime leader of ANSR, described the conflicts involving the lung associations and ANSR in the mid- and late 1970s as follows:

There was lots of in-fighting between the lung associations that affected ANSR. And the year I became president, Hennepin withdrew its sponsorship. And then it was just Minnesota and Ramsey Lung. . . . My understanding was that [the executive director of the Hennepin County ALA] just got real tired of nobody ever being able to figure who was supposed to be doing what. And I think he thought that there was so much backbiting and so much finger pointing and nobody every knowing who was going to do what. And this staff person constantly complaining that other staff people weren't doing their work, that he just decided we've done our time and got out. . . . I think it had to do with just them. They [the three lung associations] have trouble dealing with each other. . . . And for years, they found it easier to work with us than with each other. . . . It wasn't at all uncommon for Hennepin and Ramsey and ANSR to sponsor a program because as long as ANSR was in, then there are not turf problems. But there would be turf problems the minute it was just the two lungs. It was somehow adding ANSR into the mix. It took some of the . . . some of the conflict out. And maybe that's still to some degree true. I suspect it is. But I think that they're getting along better now than they did then.

Weigum elaborates on the turf issues among the ALA organizations:

But there were terrible turf issues then. . . . I mean, they actually had the tele-vision stations divided up—one got WCCO and the other got KSTP. And this one gets this paper. . . . And you can't solicit money on this side of the river and I can't solicit money on that side. And you can't talk to that company even though there are employees in this city and that city. It all comes down to money, and who's going to get what. Which is why Minnesota Lung had to be involved, because they. . . . they could provide kind of a bridge. But you see, Minnesota can't contact Metro stations—they contact the outstate sta-tions [where there isn't a local lung association].

From the time of its advocacy on behalf of the MCIA of 1975, ANSR had relatively little involvement in state legislation until the 1985 campaign to pass the Omnibus bill:

ANSR did not have any kind of an initiative in the legislature really until our involvement with the Omnibus No-Smoking Bill. We had a couple of reac-tive involvements where there were threats to the Clean Indoor Act, and we rallied the troops and showed up at the capitol and wrote letters and got hys-terical. But we didn't have any bills of our own until the Omnibus Non-Smoking Bill in 1985.

The group engaged in efforts to keep its fingers on the pulse of the mem-bership: "For quite some time we would call new members and welcome them to the group and ask them what their concerns were and were there special things they wanted the organization to 'beat the band' on."

And most often, the members were interested in enforcement of the MCIA. Many of the programmatic efforts in the years following the 1975 passage of the MCIA focused on enforcement of the new law. For example, a restaurant survey was done, and the results indicated that many restau-rants were not in compliance with the legislation. So,

[ANSR at the time was involved in] a lot of enforcement stuff. In fact, there was a committee who did a really nice job on restaurant compliance. . . . They sent a letter to every restaurant in the state. God knows how they did that. . . . They got the state list, and they mailed the thing off, telling restaurants what they need to do to comply.

Members of the group designed what may have been the first no-smoking signs, and worked to distribute them as a mechanism for encouraging the enforcement of the MCIA. ANSR was also involved in developing the rules that implement the MCIA. The Minnesota Department of Health (MDH) had meetings with people to discuss the problems, and then held meetings at a later date in which testimony was taken. Key ANSR representatives were often involved in meetings during the investigative period, before the draft rules were written.

Interestingly, the relationship between ANSR and MDH was not good at the outset. According to Jeanne Weigum:

> The relationship initially was horrible. It was terrible. The first actual annual meeting that I went to. There were two or three hundred there, and [the head of the Environmental Division, which was in charge of enforcing the MCIA] was asked to give a presentation, and whoever introduced him, introduced him as the enemy: "And now we're going to hear what the enemy has to say." . . . He did a lot of wringing his hands, saying that they didn't have any money to do the enforcing. They didn't have staff to do enforcement and why did they expect him to do all this work without giving him a staff. Well, that had been a decision that was made at the legislative level because if you'd ask, it would have to have gone through two more committees, and that would have been the death of the bill. There was a deliberate strategy on Phyllis's [Kahn's] part not to put money onto it because then it didn't need to go through those committees. But what it meant was here was the Health Department stuck with something to enforce. And it turned out to take a fair amount of their time. They started getting a lot of phone calls on it. They didn't—this wasn't their bill. This wasn't a departmental bill. . . . He was constantly frustrated by the fact that there was no staff provided to him. He just was sort of magically supposed to take care of this, shift other personnel around to do it.

This state of affairs—no legislative appropriation to support efforts to enforce the MCIA—continued until passage of the Omnibus Non-Smoking Disease Prevention Act of 1985 (discussed later in this chapter and in Chapters 7 and 9). According to Weigum, "it seemed like every session we were told there isn't money available. You know, we're looking at budget cuts, and . . . it never seemed like it would fly."

Despite the bad start, ANSR's relationship with MDH improved over time. Jeanne Weigum:

> When I got involved in a leadership role, I felt there was really no point in haggling with these people—that you needed to work with them. We needed them, and they could use us. And so we tried real hard to forge a better relationship, and as soon as I got involved that became one of my goals—to try and forge a better relationship. And, over the years, it really has. They [MDH]

in fact in their annual report to the legislature list ANSR and basically say we handled certain numbers of complaints for them and it makes it so that the only ones they handle are the more difficult ones to resolve.

Thus, we see here another aspect of the integral relationship between a social movement organization and a state agency: joint involvement in implementation of the Minnesota Clean Indoor Air Act. ANSR was not only involved in processing complaints under the MCIA, but also in producing and disseminating literature publicizing the provisions of the Act:

> We also have produced the only literature that has ever been produced about the Clean Indoor Act. They've [MDH] never done anything in the way of literature, and partly that may be because we've done it so they didn't have to. They've always distributed our literature.[6]

Weigum further describes this relationship, which illustrates the symbiotic relationship between MDH and ANSR with respect to enforcement of the MCIA:

> The disadvantage is that it costs us money. On the other hand, a couple of times on things that they've known we we're going to be using and that was to their benefit, they've helped print. So it's been mutual backscratching. There are a couple of things that they've actually printed for us. . . . I think that's real healthy. I think that it's real helpful to have an enforcement body that has equal clout that's doing the first line of enforcement—dealing with some complaints and resolving some things and saying, 'Look, we're just here to help. We're here to negotiate. We don't have any authority. We can't tell you what to do, but you can talk with us about what you want to do,' whereas the Health Department will tell you what you can't do. We can tell you what, if they come in, what they're going to tell you you have to do. We can tell you that. We can't make you do that. . . . I think there are organizations who would much rather deal with us, and there are those who would much rather deal with the Health Department. So it gives people a real choice.

Many of the complaints ANSR handles involve exposure to secondhand smoke in the workplace. As the following quotation from Jeanne Weigum illustrates, ANSR's involvement in enforcement of the MCIA is in fact a key mechanism for protecting the rights of nonsmokers:

> A call would come in from somebody and real, real typically, somebody says "Do I have any rights in the workplace?" I mean, that hasn't changed in fifteen years. It's still the same: "Do I have any rights?" And we briefly explain to them what their rights are and encourage them to give us their name and address and we'll send them information and a complaint form. . . . A lot of

people won't give us their name, but then we receive a substantial number of calls from relatives: "I'm calling for my son. He's afraid because he might lose his job. I'm calling for my wife—she's having a terrible time at work." And I think they really are calling for these people. I don't think they're just making that up. I think they're saying this is a problem for a loved one of mine and can I get some information from you.

People concerned about their exposure, or a friend's or relative's exposure, to secondhand smoke in the workplace may identify ANSR as an appropriate vehicle for pursuing their complaints in any of several ways. According to Weigum,

It's interesting. Sometimes they get us from the Cancer Society or the Lung Association. Sometimes the Health Department—they refer things to us, we refer things to them. Sometimes they've seen a little article in the paper about something or other. We've done public service announcements, so sometimes they've gotten it from there. Sometimes they've picked up something years earlier at the State Fair. Sometimes it's a friend who has said, "You ought to call these people."

After getting the call,

Typically we send them a bunch of information and a complaint form, and most people never get in touch with us again. The majority of people at that point either resolve it on their own or decide this is too hard or they change jobs or whatever. And then if they're going to follow through on it, some weeks later we get a written complaint back and do not handle complaints that are anonymous. If it's an anonymous complaint, we pitch it because we can't determine if it's true or false . . . we have no way of following up on it. The Health Department will take anonymous complaints but we won't, so we tell people when they call us that if you don't want to give your name, we can't help you. We can give you information, we can send you stuff, but we won't handle your complaint. . . . Then we send a letter to the employer saying the following has been alleged and this is what the law says. If this is true—we don't know if it's true or not—but if it is true, this is what you could do to change the situation. This is how we can help you. If you want further help from us, this is how we can help you. And then we've taken various approaches. Sometimes we've said if we don't hear from you within twelve days, we'll forward this to the Health Department. That tends to get a quick response. . . . Then typically they will call us and ask for more information. We'll send them additional information. We've had follow up with companies—little companies to 3M.

Sometimes ANSR will send a staff person out to meet with the employer, treating the employee's identify confidentially:

So we will contact the employer and say this is the complaint and is this in fact true and if not what is the situation? And then sometimes they'll say, "Well, would you come out here and help us solve this?" and then we . . . will go out and walk through the workplace and look at their workplace, work environments, and look at options and that kind of thing and help them designate areas or do whatever they are going to do.

Sometimes the call to ANSR is initiated by an employer:

The other kind of thing we get involved as often as the employee calls is the employer call. And that would be the employer calling and saying we have a problem with smoking here and I want to resolve it. What can we do—can you help us? So then we send them more literature. Then [an ANSR staff person] will go out and meet with them. And that procedure, although our level of sophistication of our material has changed very dramatically—you know, we've got just much, much better stuff then we did before. But basically, that approach hasn't changed since '76, '77.

ANSR leaves much more of MCIA enforcement in restaurants to the state or local health departments:

In the early years, we got a lot of complaints about restaurants. And we try to deal with them. We contact the restaurant. We tell them what they needed to do. It came to us over time that the one thing the Health Department seemed to really do pretty well was enforcement in restaurants, because they have inspectors in those places. They don't have inspectors in workplaces. And so why should we do doubling up on something they are already doing and doing pretty well. . . . We encourage the Health Department to do some training of sanitarians. They did, and, in general, sanitarians are doing a great job. Now, in the outstate area, it continues to be a problem. Mac lives next door to Joe who owns the restaurant down the street and Mac's the health inspector and he probably isn't going to tell that a guy's got to shape up and so there's still major problems in the outstate area. But in the Metro, it's really going pretty well. . . . You know, the sanitarians go in and they have a check-off list, and one of the things we worked on is to make sure that smoking thing was on the checklist.

However,

In fact the way that it has worked is that it's just one more thing. So the freezers aren't cold, the nonsmoking section isn't large enough and there are flies in the dining area. You know they probably wouldn't close them up for . . . any one of those things. They might for the freezers if they couldn't get the freezers cold enough because you're going to have people dying. So that's an immediate health risk, but [nonsmoking areas] fits in the category of other things that are not immediate health risks.

As a result of passage of the Omnibus Non-Smoking Disease Prevention Act of 1985, MDH was allocated a staff person for enforcement of the MCIAA, and their enforcement efforts improved considerably:

> Their overall effort has been much, much improved. . . . She goes out. She does workplace inspections. She does letters. Mostly, she does letters. You know, she is going to be doing enforcing all over the state and making site visits, she'd go out of her mind so mostly she does letters. The first letter says we've received this complaint. The second letter says you still haven't shaped up. And then it starts getting tough and says we can get an injunction to close your doors. Which they can. They've never done it and they probably never will, but they say they can and they can.

Despite these improvements, ANSR staff are in some respects critical of MDH's enforcement efforts:

> The Health Department has never had an initiative. Ever. They have never done an educational program. They have never, to the best of my knowledge . . . taken the aggressive role with the Clean Indoor Air Act. Anything in the way of outreach that's been done, we've done. And that is one of the early complaints that I had. I remember meeting with somebody from the Health Department . . . saying what I wanted to see was some creativity from the department instead of just handling complaints—doing something to initiate compliance and educational efforts. And we got the same thing always: "We don't have any money . . . to do the whole thing."

Thus, we see a kind of division of labor between a grassroots movement organization—ANSR—and a state agency—MDH—with respect to enforcement of a key piece of tobacco control legislation.

ANSR might never have started if it had not been for the ALA. In an example of how the tobacco control movement has grown out of the infrastructure of health organizations, ANSR was born and incubated in the lung association. However, schisms are common in social movements, especially in their early stages (McCarthy and Zald, 1977; Gamson, 1990). By the late 1970s, ANSR's relationship with the American Lung Association had turned increasingly sour. Jeanne Weigum:

> And I kind of made the decision at that point that we needed to do something to preserve ANSR because this thing with the Lung Association didn't look real good. There were increasing frustrations between that board and the Lung Association about wanting to control staff and wanting to control budget—with ANSR wanting to control the staff that was assigned. We wanted accountability for the time that was . . . supposedly given to us. What were these people doing? There was a period of time where there was no staff person assigned and we pushed real hard to get [an official at the Lung As-

sociation] to hire somebody. Somebody had left and she didn't get around to hiring somebody for months. And so during that whole time, it was . . . nobody was doing anything. . . . So I remember a meeting at [an ANSR board member's] house where a half-dozen of us met and talked about the alternatives and what we ought to do. And the group of us who were there decided that there were three alternatives. That it was untenable for us to remain in the organization as it was. That it was too painful for us personally to be there. There was so much tension, so much anger and still going nowhere. . . . We needed to start a new organization. Just start from scratch and say blow it off and let the Lung Association do whatever they wanted with their little program and forget it. Or try and basically steal the organization. And we played all the options again and again and again. And if we were going to do it, how were we going to do it? And basically started trying to pirate it.

The effort to wrest control of ANSR from the Ramsey County office of ALA proceeded:

After the first meeting, there may have been a list of kind of demands or expectations or something like that. And there was a big meeting then that was called, a meeting of the board where the vote was actually taken: Do we want to become an independent organization? The board had to vote on that, and then there had to be a vote of the membership so the first vote was what did the board want to do? And that was so tense. Oh, I just . . . I cannot tell you how unpleasant that was. Lots of anger, lots of blame, lots of accusing.

Some board members felt strongly that ANSR should continue as part of the Lung Association, and felt betrayed by the effort to effect a split:

[They] viewed us as usurpers, ungrateful. People who did a lot better doing selfish—self aggrandizing. There was a lot of thought that we were just trying to steal some glory. God knows what glory there was to steal. . . . The vote at the board meeting was to take it to the membership with a recommendation to become a separate 501(c)(3). And we worked our tails off to pass because we had to get people to the meeting and we had to get the right people to the meeting. . . . I don't know if you've ever been a part of an organization, on the fringes of an organization that's in the process of rebuilding itself. . . . It gets very difficult to inform people on what's really going on because anything you say sounds paranoid.

The membership did not have any sense of this conflict—it was a complete surprise. "So you're starting with a membership that has been reading newsletters, that don't know anything about any internal things. . . . So that all the informing of the membership had to take place in that window between the board member vote and the time of the meeting." The key

ANSR board members—now dissidents—had done some mailings to the entire membership, trying to lay out the issues, and encouraging them to come:

> The membership meeting was at the Hennepin County Government Center—there's a little auditorium there. And there was a blizzard. It was just a dreadful day. But we got a hundred or more to come. And we had arranged a series of speakers and we tried to sort of have a pro and a con and a pro and a con. And the vote went for separation. That was very tense. There were representatives from the Lung Association there. [A Lung Association representative] spoke against—she looked so angry—oh, she was so angry. And a couple other people from Lung were there and spoke against. But the staff didn't fight. . . . I think they felt we were going to flop. I think that they were pretty darn sure we were not going to make it.

So, ANSR became independent in 1980. The leaders of the group—after some wrangling with Ramsey Lung Association officials—were given the remaining funds that had been in the ANSR account at the Ramsey County Lung Association (all of $6,000) to get the new organization off and running. A few members of the board contributed $1,000 a piece to get the effort off the ground—to cover, together with the leftover money from the lung association, a few months salary (ANSR had not had a separate payroll while it was part of the lung association—there had only been the donated salary from the lungs, volunteers, and board members). In many ways, the transition was not easy:

> And that was another problem—that the board was used to doing the things that needed to be done. . . . The treasurer wanted to keep the books at her house. And she was basically able to keep it, like a family checkbook was her level of recordkeeping. And that couldn't be. I mean, we were not a 501(c)(3), and we've got to keep those records . . . for the U.S. government. And we've got to do payroll.

There was conflict within the personnel committee of the board (which included the person who was president at the time) on what kind of person to hire: a fund-raiser or a program person. According to Jeanne Weigum, those in favor of hiring someone with fund-raising skills

> wanted us to be $100,000 in the black in the next year, and wanted us to be able to have Pillsburys on our board of directors. And we aren't. And we will never be. You know, we've succeeded a few times in getting highly impressive people to be on our board. And they tend not to stay because it's not a high powered group. It's not the kind of organization . . . I mean, it's not like being on the board of directors of the symphony orchestra. You know, what people get out of being on our board is not . . . not the leads from their busi-

ness partners. You know, they get a sense of satisfaction of helping a small organization do well.

In the end, the decision was made to hire a person with skills in program development and implementation. One member of the board resigned as a result. According to Jeanne Weigum, "It really was a major power struggle at that point in terms of what the direction of the organization would be." ANSR changed its name shortly after becoming independent.

The Association for Nonsmokers' Rights is a title that was sort of born of the '60s mentality and that was OK . . . a more confrontational mentality. . . . A much more confrontational approach to things. And we really felt that it was important to get into corporate America with our . . . with what we had to say. And we wanted to be helping not just employees, but employers also. We saw that as a whole place where we needed to get involved. And as long as we were identified as people who weren't going to give them trouble, once we got in the door they were in big trouble. . . . And so we thought by dropping the word "rights" it made . . . it was a subtle change but one that we felt would in the long run signify a different kind of approach, and one which we had wanted to take so we would be more accessible.

The new organization forged ahead, under what could be called "primitive conditions."[7] The group had received a donated typewriter, but the period key didn't work.[8] While getting ready to do the first membership mailing, the ANSR group realized that the names they had inherited from the days when the organization was housed at ALA weren't organized, so they typed them up alphabetically for mailing—only to learn that the names had to be in order of the zip code to obtain discounted mailing costs. They would have to sort 2,000 pieces of mail by zip code.

Almost from the outset, the new organization experienced problems on the board. The board was composed of the same people as it had been during the organization's time as part of Ramsey County ALA, except the two people appointed by Lung Association were no longer on it. Thus, the board of the new organization included a number of people who had opposed the move to become independent. As a consequence, there was a lack of trust among many of its members.[9] There were also competing visions of the role of the board: some favored a policy board (where staff would be hired to do all of the day-to-day work), while others favored a working board (where, as in the past, board members would work on committees).

Finally, a decision was made to reshape the board to reflect the leaders' vision of the organization. Jeanne Weigum:

And then at that point—I mean this was the dirty stuff, and it was icky. . . . We had to get rid of the people on the board who had no concept of what we

had. We didn't want to get rid of them as people. We wanted them to continue to be involved in the organization but we needed to find a role for them
that was suitable and not the role they were in. . . . There was a committee
that met and recommended that we go from a 25-person board to an 11-per-
son board. And that was what was done at the next annual meeting, which
meant that half the people were no longer on the board. And that was the really big turning point of the organization. That changed it forever. . . . The
nominating committee then proceeded to nominate the thinkers instead of
the committee-type people. But there were hurt feelings, and there were a
few of the people who continued to be what was nominal involvement. But
basically a lot of people were turned off by it. And I still feel real bad about
that because there were people who had a contribution to make. It just
wasn't as a board member. And from that point on we really struggled to try
and upgrade the quality of the board, and we have tried unsuccessfully
pretty much to get business people on the board. We have real good success
getting health educators on the board. We could have a board of total health
educators. And they love it. . . . Right now we have a pretty good mix—we
have a couple of business people, we have a doctor, we have some health educators, and we have one politician [a Republican Party activist, city council
member in Chanhassen, a Minneapolis suburb].

Interestingly, ANSR's relationship with MDH precipitated the grassroots organization's first major proactive foray in state legislative advocacy
since the passage of the MCIAA in the early 1970s. ANSR, along with other
groups, worked with MDH to develop the Minnesota Plan for Nonsmoking and Health, which was published in 1984 (see Chapter 7 for a detailed
description of the Minnesota Plan and its development). Out of the plan
came a comprehensive piece of legislation—the Omnibus Nonsmoking
and Disease Prevention Act, which was introduced and passed by the
Minnesota legislature, and signed into law, in 1985. According to Jeanne
Weigum,

> We really had not been real strongly politically proactive up to that point. You
> know, we . . . there had been a period of just doing a lot of enforcement kinds
> of things and a lot of cooperative activities. And we worked a lot with work-
> places, but hadn't really had a presence with the legislature for a number of
> years.[10]

As can be seen from the following discussion by Jeanne Weigum, the
Health Department "sponsored" ANSR's involvement in advocating for
the Omnibus bill:

> So we had been pretty quiet, but Mike Moen [the MDH official who was
> charged with implementing the Minnesota Plan] kind of identified us as
> more likely to be helpful in the legislature than the other groups. [The other

groups, at this point, included the beginnings of the Minnesota Smoke Free Coalition-2000]. And Mike for some reason identified ANSR as the organization and people, person, who would be likely to be helpful on the bill. . . . I suspect he was aware of our original involvement with the Clean Indoor Air Act. . . . He knew we had a little bit of political background, but he really went out of his way to say look, I think you can help. There's going to be a big role for you guys to play, and we really need you. And he really went out of the way to focus on us as an organization. He also made . . . obviously, he was making efforts to bring other organizations in.

The idea of a greater involvement in state legislative advocacy caused some concerns for the organizations at the meeting called by MDH, mainly among representatives of the health voluntary organizations, who were concerned about their organization's 501(c)(3) nonprofit status:[11]

I remember real clearly one of the early meetings [that Mike called] where there was lots of hand wringing and saying we can't do this without jeopardizing our nonprofit status. And I just said look, that's just not true. You don't jeopardize it as long as you don't spend too much. And there was just so much fear. So much fear. . . . It was clear at that point we could do lobbying. It was . . . and it's still . . . unclear how much. . . . It's very murky. Despite all of the efforts to make it less murky, it's still murky. . . . It was even murkier then than it is now, but it was still clear that they could do it. And yet, the other organizations [ACS, AHA, ALA] really felt intimidated by it. . . . [They] were concerned that their organization would be jeopardized financially or their nonprofit status would be jeopardized. And I think that probably Mike [Moen] picked up that there was enough fear, that they [the voluntaries] weren't going to take any leadership anywhere.[12]

Moen coached ANSR on strategies and tactics: "He pretty much told us what to do and when he needed something done." One of the things the group did was grassroots lobbying of the membership:

We sent really neat, concise things out to our members. We did a real regular communications. We had our membership sorted by legislative district so that we could pull up people in various districts and . . . pinpoint places where we needed a push and contact people with a phone call and some letters. And our membership was real involved in the letter writing, telephoning. . . . In terms of showing up at the legislature, that's just too hard. Just very few people can ever do that. . . . Oh we would try to get people to come to hearings occasionally, but that really doesn't work either because hearings get changed. They get canceled. I mean it's just . . . the system is not really geared up for laypeople to easily participate . . . at that level. At the telephone call and lettering level, people can participate very easily, but stepping it up a little bit is much more difficult. . . . You need to have some reason for people to take the time to write a letter. I don't know about you, but I'm . . . I belong to probably six organizations that all think . . . at least six . . . that think I want to write . . . regularly write to my congressman. And most of the time, I don't. And I'm politically active. So it obviously has to be pretty darn persuasive to get somebody who's not politically active to do it. And that was the thing that we felt would be most persuasive to our members in terms of getting them to actually write a letter. Part of the promotion stuff to ANSR members was that "for the very first time there was going to be money to fund this person" [money for a real staff person to enforce the Clean Indoor Act for the first time ever].

On the advice of MDH ("Mike Moen had said we need to do a survey so we know where our strengths are"), ANSR surveyed legislators to gauge their potential support of, and involvement in, passage of the Omnibus bill. The House author had pulled the bill, so a new author was needed. The fact that, by this time, Surgeon General C. Everett Koop had been recruited to testify, and the proponents of the bill had lost their author, intensified the urgency and importance of this undertaking. So ANSR conducted the survey—not all of the legislators had filled it out, but a good number had—and presented it to Moen of MDH. In the words of Jeanne Weigum, "[Moen] ran off with it into the night someplace. And went through and based on people's answers on the survey started calling people and he found an author."[13]

There was some concern among the ANSR leadership and membership about whether its support for this bill reflected an unwarranted broadening of the mission of the organization. Much of the focus of the bill was not secondhand smoke and the health and well-being of nonsmokers, but a more general effort to prevent smoking. Jeanne Weigum reflects on this dilemma for the organization: "I would think that we might not have been as excited about the Omnibus bill if there hadn't been the clause in there that funded the Clean Indoor Act. That was real key to our being real actively involved." And, the members seemed to have liked it: "It was real important to our membership. . . . I think they really like us to be out there doing things that got attention and focused the issues, etc." Ultimately, the bill passed, which set the stage for greatly expanded tobacco control efforts in the state (see Chapters 7 and 9 for more discussion of the Omnibus bill and its impact on tobacco control efforts).

The twin themes of this book are evident in the early history of ANSR. The primary grassroots tobacco control advocacy organization in Minnesota started as a project of the American Lung Association—part of the "infrastructure" of health organizations in the state. And we already see a close intertwining of the state—in this case, the Minnesota Department of Health—and the key advocacy organization of the period (and beyond). MDH and ANSR had arrived at a symbiotic division of labor in implementing government policy—the Minnesota Clean Indoor Air Act. When

MDH staff were interested in generating support for what was to become the Omnibus Nonsmoking and Disease Prevention Act of 1985, they turned to ANSR. MDH staff coached ANSR on how to "do" legislative advocacy on this particular bill, and looked to it for leadership on both grassroots lobbying and polling legislators to identify potential authors of the bill. This complicated and close relationship between a social movement organization and a state agency, which encompasses both policy formation and policy implementation, provides a first illustration of the concept of state-movement interpenetration.

NOTES

1. This account is consistent with that of John Banzhaf (the founder and president of ASH, quoted in Troyer and Markle (1983:80), who described GASP as "a very loose affiliation of individual chapters all of whom have adopted a common name."

2. Kluger's (1996:555) chronicle of tobacco control efforts in the United States characterizes ANR as "the grassroots complement to John Banzhaf's ASH."

3. According to the foundation's quarterly newsletter, *Advances* (Issue 3, 1996), the foundation awarded $19.5 million to the center in 1996 to support a national campaign to reduce youth tobacco use. More generally, RWJF has taken a prominent role in funding nongovernmental tobacco control efforts, providing support to tobacco control research and programmatic efforts by such groups as Public Citizen, the Investor Responsibility Research Center, the Tobacco Products Liability Project and Tobacco Products Divestment projects of Northeastern University, and other groups, including my own study of enforcement of laws regulating youth access to tobacco. As discussed in this chapter, RWJF also funds the largest multistate nongovernmental tobacco control program, known as the SmokeLess States program.

4. According to my 1996 survey of state and local organizations involved in tobacco control efforts throughout the United States, 214 of 624, or 34%, subscribed to SCARC-NET.

5. In the words of the chief sponsor of the Act, Phyllis Kahn (1983:1300), "This was not the first law to attempt to control smoking in public places, but it was the first one to use the comprehensive approach of saying that smoking would be prohibited everywhere unless it was specifically permitted."

6. The first literature ANSR put out on the MCIA was a pamphlet, "The Clean Indoor Air Act and You." According to Jeanne Weigum, "It answered every question anybody could ever have had about the Clean Indoor Act and the rules. . . . The problem with it was that is all together too complicated. You know, the layperson was never going to flag through there. The only person who would ever really use it would be a sanitarian. So it was a piece of literature that was beautiful but didn't exactly suit the purpose."

7. Although the conditions were somewhat primitive, the organization did have access to a computer, personally purchased by Jeanne Weigum. "Any of the computer stuff we did, we did at my house. And that was also during the energy

crisis. And I remember people complaining that they couldn't type with blue fingers. . . . The computer really was the beginning of being able to do a good organization. I mean, it seems like a silly thing in a way, but we were computerized before any of the Lung Associations. . . . We had to. If you're going to have a half of a staff person and then another half of a staff person and then a volunteer in order to get the job done you had to have a computer."

8. Continuing the theme of "adventures with office equipment," Jeanne Weigum relates this story about the group's efforts to obtain an answering machine: "But a big problem came up over an answering machine, if you can believe that." The treasurer at the time volunteered to purchase an answering machine, by mail order from 54th Street Photo in New York. The check was sent—money was gone— they needed a machine desperately—but, when 54th photo gets too many orders, they apparently take the phone off the hook for a few weeks, until they get caught up. So, Jeanne Weigum put her answering machine in the office, "which said, 'You've reached the number for the Association for Non-Smokers Rights and Jeanne Weigum'—it wasn't a good situation. . . . So we contacted [name deleted] and told him what we wanted and Jack operates on cash. You go give Jack the cash and a day later he calls you and tells you where to pick up your machine. And sometimes he'd say go to Radio Shack and talk to Mack. And so you'd go to Radio Shack and Nat would say may I speak to Mack? Jack sent me to come get your machine and we'd go. And it was all perfectly legitimate, but he would negotiate sort of bulk buys from these places. And he'd get a lot of jewelry and electronic stuff and none of it was hot, but it was all discount. . . . Discounts with Jack. So we got an answering machine from Jack. We took it into the office and there was an answering machine. And the next day the answering machine came from 54th Street Photo. We had three answering machines. [Name deleted] had gone out and bought an answering machine without any authorization from anybody."

9. This is reflected in the following comment by Jeanne Weigum: "There were some bad [board] meetings at the beginning. . . . We were unsure of where we were going. There was a sense of fear. There was a sense of excitement. And a sense of suspicion kind of all the way around. It's who's vying for power? Power over what?"

10. ANSR had been involved in what Weigum calls "a couple of minor skirmishes," one related to smoking in libraries and another related to smoking on buses. In one such skirmish, ANSR was able to persuade the coauthors on the bill to withdraw, and the author dropped it without even a hearing held. "Everybody showed up for the hearing, and we had the room packed."

11. For an analysis of the role of the tax code and other mechanisms on the part of the state to "channel" the efforts of social movement organizations, see McCarthy et al. (1991).

12. The Cancer Society did provide a staff person time to work on this effort, along with a volunteer from ACS. Also, Arlene Wilson, from the Minnesota Medical Association-Auxiliary, was involved in the effort to pass the legislation. See Chapter 9 for a more detailed description of the campaign for passage of the Omnibus bill.

13. The author was Allen Quist, who was a newly elected legislator (a "rookie") and, coincidentally, a strong prolife advocate.

4

The Single-Issue Groups—2

In this chapter, I continue with the history of ANSR, and pick up the history of a second tobacco control movement organization: the Minnesota Coalition for a Smoke-Free Society 2000 (hereafter the Smoke-Free Coalition, or simply the coalition). We will see an enlargement of the focus of ANSR, moving into the new area of youth access to tobacco. And we will see how ANSR and the new player, the Smoke-Free Coalition, interact. The themes of the trade-offs involved in building on the infrastructure of health and the integral relationship between the state and movement will again figure prominently in this discussion.

Despite a membership base primarily concerned with clean indoor air,[1] the leadership of ANSR latched onto the newly discovered issue of youth access to tobacco in the late 1980s and early 1990s.[2] Activists and university researchers in California, Massachusetts, and Minnesota had been using "confederate buyers" to demonstrate the ease with which youth could purchase cigarettes from grocery stores, convenience stores, and vending machines in many communities. This finding, along with scientific surveys demonstrating that many youthful smokers obtain cigarettes through such commercial sources, led to the development of state and local policy proposals to reduce youth access to tobacco. ANSR played a key role in developing these policies and, especially in the Twin Cities Metropolitan Area, in successfully lobbying for their passage in many communities.

ANSR's longtime leader, Jeanne Weigum, reflects on the organization's mission:

> Well, that's interesting. The easiest answer is to promote the health, safety, and economic interests of nonsmokers. And that includes all nonsmokers, including babes in wombs. And nonsmokers such as 11-year-olds who could become smokers. That our mission is not helping smokers quit. It is not publicizing the health effects of smoking to that group. But maybe publicizing the health effects . . . of secondhand smoke. Our interest is not publicizing the economic concerns that smokers experience. . . . But we are interested in

health benefits and health insurance and life insurance and those kinds of benefits as they relate to nonsmokers. Now there have been a couple of times in our history where we've kind of pursued those economic interests but it's never been a dominant focus. We've done it for brief periods either because there was an open door and we could pursue it right then or whatever.

Interestingly, there is doubt about whether one of the key elements of contemporary tobacco control efforts—increasing taxes on tobacco products—fits into this mission, according to Weigum:

I really have a problem with tobacco tax, and I have at various times said I'm not going to get involved in supporting tobacco tax. Back two years ago, I said I'd just supported my last tobacco tax increase. This has nothing to do with ANSR's mission or very little to do with ANSR's mission. . . . It seems to me that it's becoming more and more a part of raising revenue for the state and becoming more insidious in terms of getting the state indebted on that issue so they're. . . . we're going to be more reluctant to do things to reduce smoking. It has nothing to do, or very little to, with clean air. The only place that it seems that it relates to ANSR's chosen direction is that it discourages youth from smoking. And, in fact, I wrote what I thought was really a pretty good letter to the legislature saying either increase it 24 cents or don't do it at all, because anything less is just money raising. And I have no interest in supporting that. I only have an interest in supporting it if you're doing something substantial for children. . . . I think that unless you're doing something that's got a meaning, you know, don't do it. And a nickel increase in the context of the tobacco industry raising prices every six months by a nickel. . . . A nickel tax increase is not a deterrent to kids. I'm sorry. Forget it. It's not there. And that's the reason that I would support a tax increase, or if were going to promote additional programs, such as a Health Department program. And I can get into that. I can support, but increasing the tax unless it's major. . . . You come with a dollar tax, boy, I'll be all the way for that.

Another issue that ANSR has taken up is exposure of children to secondhand smoke in family day care settings:

The big places got included in the Clean Indoor Air Act so there's no smoking allowed in day-care centers, but family day-care has never been regulated in terms of smoking. So if you take your kid to Suzy Smith's house and she takes care of three- to five-years youngsters, she can smoke anyplace. She can hold your babe in arms and smoke with an ash dripping over the baby and there's no regulation on it. . . . We now know that about a third of infants that die of Sudden Infant Death Syndrome are dying in day care. And, of course, environmental tobacco smoke has been linked with Sudden Infant Death Syndrome, so it becomes not just a long-term factor in development of a child's lungs but it also can be a factor in the immediate problems.

ANSR became involved in hearings held by the Minnesota Department of Human Services (MDHS), which was charged with licensing family day-care operations, in the late 1980s. The group spent quite a bit of time working on the issue, and had ideas about prohibiting smoking in the area in which the child is being cared for and in an automobile while caring for the child, among other things. However, ANSR became involved late in the process—it had not been involved in the issue before, so was not on the list used for mailings by MDHS. MDHS ruled that since the ideas about clean air weren't included as part of the original draft published for comment and represented a substantial change, they could not be included through the rule-making process at that time.[3] But, they could go back and do rule-making if it was done again:

> We had gotten involved too late in the process. . . . You know, Clean Indoor Air Act rules are right now in the process of sort of everybody sitting down and talking about what ought to be included. And then they're going to put together a document and then there will be public comment on the document. Where we needed to get involved with the day care is where we're involved right now in the Clean Indoor Act—at the place where you're brainstorming and talking. . . . I mean the Welfare Department is just not an organization that would think to contact us. The health department would have . . . I think. . . . You know, it's just not an issue that puts us in proximity with each other and they were . . . looking at structural things. They looked at railings and paint and those kinds of things. They weren't thinking air.

Despite this initial setback, ANSR has continued to pursue the issue when opportunities presented themselves.[4]

Scientific discoveries over the past ten years—such as the famous EPA report—have not really changed the way ANSR activists think about the issue of secondhand smoke, but have provided them with important "ammunition" in pursuing their goals in the political arena. According to one ANSR activist,

> I think we all kind of assumed that it was there, and then what remained to be done was work to be demonstrated. I think . . . I guess it was no surprise to me when they came up with research that showed that lung cancer and secondhand smoke were cause and effect. I meant that was no surprise. [And, with respect to heart disease,] you know, I guess I have always gone on the assumption that you would get it, just in lower doses. Whatever you can get with primary smoking, you can get with secondary smoking, but you would expect much lower rates because of the lower exposure. And I've always assumed that to be true. So in terms of my reaction, there's been no difference. It's just that now we've got a smoking gun, so to speak.

However, the aura of science has helped the cause:

It seems like it's [scientific evidence] given us a lot more credibility having a piece of paper that has somebody's name on it who's fairly important saying this is what they said really makes a difference. If we didn't have that kind of information with the strength the tobacco lobby has now, we wouldn't have . . . I mean we wouldn't even be at first base. It was easier to pass things before the tobacco lobby was involved. . . . Without the scientific background, we just would not have a ghost [of a chance] now. . . . And it really has been filtering in. For ten or fifteen years it's been, you know, the. . . . studies which showed minor diminution of lung function in nonsmokers who worked with smokers was the first hard piece of stuff. And we were real excited about that. . . . not excited that it was a fact but excited that we had verification of something we knew to be true.

Jeanne Weigum on the long awaited EPA report:

Well, I think that's the only hope that we have for state legislation. That is, the only hope is that the evidence is so overwhelming that they appear irresponsible not to do something. That they are neglecting their constituents. I mean, that it's just ludicrous not to do something. That's the only way, and unless the EPA report is really strong, it's not going to get us that kind of push. I mean, that's our only hope at the legislature. I cannot see the media taking the kind of interest in Clean Indoor Air that it took in the vending machine thing. Anything that relates to kids is going to be easy . . . and easier to sell than anything that relates to adults. I think we really have to try and deal with Clean Indoor Air at the local level. . . . I think unless we get something going at the local level on Clean Indoor Air Act, it's going to be real hard to get anything going on at the state.

Another issue that ANSR has undertaken is fire-safe cigarettes. Jeanne Weigum explains the issue:

The initial concern came from a firefighter who was an ANSR member, and he said, "You know cigarettes cause a lot of fires, and I've read some stuff in my firefighter magazines that indicate cigarettes don't have to start fires." . . . And then at the end of a hearing . . . a senator who I'd had no contact with previously came up to me because he had been at this hearing and testifying and carrying on about some issue had come to me and said, "Do you guys know anything about something called a fire-safe cigarette?" And I said, "Well, yeah, it does . . . exist, at least in prototype, and yes it can be done?" And he said, "Well, one of my constituents came to me and said that this was a concern of his and thought I ought to do something about it, and I'm willing if there's some scientific reason that I ought to." And he said. "It sounds like kind of a neat issue, and I'm really into environmental things and consumer protection."

And there had been two or three horrific fires, one in the district where the firefighter is from, where four family members were killed. And it was in the district where this one senator had come to us and said, "Does this make any sense?" There was another fire, in Minneapolis, where several people were killed. I had quite a bit of background on fire-safe cigarettes at this point. . . . I heard on the way [to work] that there had been just this horrific fire. And I called the Minneapolis paper, and I think I called the TV stations too and gave them the pitch that I would betcha given the description of the fire, you learn how to hear cigarette fires. You recognize them. . . . They always occur at night. They start in bedrooms and living rooms. There are things that are markers for cigarette fires. And the first description I heard of that fire said this is a cigarette fire. I called the media and said I'll bet you ten to one this is a cigarette fire and this is the real story. The real story is that it didn't have to happen. Nobody bought it, and it was a cigarette fire. And for days, there were pictures of grieving family members, funeral pictures. Pictures of rescuers that had been injured trying to rescue people, and pictures of people in hospitals with burns and broken arms and stuff because people were jumping out of windows. The timing really seemed right to do something.

ANSR was able to get two good authors for a bill—one in the House, one in the Senate. The bill passed the Senate, but ran into

> the age-old problem of a powerful person not willing to let it do its thing. . . . We saw him. . . . The tobacco people really lobbied this hard. They had three or four people working on it constantly. There were people in from faraway places with expensive suits and boot briefcases [soft, shoe-like leather] and sometimes even suitcases. A couple times people actually came to hearings with their suitcase. I mean they . . . you want to talk about carpetbaggers? They didn't even stay long in the end, paying a hotel bill. They just came with their suitcase and left. . . . And later we were told unofficially that there was a very substantial contribution made—$100,000—to the DFL. Now I don't know if it happened. I have no way of knowing, and I'll never know. Nobody will every know. Nobody will ever tell that. But it's sort of generally accepted that something like that happened, because one person stopped it.

Although ANSR went back to the legislature the next year to support the bill, the spirit was out of it: it went down to defeat in the first committee in the House and in the Senate it didn't get a single vote in a committee it had passed unanimously the previous year. In the words of Jeanne Weigum

> I kept asking for a hearing, asking for a hearing, asking for a hearing. Finally they agreed to assign it to a subcommittee. We had people all lined up. They came and testified. And we were really organized and by this time, [name

deleted] was our house author. . . . We had a statement written for her that was just dynamite. And they just played games with her. They'd interrupt her. They'd lead her in this direction and that direction and I just sat there saying, "What the hell is going on here?" . . . The tobacco guys were just sitting there smiling. I just wanted to die so I realized that we didn't have the votes with the people who were in the room so I went to [name deleted's] office and said, "You've got to come down there." . . . And he said, "This is not my game. This is a DFL game, and I refuse to be a part of it and I will not be in the room when this happens." He said, "The vote's done, Jeannie—you just don't know it. It's over." And I went and sat, red and hot and angry, and watched them do it. And after it was over I went to the chair and I said, "I know what happened here. I know that it was arranged ahead of time who was going to vote in what way and I know how the vote was arranged and it stinks and I'm not going to be quiet about it." And he said, "I'm really sorry about this. There was nothing I could do. The word came from the leadership that this bill was never going to come out of committee. And I'm really sorry, but there was nothing I could do."

Having learned this lesson about power politics, ANSR subsequently has focused on the time-honored strategy of involving "bystander publics" (Lipsky, 1968) in the debate:

We try to get public attention. That's the only thing that makes it clean. And it got clean again with the vending machine bill when they tried to get preemption. And the only reason it was clean was that the press was there every time. And that's the only thing. There is nothing else that keeps it clean. Nothing. If the press is there and talks about it and shines the light on it, it's clean. If they aren't, it's not. It just isn't.

Although protest is not a common tactic used by ANSR, there are occasions where it is used. As Jeanne Weigum relates:

We all dressed up in costumes and carried posters and marched at a golf course where the tobacco industry was sponsoring the club. Very pricy golf tournament. And after we were done, we went over to the miniature golf course on Como and Snelling and had our own golf tournament. And we just had a ball. . . . You know, we can't offer the kinds of things that the tobacco industry has to offer. All we can do is show a good sense of humor and not be obnoxious and present our ideas and if we can . . . I think we scored a lot of points with that. . . . You know, they had this flyer that went out, and we copied it. So it looked like the same thing. Got press coverage. Coalition wouldn't get involved, Heart, Cancer . . . although Lung loaned them the costumes.

The second major single-issue group in the tobacco control movement in Minnesota is the Minnesota Coalition for a Smoke-Free Society-2000. The coalition is—as the name indicates—a statewide coalition of organizations opposed to smoking. It formed in 1984 as an outgrowth of concerns and efforts by members of the Minnesota Medical Association. Accounts of its formation differ in some respects. For example, one participant describes what took place in 1984, as the task force that had been working on the Minnesota Plan was finishing up:

> The Health Department of the Medical Association called a meeting. And that was a terrible meeting. It was late at night, and they had all of these people who came and sat in an incredibly warm room in the Health Department, that board room that they have there. And we sat and sort of all droned on to each other about how something really needed to be done. Stuart [Hanson] was a real mover and shaker in this group. He wasn't chairing the meeting. The guy that was chairing the meeting, I don't remember who he was, but I think he was from the Society for the Preservation of Boredom. Because it was really a dreadful meeting, but all of the key players were present. There was a representative from Heart and Lung and Cancer and all of the players were present. And it basically was the first meeting of what became the coalition.

Stuart Hanson's account is that the Minnesota Medical Association (MMA) was the catalyst for bringing together the players and founding the Smoke-Free Coalition:

> Andy Dean [from the MDH] and I started meeting . . . and we talked a little bit about bringing together all the parties, and I kind of conceived this coalition idea, and we started getting people who were interested in tobacco issues meeting and talking about how we can work together and how to back the advisory committee recommendations. Out of those discussions came this coalition. We went to the Health Department, Heart, Lung, Cancer, Blue Cross, all being sitting down and kind of—we sort of shamed everybody into coming because we kind of said, "Well, this is where the action is." And the Medical Association, which I represented, sort of called the meetings and said, "We'd like you to come address these issues of tobacco and how can we work together in a consortium of some sort." . . . Organizations like Heart, Lung, Cancer, Department of Health, and ANSR, all of whom—and Blue Cross—all of whom were already dealing with little pieces of the smoking issue, and we kinda called them all together and said hey, we gotta work together. We gotta think about public policy and joint advocacy and joining together of all programs that can really intervene in a broad way.

From the outset, there were strong ties between the emerging coalition and the established grassroots organization—ANSR:

> And Charlie Howard [a key board member and leader in ANSR] was there, and he and Stuart [Hanson] kind of linked up. . . . Charlie really got excited

about this, and he and Stuart linked up, and the two of them went out and raised some money. Charlie worked his tail off to raise money to get the coalition off the ground, and they got some people to sign their name on the dotted line in terms of being part of the coalition. And really, Charlie was the key. Stuart was kind of the. . . . the name that gave the whole thing credibility. But in terms of energy and effort, it was Charlie who did it.

Meanwhile, Arlene Wilson, a physician's spouse and member of the Minnesota Medical Association auxiliary, brought back from Norway the concept of a smoke-free society by the year 2000:

Arlene started talking about a smoke-free society by the year 2000, and it was picked up by the Medical Auxiliary [the Minnesota Medical Association Auxiliary] in the form of a resolution and the resolution went to the Minnesota Medical Association and they passed it. And then it went to the National Medical [i.e., the AMA] and they passed it, and Surgeon General Koop picked up on the concept. And so, the concept of the smoke-free society by the year 2000 didn't necessarily carry with it an organization. But I think it was sort of simultaneously that the Medical Association, when they passed this resolution, I think felt the need to do something to implement it. And if memory serves, what they did was they held this first meeting.

Stuart Hanson distinguishes the smoke-free society idea, which was the animating idea behind the founding of the Smoke-Free Coalition, from the concerns of ANSR at the time: "They [ANSR] were ahead—they were ahead. But they were talking about clean indoor air. They weren't talking about smoke-free society. That was kind of the next leap forward."

According to several knowledgeable participants, turf issues were salient from the outset: "God, the guy from the Cancer Society . . . there wasn't a meeting that didn't go by that he didn't worry about somebody getting on his turf." Lung had had turf problems internally, but Cancer was concerned from the early days of the coalition about:

the coalition being on its turf, and concerned about it interfering with their fund-raising. To get any activities that the coalition did would be stepping on things they were already doing. And why should the coalition do something that the individual organizations were already doing?

In fact, there was sentiment that "maybe some of the organizations were doing these things, but they might not be doing them very well. And so maybe we need to have somebody do them better."
In the words of another observer,

Meeting after meeting, we'd go very far and all of a sudden we'd be talking about Cancer's turf. And Cancer more or less formed this alliance with Heart and Lung where it was sort of like they. . . . the three of them were the ones who had to worry about turf issues from this upstart coalition organization. And even though they frequently seemed to represent all three organizations, really it was Cancer that was most concerned. And I think Lung was . . . maybe they worried about it but it never was an overriding concern for them. And, oddly enough, Heart has never been very involved one way or the other. They never have been very involved. They send their money and sometimes they send a representative. It never amounted to much more than that.

The Minnesota Medical Association (MMA)—which of course had its own, distinct, funding base (its physician members), was "looked on as neutral turf. They didn't see the Medical Association as having a vested interest here."

The composition of the coalition illustrates the ways in which the movement has built on the rich reservoir of resources (including money, legitimacy, and expertise) contained within state and local health organizations. The members of the coalition—which are organizations, not individuals—included the following in the mid-1990s:

1. Health voluntary associations (the state branches of ACS, AHA, and ALA).
2. Health care provider and insurer organizations (including Blue Cross/Blue Shield, HealthPartners, Medica, the Park Nicollet Medical Center/Foundation, the Mayo Clinic, and the Minnesota Medical Group Management Association).
3. Health professional associations (including the Hennepin County Medical Society Foundation, the Minnesota Medical Association and Minnesota Medical Association Auxiliary, and the Minnesota Society for Respiratory Care).
4. Tobacco control advocacy organizations (ANSR).
5. The University of Minnesota School of Public Health.
6. Government agencies (the Hennepin County Community Health Department and the Minnesota Department of Health).

The Smoke-Free Coalition relies on several sources of funding. Historically, the coalition's main source of support has been its organizational members. For example, the coalition reported income (not counting in-kind contributions) of $210,000 in 1989 (Minnesota Coalition for a Smoke-Free Society 2000, 1990). A little under half of this amount ($95,000 or 45%) came from contributions from sponsors ($50,000), foundations/corporations ($20,000), affiliates ($10,000), hospitals ($10,000), and individuals ($5,000). The second largest source of income for the coalition was sales of products, fund-raisers, and interest, which totaled $60,000 (29%) in 1989 (ibid.).[5] Grants have been an important source of funds for the coalition. In 1989, the coalition reported grant income of $55,000 (26% of the coalition's budget), which represented half of a two-year grant award from MDH, focusing on youth access to tobacco (ibid.). During the 1990s, grants from MDH and foundations came to play a larger and larger role in funding the coalition. For example, the coalition received a $230,134, 2.5-year capacity-building grant from the Robert Wood Johnson Foundation under the foundation's SmokeLess States program. In addition to cash obtained from contributions, product sales and fund-raisers, and grants, the coalition relies heavily on in-kind contributions. For example, the coalition reported in-kind support valued at almost $70,000 in 1989 (not including volunteer hours) provided by ALA, ACS, Blue Cross Blue Shield of Minnesota, the Minnesota Medical Association, Colle & McVoy (a Minnesota-based advertising agency), MDH, and the Minnesota Department of Education (ibid.).

The Smoke-Free Coalition has somewhat more diffuse goals than ANSR. These include running smoking cessation programs and school-based educational programs. The coalition has worked on institutional policy, such as an effort to encourage hospitals to go smoke-free.

The coalition has also been active in changing public policy. In 1988 it convinced the Metropolitan Sports Facility Commission to make the Metrodome Stadium (home of the Minnesota Twins and Vikings) smoke-free. In addition, the coalition's Public Policy Committee has been extremely active in state legislation, working to pull together a more-or-less-coordinated lobbying effort of its constituent groups (see Chapter 9).

ANSR has always been closely involved in the work of the coalition. In the words of Jeanne Weigum, "As a part of the coalition, so our involvement has been real nuts and bolts from the beginning." This has included involvement in committees (as we will see in subsequent chapters, ANSR has been centrally involved in the Public Policy and Legislative Committee, which is the primary vehicle for the coalition's lobbying efforts). And ANSR members constitute something of a mass base for the coalition—for example, the single largest group that receives the coalition's newsletters *Countdown* is the ANSR membership (every ANSR member gets a newsletter).

According to Jeanne Weigum, ANSR realizes several benefits from its involvement in the coalition:

Well, it's a network that sometimes works. It's a couple more bodies that are willing to work hard on things. Some great staff members: real organizers, real cooperative, creative. . . . On something like Shoreview, where we were all hustling because we were really worried about that one . . . it was nice to be able to call [a coalition staff member] and say, "Hey, we need a couple of people in Shoreview," and she said, "OK, I'll take care of this, this, and this. And I said I'll take care of this, this, and this."

In addition, the SFC provides a degree of "legitimation" to advocacy efforts:

> On a different kind of level, it's nice to say that it's not just ANSR that supports this piece of legislation. It's all of these people. Even if they never do anything but have their name on the bottom of the page, to say that the Cancer Society supports this legislation has meaning. . . . I think we're [ANSR is] viewed as . . . well, we're real single issue. And that means in some ways, you're . . . you're less counted or discounted because you're a single-issue kind of organization, than if you're a broader-based organization.

In the words of another participant in the movement, who notes both ANSR's influential role in determining legislative priorities, and the advantages to ANSR in participating in a larger coalition:

> I think she [the president of ANSR] needs the backing of the different agencies, and I think that legislators need to know that. . . . I mean you need to be careful not to be so outspoken that you get disrespected, and I think that she has got respectable organizations in the coalition—the Department of Health has to report to very high powered people to get—when you get an agenda that's okayed by all of these agencies, that's pretty powerful, and to have each agency to have a network to follow through with—you get a lot of power behind them.

What does the coalition get from ANSR's involvement? According to Jeanne Weigum,

> I mean we supply an awful lot of energy and ideas and . . . and I think the public policy thing would be just dead in the water without us. They may say I'm dreaming for saying that. They may say I have a rather varnished view of our contribution there, but I really think that what we bring at this point is a lot of sophistication and knowledge about how the systems works. And get things done over there [at the legislature].

ANSR sees itself has having considerable influence over setting the public policy agenda of SFC-2000:

> I think if we said we weren't going to work on an issue, the odds are pretty good it wouldn't get worked on. And we've seen that on a couple of issues. You know, a couple things that people said they were . . . that were really important to them and you know we have to divide up our time. We can't just do everything. [For example, an effort that the Ramsey County Lung Asso-

ciation was going to undertake in the 1991 session to advocate for a bill that would prohibit smoking in all schools] never happened. They didn't get one author. Not one. Not even a number three or four author.[6]

Other observers have expressed a similar view. For example, one participant in the coalition's public policy committee opined: "So now what's happening, and this is very interesting, is [the president of ANSR] is basically running the coalition, in a sense [with respect to legislative issues]"

While the coalition has achieved some important successes, and has garnered national recognition, it has been criticized for not fully exploiting its own resources—in particular, the potential political power of many of its member organizations. According to one person with close connections to the Smoke-Free Coalition,

> [The] Smoke-Free board wasn't being tapped into. You have U.S. West sitting out there and you are not using them. You have major health organizations and not doing much. . . . Lobbying, or you know, paying for, or you know, a lot of different things they can be doing.

Thus, the Minnesota tobacco control movement includes two central organizations whose entire mission involves tobacco issues.[7] For the first fifteen years of its existence, ANSR focused almost exclusively on strategies to reduce people's exposure to secondhand smoke (ANSR's involvement in the Omnibus bill of 1985, described in Chapter 3, was something of an exception in that the bill addressed clean indoor air as part of a systematic tobacco use prevention program). In this respect, it mirrored state and local advocacy organizations that were active in several other states during the 1970s, such as GASP. This focus was also consistent with the preferences of ANSR's base of members, most of whom joined the organization because of their own exposure to, or concern about public policy concerning, secondhand smoke (see Elnicki, 1992). ANSR achieved a major victory early in its existence: in 1975, it was instrumental in the introduction and passage of the first comprehensive state clean indoor air act in the nation, requiring the creation of separate smoking and nonsmoking areas in public buildings. In 1985, ANSR and other groups, including MDH, succeeded in gaining passage of the Omnibus bill, which provided support to MDH for enforcement of the MCIA. However, ANSR, and the Minnesota movement as a whole, has not had a significant legislative victory since then on the issue of secondhand smoke, as we shall see in Chapter 9. It has, however, become increasingly involved in the issue of youth access to tobacco and has, in collaboration with Smoke-Free Coalition, achieved some important victories on that issue, both at the state legislature and in local communities.

ANSR occupies an interesting position in the movement. In many ways, it may be thought of as the movement's "radical flank." It has a largely independent funding base (relying primarily on dues, allocations from a health fund-raising federation, and small amounts of program income), and both its rhetoric and policy prescriptions tend to be more extreme than that of other movement organizations in the state. And yet, ANSR has played a quasi-governmental role with respect to enforcement of the Minnesota Clean Air Act (it produces and distributes the only literature on the act to educate the public about its provisions, helps companies achieve voluntary compliance with the act, and handles minor complaints about violations). In addition, MDH has relied on ANSR to develop materials and provide technical assistance to local tobacco control coalitions funded under the recent ASSIST initiative (described in Chapter 7).

The second organization, the Coalition for a Smoke-Free Society-2000, provides an excellent example of both the strengths and weaknesses of building on the infrastructure of health organizations. The coalition has achieved some important successes, and was reportedly used as a model by the National Cancer Institute for the coalition development effort of ASSIST (see endnotes, Chapter 2, 14).

However, it has suffered from leadership problems; conflicts between its constituent organizations about goals, directions, and credit; and a failure to generate a grassroots force for tobacco control. Moreover, its funding sources—government agencies, charitable foundations, and its sponsoring members—have all constrained the ways in which its advocacy efforts have been pursued.

NOTES

1. According to Jeanne Weigum, "We don't get a lot of feedback from our membership. The board seems to be real interested and involved [in the youth access issue]. . . . You know, people who choose to join our board know what we're doing and that's why they want to be on the board. . . . Those are people who have a very substantial interest in children's issues."

2. See Chapter 5 on the role of Dr. Jean Forster of the University of Minnesota School of Public Health—who was also an ANSR Board Member beginning in the early 1990s—in influencing ANSR to broaden its mission to include youth access.

3. In any event, the hearing examiner ended up rejecting the entire package of proposed rule changes, because the hearings had gone beyond the intended scope of the statute.

4. The following example, described by Jeanne Weigum, illustrates how legislators and social movement organizations coalesce around issues: "And there's some interest in it. Alice Housman seems to be interested. She's a representative. She brought it up to us. She came to our day at the capitol and said what do you

know about this? Is this a potential . . . and we gave her copies of all the stuff we had done. I mean we had tons of stuff we'd done on this. And we just got a call from a guy who seems to have not enough to do and is the Human Resources director for a company in St. Paul, and he wants to do something about this."

5.   The total for income from sale of products may be somewhat misleading, since the amounts reported represent gross rather than net income (e.g.,the costs of obtaining the products for sale—such as T-shirts for the Smoke-Free Class of 2000 project—are not reflected in these figures).

6.   Jeanne Weigum explains the rationale for this position: "We've got bigger fish to fry than that. And except in the context of a larger bill or if we felt we needed to get a vehicle moving for some reason, then I would say, Yes, let's do it. But it would not be because that was our ultimate goal."

7.   There is one other single-issue organization, which is mainly of historical interest. The Smoke-Free Generation (SFG) was founded in the early 1980s. A fellow from Sweden, who had gone to school at Mankato State University, connected with the Minnesota Medical Association on a "world movement for a smoke free generation." This individual had some fund-raising skills. According to one person, who was involved in both the SFC and SFG, this individual "went out and hustled money and used all his Scandinavian contacts with the Lutheran Brotherhood and other organizations to get some seed money." It was supported by Park Niccolet, through its Med Center Health Plan. Stuart Hanson, who was to be a leader in the MMA and the Smoke-Free Coalition, was named chairman of the board (he was, at the same time, chairman of the Smoke-Free Coalition, which resulted in considerable confusion in the community when fund-raising efforts occurred). The focus was on special events for kids (such as rock concerts), merchandise, and a school curriculum. "The idea was to create a whole social environment where kids would wear their T-shirts with the logos on so that the whole idea of a smoke-free generation would be in the community" [Hanson]. However, there were some concerns about duplication of programs (and funding sources) with the coalition, and SFG accidentally went over its budget for an event and subsequently folded because of financial difficulties. Elements of the curriculum it had developed were incorporated into the school programs of the Smoke-Free Coalition.

In the words of one knowledgeable observer: In addition to a lack of management skills, "I think that they also didn't have a broad enough mission. I don't think you can address this problem, which is a complex one, with only one idea. And they believed there was one solution." In addition, "people had pretty negative reactions to their fund-raising, because they were so aggressively fund-raising that it made people like Cancer and them feel very nervous."

5

The Health Voluntaries

The health voluntary organizations—principally national, state, and local units of the American Cancer Society, American Lung Association, and American Heart Association—are centrally involved in the tobacco control movement. The involvement of the voluntaries, as a group, has important implications for the movement. The voluntaries enjoy a highly favorable image in the public mind, stemming from their long histories, their involvement in provision of important services not provided by government, their reliance on volunteers, and their own efforts to cultivate this image. Thus, the involvement of the voluntaries in this movement has the critical function of legitimating the advocacy efforts that occur in the context of the movement. In the words of Debra Minkoff (1994:947),

> Voluntary associations that pursue service provision . . . are in a position to validate social and political participation more generally, since this associational form avoids direct institutional confrontation and encourages social change by indirect means. The underlying logic is that increases in the number and familiarity of more institutionally moderate organizations promote the acceptance of the constituency as a legitimate collective actor. Once baseline legitimacy is established, the field of activity becomes open for groups that directly challenge social and political institutions. . . . Paradoxically, as confrontational alternatives become more established, they may compete for funding and support previously earmarked for the more moderate, precursory organizations.

In addition to legitimating tobacco control as a field of action, the health voluntaries represented a kind of dense organizational "infrastructure" on which the emerging movement could build, especially in its early years.[1] Thus, as we saw in Chapter 3, the ALA gave rise to ANSR, one of two key single-issue organizations in the movement. The other single-issue organization, the Smoke-Free Coalition, formed around a nucleus of health voluntaries along with a handful of other health organizations. These preexisting organizations, with considerable stores of resources, such as money, staff, volunteers, expertise, and legitimacy, have facilitated the growth of the movement.

But the use of this infrastructure, and the resources associated with it, comes at a price. As we shall see, the voluntaries are heavily dependent on contributions from a broad cross section of the public. Largely because of concerns about alienating potential donors, each of the voluntary organizations vigilantly protects its image as a mainstream, highly legitimate organization,[2] thus constraining choices of issues and tactics. In addition, the voluntaries are wary of doing anything that might compromise their tax exempt/tax deductible [501(c)(3)] status with the Internal Revenue Service, which leads to caution and a degree of wariness in making decisions about whether to engage in lobbying on a particular issue. As tobacco control efforts have become increasingly accepted and applauded by the public in recent years, the voluntaries have been less and less burdened by these considerations—witness ACS's role in the ASSIST Project (ASSIST will be discussed in Chapter 7) and the increasingly bold positions and strategies of the voluntaries, and their umbrella coalition (the Coalition on Smoking and Health, which is described below), which evolved over the course of the 1990s. Nevertheless, the pattern of building a part of the movement on these organizations—which are central to what Stanton Glantz (1987:746) once called the "health establishment"—has constrained the movement in important ways over the years.

The health voluntaries—ACS, ALA, and AHA—have a long history of involvement at the national level in issues related to tobacco use and health. The cancer society, heart association, and lung association (which at that time was called the American Tuberculosis Association), together with the American Public Health Association, persuaded the Kennedy administration to name an expert study committee to advise the Surgeon General on the healths effects of smoking. The work of this study committee resulted in the famous 1964 Surgeon General's Report on Smoking and Health (USDHEW, 1964).[3]

More recently, the three health voluntaries have worked together on tobacco issues under the umbrella of the Coalition on Smoking OR Health. The Coalition on Smoking OR Health, which was started in 1981 as a joint effort of the ACS, AHA, and ALA, has been an active advocate of stronger federal policy on tobacco control, such as the Synar Amendment and the 1996 FDA regulations (Kluger, 1996). The coalition also publishes an annual compendium of state laws, *State Legislated Actions on Tobacco Issues*, which is widely used by policymakers, researchers, and advocates interested in tobacco control issues (Welch, 1996).

In Minnesota, the voluntaries have played an important role in the movement, although it is a role that is clearly secondary in importance to that of the single-issue groups described in Chapters 3 and 4. The nature of involvement of each of the voluntaries, at both the national level and in Minnesota, is described below.

"THERE'S NOTHING MIGHTIER THAN THE SWORD": THE AMERICAN CANCER SOCIETY

The nation's preeminent nonprofit sector organization focused on cancer was founded as the American Society for the Control of Cancer in 1913, and reorganized as the American Cancer Society in 1945 (ACS, 1990a, 1991a).

Throughout its history, ACS has funded scientific research, including studies on the health effects of tobacco use. ACS funded the seminal case-control study by Graham and Wynder, "Tobacco Smoking as a Possible Etiological Factor in Bronchogenic Carcinoma" (Ross, 1987; Wynder and Graham, 1950), which, along with three other studies published in 1950, provided dramatic evidence of the links between smoking and lung cancer (see Chapter 2). Using its own in-house research capacity, ACS accomplished the mind boggling task of enlisting 22,000 ACS volunteers in nine states to collect data (beginning in 1952, with annual follow-ups) from 189,854 white males between 50 and 69 years of age as part of a prospective study of smoking and disease outcomes (described in Ross, 1987). The results, which were presented at the 1954 annual meeting of the American Medical Association and published in the *Journal of the American Medical Association* four years later (Hammond and Horn, 1958), "created shock waves worldwide and was front-page news from New York to Tokyo" (Ross, 1987:53).[4] According to the eminent epidemiologist Sir Richard Doll (who, as mentioned in Chapter 2, was the lead author of one of the key works on smoking and lung cancer published in 1950), the Hammond and Horn study "showed that smoking was associated with a much wider variety of ills than had previously been suspected, that the association was, in nearly all cases, much closer for smoking cigarettes than for smoking tobacco in other forms, and that among regular cigarette smokers, smoking might be responsible for up to 40% of their total mortality" (quoted in Ross, 1987). Over the succeeding years, research continued to be a central part of ACS activities: in 1989, for example, more money was spent on research (a total of over $90 million) than on any other program (or administrative) area (ACS, 1990a), with a substantial portion of that money being spent on tobacco research.

The ACS has sponsored a number of important tobacco control efforts. ACS was a joint sponsor with NCI of the seventeen-state American Stop Smoking Intervention Study (ASSIST; see Chapter 7). The collaboration was approved by the ACS board of directors in 1988 (ACS, 1990a). Over the life of the project, ACS planned to provide "local staff, materials, volunteers, and in-kind support" valued at $25 to $30 million to the effort (Shopland, 1993; the collaboration of the Minnesota Division of ACS and the MDH in managing the Minnesota ASSIST Project is described in Chapter 7). More recently, ACS, along with the AMA, and the Robert Wood Johnson Foundation (RWJF), provided funding to support the creation in 1996 of the National Center for Tobacco-Free Kids (see Chapter 3; Robert Wood Johnson Foundation, 1996).

Adhering to the methodology used in the CDC's Behavioral Risk Factor Surveillance System, ACS volunteers were used to conduct telephone interviews with random samples of adults in four states (Arizona, Michigan, Pennsylvania, and Texas) to measure public attitudes about cigarette taxes, advertising restrictions, youth access to tobacco, school-based prevention efforts, and ETS (Marcus et al., 1994).

In addition, ACS has produced a number of publications that provide "ammunition" that health advocates can use in policy debates. For example, the ACS periodical, *World Smoking & Health*, has devoted entire issues to such topics as tobacco taxes: their effects on smoking by youth and adults, their economic impact, how taxes in the United States compare to those in the rest of the world, taxes on smokeless tobacco, and the use of media advocacy to achieve increases in tobacco taxes (ACS, 1994). In addition, ACS has produced a number of manuals and guides meant to provide ACS staff and volunteers and others with concrete strategies and tactics for advocating for tobacco control. For example, in 1987 ACS published a piece, prepared by staff of the Advocacy Institute, entitled *Smoke Fighting: A Smoking Control Movement Building Guide* (Pertschuk and Erickson, 1987). Another publication, entitled *Stop Illegal Tobacco Sales. A Manual for Community Action* (ACS, 1997) is designed to equip health advocates with the knowledge needed to address the problem of tobacco sales to minors.

In 1997, ACS emerged as a critic of the proposed settlement with the tobacco industry negotiated by state attorneys general (see Chapter 10), arguing that the amount of the proposed settlement was too low and that it would have a limited impact on smoking rates (*New York Times*, 1997; Harris, 1997).

In addition to the national society, ACS comprises 57 divisions, including one in each state as well as five metropolitan areas, the District of Columbia, and Puerto Rico (ACS, 1991a). At the subnational level, many state divisions of ACS have been quite active on the legislative front on issues directly or indirectly related to tobacco use. For example, the Massachusetts Division of the ACS played an important role in the 1992 passage of the 25 cent per pack increase in the state excise tax on cigarettes, which provided dedicated funding for the Massachusetts Tobacco Control Program (Koh, 1996).

The Minnesota ACS organization began in 1937 as the Women's Field Army, which affiliated with the American Society for the Control of Cancer—later to become the American Cancer Society. The financial set up of ACS—like that of the other voluntaries—has important implications for the organization's latitude in engaging in tobacco control advocacy efforts. Compared to a grassroots, advocacy organization, such as ANSR [which reported revenues of $66,576 in 1990 (ANSR, 1991)], ACS is well funded— the Minnesota division 1990–1991 financial statement reported assets of $10,780,741 as of August 31, 1991 (ACS, 1991b). The Minnesota division, like the other state divisions, is heavily dependent on financial support from the public. In 1990–1991, the division reported $9.7 million in total support and revenue. The vast majority of this sum—94%—came from "support from the public": contributions (30% of total revenues), legacies and bequests (26%), special events and other fund-raising activities (21%), and the United Way (17%) (calculated from ibid.:12). This degree of dependence on fund-raising from the general public—according to accounts of ACS insiders, organizations that work with ACS, and others—affects the manner in which ACS positions itself on issues, and the strategies and tactics it is willing to adopt to pursue its chosen ends.

Of the $9 million in expenditures of the Minnesota division of ACS in 1990–1991, almost half (45%) was funneled to National Programs (with the majority of this amount going to support national research programs, and the remainder going to "education and other programs" and "supporting services"; ibid.). Of the $4.8 million remaining in thedivision, almost half (44%) went to "supporting services" (including management and fund raising), and 56% going to programs (including local research, public education, professional education, patient services, and community services) (ibid.).

The Minnesota state affiliate of ACS has played the most active role of the three voluntaries in tobacco control efforts. A staff member of the state affiliate has been active in the Smoke-Free Coalition's Public Policy Committee, both lobbying the state legislature, and educating and mobilizing cancer society volunteers (mainly members of the ACS Public Issues and Public Education Committees) on tobacco issues. Most recently, ACS and MDH have jointly sponsored the ASSIST Project in the state (described in detail in Chapter 7).

Public Issues is the "legislative arm" of ACS (ACS, no date). At the level of the Minnesota division, it encompasses the Public Issues Committee and the Quick Response Team. The Public Issues Committee includes ACS volunteers from the eight U.S. congressional districts (ibid.), and is responsible for "inform[ing] the Division Board of Directors, Unit Board of Directors and Quick Response Team on legislative affairs concerning the Society. It is also responsible for assisting in the recruitment and training of Quick Response Team members from each Unit of the Minnesota Division" (ibid.).

According to the ACS Minnesota division's 1990–1991 annual report, the Public Issues Committee worked to expand "the Quick Response Network," which responds to state and national concerns of ACS (including tobacco control measures); volunteers from the committee, as part of the Smoke-Free Coalition, participated in "A Day at the Legislature," advocating on behalf of amendments to the MCIAA and an increase in the cigarette excise tax, and supported efforts to ban vending machines and other restrictions on tobacco sales to minors (ACS, 1991b:10). According to the 1990 report, highlights in the public issues area included "work done on a community level to totally ban or significantly reduce the sales of cigarettes through vending machines" in more than thirty Minnesota municipalities, the division's Quick Response's Team's involvement in "the passing of state legislation to require supervision of vending machines in public places," and the successful effort to work with the Minnesota Timberwolves NBA team to have the new Target Center arena be smoke-free and free of tobacco advertising—"the first such action by a sports facility in the country" (ibid.:8).

In addition to the Public Issues Committee, the Public Education Committee had some involvement in tobacco issues, although, as the name suggests, these focused largely on public education. For example, the Tobacco Subcommittee of the Public Education Committee has focused its efforts on such issues as ACS tobacco education programs (Special Delivery, FreshStart, Tobacco Free Teens, and Smart Move), D-Day,[5] local health affairs, and a speakers bureau.

The ACS employee who staffs the Public Issues Committee describes it as follows:

> The committee right now stands at about 11 people, and it's really an active committee. . . . We're trying to make sure we have balance in the whole state, but also people that come to the committee with a particular expertise in some cases, too. So we have a breast cancer coalition rep. and whatnot. Beyond that, the way we meet is five times a year regularly.

This ACS staff person went on to describe how the Public Issues Committee chooses which tobacco policy issues to pursue:

> The list for this coming year that was presented at the last Smoke-Free Coalition [meeting]. I brought that whole list to the committee and we sort of moved it as a slate that we would be willing to work on those issues. . . . So

many groups are able to actually have legislative agendas out at the beginning of the year, and this is what we're working on, you know. In a sense, by packaging the Smoke-Free Coalition issues and these federal public issues, you know, we do have almost our broadest menu. We're still missing a few things that we're not getting . . . but I'm trying to move more towards having some action be taken "front end" so that we can act on things, because often, as you know, they come up with two weeks warning, and I'm lucky if I can get one or two people on the phone.

The Quick Response Team is a "grassroots network." Key volunteers from across the state are identified to be "Quick Responders and are called upon on an 'as-needed' basis to respond to legislative concerns affecting the society. This enables letters, phone calls and personal visits to be arranged through a preexisting network of volunteers, willing and able to make contact with their elected representatives" (ACS, no date). Appropriate issues for the Public Issues Committee and the Quick Response Team to address include categorical issues, which "relate to cancer; the cancer patient; and the potential cancer patient" (ibid.). These include government funding for cancer control efforts, tobacco control legislation and regulation, "unproven" methods of cancer management (such as Laetrile), discrimination against cancer patients and survivors, and health insurance needs of cancer patients (ibid.). Institutional issues are issues that "affect the Society's ability to carry out its business and programs," and include taxation of nonprofits and contributions to nonprofits, restrictions on lobbying by nonprofits, and similar issues (ibid.). The Minnesota Quick Response Team consisted of 142 volunteers in 1990 (ACS, 1990b).

The national office of ACS provides strong guidance on the content and methods used in legislative advocacy efforts. The National Public Affairs Office in Washington, D.C., publishes a handbook on public affairs and public issues, which explains the federal legislative process, the state legislative process, "communication skills and strategies" for communicating with public officials orally or in writing, cultivating relationships with public officials, developing a public issues grassroots network, developing and working with coalitions of organizations, working with the media, and navigating the limitations imposed on lobbying by federal legislation (Madigan and Wilson, 1990).

People involved in ACS tobacco control efforts at the local level—particularly staff—often look to the national organization for guidance on policy issues. According to the individual who staffed the Public Issues Committee of the Minnesota division:

One of the things that I do . . . is that I call them [the National Public Issues Office] a fair amount when there are issues in front of me that I think I need some opinion on. The first thing that I do is check that what we're hearing at the state level matches with what the American Cancer Society's policy is on a particular issue.

This is not to say that policy priorities set by the national organization complete determine the scope of issues to be undertaken at the state level:

> Some of our policy statements are so vague and short. I should show you some of the ones about, like, clean indoor air, for instance . . . is so vague it's just sort of like "Yes! We Support any effort! Thanks!" That gives me a lot of room to move. . . . Sometimes what I'll do is call the national office if we're faced with two or three issues and we can only really pursue one to offer some priority, to sort of check on priorities. . . . You know, I look for some help from them on prioritization quite often and then bring that answer to my committee. So we rely on the staff out there.

In part because of the volunteer focus of the organization at the state level, the division does have autonomy in many respects. For example, it can choose not to work on something that is a priority for the national organization (these bills were not related to tobacco, but illustrate this point nonetheless):

> There have been two bills at least I can point to where National has been saying that "you really should be working on this," and I have had to say that it is up to my volunteers ultimately, which they know.

The national office often serves to link subnational units that are working on similar issues, facilitating the exchange of information:

> Quite often they'll know of things that other states have done, or they'll suggest, "I think so-and-so had this issue in their legislature, why don't you call them?"

ACS staff are required to negotiate a number of constraints on permissible activities of the organization. For example, one ACS staff person explained that the organization strongly supported the MDH tobacco counteradvertisements that were part of its Nonsmoking and Health Program (described in Chapter 7) in part because ACS could not purchase time to run such ads:

> We do not spend donor dollars on commercials. We can't buy advertising. . . . The only way we can buy advertising is to have corporate underwriting or an individual donor underwriting.

This same staff member discusses the extent to which ACS's advocacy efforts are affected by the limitations on lobbying by 501(c)(3) nonprofit organizations. This involves reporting lobbying expenditures to the national office:

> We have to turn in quarterly, for lobbying purposes, monetary breakdowns of where our money went, what we spent on what, but that usually doesn't have a content component. I tend to on the margins say what the alert was about, but it doesn't go in depth. Really, it's surprisingly little that we get asked to send them in the way of any kind of reporting mechanism. . . . You know, I guess that I'm so careful to check with them on anything that it hasn't come up. I suppose there have been times with other divisions maybe where they've heard about it later and gotten themselves in trouble.
>
> We file nationally, and then they have to add up all of our things locally and at the national level. . . . I've got a whole big thick thing on what is grassroots, what is direct. . . . We elected to come under the guidelines. . . . There are two different ways of doing it, and one was to stay with some percentage, and this other one is to come under these guidelines and you have certain percentages you can spend. We're so far away from even beginning to touch the edges of the percentages, it's really not an issue. I mean, I can't remember, but it's like 10%—one of the two figures is something like 10%. Well, with an organization that raises $9 million effectively, we're not going to do it. I wish my budget were that big. . . . They still require the paperwork, but it's never been challenged.

As described in Chapter 3, ACS has had a long-standing involvement in the Smoke-Free Coalition. However, for a period of time in the late 1980s, ACS formally withdrew from its involvement in the coalition. In public documents, the reasons for this action were described as "concerns over governance and management policy" (ACS, 1990b). Observers attribute the pullout to a number of factors, such as concerns over fund-raising as well as the tendency on the part of organizations that feel constrained from doing advocacy themselves—such as ACS—to "outsource" advocacy efforts:

> They wanted [the executive director of the Smoke-Free Coalition at the time, and a former staff member of ACS] to do public policy stuff. And there was kind of the implication as I read it that they wanted [the executive director] to do the public policy stuff so they didn't have to . . . have somebody else, pay for somebody else to do it kind of thing. Well, it doesn't work that way, you know. If [the executive director] was the best public policy person in the world, it would still mean that he would have to turn to them and say contact the members, we need this. That's the way it works. It doesn't work by hiring somebody to go and do it.

Why did ACS not want to conduct advocacy efforts itself?

I think they continue to be frightened of it from a fund-raising point of view—their 501(c)(3) stuff. I think it's just not a priority for them. They were willing to pay $5,000 a year for somebody else to do it, which is what it amounted to. And they felt [name deleted] was spending all his time doing this other stuff instead of public policy stuff, and he shouldn't spend his time doing that. They really wanted him to do the public policy stuff.

One movement activist, with years of experience working in the field, offered this overall assessment of ACS's involvement in policy advocacy:

There was a survey done on who you trusted most in public interest people. And I think the Cancer Society was the most trusted organization on public policy issues. I almost fainted. At least in this state, they haven't done anything. You know, they ought to use that trust. They haven't . . . they aren't spending their capital. They've got lots of capital, and I just wish they'd spend it.

THE CHRISTMAS SEAL PEOPLE: THE AMERICAN LUNG ASSOCIATION

The American Lung Association began its existence in 1904 as the National Association for the Study and Prevention of Tuberculosis, later to become the National Tuberculosis Association and finally, the American Lung Association (ALA, no date). Its promotional materials state that it is "the first nationwide voluntary health agency in the United States organized to fight a specific disease" (ibid.). The organization is closely associated in the public mind with its Christmas Seal Campaign. As its initial name suggests, the organization was first concerned with tuberculosis, but later expanded its mission in its role as "guardian of this nation's lung health." These issues include air pollution, occupational lung hazards, prevention and treatment of asthma, and, of course, smoking and exposure to secondhand smoke (ibid.).

ALA is involved in educational efforts on smoking, as well as smoking cessation programs. For example, the ALA Freedom from Smoking cessation program is, along with the ACS FreshStart program, one of the most widely used public service smoking cessation programs in the nation (Lando et al., 1990b).

Like AHA and ACS, ALA was slow to take on a significant role with respect to political advocacy (Kluger, 1996:506).[6] However, the national organization has become increasingly emboldened over the past ten or so years. By July 1997, the national office of ALA had organized a protest event on Capitol Hill, in which health advocates from eighteen organizations, along with children, chanted slogans and shook chains of hospital bracelets, each of which was inscribed with the name of someone who had died, or whose life had been diminished, as the result of tobacco use or exposure to secondhand smoke. The bracelets were collected by ALA chapters in each of the fifty states. The demonstration was organized to support legislation introduced by Senator Ted Kennedy, which would have increased the federal excise tax on cigarettes by 20 cents per pack, with increased revenues going to support health care for uninsured children (American Public Health Association, 1997).

The Minnesota lung organization was founded in 1906 and went through a series of name changes over the next seventy-five years.[7] By 1990, the American Lung Association of Minnesota had grown substantially. Nevertheless, ALA's budget is considerably smaller than that of ACS—$2 million in expenditures in fiscal year 1990. Like ACS, ALA of Minnesota remitted a portion of its budget—about 12%—to the national organization (ALA of Minnesota, 1990). With the $1.7 million available to spend at the state level, ALA of Minnesota allocated about 80% to program services and 20% to supporting services (including fund-raising and general and administrative expenses; ibid.). Program expenses are reported in four categories: environmental health, lung disease, community health services, and smoking or health [the last of which received $326,000, or almost a quarter (23%) of funds spent on programs by the state organization].[8]

Like ACS, ALA is heavily dependent on public support. Of $2 million in revenues in 1989–1990, almost three-quarters (72%) came from public support—primarily contributions, but also from "contribution allocation from affiliates," special events, and memorials and bequests (calculated from ibid.).

The Minnesota lung association includes two substate affiliates—ALA of Ramsey County and ALA of Hennepin County. Organizationally, they resemble the larger, state-level organization. For example, ALA-Ramsey County had a half-million dollar budget in 1989–1990. Like the state organization, it was heavily dependent on public support—its Christmas Seal Campaign and other public support provided about three-quarters (76%) of the organization's budget. Sixteen percent of its 1989–1990 expenditures went to state and national programs. Of the remainder, the largest amount—$163,300—was spent on antismoking programs (ALA of Ramsey County, 1990).

The state organization, as well as the Hennepin and Ramsey County associations—have played important roles in the tobacco control movement over the past twenty-five or more years. As described in Chapter 3, the Hennepin County office of ALA spawned ANSR in 1973. The Minnesota Lung Association has been a long-time member of the Smoke-Free Coalition, and staff have been active in lobbying the state legislature on tobacco issues, although this has waxed and waned over the years depending on the inclinations of managers and staff. ALA, lacking the volunteer com-mittee structure of ACS, has generally not had much success in mobilizing volunteers on tobacco issues.

In addition to the policy advocacy described above, ALA has been in-volved in a number of programmatic activities, including an educational program called Tobacco-Free Teens (mostly "marketed" out of the Ramsey County Lung Association), and quit-smoking programs, such as the Fresh-Start program mentioned earlier. According to one key staff person at the lung association, the organization has an especially strong focus on tobacco prevention efforts in the schools: "The lung association is very strong in the school systems with tobacco issues: tobacco-free schools, tobacco-free teens, smoke-free class 2000, all of that stuff."

In addition to its base in the Minneapolis-Saint Paul Metropolitan area (with Minnesota and Ramsey Lung sharing different floors of the same building in Saint Paul, and Hennepin Lung in Minneapolis), there are two regional offices outstate: one in Duluth and another St. Cloud. These out-posts have, according to one knowledgeable observer, been involved in some focused advocacy efforts, such as the 1990 effort to defeat a tobacco industry-sponsored bill that would have imposed weak restrictions on vending machine sales of cigarettes and preempted stronger local-level re-strictions (see Chapter 9). With coaching from ANSR,

> They did a lot in activating their community to be very active in this piece of legislation. Then they brought people down from their community to testify or to be there for press conferences that happened or different things like that, at a local level to influence their legislators

The Minnesota Lung Association has been a long-time member of the Smoke-Free Coalition. However, this involvement, at times, has been viewed with some ambivalence within ALA:

> We spend so much time helping the coalition, we have a PR person that does their slide-tape shows for the coalition, a lot of their P.R. stuff. . . . [Name deleted] goes to coalition meetings dealing with smoking issues—smoking prevention and cessation. [Name deleted] would go for different school stuff, and [name deleted] would go for legislation. Well, what happens is we get so submerged with putting all of our efforts in coalition effort that the Lung Association gets lost—everything goes on coalition letterhead, which is a big deal to the Lung Association. So what we're doing right now in staff meet-ings at the Lung Association is saying, "Do we want to pull out?" We already pulled out on contributions—we're not a primary contributor, we're only an affiliate. Now we're talking "How much staff time do we want to go over there, and do we want to start concentrating on Lung Association efforts?"

There was a sense that the Lung Association benefited with respect to involvement in the legislative activities of the coalition, but not in other areas:

> Its lobbying efforts—that's the biggest thing that the coalition is able to contribute to us as the Lung Association. Otherwise, we do all the other stuff. . . . We for sure want to be in, in regards to legislative issues. But everything else, they want to pull out—limit who goes, and how much time we spend.

According to an ALA staff member, ALA's involvement in the coalition provides a mechanism for establishing its (ALA'S) legislative agenda on tobacco issues:

> We get most of our legislative agenda from the coalition, and what happens is we go to the coalition and we write letters, and we do as much as we can do in regard to staff time, but really the coalition drives the bills, and really a lot of it is [the president of ANSR], because that is her full-time job. It's not my job, and it's not [name deleted] full-time job everyday. If I were to do that, I'd have to . . . and I wanted a bill passed, I wouldn't be able to do the rest of my job. . . . And that's where the history and the knowledge is. That's years of experience sitting at the coalition.

Staff have had some involvement in lobbying the state legislature on tobacco issues, although this has waxed and waned over the years depending on the inclinations of managers and staff. The legislative liaison in the early 1990s had been hired with very little lobbying experience, and relied on coaching by the then-chair of the legislative committee of SFC in her first legislative session:

> So what happened [in the 1990 legislative session] is I basically represented the lung association via [the chair of the legislative committee of the SFC at the time], and I bounced all of my ideas off of him, and did everything through him and then he would give me feedback as to how to lobby, because I'd never lobbied, and give me feedback on what the legislators were saying.

The lobbying effort in the early 1990s was mainly reactive:

> I had gotten the impression that I was supposed to be proactive, and working for all three lung associations on all respiratory issues, which is a huge job. Well, in reality that's not what happens at all because I'm too spread out. The other two lung associations don't direct me, my committee doesn't direct me, so what happens is I'm just reacting to so called "action alerts" coming from national or coming from what's happening here in Minnesota.[9]

ALA, lacking the volunteer committee structure of ACS, has generally not had much success in mobilizing volunteers on tobacco issues. However, there was often an assumption that each of the three voluntary organizations had an extensive network it can easily tap into for grassroots lobbying:

> What I felt was happening was when we go to the coalition—Smoke-Free Coalition—the lung association is really pretty visible staffwise—I mean, they are always sending staff over there and that's where we get a lot of our direction in regard to which issues we're going to support at the capitol. But what happens is the coalition wants you to do various levels of activism, okay, all the way to concrete lobbying and walking the halls. Well, that takes a lot of time, and our legislative network that we should have in place throughout the state to activate isn't updated at all. . . . So when I walked into the position, the legislative network wasn't really functioning as it should be. So, what happened is I didn't have much to work with, and it was a lot of frustration that I was feeling, not overtly, but just from my own intuition that the coalition was frustrated with the voluntary agencies—"Why aren't they working harder? What is their role?"[10]

Interestingly, there was also a sense expressed that ALA leaders "want to say they can do more than they can do. They want to present themselves as being much more active than they actually can be" to supporters, the community at large, and the national lung association.

However, according to one person familiar with the health voluntaries efforts on tobacco control efforts:

> I also think that the Lung Association of Minnesota is not committed to legislation. It's only committed on the point of writing letters. . . . I think you get into some politicking about people contributing to the lung association, and if you're lobbying are you going to be lobbying for the right reasons and are they going to agree with your politics? I think it gets confusing and there is concern when you go out into greater Minnesota.

This informant did not see concerns about tax deductibility being an important factor in the limited enthusiasm about lobbying:

> To be honest, I don't mean to be so skeptical about the whole function of the system and the thought process behind it, but I don't think they've gone to that level, of thinking of it in that way. I think if they were really committed to it, and had a strong system to push lobbying, I think they'd work around it, plus Lung Association could really lobby a lot and do a lot for Minnesota. It's just not committed to put that much time and effort into it.

FIGHTING HEART DISEASE AND STROKE:
THE AMERICAN HEART ASSOCIATION

The American Heart Association was founded in 1924 (AHA, 1992). According to AHA promotional material, by 1992 the organization had over 2,000 state and metropolitan affiliates, divisions, and branches in the United States, and about 3.5 million volunteers (ibid.). The three "enterprises" of AHA are cardiovascular science, cardiovascular education and community programs, and revenue generation (ibid.).

AHA at the national level sponsors a considerable amount of research on cardiovascular health and disease [$69 million's worth in 1989 (AHA, 1989)], including work related to smoking, exposure to secondhand smoke, and health. The flagship journal of the association, *Circulation*, has published influential research (and research synthesis) and policy analyses on the health effects of smoking and exposure to ETS (e.g., Glantz, 1987; Glantz and Parmley, 1991). While the association, like the other voluntaries, has been criticized for its relatively late arrival to political advocacy (e.g., Kluger, 1996; Glantz, 1987), it has become increasingly active in the past decade.

According to its 1991 annual report, the Minnesota affiliate of AHA had a budget of $4.5 million in 1991. About one-quarter of this amount was used to support AHA national efforts. Of the remaining funds, about one-quarter was spent on management and fund-raising, and three-quarters on programs: public education, research, community service, and a small percentage for professional education (calculated from AHA Minnesota Affiliate, 1991). As was the case with the other voluntaries, the Minnesota AHA organization relies on public support for the majority of its funds (84% of its funding in 1991 came from individuals; United Way, Combined Federal Campaign, and Community Funds; and Planned Gifts (ibid.).

The Minnesota affiliate of AHA has played a relatively minor role in the movement. While it, like ACS and ALA, has been a long-time member of the Smoke-Free Coalition, it has never mounted much of a lobbying effort at the state legislature, either by staff or volunteers.[11] In an early 1990s interview, one interviewer described AHA's involvement as follows in legislative matters: "I don't see them at meetings really. They pay the money."

However, in the past few years, the Minnesota Affiliate has begun to adopt a more activist posture. For example, by 1997, the Minnesota Affiliate was involved in sponsoring the "Putting Health First: No Tobacco Money in Politics Pledge Initiative" (Edwards and Burfeind, 1997). This initiative responded to the Minnesota Affiliate board's "frustration with the power of the tobacco industry in Minnesota." AHA volunteers contacted the "identified candidates for governor" and asked each of them to pledge not to accept campaign funds from the tobacco industry or their lobbyists.[12]

Two themes emerge from this examination of the role of the health voluntaries in the tobacco control movement in Minnesota. These organizations represented an organizational "infrastructure" on which the emerging movement could build in its early years. Thus, ALA gave rise to ANSR, one of two key single-issue organizations in the movement. The other single-issue organization, the Smoke-Free Coalition, formed around a nucleus of health voluntaries along with a handful of other health organizations. These preexisting organizations, with considerable stores of resources, such as money, staff, volunteers, expertise, and legitimacy, facilitated the growth of the movement. In particular, the legitimacy of these organizations has helped legitimate both the movement as a whole and particular legislative initiatives. But, once again, the use of this infrastructure, and the resources associated with it, comes at a price. Each of the voluntaries has some concern about its tax exempt/tax-deductible [501(c)(3)] status with the Internal Revenue Service, which may constrain the amount of lobbying they can take part in. Even more importantly, each vigilantly protects its image as a mainstream, highly legitimate organization, thus constraining choices of issues and tactics.

As tobacco control efforts have become increasingly accepted and applauded by the public in recent years, the voluntaries have been less and less burdened by these considerations—witness ACS's role in the ASSIST Project (although, as we will see in Chapter 7, ACS was still hindered by a number of factors in the degree to which it was willing to "push the envelope" of advocacy in this effort). But the constraints of these voluntary agencies always seem to be close to the surface. For example, ACS, AHA, and ALA sponsored a conference in March 1993, which included as speakers a health economist at the University of Minnesota who was an expert on tobacco and alcohol taxes, as well as the Director of Special Projects of the Advocacy Institute's Smoking Control Advocacy Resource Center, who was a strong proponent of increased taxes. Materials produced by the Coalition on Smoking OR Health, which strongly argued the merits of increased tobacco taxes, were distributed (Coalition on Smoking OR Health, 1993). Panelists discussed strategies for dealing with sometimes knotty arguments against increased tobacco taxes, such as the apparent regressivity of such taxes. Despite the clear intent of the conference—to motivate and equip people to advocate for increased taxes—which is one of the four goals of the national ASSIST project—the conference was given a neutral title: "Tobacco Taxation: It's Time to Explore the Issues." The subclause, "An Educational Conference," was featured prominently on all of the materials that were distributed.

NOTES

1.   See Walker (1983, 1991) for a more general analysis of the provision of start-up resources by established groups to related efforts.

2.   In 1996, leaders of ACS may have seriously jeopardized this image—at least for a time—by agreeing to endorse commercial products made by two different companies. The society announced that it would lend its name (and logo—the sword) to Smith-Kline Beecham Consumer Healthcare for marketing the Nicoderm nicotine replacement patch and Nicorette, the nicotine gum, which had both recently been approved and made available for over-the-counter sales (Elzay and Swanson, 1996; Associated Press, 1996a). In addition, the society would enter a "partnership" with the Florida Department of Citrus (the Florida orange growers and producers' association; Elzay and Swanson, 1996; Associated Press, 1996a). Of course, increasing fruit and vegetable consumption, and quitting smoking, help prevent cancer. However, ACS's entry into these "partnerships" (which ACS representatives argue do not constitute endorsements—see Elzay and Swanson, 1996), which involved the provision of substantial financial support (at least $4 million) to support ACS programs, received considerable press attention and criticism on ethical grounds (Associated Press, 1996a).

3.   Two Minnesota connections are worth mentioning. First, Dr. Harold Diehl, former dean of the University of Minnesota medical school, as Vice President for Research and Medical Affairs for the ACS, was active in lobbying for the appointment of the study committee. Second, Dr. Leonard M. Schuman, of the University of Minnesota School of Public Health, served on the committee. Schuman was to later serve on Minnesota's Technical Advisory Committee on Nonsmoking and Health, which formulated the Minnesota Plan for Nonsmoking and Health (MDH, 1984; see Chapter 7). As explored in Chapter 6, the ready availability of sympathetic experts on the health effects of smoking and other issues has been an important asset for the movement in Minnesota and nationally.

4.   It should be noted that the account from which this quotation is taken (Ross, 1987) is the official history of ACS.

5.   D-Day ("Don't Smoke Day") was developed by a local newspaper publisher in Monticello, Minnesota, and first held in 1974. It became a statewide event and served as the basis of ACS's "Great American Smokeout," which began in 1977. D-Day is jointly sponsored by the ALA of Minnesota and the Minnesota Division of ACS (Minnesota D-Day Steering Committee, no date).

6.   This is Kluger's (1996:506) account of the posture of the three voluntaries in the late 1970s, as the issue of secondhand smoke was spurring a groundswell of activism among grassroots organizations: "The ACS, along with the American Heart Association (AHA) and the American Lung Association (ALA), had size, organization, and a universally acknowledged mission to educate the public. What they had no experience at, and little stomach for, was political crusading; what they shared was a determination to avoid controversy—and smoking remained an emotional, divisive issue. The Big Three's tax-exempt status, furthermore, might have been imperiled if they had overtly lobbied Congress on the smoking issue (or any

other); the health voluntaries could have brought legal action against the cigarette companies or testified against them, but such measures were seen as antithetical to the voluntaries' basic task and might have cost them dearly."

7. The name was changed to the Minnesota Public Health Association in 1914, the Minnesota Tuberculosis & Health Association in 1951, the Minnesota Respiratory Health Association in 1967, the Minnesota Lung Association in 1974, and the American Lung Association of Minnesota (its current name) in 1981.

8. It is possible that this underrepresents the amount spent on tobacco control activities, since some of these activities might have been classified under one of the other expense categories. For example, ALA categorizes indoor air quality, including secondhand smoke, under the rubric of environmental health.

9. Specifically, "lung association's policy issues are driven by MPCA (the Minnesota Pollution Control Agency) . . . the environmental stuff is taken care of there. And the (Smoke-Free) Coalition (on tobacco issues) . . . .How the Coalition functions determines how lung association functions [on legislative issues] a lot."

10. The legislative liaison at the time describes the status of the "grassroots network": On the legislative network: "Well, my understanding of it is it's set up by issue: people that are interested in smoking, environment, community, school health issues—different categories. Who's on it can range from the actual legislators to people that call up and say, 'I'm interested in legislative issues. Put me on your list.' But it hasn't been updated and it's very old, and some of those people are dead that are on the list. So what I was trying to do is update that list. And I think the setup, the framework, came from National—help the states understand how to set up their network."

11. Despite the fact that, in 1997, the organization reported having over 60,000 volunteers in the state (Edwards and Burfeind, 1997).

12. According to an op-ed piece in the August 16, 1997, *Star Tribune* (Edwards and Burfeind, 1997), seven candidates—Mark Dayton, Mike Freeman, Hubert Humphrey III, Dean Johnson, Ted Mondale, Tim Pawlenty, and Allen Quist—signed the pledge. The article did not state whether the person who was eventually elected—Jesse Ventura, a former professional wrestler and a surprise winner as a third-party candidate (Reform Party)—declined to sign the pledge or if he wasn't approached.

6

The Health Professionals and
Health Care Organizations

Health professionals—physicians, nurses, respiratory therapists, health educators, and others—play a key role in the tobacco control movement, both individually and collectively. In fact, many key players in the movement are health professionals (Morain, 1993). In addition, organizations representing health professionals have also come to play an important role in the movement, both at the national level and in Minnesota, as described below. Finally, health care organizations, such as managed care and health insurance organizations, have come to figure more prominently in the movement, especially in recent years.

HEALTH PROFESSIONALS AND THEIR ORGANIZATIONS

As discussed in Chapter 1, research on social movements has often examined the ways in which movements are built on preexisting patterns of social relations (or social "infrastructure"). One important aspect of this is the recruitment of participants in a movement from existing informal or formal social groups, such as friendship networks, neighborhoods, work networks, churches, unions, and professional associations.[1]

There are a number of reasons—some obvious, some not so obvious— why movements tend to draw participants from existing groups of people. First, beliefs and attitudes that are consistent with the goals of a movement tend to "cluster" within particular social groupings. For example, members of Catholic and conservative Protestant churches may be more likely than other groups to possess attitudes and beliefs that are consonant with the goals and objectives of the Pro-Life Movement (McCarthy, 1987). People who share beliefs will be much more sympathetic than those who do not to the definition of the problem, and strategies for its solution, offered by social movement organizations (Snow et al., 1986).[2]

However, shared beliefs about an undesirable state of affairs, and the appropriate means of addressing that state of affairs, are not sufficient to impel people to action. Only small fractions of those who agree with the goals of a movement actively participate at any level—whether by becoming a member of and paying dues to an organization, volunteering to help with the operations of the organization, or taking part in lobbying and protest efforts (Klandermans and Oegema, 1987; McAdam, 1986). Structural availability—being a part of social groupings that "expose the individual to participation opportunities or pull them into activity" (McAdam and Paulsen, 1993:644)—plays a decisive role, over and beyond attitudinal affinity, in explaining who participates in a movement and who does not (Snow et al., 1980; McAdam, 1986). Thus, people who live in families, worship in churches, belong to associations, or work in offices with a participant in a social movement are often in a position to discover that they have a shared grievance, learn about how a problem and its solutions are understood within a movement (i.e., the way the problem and strategies for its solution are "framed"), and about opportunities for getting involved (Snow et al., 1980; Oegma and Klandermans, 1994; Opp and Gern, 1993; McAdam, 1986; Gould, 1993). In addition, individuals in these groups may be exposed to social encouragement and rewards for participating in the movement (Oliver, 1984; Hirsch, 1990). Since social movement organizations may deliberately target particular social groups for recruitment efforts, membership in a particular group may dramatically increase the probability that an individual will be exposed to a recruitment attempt (Oberschall, 1973; McCarthy, 1987; Morris, 1984).

In the case of the tobacco control movement, health professionals represent a key reservoir of volunteers who can be recruited into activism. First, there is often an affinity between the beliefs and attitudes of health professionals and the goals of the movement. After all, an underlying ethos of the health professions is to improve health and prevent disease. In addition, tobacco control activism may be viewed as a natural outgrowth or expansion of the traditional roles of health care providers, who come to move their efforts "upstream" to actively prevent, rather than just provide medical treatment for, emphysema, lung cancer, heart disease, and other medical conditions related to tobacco use. In the words of Judith Ockene:

> In the larger sense, the physician's role in smoking intervention implies political involvement and the influencing of public policy. Political involvement can be at the local level, such as working for the rights of non-smokers to be protected from the possible effects of passive smoking, or introducing anti-smoking programs in the schools. On the national level, changes such as restrictions on cigarette advertising and counter-advertising, warning labels, and government actions can contribute to cigarette smoking cessation. There

are many public policy alternatives for change in the environment on which physicians and other health care providers can have an effect. (1987:783)

Many health professionals who do become activists are especially effective; not only do they have firm convictions based on their lived experience of treating people suffering from the health effects of smoking and smokeless tobacco use, but they also tend to be highly educated and articulate, and are viewed as "neutral medical professionals." Defining tobacco use—such as adolescent smoking—as a medical or public health issue rather than a social or moral issue tends to be an effective strategy, and one that elevates the authority of health professionals, who are viewed as having special standing and expertise to speak on these issues.

In addition, the structural location of health professionals militates toward their involvement in tobacco control efforts. As explained below, many of the professional associations to which they belong have become involved as organizations in tobacco control efforts, and encourage their members to become involved in policy advocacy. Because many health professionals are involved, their colleagues are likely to be exposed to conversations about the issue, personal recruitment efforts, and opportunities to engage in activism. Finally, as we will see, health organizations may use their networks of members to identify potential activists in strategic locations and engage in targeted recruitment efforts to enlist these individuals in lobbying efforts.

HEALTH PROFESSIONALS AND ORGANIZATIONS AT THE NATIONAL LEVEL

The American Medical Association (AMA) wields considerable political clout on national issues related to health (Laumann and Knoke, 1987; Wolinsky and Brune, 1994). About 40% of U.S. doctors are dues-paying members of the AMA (Coleman, 1997). Although the AMA has in recent years become an important force on tobacco control issues—as detailed below—it has been criticized for not taking a stronger position in the earlier years of the movement. For example, the AMA did not divest its tobacco company stocks until 1981, following a divestiture campaign by DOC (Morain, 1993; Wolinsky and Brune, 1994). Moreover, the AMA has been criticized for supporting congressional candidates who are supportive of the tobacco industry (Coleman, 1997; Sharfstein and Sharfstein, 1994).

In the late 1980s and the 1990s, the AMA has come to have an important role in the movement. The flagship AMA journal—the prestigious *Journal of the American Medical Association*, or *JAMA*—has disseminated findings from several seminal studies of, and editorials on, youth access and other tobacco control issues (DiFranza et al., 1987; DiFranza and Tye, 1990; Feighery, Altman, and Shaffer, 1991; Koop, 1989). The association has also organized conferences bringing together tobacco control advocates and sympathetic legislators, which have resulted in policy recommendations on youth access and other tobacco policy issues (Houston, 1993; Lynch and Bonnie, 1994). The AMA is the national program office for the RWJF-funded Smokeless States program, a multistate program that is the largest private sector effort to stimulate tobacco control efforts in states and local communities (AMA, 2000). The AMA has provided financial support to a number of youth access initiatives, including the Center for Tobacco-Free Kids (Robert Wood Johnson Foundation, 1996). Finally, the AMA spent $8.5 million on lobbying in Washington in the first half of 1996, which was surpassed only by Philip Morris, which spent $11.3 million. A significant part of the AMA's lobbying effort focused on tobacco control efforts (Coleman, 1997).

Other national organizations, including the National Medical Association, the American Public Health Association (APHA), and the American Society of Clinical Oncology, have issued policy statements, exhorted their members to action, and, in some cases, engaged in lobbying at the national level on tobacco control issues (Veal, 1996; American Society of Clinical Oncology, 1996).[3]

State and local medical societies have also made important contributions to the movement. They, like the AMA, have disseminated information on approaches to tobacco control in their journals (e.g., Lynch and Hopkins, 1996; Cismoski and Sheridan, 1993, 1997; Goldstein et al., 1998; Jones, Dunayer, Hill, and Oatman, 2000; also see Simpson, 1995). Published analyses of tobacco control efforts in California, New York, Minnesota, Florida, Illinois, Arizona, and Texas note an important role—but often supportive, not a lead role—of state medical societies in tobacco control efforts (Samuels and Glantz, 1991; Novotny and Siegel, 1996; Jacobson, Wasserman, and Raube, 1992).[4]

MINNESOTA

Individual Involvement

Individually, health professionals represent the largest occupational group active in the movement. My 1992 survey of members, volunteers, and other people with formal affiliations with organizations active in the movement found that fully 16% were health professionals. While this included significant numbers of nurses, respiratory therapists, and other allied health workers, physicians have played an especially salient role. Jeanne Weigum, the president of ANSR, on the importance of physicians in movement action at the local level (such as advocating for local tobacco control ordinances):

> In some communities, the key person—the key activator—has been a doctor. You know that was true in Owatonna. The person who got it started was a relatively inexperienced community doctor who really cared passionately and he got something going and fairly late in the game contacted us. You know he had done all of the spade work, and then he kind of panicked and said "I think I need help." But he had done what needed to be done.

Another example of the involvement of health professionals took place in 1994, when a group of nurses at the Hennepin County Medical Center in downtown Minneapolis agitated for the removal of a Marlboro ad on a nearby billboard (Klobuchar, 1994).

Organizational Involvement

Organizations of health care professionals have played a pivotal role in tobacco control efforts in Minnesota. As described in Chapter 3, the Smoke-Free Coalition grew out of the Hennepin County Medical Society in 1984. Like the AMA in microcosm, the Minnesota Medical Association (MMA) has a large membership—about 6,000 members (Slovut, 1997)—and wields considerable influence on health policy in the state. For example, it was one of the primary players in health care reform efforts in the early 1990s (Miles et al., 1992a). The MMA was the eighth largest spender on legislative lobbying in Minnesota in the period July 1991 through June 1992, reporting expenditures of $62,297 (Sandok, 1992).[5]

The leaders of the MMA have at times been key leaders in tobacco control efforts in the state—for example, Dr. Stuart Hanson, a lung specialist at Park Nicollet Medical Center who has been a leader in the Smoke-Free Coalition since its beginnings (as discussed in Chapter 3), served as president of the state medical society in the early 1990s. Hanson has also served as president of the Hennepin County Medical Society. Organizationally, the MMA, the MMA Auxiliary, and local medical societies have been members of the Smoke-Free Coalition. The MMA originally donated office space to the coalition, and for years provided accounting services, as well as a $10,000 cash contribution as a supporting member every year.

Interestingly, the MMA's involvement in tobacco control issues was sparked by actions taken by the Hennepin County Medical Society's "Auxiliary," which consisted of the spouses (almost entirely wives) of members. According to Stuart Hanson,

> The Hennepin County Medical Society Auxiliary passed a resolution to work for a smoke-free society by the year 2000, and this came from Arlene Wilson.

Arlene Wilson had been to Norway, where her family had contacts, and so all the recommendations by the Norwegian Medical Society—that they work for a smoke-free society by the year 2000. . . . When the Auxiliary passed this they asked the Hennepin County Medical Society to bring this to the Minnesota Medical Association as a resolution, which they did. The resolution was passed, and I was at the meeting—sort of like an apple pie and motherhood resolution. But they added the stipulation that we bring it to the American Medical Association. Now I was an alternate delegate from the state to the American Medical Association, and I was the newest alternate delegate and I had just started and was going to my second annual meeting when we had to bring this issue to the AMA. . . . The head of the delegation designated me to shepherd the resolution at the AMA meetings. Now the AMA meetings are meetings of, at that time, about 350 delegates and another 350 alternates plus all the hangers on—probably 3,000 people. But it's a very formal process going through reference committees. So, they take in a resolution proposed by a state—not this coming from the state of Minnesota, so it had credibility as a Minnesota resolution. . . . It was then referred to a reference committee, and was referred to a reference committee in public health.

Hanson continues:

I had to testify, and the reason I was designated as the person to testify is one, I was a pulmonary specialist, so I had some knowledge about the effects of tobacco and so I could legitimately put together testimony and say it and answer questions. Two was that the chairman of our delegation was a smoker, and was not about to take this on himself and was trying to get someone else in his delegation to be the lightening rod, so to speak. This was a difficult issue, because he was aware that within the American Medical Association, there was a lot of interest to not meddle in this area too much. There had been a lot of resistance to change and to have the American Medical Association in the `80s address the issues of tobacco . . . he'd been around long enough to know he was gonna use me up a little bit on this issue. . . . I think the reason this went through the AMA, even because there had been all those other resistances to taking a forthright stand against tobacco, is that it was so general, and it had 17 years to run, and if you voted against a smoke-free society, you know . . . it was pretty hard to vote against.

After the resolution passed the AMA house of delegates (this was in 1983):[6]

We put together kind of an implementation plan, and said, "Where can we implement this?" And we said, "Well, we gotta do it within our own office—I mean, the Minnesota Medical Association. And since I'm the key person on this, we'll do it at the Park Nicollet Medical Center."

So Hanson led an effort, which was ultimately successful, to make both the Park Nicollet Medical Center (which at the time had about 1,800 employees, including 200 physicians, spread across 19 offices), and the Minnesota Medical Association smoke-free.

He and his MMA colleagues also led an effort to move the AMA along on tobacco issues:

> The number of resolutions [submitted by state delegations to the AMA] began to grow. And over the next several years, we saw a little bit of movement here. They'd accept, oh, we'll work toward increasing taxes on the cigarettes on the federal level, we'd do something else, but no real bold movement. Now the Surgeon General, Koop, sits in the House of Delegates in the AMA and would come to the meetings of the reference committee where these things were discussed. So we had over a period of a couple of years this kind of pressure building and resistance at the governance level and at the staff level of the AMA to change.

Why the continuing resistance on the part of the AMA? Hanson's view is as follows:

> The AMA in the early 80s, before this came up, had already divested itself of tobacco stocks. . . . But, it turns out that many of the leaders at the AMA smoke. And to implement smoke-free board meetings was an imposition, and it turned out that between six and eight of fourteen board members at the time when the material hit the fan, so to speak, in about 1986, there were successive presidents of the AMA who were cigarette smokers. One was a lung specialist—surgeon. There were board members who smoked and smoked at board meetings so that was a smoke-filled room—the AMA board meeting was a smoke-filled room—and it was nonsmokers were offended, and had raised the issue and were not able to change the environment that they were working in. And then there were two members of the AMA who owned a tobacco farm down in Georgia. So you had both addicted smokers and you had tobacco owners who were in leadership roles in the AMA, and they were resisting.

Hanson ended up voicing his concerns at the public health reference committee of the AMA, and the press ultimately picked up the issue, reporting on who on the AMA board owned tobacco farms (see Wolinsky and Brune, 1994). This media attention had the impact of opening up the governance structure of AMA to more aggressive movement on tobacco issues.

The MMA has a lengthy history of involvement in tobacco control. Some of this has been symbolic activity—for example, at the 1974 annual meeting, the House of Delegates voted unanimously for a resolution encouraging hospitals to restrict smoking by visitors and staff to designated areas and only allow smoking by patients with their physician's approval (Anonymous, 1974). As described in Chapter 4, the MMA played a key role—as a catalyst—in the formation of the Minnesota Smoke-Free Coalition.[7] And, fast forwarding another decade, delegates at the 1997 annual meeting voted to "encourage the Legislature to raise the minimum age for smoking from 18 to 21 on grounds that people are unlikely to become addicted to the nicotine in tobacco if they don't begin smoking in their teen years" (this was the second year in a row that the delegates passed this resolution; Slovut, 1997). The delegates also passed resolutions regarding prevention of children's exposure to secondhand smoke (1) "urging parents to keep their homes free of smoke" and (2) "state regulations banning smoking 24 hours a day in licensed day-care centers" (ibid.).

Despite their importance, associations of health professionals have sometimes played a rather passive role, representing a network that can be tapped into, rather than initiating action among their members. According to one knowledgeable observer, Jeanne Weigum, president of ANSR:

> The Medical Association is a resource that we call . . . and say we need a doctor in Sunfish Lake. Who do you have that's a possibility? As so . . . then they will supply us with a name. But they have never gone out and instigated a project like this. . . . You know, they don't even send one of their lobbyists. They've got lobbyists. They don't do that at the local level. That's not part of what they do.

The University of Minnesota School of Public Health has also provided important support to the movement. For a number of years, faculty and other members of the school have produced a considerable amount of research on questions surrounding the initiation, maintenance, and cessation of smoking (e.g., Blackburn, 1983; Folsom et al., 1984; Luepker, Johnson, Murray, and Pechacek, 1983; Mittelmark et al., 1982; Pechacek et al., 1984; Perry et al., 1986; Lando et al., 1990b). In an article describing the Minnesota Plan for Nonsmoking and Health written by MDH staff (Dean et al., 1986:271), the University of Minnesota is described as follows: "The University of Minnesota, a short walk from the Minnesota Department of Health, is a major center for research on the prevention of smoking in youth and on adult smoking cessation." This, among other things, is presented as one of the reasons why Minnesota in the mid-1980s "is well positioned for confronting the smoking problem" (ibid.). Data from these studies have been used by tobacco movement organizations in both their lobbying and public education efforts (e.g., see MDH, 1984).

Moreover, school faculty, fellows, staff, and students have been involved in research on issues of tobacco policy (Blaine et al., 1997; Boyle et al., 1995; Elnicki, 1992; Pham, 1996; Lando et al., 1990a; Forster et al., 1989, 1991, 1992, 1996; Forster and Hourigan, 1994; Forster and Wolfson, 1998).[8] In fact, a number of faculty members played active, instrumental roles in the passage of controls on vending machines in White Bear Lake and its diffusion to a number of other Minnesota communities (Lando et al., 1990a; Forster et al., 1990). Finally, a few faculty and staff of the school are actively involved in the movement organizations, such as ANSR and the Smoke-Free Coalition. Many former students have gone to work for the Minnesota ASSIST project and other tobacco control initiatives.[9]

Information—particularly information legitimated by being classified as "science"—is a vital resource for social movement actors. According to Jeanne Weigum, president of ANSR:

> I don't think they [the University of Minnesota] really had a substantial role until Jean [Dr. Jean Forster of the UM School of Public Health, who was to become a leading tobacco control researcher and activist] came on board, other than the economists who got involved with that original task force at the Health Department. They provided some real good expertise there to the Health Department. They were a real solid source of information that the Health Department really had no independent access to. So that was real important. You know, we've got some individual members who are university professors, but until Jean came on board, we didn't have any solid ties to the U at all. She was the first. And, you know, it's been wonderful. There's nothing like having accurate information to go on.

The new link with the UM SPH also led to a broadening of the mission of ANSR, and the Minnesota tobacco control movement as a whole. Jeanne Weigum explains:

> She [Jean Forster] also set a new direction for us. Youth access was not one of our [ANSR's] priorities. Might have evolved in that direction at some point—you know, we tossed it around and around again. But Jean's research really did form a focal point for us, and give us a point to run from. Seems to me we had done a survey in terms of what our members thought we ought to do. If I remember right, they saw a broadening of direction as being appropriate, but the first priority would still be Clean Indoor Air stuff, which is what we really tried to do.

In conclusion, the large number of health professionals and organizations in Minnesota has served as an important element of social "infrastructure" on which the movement has been able to build and grow.

HEALTH CARE ORGANIZATIONS

Health care organizations—especially managed care organizations (MCOs) and health insurance companies—have played an important role in the tobacco control movement in Minnesota. In the early years of the movement, the role was relatively inconspicuous. Blue Cross and Blue Shield of Minnesota, MedCenters Health Plan, and the Park Nicollet Medical Center were early sponsoring members of the Smoke-Free Coalition, but on the whole, did not play a very active role in the coalition or in the movement at large. However, in recent years, Blue Cross/Blue Shield (BCBS) and several of the large MCOs have come to play a more prominent role.

BCBS is the state's largest health insurer, and its HMO, Blue Plus, is the third largest health plan in the state, after Medica and HealthPartners (Howatt, 1997; Christianson et al., 1995).[10] By the mid-1990s, BCBS had taken on a more prominent role in lobbying for state-level tobacco control measures than it had played in earlier years. This may significantly increase the clout of tobacco control forces in the state, since BCBS has for a number of years been a significant force at the state legislature. For example, it was the fifth largest spender on legislative lobbying in Minnesota in the period July 1991 through June 1992, with expenditures of $91,612.[11]

BCBS was also the prime mover behind the formation of the Tobacco Tax Coalition for a Healthy Minnesota in 1993. This group emerged out of an early 1990s legislative effort to extend health insurance to the uninsured and control health care costs. Legislation was passed in 1992 (and subsequently modified in 1993 and 1994) that established a subsidized health insurance program for uninsured children and parents (MinnesotaCare), instituted cost control measures for health care in the state, and established the Minnesota Health Care Commission (Blewett, 1994; Chun and Pender, 1994; Miles et al., 1992b). The health care coalition was composed of twenty-five members including health care providers, payers, and consumers, and was charged with developing a detailed plan to contain health care costs in Minnesota (Blewett, 1994).

One key player in the Tobacco Tax Coalition explained its genesis as follows:

> The [Tobacco Tax] Coalition began in fall of 1993 following the Minnesota Health Care Commission's report to the legislature on both cost-containment and funding for universal coverage through the MinnesotaCare system. And their report to the legislature came up with a single answer to those questions, which was tobacco taxes, to both control medical care costs in the long term and to fund the expansion of MinnesotaCare towards the end of universal coverage by 1997. And that recommendation was for a forty cent [per pack] tax per year over five years for a total of two dollars by the end of that time.

Thus, the Tobacco Tax Coalition was formed to spearhead a campaign to enact state legislation raising the state excise tax on tobacco, with a portion of the increased tax revenues to be earmarked for programs to increase health care access and to prevent chronic disease.[12] In part because of the promise of earmarked funds resulting from a tax increase, the tax coalition was able to enlist organizations that had not previously been active on to-bacco control as members, including many health care organizations, but also organizations concerned more broadly with children's issues (such as the Children's Defense Fund, Congregations Concerned for Children, and the Minnesota Education Association). BCBS was not the only catalyst be-hind this effort—representatives from ANSR and the Smoke-Free Coali-tion, as well as an official from a local public health department, who had chaired the subcommittee of the MHCC that had developed the tobacco tax recommendation, were also closely involved in this effort. Neverthe-less, BCBS provided important resources to get the coalition up and mov-ing, including space, donated personnel, and start-up funds.[13]

The most dramatic step in the increasingly prominent role of BCBS in tobacco control advocacy was the suit it filed jointly with the Minnesota Attorney General against the tobacco industry in August 1994. The defen-dants included all of the major tobacco companies—Philip Morris, R.J. Reynolds, Brown & Williamson, B.A.T. Industries, the American Tobacco Co., the Liggett Group, and Lorillard Tobacco Co.—as well as the indus-try's trade associations (the Council for Tobacco Research and the Tobacco Institute). The suit was strikingly different from all of the numerous suits that had previously been brought against tobacco companies. Past suits had been brought on behalf of individual plaintiffs suffering from tobacco-related illnesses, and accused tobacco companies of marketing dangerous and addictive products. The Minnesota suit, on the other hand, was brought on behalf of two of the largest purchasers of health care in the state—BCBS and the State of Minnesota. It charged that the tobacco com-panies had conspired for forty years to deny consumers critical informa-tion on the health risks of smoking and to stifle the development of safer cigarettes. The suit alleged that this conspiracy violated state consumer fraud and antitrust laws. The suit was of tremendous size and scope com-pared to past suits. According to Michael York, who was one of the at-torneys representing Philip Morris, "You've got literally every tobacco company, all brands, all time, involved in this case. Usually, you have one or two involved, limited to the [individual] plaintiff's smoking history" (Phelps, 1996c).

In May 1998, the tobacco industry settled the suit, agreeing to new re-strictions on marketing and a financial settlement of $469 million paid over a five-year period to Blue Cross and $6.1 billion paid over twenty-five years to the state (Rybak and Phelps, 1998; see Chapter 7).

Why did BCBS of Minnesota take the unprecedented step of collaborat-ing with the state Attorney General in suing the tobacco industry? There were concerns that the suit would require considerable resources, might not be unsuccessful (given the record of the industry in court), and could even invite retaliation—such as the tobacco industry working with allies in the state legislature to institute undesirable regulations on BCBS and other health care purchasers (ibid.).

But the Minnesota BCBS organization had a long history of concern and involvement in the tobacco issue. According to Rybak and Phelps, it was the first health plan in the country to offer nonsmokers a discount in their premiums. As described in Chapter 4, BCBS was one of the founding members of the Minnesota Smoke-Free Coalition-2000. Thus, the regulatory aspect of the suit—to constrain the behavior of the tobacco industry, thereby reducing uptake and maintenance of the smoking habit—was consistent with the organization's long-standing interests in reducing tobacco use as a means of controlling health care costs. BCBS and the State of Minnesota are the two largest purchasers of health care in the state (Humphrey, 1994). In the suit against the tobacco industry, they argued that from 1978 to 1994, their expenditures associated with the treatment of and care of persons with smoking-related illnesses totaled $1.77 billion (Rybak and Phelps, 1998). Thus, any reductions in tobacco use that resulted from the suit could help BCBS in its goal of controlling costs. In addition, to the extent that money from a settlement is used to reduce premiums, BCBS could achieve a competitive advantage in the health care market (McCallum, 1998).[14]

Finally, BCBS stood to enhance its public image by heroically taking on what had come to be widely viewed as an immoral and criminal enterprise: the tobacco industry. In an era of increasing regulation of health care—including periodic discussion of opening up the market in the state to for-profit MCOs (Blewett and Hofrenning, 1997)—the large nonprofit health plans work hard to position themselves before the public and state policymakers in a favorable light (Marmor, 1991; Schlesinger, Gray, and Bradley, 1996).[15]

In addition to becoming more prominent in the Smoke-Free Coalition and the Tobacco Tax Coalition, in the last few years MCOs have been increasingly visible on the issue of youth access to tobacco. For example, during the 1996 state legislative session, representatives of MCOs, along with the Attorney General, were prominently featured at news conferences designed to promote a bill on youth access to tobacco (see Chapter 9). In 1996, the Allina Health System, which includes a large HMO [Medica, which enrolled 44% of health plan members in the state in 1996 (Howatt, 1997)], several community hospitals, and a large group practice, selected tobacco control as its first "systemwide health improvement initiative" (Jeddeloh and Roski, 1998). This is an effort to reduce tobacco use that runs the gamut from clinical smoking cessation programs to community-based tobacco use prevention efforts (Jeddeloh and Roski, 1998; Roski and Jeddeloh, 1997, 1999). The Allina Foundation provided $20,000 in early 1997 to fund groups in Granite Falls, Anoka County, St. Cloud, Wright County, and Duluth that had been funded by ASSIST, but did not receive continuation funding because requests for funds exceeded the funds available. ANSR approached Allina Foundation on behalf of these groups, and obtained funding for them to work locally to reduce tobacco consumption by minors. ANSR is administering the grant (ANSR, 1997).

HealthPartners was the second largest health plan in the state 1996, with an enrollment of a little under one-third of Minnesota health plan members (Howatt, 1997). As mentioned above, HealthPartners is a long-standing member of the Smoke-Free Coalition. By the mid-1990s, the organization had begun to break out of a largely supportive role, supporting such independent initiatives as a televised smoking counteradvertisement campaign aimed at youth (particularly girls) (Sandell, 1996), articles in the quarterly magazine sent to members that urged members to "contact your representatives to encourage them to protect Minnesota's children by pushing for tough access laws and a tobacco tax increase" (Anonymous, 1996a), and, in concert with other MCOs, an increasing presence at the state legislature on tobacco control issues (Sandell, 1998). Finally, in March 1998, HealthPartners and Allina's HMO (Medica) followed BCBS's lead and filed suit against the tobacco industry, this time in federal court (Sandell, 1998; Rybak and Phelps, 1998).

How can the increased involvement of health care organizations in the past few years in tobacco control efforts be explained? While these organizations were always part of the health "infrastructure" on which the movement has built, they have increasingly taken on active, high-profile roles in the movement. The growing popularity of "population health" initiatives by health care organizations—particularly MCOs—may provide a partial answer to this question. Historically, an emphasis on health promotion and disease prevention has been seen as a integral and desirable aspect of managed care. However, this emphasis has usually taken the form of health education and preventive services, usually delivered in a clinical setting: health screening, smoking cessation, nutrition classes and counseling, prenatal classes, and the like. In the 1990s, some MCOs began to move beyond this narrow range of prevention efforts to focus their prevention efforts on larger units:work sites, neighborhoods, cities, and states (Bowser and Gostin, 1999; Schlesinger and Gray, 1998; Wolfson, Hourigan and Johnson, 1998).

Wolfson and colleagues (1998) suggest that several factors may contribute to MCOs' recent interest and involvement in communitywide disease prevention and health promotion efforts. First, these initiatives, under certain circumstances, may be perceived as a good business strategy. An important part of the underlying logic behind managed care, embodied in the federal Health Maintenance Organization Act of 1973, is that situating responsibility for insurance and provision of health care within a single organization creates an organizational incentive for the prevention of disease in the enrolled population (Green and Kreuter, 1990; Starr, 1976; Luft and Greenlick, 1996). In the 1970s and 1980s, the major strategy MCOs have used to improve the health of enrollees to prevent disease and improve health has been the provision of health education and preventive services, such as prenatal classes, mammography, immunization of children and seniors, and promotion of bicycle safety helmet use (Thompson et al., 1995; Johns et al., 1992). The movement into population health initiatives seems to reflect a growing awareness that communitywide health campaigns, including efforts to change public policies in such areas as tobacco use and violence, have considerable potential for improving the health of communities (Stodghill, 1996; Wolfson et al., 1998). Thus, MCOs are not limited to providing smoking cessation classes and counseling to their members; they may come to understand that they have a financial interest in increasing the state excise tax on cigarettes, for example.[16]

The financial incentive for MCOs to get into "the public health business" is most pronounced where there is high market penetration and where a few MCOs dominate the health insurance market. As stated in a mid-1990s health care industry publication,

> By the time managed care plans enroll 70 or 80 percent of a metropolitan population, health plans with large market shares will find their subscribers' health risks effectively mirror those of the larger community. If a plan has 25 or 30 percent market share in an area where managed care plans enroll the vast majority of a community's citizens, the health plan will discover that it is really in the public health business. (Goldsmith, Goran, and Nackel, 1995:22)[17]

In addition, population health initiatives may help legitimate MCOs—particularly nonprofit MCOs—in an environment of increased accountability and demands for regulation (Bowser and Gostin, 1999; Schlesinger and Gray, 1998). Nonprofit health care organizations throughout the country have been criticized—often by the for-profit sector of the industry—as having an unfair advantage because of their preferential treatment—particularly exemption from federal and state income taxes and county and municipal real estate taxes (Marmor, Schlesinger, and Smithey, 1987; Potter and Longest, 1994). Historically, the central rationale for favorable tax treatment of nonprofit health care organizations was that they provided free medical care to indigent patients (Schlesinger et al., 1996; Potter and Longest, 1994). However, the implementation of Medicaid, Medicare, and other federal programs that assume much of the responsibility for paying for medical care for the poor has weakened this justification (Schlesinger et al., 1996; Potter and Longest, 1994). Broader ideas of "community benefit" have come to fore as an alternative basis for tax exemption. Increasingly, norms of community benefit have been advocated—for nonprofit MCOs, in particular—by the federal, state, and local governments as well as hospital and managed care associations (Bowser and Gostin, 1999; Schlesinger et al., 1996; Schlesinger and Gray, 1998; Potter and Longest, 1994; Wolfson et al., 1998).

These motivations for involvement in tobacco control efforts, ranging from providing smoking cessation services to enrollees to lobbying the state legislature for measures to reduce youth access to tobacco and to increase the state excise tax on cigarettes, have been articulated by representatives of MCOs. For example, a series of recent articles on tobacco control efforts sponsored by Allina make reference to the potential cost savings from such measures:

> Interventions designed to control tobacco use can have a positive effect on [clinical outcomes (morbidity and mortality), functional status outcomes (quality of life), modifiable risk factor outcomes (e.g., smoking), patient experience outcomes (satisfaction), and cost-effectiveness outcomes (cost savings)]. The impact of tobacco use on Allina's clinical priorities—cardiovascular disease, diabetes, cancer, pediatric asthma, and pregnancy care—has been well documented. Each clinical action group formed at Allina to address these five priorities has cited the need to tobacco use control. (Roski and Jeddeloh, 1997)

In addition, the importance of appealing to individual consumers and corporate purchasers of health care has been articulated as well:

> Allina is faced with the need to demonstrate value to individual consumers and large-scale purchasers of medical care. State and federal Medicaid and Medicare administrators, employers, and such business coalitions as Business-Health Care Action Group expect healthcare organizations to provide various prevention services and health improvement programs of known effectiveness. For these groups and individual patients alike, tobacco use control is becoming or has become an expected healthcare service. (ibid.)

Finally, the value of demonstrating that an MCO is socially responsible, committed to the communities that it serves, and on the cutting edge of efforts to promote health has been acknowledged as well:

> In summary, by simultaneously engaging in multiple efforts across many of its settings—namely clinics, hospitals, and health plans—in addition to partnering with key community stakeholders, Allina can demonstrate the value that an integrated healthcare system can bring to the improvement of the health of its patients, members and communities it serves. Allina's efforts hold the promise of effectively connecting improvement strategies rooted in

a medical or public health model. Allina's efforts are poised to advance the emerging paradigm of population health improvement, to provide significant community benefit, and to allow Allina to be recognized as a socially responsible healthcare organization. (ibid.)

The managed care industry in Minnesota appears to be a leader among the states in forging public health initiatives in such areas as childhood immunization, violence prevention, and tobacco control policy (Wolfson et al., 1998). Several factors are likely to have contributed to Minnesota's managed care industry relatively advanced degree of involvement in population health. First, the state displays extremely high market concentration. By the early 1990s, HMOs in Minnesota had achieved high levels of market penetration. In 1993 the average level of penetration in each of the fifty states was 17.4%; Minnesota, however, was sixth among the states in penetration, at 30.1% (Group Health Association of America, 1994:27).[18] Market penetration is even more striking if we consider the Twin Cities metropolitan area. Among the fifty-four largest MSAs in 1991, the Minneapolis-St. Paul MSA ranked fourth (at 46% penetration), exceeded only by Rochester, New York (at 54%), Worcester, Massachusetts (at 51%), and San Francisco-Oakland-San Jose / Sacramento (at 49%) (ibid.:29).

Minnesota is unique among the states in that state laws requires all MCOs to have nonprofit status (Aspen Systems Corporation, 1996). As described above, strong norms have emerged that nonprofit MCOs demonstrate "community benefit" by engaging in community health initiatives, such as tobacco control efforts. In 1996, these norms were embodied an amendment to MinnesotaCare legislation (Minnesota Statutes §62Q.075[2] 1996) that requires each MCO in the state to prepare and submit a "Community Collaboration Plan,"

> a plan describing the actions the managed care organization has taken and those it intends to take to contribute to achieving public health goals for each service area in which an enrollee of the managed care organization resides. This plan must be jointly developed in collaboration with the local public health units, appropriate regional coordinating boards, and other community organizations providing health services within the same service area as the managed care organization.

In addition, the connections of for-profit HMOs with the tobacco industry that are found in some states may constrain HMOs' involvement in tobacco control efforts in those states. Prudential and other insurers, which are also major owners of for-profit HMOs, are heavily invested in the tobacco industry (Boyd, Wesley, Himmelstein, and Woolhandler, 1995). At least in some cases (such as Aetna and Philip Morris), these companies also have directorship interlocks with the tobacco industry (ibid.). And HMOs and tobacco interests share lobbyists in a number of states (Goldstein and Bearman, 1996; Pallarito, 1993).

We have again seen in this chapter how the movement has built heavily on the dense health care and public health "infrastructure" in the state of Minnesota. The movement has drawn on health care professionals—especially physicians—and their professional associations. The health care organizations—BCBS, and to a lesser extent Allina and HealthPartners, initially played a backstage role in the movement, but have increasingly come to prominence, as evidenced by the landmark suit against the tobacco industry undertaken jointly by BCBS and the Minnesota Attorney General. I argue that the entry of these organizations into the fray may be explained, in part, by the growing trend in the managed care industry of population health initiatives as well as distinctive aspects of the Minnesota health care system that encourage such efforts. The growing involvement of these organizations is significant, in that they devote considerable resources to lobbying—they have historically been major players at the state legislature—and they appear to be less constrained then the voluntaries when it comes to engaging in political advocacy on behalf of tobacco control.

NOTES

1. My use of the term "recruitment" here refers both to self-recruitment and to recruitment by an existing participant in a movement.

2. In the language of framing analysts, "frame alignment" between movement actors and potential participants—i.e., achieving a common understanding of the nature of a social problem and preferred strategies and tactics for its solution—is facilitated by shared underlying beliefs, or "master frames" (Snow et al., 1986; Snow and Benford, 1992).

3. As noted at the beginning of this chapter, there often is a progression among health professionals from treating the sequelae of tobacco use, to providing counseling on prevention and cessation, to engaging in policy advocacy to prevent tobacco use. Thus, new "recruits" to the movement may be a by-product of widespread efforts to expand the role of many groups of health professionals, to encourage provision of educational materials, counseling, etc., aimed at preventing the use of tobacco by adolescents, and cessation by adolescent and adult smokers. Examples include primary care providers, such as pediatricians (Gregorio, 1994), family practitioners (ibid.), dentists, and oral hygienists (Dolan, McGorray, Grinstead-Skiger, and Mecklenburg, 1997; Gregorio, 1994; Hovell et al., 1995); nurses (Sanders, Peveler, Mant, and Fowler, 1993); pharmacists (Smith, Chatfield, and Pagnucco, 1995); and obstetricians and nurse midwives (Secker-Walker et al., 1995). In 1996, the Agency for Health Care Policy and Research issued a clinical practice guideline stating that "clinicians should ask and record the tobacco-use status of every patient" and "every person who smokes should be offered smoking cessa-

tion treatment at every office visit" (Fiore et al., 1996:iii). The development and testing of brief, structured interventions delivered by physicians or other clinicians was supported by a research funding initiative launched by the National Cancer Institute in 1983 (Glynn, Manley, and Pechacek, 1990).

4.   As we shall see in Chapter 10, there are situations where the interests of organized medicine and tobacco control diverge—as came to be the case in California—leading to competition and conflict between medical and tobacco control groups (Traynor and Glantz, 1996).

5.   By way of comparison, Blue Cross / Blue Shield was the fifth largest spender on legislative lobbying in Minnesota in 1992 ($91,612), and the top tobacco interest, R.J. Reynolds Tobacco Company, was tenth ($56,448 (Sandok, 1992).

6.   Hanson and others in Minnesota argue—with considerable pride—that the trajectory of the "smoke-free society by the year 2000" idea went from Norway to the Hennepin County Medical Auxiliary to the Hennepin County Medical Society to the MMA to the AMA, where Surgeon General Koop, who attended the AMA public health reference committee meetings, picked up the idea and, beginning in 1984, challenged APHA, ALA, and others to work to achieve it at the national level.

7.   The MMA had been involved in a few earlier coalition efforts, providing a kind of template for how such efforts are accomplished. One was a commission on health care costs, which included attorneys, business representatives, and MMA members. The second was a commission focusing on tort reform / professional liability.

8.   In the interests of disclosure, I remind the reader—as I mention in the Introduction—that I was a member of the UM SPH faculty in the early and mid-1990s. Thus, many of the people I mention here were direct colleagues, with some of whom I continue to collaborate.

9.   The strong researcher-activist connection is not idiosyncratic to Minnesota. For example, Dr. Stanton A. Glantz, of the Cardiology Division of UCSF, is a past president of ANSR (Glantz, 1987) and a leading tobacco control advocate nationally. Dr. John Slade, who is vice president of New Jersey GASP (Hyman, 1997) and past president of STAT, is a faculty member in Internal Medicine at the University of Medicine and Dentistry of New Jersey / Robert Wood Johnson Medical School. Dr. Richard Daynard, who is also a past president of STAT and directs the Tobacco Products Liability Project at Northeastern University, is a professor of law at Northeastern. My colleague at Wake Forest, Dr. David Altman, also served as president of STAT. Papers jointly authored by academic researchers and members of activist organizations are common in the tobacco control and public health literature (e.g., Altman et al., 1989; Pierce et al., 1994; Lando et al., 1990a; Forster et al., 1990).

10.   Although BCBS is classified as an insurer, Strang (1995:179) argues that it resembles an MCO in important respects: "Minnesota's Blue Cross responded to HMO growth by adopting many of the practices of HMOs. In the late 1980s, Blue Cross began to aggressively contract with hospitals rather than paying standard fees, and to withhold 10% of physicians' income against plan losses. As a result, Minneapolis-St. Paul's conventional fee-for-service sector has moved to a form of 'managed care' that is hard to distinguish from the structure of many IPAs [Independent Practice Associations]."

11.   This exceeded the top spender among tobacco interests that year: R.J.

Reynolds Tobacco Company, which with $56,448 in legislative lobbying expenditures was the tenth biggest spender (Sandok, 1992). Of course, BCBS lobbied on a variety of issues unrelated to tobacco.

12. The health care commission recommended that in the first year of the tax increase, 30% of the revenues be allocated to "Consumer Education and Wellness— Tobacco Use Prevention Initiatives and Programs)," "Violence Prevention," and "Improved Birth Outcomes." The remaining 70% of the revenue would go to supplement the legislative appropriation for the MinnesotaCare health insurance program (Minnesota Health Care Commission, 1994).

13. Unfortunately, this effort did not succeed in achieving an increase in the tobacco tax. As of December 1998, the tax remained at the level set in 1992: $0.48 per pack (see Chapter 9).

14. Other options would be to fund smoking cessation programs, education, and research. Since BCBS is a nonprofit, it cannot distribute the proceeds of a settlement or award to stockholders (McCallum, 1998).

15. Analysts of BCBS organizations argue that they have throughout their histories been concerned with projecting an image of community service in order to justify their privileged tax treatment (they are nonprofits) compared to other health insurers and ward off regulations that would affect their tax status or the advantages they enjoy (Brown, 1991; Marmor, 1991; Schlesinger et al., 1996). The theme of the value of nonprofit health care organizations demonstrating "community benefit" will be revisited later in this chapter.

16. According to a leading expert: "Examining the literature on a wide array of smoking cessation interventions, ranging from public health media campaigns to resource-intensive, physician-led office interventions, one observes a consistent pattern of findings in which the cost per life-year saved is less than, or at least no greater than, virtually all of the healthcare interventions for which cost-effectiveness has been assessed" (Warner, 1998:S50).

17. In addition to reducing demand for curative medical services, population health initiatives may contribute to the "bottom line" of health plans in other ways, including reducing the amount of uncompensated care they provide and increasing the attractiveness of health plans to employers and individuals when choosing plans (Schauffler and Rodriguez, 1994, 1996; Wolfson et al., 1998).

18. The states with higher levels of market penetration were California (35.0%), Massachusetts (34.1%), Arizona (32.9%), Maryland (32.0%), and Oregon (31.5%) (GHAA, 1994:27).

7

The State

Government has been heavily involved in tobacco control efforts, particularly at the federal and state levels. In this chapter, I will outline federal involvement in tobacco control, and then move to an in-depth examination of state government involvement in tobacco control. As I argued in Chapter 1, existing images in the social movement literature of government involvement in social movements—as a target, as a provider of constraints and opportunities, or as a facilitator or sponsor—provide an incomplete, and somewhat misleading, picture when we look at the tobacco control movement. In this chapter, we will see the state playing all three of these roles, but we will also see involvement in joint advocacy and close collaboration with movement organizations—a relationship that I describe as state/movement "interpenetration."

FEDERAL INVOLVEMENT IN TOBACCO CONTROL

Federal involvement in the tobacco control movement has grown dramatically in the recent period (Kagan and Vogel, 1993; Novotny et al., 1992). This involvement primarily has taken three forms: direct regulatory action (by rule or statute), sponsorship and publication of research and other materials, and attempts to catalyze state- and local-level collective action by providing technical assistance and funding.

Examples of direct regulatory action include Federal Trade Commission restrictions on cigarette advertising issued in 1955 and 1960 (Troyer and Markle, 1983), the 1965 passage of the Cigarette Labeling and Advertising Act (Fritschler, 1989), and Interstate Commerce Commission restrictions on smoking on common carriers issued in 1974 and 1976. Regulations issued in 1996 implementing the "Synar Amendment" require states to demonstrate higher levels of enforcement of minimum-age-of-sale laws for tobacco (Jacobson and Wasserman, 1997; Forster and Wolfson, 1998). In 1996, the Food and Drug Administration issued far-reaching regulations restricting tobacco retailing and advertising in order to reduce tobacco access and use by youth (USDHHS, 1996). In a significant setback to the movement, the Supreme Court overturned these regulations in March 2000, ruling that the FDA lacks the authority to regulate tobacco products (Gottlieb, 2000).

In addition, the state, especially federal agencies and authorities such as the Surgeon General, the National Cancer Institute, and the Centers for Disease Control and Prevention, have played pivotal roles as sponsors and publishers of research and other materials that have been widely used by activists in advocating policy changes at the federal, state, and local levels. Examples of such materials include the widely read and cited, and highly respected, Surgeon General Reports on Smoking and Health. The first report (USDHEW, 1964), issued in 1964, is often depicted as a watershed in the history of tobacco control efforts (Nathanson, 1999; Troyer and Markle, 1983; Kluger, 1996), with far-reaching consequences for policy, the behavior of the tobacco industry, and long-term trends in smoking rates. The 1986 report, *The Health Consequences of Involuntary Smoking* (USDHHS, 1986), helped disseminate the scientific underpinning for movement organizations' claims about the health effects of secondhand smoke. The 1994 report focused on youth tobacco use (USDHHS, 1994), and included as policy recommendations much of the movement agenda, such as increasing taxes on cigarettes and smokeless tobacco, restricting advertising targeted at youth, and limiting the commercial availability of tobacco to youth.

In addition to the Surgeon General reports, a number of other reports and data sources have provided important ammunition for tobacco control advocacy efforts. A 1986 National Research Council report (National Research Council, 1986) and a 1993 Environmental Protection Agency report (EPA, 1993) provided extremely important ammunition to activists' efforts to influence state legislatures and other bodies to enact measures to limit population exposure to secondhand smoke. Similarly, the 1994 Institute of Medicine report, *Growing Up Tobacco Free: Preventing Nicotine Addiction in Children and Youths* (Lynch and Bonnie, 1994), provided support for, and legitimation of, movement efforts to increase taxes on tobacco products and promote policy and enforcement efforts aimed at reducing the availability of cigarettes and smokeless tobacco to youth.

Government agencies also collect or contract for the collection of data on the prevalence of adult and teenage smoking. Prominent examples include the High School Senior (Monitoring the Future) study sponsored by the National Institute on Drug Abuse, the Behavioral Risk Factor Survey sponsored by the CDC, and the National Health Interview Survey sponsored by the USDHHS. The Youth Risk Behavior Surveillance System, which was established by the CDC in 1990, allows the tracking of high school students' use of tobacco (as well as five other categories of health risk behaviors) over time (CDC, 1994c). At the state level, legitimated data on the prevalence of smoking and smokeless tobacco use—especially among youth—has been critical to the efforts of activists to frame the issue as a compelling health problem (see Chapter 2 for an overview of these data).

In addition to data on prevalence, estimates of mortality, morbidity, and economic costs associated with tobacco use are a key resource provided by government agencies. The health departments of all fifty states reported in a 1989–1990 survey that they used the SAMMEC (Smoking-Attributable Mortality, Morbidity, and Economic Costs) software package to generate state-specific estimates of the economic and health costs of smoking (CDC, 1991b). Finally, tobacco control activists, as well as government authorities, routinely cite the estimate of nearly 419,000 deaths attributable to smoking in the United States in 1990 (CDC, 1993a).

Perhaps even more important than the creation and dissemination of knowledge are government efforts to catalyze collective action on tobacco control by providing technical assistance and financial support to state governments, local governments, and nonprofit organizations. Such efforts have proliferated in recent years. Some of these, such as the Community Partnership Program sponsored by the Center for Substance Abuse Prevention, focus on alcohol and illicit drugs in addition to tobacco use. Others focus exclusively on tobacco use. These include the $45 million Community Intervention Trial to Reduce Heavy Smoking (COMMIT), sponsored by the National Cancer Institute (Lichtenstein, Nothwehr, and Gray, 1991; COMMIT Research Group, 1995). While the primary focus of COMMIT was smoking cessation, it did incorporate community organizing and media advocacy efforts as well (Thompson, Wallack, Lichtenstein, and Pechacek, 1991; Wallack and Sciandra, 1991).

The American Stop Smoking Intervention Study for Cancer Prevention (ASSIST), jointly sponsored by the National Cancer Institute and the American Cancer Society, brought federal involvement in tobacco control advocacy to a new level. ASSIST represented a massive infusion of federal resources into state and local tobacco control advocacy efforts. A survey by the Association of State and Territorial Health Officials (1994:15) asked states about state health agency tobacco control expenditures in 1990 (i.e., fiscal years 1989–1990) and 1992 (i.e., fiscal years 1991–1992). State funds (excluding California)[1] spent on tobacco control increased from $3.5 million in 1990 to $4.1 million in 1992 (an increase of 17%). In contrast, federal and "other funds" grew from $2.8 million in 1990 to $9.8 million in 1992, an increase of 250%! This increase coincided with the 1991 awards of planning contracts to seventeen states participating in ASSIST.[2] The health department in each of the seventeen ASSIST states received approximately $400,000 per year for the two-year planning period (1991–1993) and an av-

erage of about $1.2 million a year over the course of the five-year imple-
mentation phase (1993–1998), for a total of approximately $115 million in
funds awarded to the states with an additional $20 million going to coor-
dination and technical assistance (Manley et al., 1997a; USDHHS, 2000).
Thus, ASSIST has been aptly characterized as "the largest, most comprehensive tobacco control project ever undertaken in the United States"
(Manley et al., 1997a:S8).[3]

The Center for Substance Abuse Prevention (CSAP), which is part of the
Substance Abuse and Mental Health Administration of the U.S. Department of Health and Human Services, has promoted efforts to reduce youth
access to tobacco in a number of ways. In connection with its responsibility for implementation of Synar, CSAP published and distributed monographs to assist states in complying with the Synar requirements. These
reports contain information on the importance of preventing tobacco sales
to minors, policy approaches to reducing sales, merchant education, enforcement, and community education (CSAP, no date), as well as instruc-
tions on how to go about measuring compliance with the regulation
(CSAP, 1996).

State governments have also been actively involved in promoting and
pursuing activism, policy, and social change on tobacco. In 1989, the Association of State and Territorial Health Officials established a network of
state health department officials responsible for communication between
and state health departments and CDC and other government agencies on
tobacco control (CDC, 1991b).

THE STATE AND TOBACCO CONTROL IN MINNESOTA

In Minnesota, three state agencies have been active in tobacco control
efforts: the Minnesota Department of Health (MDH), the Minnesota Attorney General (AG), and, to a lesser extent, the Minnesota Department of
Human Services (MDHS). MDH's involvement in the movement can be
traced back to the publication of the *Minnesota Plan for Nonsmoking and
Health* in 1984 (MDH, 1984).[4] The plan emerged out of a concern on the part
of MDH to address chronic disease. This concern with chronic disease was
not idiosyncratic to MDH, but was shared by a large and growing contingent of public health researchers, practitioners, and policymakers.[5] The
National Heart, Lung, and Blood Institute (NHLBI) of the NIH had funded
large research and demonstration projects that sought to "develop and test
population-wide educational programs to reduce cardiovascular morbidity and mortality rates" in Minnesota, Rhode Island, and California (Blackburn, 1983:398).[6] The NHLBI was also supporting the National High Blood
Pressure Education program (which began in 1972—see DHHS, 1997) and

would in 1985 initiate the National Cholesterol Education Program (USD-HHS, 1993b).

MDH had in 1981 embarked on a mission to "develop a systematic approach to controlling chronic disease risk factors, and to identify a unique, useful role for a State health department in health promotion, a field in which many other public and private groups were already active" (Dean et al., 1986). The Commissioner of Health appointed an expert panel to define the major health problems in Minnesota; smoking was considered by the panel to be the most important of the nine areas identified (ibid.). MDH reported the results in 1982, and in 1983 the Minnesota Center for Nonsmoking and Health, consisting of two half-time research scientists (a psychologist and an epidemiologist) and a health educator-administrator, was established (ibid.). This provided the nucleus on which governmental tobacco control efforts in Minnesota would build.

The staff of the center began doing groundwork on the epidemiology and economics of smoking in the state and methods for preventing or controlling smoking. They also helped select and organize (and subsequently staffed) the Minnesota Technical Advisory Committee on Nonsmoking and Health (ibid.). The committee included twenty members, with backgrounds in business (including major corporations in the state and business sectors with a direct economic interest in tobacco use, such as groceries and the hospitality industry), education, advertising, insurance, labor, economics, law, state government, medicine, and public health (ibid.; MDH, 1984). The panel included one legislator (Senator Thomas A. Nelson of St. Paul), five faculty from the University of Minnesota (three from the School of Public Health, one from the Department of Medicine, and one from the Department of Agricultural and Applied Economics), and two individuals who were past or present leaders of ANSR—then known as the Association for Nonsmoker's Rights.

One member of the panel described the process as follows:

My understanding was that [Andy Dean] was asked by the commissioner to do a comprehensive study and develop a plan for how to deal with smoking in Minnesota, and he was supposed to put together this task force. . . . And then we had a couple of legislators and a couple of retailers—retail merchants association—it was really a broad group. They had a couple of economists. Some from the University of Minnesota. Kind of a bunch of health people and a couple of educators. It was just a really a broad task force. . . . In the end we came out with a report. The department put a lot of time into it. Boy, they put in major time. . . . I think they probably had two people full-time during the course of this task force and then other people part of the time. . . . It seems to me it took them about a year, a year and a half to do this report and then came out with the Minnesota Plan for Nonsmoking and Health.

The completed plan included a thorough review of the state of knowledge on the health benefits of nonsmoking;[7] patterns of smoking and smoking-attributable deaths and disability in Minnesota; economic costs attributable to smoking in Minnesota; the economics of tobacco; and methods for the promotion of nonsmoking (MDH, 1984). Some of the highlights among the findings were that smoking is the "single largest preventable cause of mortality" in the state, accounting for about 15% of deaths as well as 9% of disability; that reductions in smoking would reduce mortality and disability among smokers and health consequences and discomfort among nonsmokers exposed to secondhand smoke; and that substantial costs savings could be achieved by reductions in the prevalence of smoking (for example, an estimated $67.8 million would be saved if 10% of current and potential smokers were motivated to abstain from smoking; MDH, 1984; Dean et al., 1986).

The plan classified methods for the promotion of nonsmoking into five categories: "educational and behavioral interventions," "economic strategies," and "regulatory/legislative strategies" (MDH, 1984). A series of recommendations flowed from the discussion of these methods. Under the category of "school and youth education," there were recommendations to provide six or more hours of "scientifically-evaluated nonsmoking education" in the seventh grade, regulate smoking in schools, and "reinforce school efforts through community programs" (ibid.:109). In the area of public education, there were recommendations to conduct a long-term public communication campaign, provide physicians with better skills to identify and treat smoking addiction, support nonsmoking campaigns by the local public health infrastructure (Community Health Service agencies and other community organizations), encourage smokers to use effective methods for quitting, and encourage nonsmokers to assist in implementing the Minnesota Clean Indoor Air Act (ibid.:116). Recommendations in the regulatory area included encouraging smokefree worksites improving the effectiveness of theMCIAA, and enacting a state law prohibiting distribution of free cigarettes (ibid.:130).[8] Finally, the plan included several recommendations regarding economic incentives and disincentives to smoke: increase the state excise tax, fund nonsmoking programs, and implement economic incentives (through insurance and other means) to reward nonsmoking (ibid.:147).

The originators of the plan promoted it as a model for other states in widely read reports and professional journals (e.g., Dean et al., 1985, 1986; Shultz et al., 1986).[9] Computer software to estimate smoking-attributable mortality, morbidity, and economic costs was developed by MDH and made available to other state health departments and public health professionals (Shultz et al., 1986). The plan, and MDH's related efforts, contributed to the development and use of economic arguments for tobacco control. The plan also led to the creation of the Section for Nonsmoking and Health within MDH in 1985.

The plan was widely distributed—two thousand copies of the full report and recommendations were distributed in the first eight months following the release of the report. As discussed in Chapter 3, the plan, together with actions on the part of the Minnesota Medical Association and others, was one of the catalysts for the 1984 founding of the Minnesota Coalition for a Smoke-Free Society by the Year 2000.

The plan also led to legislation introduced into the Minnesota legislature, with the support of the governor. Surgeon General Koop came to the state and spoke to the House of Representatives and the Minnesota Press Club in support of the plan, the SFC, and the proposed legislation (Dean et al., 1986; Shultz et al., 1986). This legislation—the Omnibus Nonsmoking and Disease Prevention Act—was enacted in June 1985 (see Chapter 3). Among other things, it provided a two-year appropriation of $2.7 million to MDH (Dean et al., 1986), which enabled the creation of the Section for Nonsmoking and Health. The Omnibus Act also provided $1.3 million over two years for the Department of Education to implement nonsmoking programs.

The Omnibus Act included a formula that was to be followed by a number of other states (in some cases at a much grander level—such as in California, Massachusetts, and Arizona[10]). A little over one-third of one cent of the five-cent tax increase would be used to fund tobacco use prevention programs to be conducted through the MDH and the Minnesota Department of Education (MDE; MDH, 1991; Cummings, 1993).

The initiative, implemented by MDH and MDE, has been the focus of national attention. It has been characterized as the first "comprehensive, legislatively funded initiative to curb tobacco use" (Harty, 1993:271). According to Cummings (1993:270), "one of the objectives of the ASSIST project is to help the states establish tobacco control programmes similar to [the one that] existed in the MDH."

MDH instituted a competitive application process, and based on applications received, in 1986–1987 awarded $50,000 to the Minnesota Smoke-Free Coalition 2000 to work with Minnesota hospitals to become smoke-free. A total of $175,000 was awarded to Community Health Services agencies[11] and, in one case, city government, to implement programs involving work-site nonsmoking programs, school programs, development of community task forces, public education campaigns, and training of health professionals (MDH, 1987). In the second cycle of funding (1998–1989), the Smoke-Free Coalition was awarded $100,000 for a statewide effort to promote nonsmoking in chemical dependency treatment programs, and to cosponsor a conference on nicotine dependence. In addition, a total of $412,881 was awarded to CHS agencies to implement community-level programs (MDH, 1991). In the third funding cycle (1990–1991), MDH funded the Smoke-Free Coalition in the amount of $110,000 to "work with statewide networks to prevent youth tobacco use" (ibid.:79), and five CHS or county agencies $400,000 to implement programs (ibid.).

As an outgrowth of the plan and the Omnibus Nonsmoking Act, Minnesota launched the first state-sponsored tobacco use prevention campaign to use paid advertising (Cummings, 1993). MDH worked with a professional advertising firm to develop a series of tobacco use counter-advertisements that were aired on radio and television and displayed on billboards and bus shelters throughout the state (MDH, 1991; Harty, 1993). These ads—the best known is probably an ad picturing animals, such as a pig, a deer, a collie, and a goose with smoking cigarettes dangling from their mouths, and a caption saying, "It Looks Just as Stupid When You Do It"—won awards at the Cannes International Advertising Festival, the New York Art Director's Show, and the International Radio Festival of New York, and were finalists for Clio awards (MDH, 1991). They have also been rebroadcast by state and local health departments in New York, Utah, and Pennsylvania; the Roswell Park Cancer Institute; ACS divisions in Florida, California, and Texas; and by the Jamestown, North Dakota, Tobacco Free Coalition, and they have also appeared in Belgium, Australia, and Israel (MDH, 1991; Harty, 1993).

However, the budget for the MDH nonsmoking program, which was $1.6 million from fiscal year 1986 through fiscal year 1990, was cut to $1.1 million in fiscal year 1991, $968,000 in fiscal year 1992, $900,000 in fiscal year 1993, and $205,000 in fiscal year 1994 (Cummings, 1993; Harty, 1993; MDH, no date). These decreases began with actions on the part of the governor to divert a portion of the resources from the tobacco control to other areas of the state budget, and to end earmarking of a portion of cigarette excise tax revenues for tobacco control (Cummings, 1993). In the early 1990s, the legislature continued to diminish funding for the tobacco control effort until the final blow in 1993. According to Kathy Harty, who was the manager of the MDH Section for Nonsmoking and Health from the time of its creation in 1985 until her departure to become the deputy program director for the National Program Office in Tobacco Prevention and Control of the American Medical Association, "in 1993 the legislature all but eliminated the programme by cutting funds for the advertising campaigns" (Harty, 1993).

It is true that state government tobacco control efforts received a bolus of resources beginning in the early 1990s from the ASSIST contract, which is described below. In fact, this influx of resources in the context of state budget problems was used as one of the rationales for diverting state tax dollars (from the cigarette excise tax) from tobacco control to other areas (Cummings, 1993). However, as pointed out by Cummings (ibid.), (1) AS-

SIST funds could not be used to support the kinds of media campaigns that MDH had been sponsoring, and (2) ASSIST funding would be for a limited number of years (two years of planning and five years of implementation funding). More generally, this example raises the issue—to which I will return in Chapter 10—of the precariousness of tobacco control efforts that are situated to an important extent within state structures, and thus are subject to the vicissitudes of budget cycles and legislative and bureaucratic politics.

The MDH is a member and a key player in the Smoke-Free Coalition. The director and assistant director of the Division of Health Promotion and Education often attended meetings of the legislative committee of the SFC.

As noted above, Minnesota is one of seventeen states to receive an AS-SIST contract from the National Cancer Institute. As we will see, the infusion of federal funds under the ASSIST project has provided MDH with the resources to actively promote tobacco control efforts in a large number of local communities throughout the state.

NCI awarded the ASSIST contract to MDH in 1991. It had been anticipated with excitement among Minnesota tobacco control advocates for some time:

> Back when I was working at Smoke-Free 2000, we kept hearing that ASSIST was coming. It was a different name, but the Feds were modeling something after Minnesota. And that it was going to be a national project. So, I kind of always knew that it was coming. And then, finally, it came. Years later.

The intervention period was scheduled to last five years, from October 1993 through 1998. A principal goal of the project was to reduce the rate of tobacco use among Minnesota adults—which was 22% at the time the program began (MDH, 1993)—to 17% by 1998 and to 15% by 2000. In the Minnesota project, as in the program as a whole, there were four main strategies for achieving these changes: (1) eliminate environmental tobacco smoke; (2) reduce tobacco advertising and promotion; (3) reduce youth tobacco access and availability; and (4) create economic disincentives (MDH, 1997).

In the beginning, there were struggles to define the ASSIST project in Minnesota: what it was to do, who would be involved, and how things would get accomplished. In the words of one person who was closely involved in the process,

> When I went to women's task force meeting . . . [in the] spring of '92, it was chaos. And there was actually open yelling, back and forth. . . . There was no definition. There was no definition. . . . I think it's that thing about how much control can we get? And how much do you allow the community to take control? And I think you need to provide a strong framework for the commu-

nity. They knew they wanted a community. They went with all the priority groups and decided to have, you know, task forces. I just didn't think you could organize women all over the state without some grassroots, or some activity to hinge it to.

The thrust of the Minnesota ASSIST project differed in important ways from that of the MDH tobacco control program that had been in place since 1985 (but was decimated by budget cuts, as described above):

> The difference was strictly media versus community activity and policy. [The MDH nonsmoking program] was definitely media, but not into policy. They were aggressive campaigns. That's kind of what they were doing. And they had support functions, whatever state governments do—send out things, respond to questions, and, so, they did those things, too.

Further illustrating the difficulty of organizing at the state, versus, or ahead of, the local, level:

> I didn't know how you organized women [at a statewide level]. I still don't. I felt like you needed geographic organization. Where people can come to the table and say, "We know about this because we need to learn about this in our community first." And then maybe there could be a women's task force now, where there's a bunch of people involved for something concrete. . . . And if you want activists, you have to get concrete.

So, the manager of the ASSIST effort at the time made a decision to make a conceptual shift from organizing people outside their geographic and immediate political environments to really focusing on communities. In her words, the goal was "to create the grassroots."

However, the project, like that in many of the ASSIST states, was a year behind the national timeline. So:

> We tried to hustle to get locals going. To try and get something going in a lot of communities within our primary intervention region. . . . [This was] prior to the subcontracting. We knew that by the time, a year from then, we were going to have to have people applying for money. So, whatever we were going to do, we were going to have to get it into place in a big hurry. So, that was the initial goal—to get staffed up and to get things rolling so that by the time money was available we would have people ready to apply for it. And get it out to the community.
>
> And so, it seems as though we just did an awful lot of recruiting that first period of time. . . . We would go and meet with local community health departments to try and see what, is this something that you would be interested in, could you try and form a coalition so you guys could be ready to apply.

You know, there will be money coming. We can kind of help you get some stuff off the ground and laying the groundwork.

The response in the local Community Health Services agencies and health departments varied. The program's emphasis on policy change didn't always resonate within these local agencies: "We tried to paint a policy angle for them, which was hard for them to 'get.' But that is the angle we went after. And how much fun this can be and how it can be really important for the community."

So, a decision was made to conduct a policy conference to raise the level of awareness—and interest—in policy approaches to tobacco control within the local public health system:

> Spring of '93, all of a sudden, it was like, you guys, we have to do a policy conference. No one gets it. We were still getting all of these ideas [from the local agencies] about what are we going to do in schools? Finally, we just said, "We have to do a policy conference." . . . So that if they had to write proposals, they would understand what they needed to write on. Because we were just hammering away at no education. We were ripping people off that electromagnet. . . . You've heard this analogy, haven't you? There is this big huge electromagnet down the education/cessation path and it just sucks people right down. And it is so hard to pull them off. . . . So hard to get people to make that leap. But, once we could get people ripped off that magnet, it was really a lot more fun.

The conference took place, focusing on a variety of tobacco control policies and on the strategies that could be done at the local level and the state level to obtain policy changes. About thirty people came, mainly from CHS agencies. ANSR, with a strong stock of experience in policy change related to both secondhand smoke and youth access to tobacco, was enlisted to help raise consciousness about policy approaches.

> ANSR helped with our policy conference, and was always kind of there helping in some way. I think Jeanne [Weigum] was frustrated with us and our process. I know that. I just think she went to one ASSIST meeting for Ramsey County and said this is ridiculous, this is all wrong. It was all these people and they worked for "magnet." They were sucked down and wanted to do school programs. It was just going to take time to get them off.

The complementary relationship of the state and movement organizations is further illustrated by this comment by the manager of the ASSIST effort at the time:

> And Smoke-Free, it was just in my mind we were just going to have to build a thing to complement Smoke-Free. That was my goal from the outset. How

are we going to complement the image Smoke-Free has and, in theory, the political clout they had? By getting enough grassroots to support them when they bring up state law. My whole goal was to build something at the local [level] that people can understand as their home base. Maybe . . . try policy change there, but really to fire in to help the state action. That was the goal.

This raises the intriguing prospect of state agencies working to develop the grassroots base that the movement (with the exception of ANSR members, who are most concerned with secondhand smoke issues) had, to a significant degree, lacked.[12]

MDH divided the ASSIST money allocated for subcontracts in their first funding cycle—$450,000—into two pots: one for grassroots coalitions and one for special projects, both of which were intended to further the four goals of ASSIST described above. The vast majority of funds were earmarked for the Minnesota ASSIST "corridor," which stretched from St. Cloud to Rochester and was home to two-thirds of the state's population (MDH, 1993).[13] However, $20,000 was also set aside for small pots of money to fund some activities outside the corridor.

There was pressure from various quarters to focus the effort on the state as a whole, rather than the defined geographic area that had been selected:

> There was a fair amount of chatter out there about, "Oh, ASSIST is only working in the metro areas." That was the word that got back to me. I was just glad that I didn't hear it. So, no one came to us and said, "You've got to do it differently." Because we would just wave our contract [with NCI] at them. And, [we] were already many counties over what most [states] were doing.

The debates about how to focus resources—allocate them statewide, or focus on a smaller geographic area—illustrate the constraining influence of the health voluntaries—in this case, ACS—and government agencies (MDH):

> But then ACS applied a lot of pressure to work outside the corridor. They are a statewide organization, there needs to be more effort in the rest of the state. How is this going to fly? So there was a lot of pressure from them. And a lot of just state health department pressure. . . . I think the statewide pressure, the state health department's under pressure to work with the whole state. There is the whole, kind of, "You're the urban setting, you get everything" kind of mentality. . . . And NCI was very specific. Most . . . states only had four counties funded. And we had this huge corridor to begin with. So, my thought was let's appease some people in the out-state and give them $2,500. You know, a small amount to try and take some of the pressure off. Get a little more out-state political help. And that went pretty well. I mean, I think we didn't have enough money for them. But, we just couldn't do the whole state.

ASSIST was designed as a "partnership" between state health departments and state cancer societies. For example, the executive committee of the Minnesota ASSIST project consisted of four staffers at MDH, four at ACS, and, in theory, at some point, there would have been two people from the community. A significant concern for ACS was public acknowledgment of their involvement in ASSIST:

> It may seem trivial, but it's like . . . the quintessential issue was their publicity. Their reason they were in this, they needed name recognition. And, by God, if they are going to do this, they are going to get their name out there and they're going to get their sword out there. And, once we got over it, it's like, we just have got remember they need the recognition. They need the recognition.

When I look back . . . it was getting to know one another. We didn't trust them, they didn't trust us. I knew their network didn't work, and it was always the warning for them to say, "We have this volunteer network."

This was finally acknowledged by one of the ACS staff involved in the effort: "These people are gray-haired ladies who collect money, you can't parade this as a volunteer group that we can use."

However, this relationship continued to improve over time:

> So then they just worked really hard to get us to understand the sword. We needed to understand that they were there, and what they were about. And, they became more activist. [Name deleted]'s leadership was huge in that—cutting them loose to be activists. . . . And now, [ASSIST staff] call ACS to push [the leadership of MDH]. I mean, now, you can go to your partner and say, "It's falling apart." You know, now, there is a good reason why this partnership works. It takes the power away from MDH. Because no one at MDH could have all the say on the money going out. And the power is really diffuse. It is a weird structure for MDH to have to have an executive committee. . . . Because I know no one could ever understand why we didn't have to get commissioner's approval. Like, commissioner doesn't have a say in the executive committee.

One of the examples of ACS being freer to pursue certain kinds of advocacy activities was that they were able to send out Action Alerts, on federal and state legislative proposals, to all ASSIST subcontractors. An important example of this took place in the 1996 session, when advocates were working on an important youth access bill and trying to make sure that preemption did not pass (see Chapter 9).

However, ACS efforts were hamstrung by a low level of staffing. For example, the ASSIST project manager at ACS, who was funded out of ASSIST / ACS funds, was also the director of prevention—and had quite a few duties above and beyond ASSIST. The funds supporting this position did not come from the federal contract—ACS has had a long policy of not taking government funds—but out of the ACS contribution to ASSIST. This level of staffing resulted, at times, in limiting ACS input on the project. According to one ASSIST staff member at MDH,

> Because of the low level of staff time that they have, a lot of times it's sort of running things by them, saying, "We're thinking about this project. What's your input, and how can we make sure that the ACS name is out there?"— that type of thing. . . . Because all of the money and all of the staff is concentrated in this one area [i.e., MDH], it's much easier to forget to include ACS when we should and continue to keep that in the front of our minds, that we need to get their buy-in on our things

At this stage, the MDH ASSIST project manager had two pressing objectives:

> Well, I thought that the two roles were (1) getting money out, and (2) starting to foster more and more community education about what is policy and what is tobacco. So, I was bringing speakers like, [Greg] Connolly [the activist commissioner of health from Massachusetts] and stuff to try to help rally the troops and anybody we could get at the [quarterly statewide] meeting to better understand an activist perspective.

Contracts for the 1996–1998 funding cycle included nine cities, counties, or multicounty projects in the primary intervention area, four counties in the secondary intervention area, and six special projects: the ALA, ANSR, the Smoke-Free Coalition, the Minnesota Institute for Public Health, the Council for Preventive Medicine, and the Minneapolis American Indian Center. Eighteen of the nineteen projects were characterized by Minnesota ASSIST as including a policy focus on youth access to tobacco, and nine were characterized as including a policy focus on ETS (MDH, 1996a).

As part of the ASSIST project, MDH provided funding to both of the key single-issue groups: SFC and ANSR. ANSR was funded to be a resource on tobacco control strategies and tactics to all ASSIST contractors. ANSR developed manuals on how to pursue local public policy changes: the *ASSIST Community Action Book: A Handbook for Community Tobacco Control Activists* (Association for Nonsmokers-Minnesota,1993a) and *Community Tobacco Control: A Handbook for Community Action* (Association for Nonsmokers-Minnesota, 1994b). ANSR also received ASSIST funding to implement a Smoke-Free Apartment Project (MDH, 1996b). SFC was funded to train youth on tobacco control advocacy—the Kick Butts program. An organization called Health Futures was funded "to work with HMOs to get them to adopt tobacco control as an issue for their plans, to take that on and integrate prevention." Contracts were also awarded to health professional organizations (e.g., a small contract to the dental hygienists' association). And money went to organizations representing communities of color, including the Urban Coalition, which was funded to conduct a tobacco billboard survey in St. Paul.[14]

If funded community projects focused on youth access to tobacco, there was an expectation that they would engage in one of the standard tactics of the movement: conducting purchase attempts by youth (see Chapter 2):

> We let the communities define how they wanted to use it. We kind of gave them ways it could be used. But, if they didn't do the buys, we just felt like there is no way to monitor the progress, there was no way to push the [city or county] council, there was just no evidence that there was a problem or that they were solving the problem.

At the local level, the secondhand smoke issue did not enjoy much resonance: "I mean, people tried some education stuff. We allowed a lot of that the first year. . . . But no one really did much, no one tried local ordinances on that."

MDH staff were wide open to local communities choosing priorities from within the list of national ASSIST priorities. However, there was some pressure from above:

> You know, NCI wanted to see unified efforts. And they were contrary to giving local control. I felt like we handed them a framework, and said, "You need to do policy on these areas. What works for your community?" And, I think, the last year, I was moving towards—can we get them to either do tax or youth access? As one of the two, you know, choose one priority and they can do something else. But we need them to start matching our state agenda.

Tax increases (or, as they were sometimes euphemistically known, "economic disincentives") were one of the focuses mandated by NCI. However, there were significant obstacles to open advocacy of tobacco excise tax increases in the Minnesota ASSIST project. The former ASSIST manager described the approach used as follows:

> Very carefully. . . . See, my feeling was, if they were working on anything for their community, you could nab them to help with the tax. There was my goal. Get them activated about tobacco in general. Get them doing a project in the community. Then, on their own time, or somebody else's time, move up to the capitol and do what needs to be done on tax, or write letters. So, we used networks to try to get to them . . . a bulletin board system. . . . I mean, we tried to keep people updated that way about things they could do.

Another staff member at ASSIST described it as follows:

There are all these—kind of—layers. Blue Cross/Blue Shield is very interested in the tax, so they worked very closely with Smoke-Free. Tax is an area
of ours, so [an MDH staff member] may provide resources to them, but the
tax is not part of our policy agenda. So, we could only really provide information and it would be Smoke-Free, through other funding sources, that
would be more proactively doing advocacy. . . . Even though NCI says that
one of our policy areas should be the tax, the fact that Governor Carlson is
against any new taxes means we don't work on that as actively as a policy
area. And that we call it "economic disincentives," and it's clear that we
would never advocate for tax if we were talking to the media or anything like
that.

Another way of dealing with the tax issue, with respect to local ASSIST
contractors, involves the distinction between advocacy and education:

Well, they [subcontractors] were certainly under the same constraints, in that
they cannot lobby. They can't use ASSIST funds to lobby federally, or on a
state level. So we've provided them with information. Some of them did
some forums that talked about different tobacco control policy options and
included the tax as one of them, without advocating for a tax. So it's the issue of education versus advocacy.

The leadership of the governor and the state health commissioner
shaped the latitude of the ASSIST program in significant ways. According
to one key participant in ASSIST,

[The 1990 election of a Republican, Governor Arne Carlson, was] significant,
because that changed. [Sister] Mary Madonna Ashton [the state health com-
missioner] was kicked off, and the appointments Arnie has made have been
notoriously bad. [Commissioner Ashton] was an absolute aggressive per-
former for tobacco [control], you couldn't have wanted more out of a commissioner. You could always want more, but she was really out there. I mean
she let those ads go, and she let them work hard on the tobacco tax. She really . . . she was a leader, in a way. I mean, I think the activists got tired of her,
but she did a great job. I think that the change was huge—[name deleted] has
said he's never seen a more eroded state health department in his twenty-
two years there—he's never seen it worse. . . . He's never seen a more politi-
cized administration.[15]

For the first several years of his administration and of the Minnesota
ASSIST project, Governor Carlson was a proponent of fiscal conservatism,
which hindered, to a considerable extent, the ability of MDH to advocate
for increases in state tobacco taxes:

That we can not have somebody saying anything about the need for tobacco taxes is pretty indicative. I mean, we had to keep our heads down, that whenever something happened, we would get e-mail saying "You are not supposed to talk to the media." You know . . . e-mail from the commissioner's office: "Behave."

Partisan political considerations also presented challenges to implementation of the ASSIST project. For example, ASSIST staff were excited about, and interested in building on, the lawsuit against the tobacco industry that Attorney General Humphrey and Blue Cross/Blue Shield were planning. Or, at a minimum, responding to press inquiries about the ways in which the suit might help advance tobacco control efforts in the state. However, the Attorney General was a member of the DFL, and was known to be a possible candidate for governor in the next election (in 1998). As a consequence, ASSIST staff received the following message from the commissioner's office:

You know, the AG's office let us know they were going to make their big announcement on the law suit, hours ahead of when it was going to happen. And we got an e-mail shortly after that saying, "There's something coming down, don't talk." . . .

And I think it was really weird to have Humphrey come down one way, and us being silent on it. I mean, when Humphrey came out and announced his lawsuit, we were told to be quiet. And we were told never to mention it.

And, of course, MDH staff were constrained from lobbying, or even having a presence at the legislature:

Well, we just don't go over there [to the legislature]. And, I think it was just triply reinforced when the new governor and commissioners, they just reinforced that you don't go over there. . . . We couldn't get any grantees to go over. . . . And it was very confusing, because they're being paid by ASSIST dollars. With those dollars, they can't go over there. So if they fall on somebody else's time, you go over or on your free time.

To some extent, the MDH culture of working with the local infrastructure of public health—the Community Health Services (CHS) system—imposes some constraints:

That's one thing, I think, that I want to make sure you know. We tried to work with the CHS agencies. That was a given, that was the structure at the Health Department—you need to work through them whenever you can. When we couldn't, it was swell, because we could go out and hire "Mom" and be a lot more successful. . . . You know, some community member who is more free-wheeling, who can just do things. Who isn't, you know, you pay a half-time mom and you get half time out of that mom. You pay a half-time CHS person who is going to all the government that they have, it changes. You don't get the same kind of effort, and there is a lot more constraint than most people. So there were times when we would pull funding, and I would be in on the carpet, and have to fund a CHS agency. I would be in trouble for not. I'm like, "They're not doing anything." That didn't matter. On the other hand, "moms" were paid as a consultant. And they had to, you know, bring coalition people together. But, it was a much more productive way to do it.

This informant went on to explain the Health Department's philosophy:

The Health Department, I think, in theory is supposed to serve the local [public health agencies]. . . . And so the money, in theory, should stay within the state health system. The local, that's the theory, that you show a lot of dedication to those local folks, struggling out there, they are trying to get to work for the public health, and you should be loyal to them. And so we give them money and people wouldn't do policy. . . . I think, in [name deleted] County, is a good example. You could just beat your head against the wall trying to get them. . . . They would never do policy, they wouldn't do the things that needed to be done. And finally, I just said, "You're not going to be funded." And she called back and I ended up on the carpet . . . I understand it. But, at the same time, they can't do policy advocacy the same way a mom can. You know, you've got your county commissioners, who support the local CHS. And you tick that little local system off, and you've got trouble. So, I understand the constraint at the local level. But, if they can't do the job, get them out of the kitchen.

Elaborating on what motivates these freewheeling activists—these "moms":

I think that's key, they've got energy. And, I mean, it is nice to have a part-time job where pay is decent, but it's way beyond that. They drove to the state legislature on their own time. I mean, they were doing things clearly on their own time. So, you were getting the volunteer side out of it too. And that is where it wasn't the paycheck, there was a bigger reward and commitment to the issue.

And on whether there is any advantage to working through the CHS system:

I just don't think there is. I mean, other than if you don't know where to go in a community. You know, people talk about institutionalization. I don't think it's institutionalized. I think it will go away as soon as the money is gone. These people will be off working on AIDS. And I don't know how many of them even bothered, on their own time, to write to senators. . . . I'm real skeptical.

In a dramatic display of the constraints faced by local government units, Wright County's funding was pulled by the County Commission, shortly after their contract was awarded:

> Why should the state be handing out money when the federals are supporting tobacco farmers? So then, that community, including the CHS worker, went out and found someone else. That was cool. But they got ordinances passed and then history came in and rolled over them and got them repealed.

Until the fall of 1995, there were no constraints on ASSIST pursuing changes in local ordinances. But then, in October 1995, MDH received a letter from the law firm that, on behalf of a local retailer, brought a lawsuit against the Preston City Council for restricting point-of-sale advertising of tobacco products (see Chapter 9 for a description of the ordinance campaign in Preston). This letter asserted that, under the Federal Acquisition Streamlining Act (see Chapter 10), lobbying at the local level with federal support was prohibited:

> And so then we informed NCI—we really were the first people to hear about this restriction, and his interpretation of it. And so, since then, we have been operating under the assumption that we cannot lobby at the local level. A few weeks ago [this interview was conducted in 1996] we received a letter from NCI saying that those restrictions in fact do not apply. Their interpretation was that it would only apply to new contracts, and because the original AS-SIST contract with the state started back in '90 or '91, that these new restrictions didn't apply to any of the work that we were doing. So we're in the process of letting subcontractors know that and then they need to decide if they do want to do some local lobbying.

However, the subcontracts would need to be amended to allow lobbying, because the current subcontracts, which were entered during the period in which MDH staff believed local level lobbying was prohibited, excluded lobbying activities as part of the scope of work. So, over a period of about four months, after several years of providing encouragement, training, and exhortations to do local policy work, local ASSIST projects were prohibited from advocating for passage of local ordinances. So, for example, a local ASSIST project working on youth access to tobacco could not pursue stronger ordinances during this period:

> [The original wording] would say something like "Engage City Council members to pass an ordinance related to youth access in communities." So, knowing that they couldn't do that, they could still do compliance checks and they could publicize the results. And there may be opportunity at the City Council for citizens to raise the issue about what should be done about this. They could engage in merchant education, which a lot of people were

doing previously too, so encouraging merchants not to sell. And what they need to do to train their employees and look for ID and that type of thing.

A 1995 offensive mounted by the Minnesota Grocers' Association also illustrates the vulnerability and constraints faced by government-sponsored advocacy efforts. Based on quarterly reports that the Grocers' Association, over a two- or three-year period had "FOIAed" (i.e, requested information under the Federal Freedom of Information Act or similar state data practices acts; see Aguinaga and Glantz, 1995) quarterly reports that ASSIST subcontractors had submitted to MDH. One of the incidents that led to the complaint was an effort, by ACS, to conduct a "patch through" for people to express their support for an increase in the excise tax on cigarettes:

> [ACS] had like a telephone bank set up so that supporters of the tax could be called and said, "We want to patch you through to your representative right now so that you can leave them a message saying that you support an increase in the tobacco tax." We didn't—the Health Department didn't fund that in any way, but we reported it in our quarterly report [to NCI] and that was really the big sticking issue for [the director of the Minnesota Grocers' Association], when he made his claim that we were misusing federal funds. He wanted all of the background information on this phone bank, and we didn't have any information on it because we didn't fund it. So it was partly that we didn't, and it was partly that we maybe could have made it clearer that ACS solely funded that effort and we were discussing some of the broader tobacco control efforts in the state in our quarterly report. And there was a combination of his creating an accusation when he wanted to. He sent 500 pages of documents to the governor and to the state auditor. On the cover letter, he copied all of our representatives and senators [at] the federal level.

Although there were not repercussions—MDH had not violated federal law:

> There was a lot of work and a lot of stress involved in looking through all the contracts, answering/counterclaiming all of these issues, writing memos saying, "This is what so-and-so did or this is what I did at the League of Minnesota Cities meeting, and not what [name deleted] claims in his letter." . . . Between that and the Ethical Practices Board, it was roughly what we did for two months. It was a huge drain on taxpayer money, there's no question about that. If you talk about—all their claims that we're misusing taxpayer funds. The amount of time that he tied up in taxpayer money was much bigger.

Although this complaint was successfully deflected, a second round was soon to come: a complaint by the Minnesota Grocers' Association to the Minnesota Ethical Practices Board (Baden, 1995; Dawson, 1995; deFiebre, 1996). Sixteen subcontractors received complaints against them for unethical practices, claiming that they had engaged in lobbying activities at the state level, and therefore should have been registered as lobbyists. None, according to MDH staff, were really lobbying. The closest case was the Youth Rally at the capitol, part of Kick Butts, sponsored by SFC: "But they were never making any calls to action. The kids were—they just met their legislators and they talked to them about why there isn't any funding for tobacco education." The ethics board cleared almost all the allegations—the exception was that the Smoke-Free Coalition was required to disclose a $40 lobbying expense, although no penalties were applied. However, the complaint succeeded in diverting the energies of many of the activists from their tobacco control efforts—including preparing for the 1996 legislative session. According to Jeanne Weigum of ANSR (quoted in de-Fiebre, 1996:A-8), "It was a fairly bogus complaint. They didn't care what the facts were. They just wanted to keep us busy."

Some of the ASSIST staff have raised questions about the heavy focus on youth access to tobacco:

> I mean, it's a huge emphasis of the project. It's really the overarching one, particularly when you're talking about local ordinance work. That's entirely the focus of local ordinance work. . . . I mean, it's really a national issue, too, in that there's such a big emphasis on youth access and that approach. But we don't really have the research to back up whether or not restricting youth access actually does decrease youth smoking rates.

However, questions about the effectiveness of the approach are counterbalanced by an awareness of the strong appeal of a focus on youth access:

> I think that really does have an appeal to the general population when you're talking about kids and talking about the fact that you are not interested in prohibition and this is not about adult smokers, that people can—I believe that they can—latch onto that. When I was talking to local officials with the [Minnesota] League [of cities], that's what I would start out with, because I knew that I was talking to a high smoking population. It was pretty rural and small town, and . . . I said, "We have strong supporters at the local level who started smoking when they were 12 and 13 and they know how hard it is to quit, and they don't want to see that happen to their kids." And I think that when you frame it that way for people, they're much more likely to . . . get on board and to say, "Yeah, that makes sense and, yeah, I had a similar experience and yeah, I wish I hadn't started when I was 15, yeah, I did finally quit but it took me 25 years to quit and a heart attack." I think that I got less opposition to hearing what I had to say by framing it that way. And I know, talking to other people in local coalitions—you know, people who have smoked for a really [long time]—they feel really vilified, and for good reason, I think. If it isn't the youth focus, then at least the tobacco industry that we're fighting, not the people who smoke.

The Minnesota Attorney General (AG) is a second state agency that is heavily involved, in a proactive way, in tobacco control advocacy in the state and beyond. As discussed in Chapter 9, the AG has a history of joint advocacy efforts with movement actors on state legislative issues. For example, the AG approached ANSR in 1986 to enlist ANSR's help in lobbying for a bill that would require warning labels on smokeless tobacco products (as discussed in Chapter 9, ANSR succeeded in expanding the scope of this bill considerably).

More recently, the AG's office became vigorously involved in the issue of tobacco sales to youth. The Minnesota AG was part of a working group of twelve state AGs that prepared a publication entitled *No Sale: Youth, Tobacco and Responsible Retailing* (Working Group of State Attorneys General, 1994). Along with AGs in Massachusetts, New Mexico, New York, and Vermont, the Minnesota AG's office joined the swelling number of government agencies in the state (including MDH, MDHS, and several local governments) in conducting cigarette compliance check operations ("Teens Buy Cigarettes Easiest," 1996). The Attorney General and his staff began to appear in local communities to add momentum to local efforts to restrict youth access to tobacco. Attorney General Humphrey also submitted a friend-of-the-court brief in support of the 1996 proposed FDA rule regulating the marketing and sale of tobacco products to youth after it was challenged in U.S. District Court in Greensboro, North Carolina (Associated Press, 1996b).

In addition, the AG, in conjunction with a number of other state attorneys general, has worked to publicize the issue of children's exposure to secondhand smoke, and to encourage fast food restaurants and other businesses commonly patronized by youth to adopt voluntary smoke-free policies (Tobacco Working Group of the National Association of Attorneys General, 1993).

A paramount example of the Minnesota AG's involvement in tobacco control advocacy is the lawsuit—jointly filed with Blue Cross/Blue Shield—against the seven largest tobacco companies and two trade organizations. This groundbreaking action was the first such suit in the nation to allege antitrust conspiracy and consumer fraud. It sought to recover health care costs for tobacco-caused disease borne by the state (i.e., health care expenses of state employees and Medicaid and MinnesotaCare recipients). Many of the states that filed their suits after the Minnesota suit patterned them after Minnesota's (Humphrey, 1997a, 1997b). Significantly, it appears that the suit was largely if not entirely self-initiated—that is, *not* a direct reaction to pressure from movement organizations.

Humphrey played a prominent role in discussions among the state attorneys general about settling their suits against the industry (Aamot, 1997; Gordon, 1997). Humphrey argued that the group settlement that was being discussed in 1997 was the result of "a flawed negotiating process," and that the proposed settlement itself was deeply flawed. Specifically, he argued that "the settlement undercuts the authority of the FDA," the "youth smoking provisions are a sham," "the offer of immunity is unacceptable," "the payment is too small," "the tobacco industry's ability to pay should not be based on U.S. cigarette revenues alone," and that the "marketing restrictions aren't likely to work" (Humphrey, 1997a, 1997b). Largely because of his vocal role in the settlement debates, Humphrey was characterized as "the most widely-quoted public official in the country in opposing the tobacco industry" (Political Communications, Inc, 1996).

In May 1998, the tobacco industry settled the Minnesota suit, agreeing to pay over $6 billion and to comply with new restrictions on marketing. Humphrey said that the industry "surrendered on our terms," and that the agreement will "protect future generations" and impose "tough reforms on the industry" (Groeneveld, 1998).

In general, the AG's office is less constrained than most other government agencies, such as MDH. According to one close observer within the executive branch,

> The Attorney General's office is much more proactive around tobacco control [compared to MDH]. And, because he's an elected official, and he has that on his agenda, he's much more "out there" as far as what he is willing to say versus what the Health Department really could say or do, particularly with working on legislation.

A number of state agencies play a smaller role in the movement. For example, the Chemical Dependency Division of the Minnesota Department of Human Services (MDHS) collects and disseminates data on tobacco use, which are sometimes used by movement activists. Moreover, the department is charged with implementation of the "Synar Amendment," which requires states to demonstrate higher levels of enforcement of tobacco age-of-sale laws. As a result of this new departmental responsibility, representatives from MDHS periodically attended strategy meetings of the legislative committee of the Smoke-Free Coalition, which was discussing the teen access to be introduced in the 1994 legislative session.

As far as MDHS involvement in tobacco control more generally—specifically, on the youth access issue—one key actor at MDH characterized it as follows:

> I think they were vaguely supportive. It was always disguised whether or not they really were. [Name deleted], our contact over there, seemed to be supportive, his thoughts seemed to be supportive, but they weren't proactive.

The Minnesota Department of Education plays some role in generating and disseminating data on tobacco use (e.g., the Minnesota Student Survey). The Department, as a partner with MDH in implementing the Minnesota Tobacco Use Prevention Initiative, was involved in promoting school-based tobacco use prevention programs and changes in tobacco use policy within schools (MDH, 1991; Griffin, 1990; Griffin, Loeffler, and Kasell, 1988).

Finally, many local governments—CHS agencies, health departments, and others—have gotten involved in tobacco control efforts, either as part of the Minnesota ASSIST project (described above) or independently. One of the most activist health departments has been the Hennepin County Department of Community Health Services.

How well do conventional images of the state-movement relationship described in Chapter 1 characterize the pattern observed in the tobacco control movement? The state is certainly a target of the movement, which seeks changes in public policy regulating tobacco advertising and retailing, taxes on tobacco products, and smoking in public places. However, fractions of the state are often allied with the movement in efforts to change the policies of other fractions. At the federal level, the Department of Health and Human Services and movement organizations target Congress and the U.S. Department of Agriculture to reduce price supports and other subsidies for tobacco production. Similarly, federal agencies, such as the National Cancer Institute (NCI), the Centers for Disease Control and Prevention (CDC), and the Food and Drug Administration (FDA), often work closely with movement organizations to influence state legislatures and state executives to change state laws regarding youth access to tobacco, tobacco taxes, and indoor smoking policies. Finally, NCI and CDC provide financial resources, scientific expertise, and technical assistance to enable state and local health departments to work closely with movement organizations to change local policies governing youth access to tobacco and clean indoor air.

Similarly, the image of state as definer of the rule of the political game is an accurate, but incomplete, depiction of state / movement relations. The rules of the U.S. federal system—allocation of authority across branches and levels of government, the system of political representation, campaign financing systems, rules about which groups and which activities are eligible for nonprofit tax status, and so on—clearly affect the organization, ideologies, and strategies of the movement. This point, which is largely self-evident, is demonstrated by the differences between the movement in France, with a unitary, centralized state, and the relatively decentralized, divided governance system of the United States (Kagan and Vogel, 1993).

The state as sponsor or suppressor of the movement is also an incomplete picture. In the tobacco control movement, the image of state as sponsor is especially germane. State agencies—NCI, CDC, and CSAP—provide funding for literally hundreds of state and local coalitions involved in tobacco control advocacy. But the relationship between the state and the movement is deeper than the relationship of funder and recipient suggests. The state initiates many actions, even without the encouragement of movement organizations—the Minnesota Attorney General's lawsuit is an example (albeit the suit was joined by Blue Cross/Blue Shield). The state directly produces or sponsors the production of the scientific knowledge that activists routinely use in their efforts to educate the public and change public and institutional policies related to tobacco use. The state develops or codifies tactics and then promotes their use among other state agencies and movement organizations—the "confederate buys" described in Chapter 3 are an important example. In addition, state actors and leaders of movement organizations often collaborate closely in developing political strategies—MDH's involvement in the Smoke-Free Coalition—particularly the legislative efforts of the coalition (described in Chapter 7)—are an example.

Thus, "interpenetration" is a more accurate characterization of the state-movement relationship than any of the conventional characterization described above. In tobacco control, it is hard to know where the movement ends and the state begins. Although much of the movement is rooted in civil society—professional groups, the health voluntaries, health care organizations—it is next to impossible to think about the movement without thinking about the state. The state is not limited to being an external force that acts on or is acted upon by the movement, but is in fact an integral part of the movement.

An important theme of this chapter—which will be revisited in Chapter 10—is the trade-offs involved in movement organizations allying themselves closely with government agencies. Are there costs that may counterbalance the tangible advantages resulting from state involvement? In fact, as we have seen in this chapter, activists and activist organizations are constrained in the issues, arguments, strategies, and tactics they select because of their ties with state agencies.

NOTES

1.   California is an outlier with respect to state monies spent on tobacco control (particularly in the early 1990s). Passage of a voter initiative in 1988 resulted in a very large increase in the state excise tax on cigarettes, a major part of which was devoted to supporting tobacco control efforts at the local level. Subsequently, Massachusetts and Arizona passed similar measures.

2.   The seventeen ASSIST states were Colorado, Indiana, Maine, Massachusetts, Michigan, Minnesota, Missouri, New Jersey, New Mexico, New York, North Carolina, Rhode Island, South Carolina, Virginia, Washington, West Virginia, and Wisconsin.

3.   In 1999, following the completion of the ASSIST project, major federal to-

bacco control efforts were consolidated into the National Tobacco Control Program (NTCP), administered by the CDC (USDHHS, 2000). Under this program, all fifty states received awards averaging $1.13 million in fiscal year 2000 (following awards received in fiscal year 1999)—nearly as much as the seventeen ASSIST states received each year during the five-year ASSIST implementation period (USDHHS, 2000).

4. MDH had also been involved since passage of the Minnesota Clean Indoor Air Act in enforcement of the act, as described in Chapter 3.

5. The growing focus on chronic disease had both epidemiologic and economic underpinnings. The United States, like the other industrialized countries, had undergone an "epidemiologic transition" in the first half of the twentieth century, reflected in declines in death rates from infectious diseases and increases in death rates from chronic diseases, such as heart disease and cancer (Susser, 1985; Omram, 1971). And the contemporary health education/health promotion movement was a response, in important part, to concerns about uncontrollable medical costs borne by businesses, governments, and individuals (Guinta and Allegrante, 1992).

6. According to some observers, NHLBI was in the forefront of efforts within the NIH to apply and translate scientific knowledge on a broad scale to improve public health. In fact, Blackburn argues that the leadership of NIH in the 1970s did not support applied public health activities on the part of the constituent institutes of NIH (Blackburn, 1983).

7. The choice of the term "nonsmoking" was deliberate. According to Dean and colleagues (1986:273): "To provide a positive and somewhat novel perspective, results were structured around nonsmoking whenever possible, presenting potential benefits of nonsmoking rather than the negative impact of smoking. Because nonsmoking was the goal, the epidemiologic and economic projections focused on the results of achieving the goal."

8. The extent to which the recent focus on youth access to tobacco represents a significantly different way of understanding the issue of youth smoking is illustrated by the treatment of youth access in the Minnesota Plan. All of the key pieces of information that underlie the contemporary focus on youth access were mentioned in the report: The smoking habit usually begins in the childhood and adolescent years (MDH, 1984:89), and restrictions on furnishing tobacco to minors are often not well enforced (ibid.:104). Yet, only one of the recommendations of the plan—that the state should follow Minneapolis's lead and ban free distribution of cigarettes—addressed the issue of youth access to tobacco.

9. As this example illustrates, the diffusion of tactics and strategies within the movement seems to have been facilitated by the extensive involvement of professionals with an interest in generating publications, including policymakers and academics.

10. California instituted a large state tobacco control program following passage of Proposition 99 in 1998, which increased the state tax on cigarettes by $0.25 a pack and allocated 20% of the revenues—over $100 million a year—to support school-based tobacco use prevention programs, antismoking media campaigns, and grants to local health departments and community agencies (Hu et al., 1994; Traynor and Glantz, 1996). Subsequently, voters in Massachusetts (in 1992), Ari-

zona (in 1994), and Oregon (in 1996) have approved similar ballot initiatives (Pierce-Lavin and Geller, 1998)

11. Community Health Services agencies are the "infrastructure" of public health at the county level in Minnesota.

12. In an interesting twist, ANSR has shared its mailing list on at least some occasions with MDH for its mailings advertising the quarterly ASSIST statewide meetings—further illustrating the close linkage between state and movement actors in Minnesota tobacco control efforts.

13. The "primary intervention region" for Minnesota ASSIST included twenty counties: Anoka, Benton, Carver, Chisago, Dakota, Dodge, Goodhue, Hennepin, Isanti, Olmsted, Ramsey, Rice, Scott, Sherburne, Stearns, Steele, Wabasha, Washington, Winona, and Wright (Minnesota Department of Health, 1993a).

14. ASSIST staff and others expressed a diversity of opinion on whether there was an adequate focus in the program on tobacco use in communities of color. Some believed that, given the relatively small minority population in the state as a whole, the degree of focus on these populations in ASSIST was adequate. However, others expressed contrary views: "It's been consistent with us that that's lacking. I think we could have done more to . . . it's just . . . I see it as a general problem within public health, that we don't know how to reach certain populations, and we don't do it very well. And, particularly, Minnesota, it's easy to kind of say, 'Well, that's just such a small percentage of the population that it doesn't make sense to be focusing our resources there.' But there's a much greater burden that they [racial / ethnic minorities] experience because of tobacco-related diseases, and the whole socioeconomic issue that increases that burden is important to look at, too."

15. This analysis is consistent with that of Cummings (1993), who cites as one factor in the demise of the MDH tobacco control program the fact that "when Sister Mary Madonna Ashton retired from the state health department, there was no one left in high places to fight for the programme, and those hungry for its resources moved in for the kill."

8

The Opposition

The main source of opposition to the tobacco control movement is economic interests who benefit from the agricultural production of tobacco and manufacture and sale of cigarettes and other tobacco products. First and foremost among these interests are a small number of cigarette manufacturers responsible for the vast majority of cigarettes sold and consumed in the United States and their trade associations.[1] The tobacco industry has been quite successful in heading off meaningful federal-level controls on tobacco over the past twenty-five years—although the 1996 rules on tobacco and youth promulgated by the Food and Drug Administration (FDA) were a major exception until they were overturned in March 2000.

With a few exceptions, the industry has also enjoyed considerable influence in most state legislatures. However, the industry often lacks the manpower and credibility to consistently head off local legislation that it perceives to be harmful to its interests (Sylvester, 1989). This national pattern is reflected in Minnesota's experience.

The cigarette manufacturing industry is clearly an oligopoly (Warner, 1993). In 1997, the top four firms' combined market share was 98%. Philip Morris was the industry leader with a 49% market share (Philip Morris products include Marlboro, Benson & Hedges, Merit, Virginia Slims, and Parliament "premier brand" cigarettes, as well as the Basic and Cambridge discount brands), R.J. Reynolds Tobacco Company had a 24% market share (RJR products include Winston, Camel, Salem, More, and Doral, as well as a number of discount brands), Brown and Williamson Tobacco Co. with a 16% market share (products include Lucky Strike, Carlton, and Kool), and Lorillard Tobacco Co. with a 9% market share (products include Kent, Newport, Old Gold, and True) (Knight, Patricia, and Mayer, 1998).

The cigarette companies are among the giants of contemporary business. For example, Philip Morris was ranked ninth among the Fortune 500 companies in 2000, with revenues of $61.8 billion (Fortune 500, 2000). Economic interests in tobacco are concentrated in the southeastern states

(Warner, Fulton, Nicolas, and Grimes, 1996). The cigarette companies' manufacturing operations are primarily based in the Southeast, with plants in North Carolina, Virginia, Kentucky, and Georgia (Knight et al., 1998; U.S. Department of Commerce, 1998). Similarly, tobacco farming is centered in the Southeast, with six states—North Carolina, Kentucky, Tennessee, South Carolina, Virginia, and Georgia—accounting for 94% of cash receipts from tobacco in 1997 (U.S. Department of Agriculture, 1998). However, the tobacco industry economic sector that provides the largest number of jobs is retailing (Warner, 1993). Grocers, convenience store owners, and other retail interests have figured prominently in opposing some tobacco control measures in many states, including Minnesota, as we shall see later in this chapter.

The industry has mounted two forms of opposition to tobacco control efforts. The first is what I term "intellectual opposition," which largely centers around the production of knowledge that minimizes or completely denies the harmful consequences of smoking, smokeless tobacco use, and exposure to secondhand smoke.[2] The second form of opposition is overtly political, and includes efforts to elect sympathetic legislators and influence legislative and regulatory decisions at the federal, state, and local levels. Each of these forms of opposition is discussed below, with special reference to their application in Minnesota over the past twenty-five years.

Intellectual Opposition

The tobacco industry, like other powerful industries that wish to undermine scientific research that may reveal the potential harmfulness of their products or services—engages in what Proctor (1995) has called "Trade Association Science."[3] Following publication of studies in the 1950s linking smoking to lung cancer (see Chapter 2), the tobacco industry sponsored the formation of the Tobacco Industry Research Committee in 1954 (Proctor, 1995; Glantz et al., 1996; Bloch, 1994). The annual budget of the committee—which was renamed the Council for Tobacco Research (CTR) in 1964—grew to $11.3 million in 1985 (Glantz et al., 1996) and almost $20 million in 1994 (Proctor, 1995). The Tobacco Industry Research Committee and CTR funded over one thousand academics and other researchers (ibid.).

Much of this research appears, at first pass, to be unobjectionable. A Scientific Advisory Board, which (before CTR was disbanded as part of the 1998 Master Settlement Agreement) included three members of the National Academy of Sciences (ibid.), performs a scientific peer review function (Proctor, 1995; Bloch, 1994). However, only a small proportion of CTR-funded research projects actually focus on the health effects of tobacco use (Bloch, 1994). In pronouncements to policymakers and the public, the tobacco industry points to CTR's active involvement in studying the health effects of tobacco use—when this is in fact not the case (ibid.). The industry also enjoys a "halo" effect from pointing to the hundreds of legitimate institutions it funds (ibid.).

A second avenue for CTR-supported studies circumvents review by the Scientific Advisory Board. Instead, the Special Projects Division, which is directed by lawyers, recruits researchers for particular studies that could cast doubt on the links between tobacco use, exposure to secondhand smoke, and negative health outcomes (Glantz et al., 1996; Bloch, 1994). It is this mechanism that the *Wall Street Journal* has called "the longest running misinformation campaign in history" (Freedman and Cohen, 1993).

Documents that became public as part of the settlement of the Minnesota suit against the tobacco industry revealed that the tobacco industry paid thirteen researchers a total of $156,000 to write letters to scientific journals questioning the harmful effects of exposure to secondhand smoke. This included a $10,000 payment to Dr. Nathan Mantel, the codeveloper of the Mantel-Haenszel test (commonly used in epidemiologic studies), to submit such a letter (with input from lawyers representing the tobacco industry) to the *Journal of the American Medical Association* (Kiernan, 1998).

In addition to supporting research that minimizes the health risks of tobacco use, the industry has supported research that had the potential of creating doubt about the harmful effects of secondhand smoke. For example, the industry has played an active role in promoting the concept of sick-building syndrome, which is presented as an alternative to secondhand smoke exposure as an explanation for discomfort and illness experienced by people who work indoors (Levin, 1993). The industry heavily funded the Center for Indoor Air Research, until it, like CTR, was disbanded in the wake of the Master Settlement Agreement.

> The evidence suggests that the tobacco industry mounted a vigorous response to EPA's draft assessment of the health risks of environmental tobacco smoke (Bero and Glantz, 1993; Durbin, 1993). While 69 of the 107 comments submitted argued that the conclusions of the draft report were incorrect, the majority of these—49 of the 69 (71%)—were submitted by individuals with an affiliation with the tobacco industry (Bero and Glantz, 1993). Moreover, the critical comments were, on close inspection, less likely to conform to the norms of science—such as referencing peer-reviewed publications (ibid.).

In addition to supporting "trade association science," the tobacco industry has worked to influence the way media portrays tobacco use. For example, for a period of about four years in the early 1990s, K-III Communications, whose majority shareholder was Kohlberg Kravis Roberts & Co. (which had earlier effected a leveraged buyout of RJR Nabisco), owned the *Weekly Reader*. The *Weekly Reader* has the highest circulation of any student newspaper in the United States, and is sold in about 80% of elementary schools (DeJong, 1996). During the period of financial ties with the tobacco conglomerate KKR, the *Weekly Reader* shifted its coverage of tobacco issues: it emphasized the attractiveness of tobacco as a "forbidden fruit" for teenagers, and gave relatively little attention to the health consequences of smoking and smokeless tobacco use (ibid.).

The industry has voiced other themes that detract from the appeal of policies that would discourage tobacco use. For example, the industry's emphasis on "parental responsibility" suggests that adolescent smoking is not a matter for the state, but for parents (Goodman, 1995). The theme of "accommodation" of smokers by nonsmokers suggests that, if we could just all get along, there would be no need for clean indoor air legislation. Finally, the theme of free speech is used as a powerful argument against restrictions on advertising tobacco products. Perhaps the most noteworthy example of an industry group playing on this theme is the 1991 Bill of Rights Tour, which was sponsored by Philip Morris (Ehlert, 1991).

The industry also engages in efforts to demonstrate that it is working with retailers to prevent tobacco sales to minors, thus obviating adoption of new laws or ordinances that would regulate retailers. A prominent example is the "It's the Law"–type voluntary compliance programs, which have been sponsored by Philip Morris, RJR, and the Tobacco Institute (DiFranza, Savageau, and Aisquith, 1996). In these programs, educational materials are distributed to tobacco retailers, who are asked to display stickers advertising the program and informing customers that they must be 18 in order to purchase tobacco products.[4] Finally, the industry engages in efforts to shift the blame for illegal sales of tobacco products from the tobacco companies and the retailers to the youth who buy them (Mosher, 1995).

In summary, the tobacco industry has used its prodigious resources to mount "intellectual opposition" to the efforts of tobacco control advocates to reduce levels of tobacco use in the United States. This opposition is intended to cast doubt on the links between tobacco use, exposure to secondhand smoke, and health, and to undermine the arguments for measures to control tobacco use.

Political Opposition

The landmark Minnesota Clean Indoor Air Act, enacted in 1975, was the first comprehensive state clean indoor air act in the nation. It required the creation of separate smoking and nonsmoking areas in public buildings. The act, which has served as a model for other states, represented an important victory for the tobacco control movement. According to one close observer (quoted in Jacobson et al., 1992), "The tobacco companies ignored the bill. . . . In 1975 the whole world was swathed in gray haze and the 'buoyant industry,' as they called themselves, saw no bogey man behind the little bill in Minnesota"

After that lapse, the tobacco industry mobilized effectively to fight state tobacco control legislation in Minnesota and other state legislatures. Because Minnesota, along with a handful of other states, had led the nation in tobacco control advocacy and policy, the industry has devoted considerable resources to its political agenda in the state. A recent study using publicly available state-level lobbying data from 1994 (Goldstein and Bearman, 1996) found that most of the lobbying in the states was conducted on behalf of four organizations: Philip Morris (34%), the Tobacco Institute (21%), RJR (17%), and the Smokeless Tobacco Council (15%). In addition, this study found that the number of tobacco industry lobbyists in Minnesota—twenty-five—exceeded that of every other state.[5]

Analyses of spending over several legislative sessions bear this out. For example, during the 1991 legislative session in Minnesota, the first and fourth largest spenders on legislative lobbying were tobacco companies—Philip Morris and RJR.[6] From July 1990 through June 1991, tobacco companies worked to prevent Minnesota from adopting what would have been the highest cigarette excise taxes in the nation. As a consequence, Philip Morris took the number one spot for legislative lobbying during that period (with expenditures of $183,326) and RJR took the number four spot (with expenditures of $75,330) (McGrath,1991)[7] During the July 1991 through June 1992 period, RJR was the top spender among tobacco interests, and the tenth largest overall spender ($56,448; Sandok, 1992).[8]

The tobacco industry's lobbying efforts in Minnesota were not only noteworthy for the amount spent, but also for who was doing the lobbying. North States Advisors is a lobbying firm that possesses considerable experience, savvy, and clout. The founder and president (as of 1992) is Thomas Kelm (Coffman and Collins, 1992). Kelm's "Father was one of the founders of the DFL (Democratic Farm Labor) Party" (ibid.). Kelm served as chief of staff for Governor Wendell Anderson (ibid.). North States' client list includes a number of heavy hitters in Minnesota commerce and government, including Northwest Airlines, the City of Minneapolis, Control Data, Carlson Companies, and the Tobacco Institute (ibid.). According to a Saint Paul Pioneer Press investigative piece on lobbying, North States—counting contributions from the firm as well as employees' individual contributions—was the biggest contributor to winning legislative candidates in 1990 among lobbying firms ($63,658).

Jeanne Weigum, the president of ANSR, provided this assessment in a *Saint Paul Pioneer Press* story on lobbying: "'We are constantly out-gunned . . . they kill us. . . . Our bills sail through the Senate. . . . But those proposals usually stall in the House.' Weigum blames the setbacks on the tobacco lobby and its deep pockets" (ibid.:23). One especially successful tactic of the industry at the state level has been to target key committee chairs to kill legislation. Because of the power afforded committee chairs to decide which bills to hear and report out to the full body (House or Senate), the industry has targeted committee chairs, as well as the leadership of both parties (who sometimes instruct committee chairs on which bills to report out of committee), with campaign contributions.

In some of the legislative battles in the late 1980s, the movement had a strong ally in the legislature who was a

> fiery orator. . . . He's persuasive. . . . But, he's been very silent for the last few years, and I don't know why. He signs onto our bills, but he hasn't really done anything. And if that's because it just hasn't been the kind of thing that he wanted to get involved with. He's really busy into the insurance thing. That's his kind of specialty . . . insurance. And then we were told last year by another senator that he'd gotten some major help on a campaign from one of the tobacco companies and that may have made it harder to pursue things he really cares about. He hasn't been bought, but it may make it harder for him to take on those kind of issues.

While the tobacco industry's efforts in Minnesota may have surpassed those in other states, the strategies it employed were similar. Victor L. Crawford, who was a contract lobbyist for the Tobacco Institute in the late 1980s, provided *JAMA* with an interview on Tobacco Industry lobbying efforts. At the time, Crawford was dying of squamous cell carcinoma of the tongue (that had metastasized) that, according to his physician, was "a textbook case of cancer caused by smoking" (Skolnick, 1995:199). According to Crawford (ibid.:199–200),

> The Tobacco Institute monitors every state, and everything that comes up on the state level, in the statehouse, courthouse, county council, county executive, little townships, anything that relates in any way to smoking, tobacco, or to their industry, for example, vending machines, they approach like a big cat at a mouse hole: when they see something move, they pounce. Thanks to the technology of communications and computers, as soon as that mouse sticks its head out of the hole, boom, they know.

The industry has sought passage of relatively weak restrictions at the state level that would preempt stronger measures at the local level. The local level in many ways is the industry's Achilles heel. According to Crawford,

> We could never win at the local level. The reason is, all the health advocates, the ones that unfortunately I used to call "health Nazis," they're all local ac-

tivists who run the little political organizations. They may live next door to the mayor, or the city councilman may be his or her brother-in-law, and they say, "Who's this big-time lobbyist coming here to tell us what to do?" When they've got their friends and neighbors out there in the audience who want this bill, we get killed. So the Tobacco Institute and tobacco companies' first priority has always been to preempt the field, preferably to put it all on the federal level, but if they can't do that, at least the state level, because the health advocates can't compete with me on a state level. They never could. On the local level, I couldn't compete with them. And that's why all your antismoking legislation without exception has started at the local level, all across the country. The Congress itself has done virtually nothing. Even the states are just starting to act. But back in the 1980s, it was the little counties, municipalities, townships, where your antismoking legislation was coming from. And that's what was driving the tobacco guys crazy, because they had to pay people like me to run around and fight the damn things. And every time I'd put out a fire one place, another one would pop up somewhere else.

This dynamic is apparent in Minnesota. According to one knowledgeable observer, the industry, which now fights the movement at the local level as well as the state level, is not very effective at the local level:

Because they're carpetbaggers, and they're obviously carpetbaggers. And money is not an issue. And money isn't an issue in a local political campaign except in Minneapolis and St. Paul. . . . I can tell you having somebody from New York coming and sitting in on a council meeting in White Bear Lake does not impress the council in White Bear Lake.

At the local level, representatives of the tobacco industry work closely with state and local retailing interests, most notably the Minnesota Grocers Association and the Minnesota Retail Merchants Association. This strategy is important because it bolsters the impression that local interests, not just outside interests, oppose local ordinances regarding clean indoor air and youth access to tobacco.

The Minnesota Grocers Association represents about two thousand convenience stores and grocery stores throughout the state (Dawson, 1995). In addition to its activity at the local level, the association has been active at the state level; for example, in 1995 it challenged the legality of federal funds supporting advocacy for changing state and local laws under the Minnesota ASSIST program, as described in Chapter 7 (ibid.).

Even though retailers, such as grocers, convenience store owners, and restaurant owners, may have more credibility than tobacco company representatives at the local level, their influence is limited, according to one experienced observer:

Those people do have an impact but they tend to be viewed as self-serving. And your local council people really are community-oriented people who are being watched on their cable television. And a lot of those speeches they give are for the cable audience. [In Chanhassen] it was real obvious that the speeches weren't just for the people in the room—that the audience really is the community. And I don't think there's any political hay to be made by somebody appearing to be soft on drugs, whether it's tobacco or alcohol, and where it comes to kids. . . . I think communities want their people to be strong on these issues so I don't think the tobacco industry is very likely to make much headway with it.

At the state legislature, the Teamsters' Union has been a consistent opponent of enhancements to the Minnesota Clean Indoor Air Act:

Teamsters give money and Teamsters tow the tobacco line. Always. . . . There's got to be some kind of financial link there. I can't believe that this is all done out of the goodness of the Teamsters' heart. And it's not the Teamsters' issues—I'm sorry.[9]

In Minnesota, as in a number of other states, smokers' rights groups have evolved (the Minnesota Smokers' Rights Coalition). Media accounts have published estimates of as many as six hundred smokers' rights groups throughout the country (Delvecchio, 1991; Cardador, Hazan, and Glantz, 1995; Malouff et al., 1993). These groups rely heavily on tobacco industry funding and technical assistance. While the groups are generally dismissed as tobacco industry front organizations by state and local policymakers, group leaders do have some visibility, and work hard to portray tobacco control efforts in a negative light. For example, according to one Minnesota advocate of smokers' rights writing in a popular magazine, *Minnesota Monthly* (Holm, 1993:55):

Whether you like the news or not, working and rural people still smoke, and are not pleased with being improved without their consent by well-to-do metro life-stylers. . . . Those who do the real work of America—which does not include facilitation, coordination, or task-forcing—are not about to be bamboozled out of their small pleasures by humorless improvers.

In August 1996, after the Target discount chain (which is part of Dayton Hudson Corporation, based in Minneapolis) announced its 714 stores would stop selling cigarettes (Hodges, 1996), Archie Anderson of the MSRC said: "By tonight, we'll have called a nationwide boycott on Target because they've decided to be politicians instead of retailers. . . . If they were so concerned about kids, they'd put Vicks inhalers and No Doz under lock and key, too" (ibid.:A-17).

Finally, a few opponents of particular tobacco control policies surface occasionally, but they are not directly allied with the tobacco industry. For example, at the national level the ACLU, and in Minnesota the Minnesota Civil Liberties Union, have opposed tobacco control efforts that they see as infringing on civil liberties—particularly free speech. For example, in Preston, Minnesota, a local ordinance that would prohibit "point-of-purchase" advertising of tobacco products was opposed by the Minnesota Civil Liberties Union on First Amendment grounds (Associated Press, 1995). In general, opposition has been fairly narrowly focused on such First Amendment issues, and has seldom been an important force in the maneuvering of movement advocates and opponents.

Similarly, advertising interests, such as the American Advertising Federation, American Association of Advertising Agencies, Inc., Association of National Advertisers, Inc., Magazine Publishers of America, Outdoor Advertising Association of America, and Point of Purchase Advertising Institute, joined the suits filed by the tobacco industry, grocers, and convenience stores against the FDA to enjoin implementation of the FDA regulations concerning marketing and sale of tobacco products to youth.[10]

Most movements experience organized opposition (Meyer and Staggenborg, 1996).[11] In the case of the tobacco control movement, the primary opposition is a powerful economic industry—the tobacco industry. While cigarette manufacturers represent a fairly narrow set of interests, they enjoy tremendous political opportunity in the U.S. political system because of their enormous wealth and sophisticated lobbying apparatus. The ability to affect decision-making "behind the scenes," through campaign contributions and other means, translates into considerable political power in the halls of Congress and state legislatures. However, the industry's political opportunity is considerably diminished at the local level. Campaign contributions—especially in smaller cities—are significantly less important to local officials. Moreover, industry lobbyists lack credibility at the local level; hence, the industry cultivates state and local actors with whom they share interests on certain issues, such as grocers and convenience store owners.

The movement caught the industry napping in Minnesota in the mid-1970s, when the Minnesota Clean Indoor Act was enacted. As we will see in Chapter 9, the formidable opposition mounted by the industry has created substantial barriers to legislative successes at the capitol, leading to growing advocacy in city hall.

NOTES

1.   As a result of the Multistate Master Settlement Agreement of November 23, 1998, the tobacco industry trade associations—most notably, the Tobacco Institute—have been disbanded.

2.   Obviously, the idea of "intellectual opposition" has much in common with the framing approach to understanding social movements (Snow et al., 1986; Snow and Benford, 1992; Gamson and Meyer, 1996; Benford and Snow, 2000). It represents a sort of "framing contest" between the industry and movement actors (including government agencies), each of whom promotes understandings of the problem and its solution—in this case, tobacco use—in competing ways.

3.   The examples that Proctor focuses on in his book, in addition to tobacco, are asbestos and petrochemicals (Proctor, 1995).

4.   In a study of 156 tobacco retailers in central Massachusetts, DiFranza and colleagues (1996) found that only a small percentage of retailers were participating in the program, and that those who were participating were no less likely than others to sell cigarettes to underage study confederates.

5.   This study did not take into account the fact that states vary in their requirements for who must register as a lobbyist—thus, the results should be interpreted with caution.

6.   These data are from the Minnesota Ethical Practices Board. The amounts reported do "not represent the total expenses of associations and individuals who lobbied the Legislature. The ethical practices report does not include campaign contributions, nor does it include the salaries of those who conduct the lobbying. The report only discloses spending on entertainment, mailings, telephone calls, gifts and other items" (McGrath,1991).

7.   A key organizational actor in the movement—the MMA—was the seventh biggest spender (expenditures of $56,340). Blue Cross/Blue Shield was not in the top ten.

8.   Blue Cross/Blue Shield was the fifth largest spender on legislative lobbying in Minnesota in 1992 ($91,612), and MMA was the eighth largest spender ($62,297).

9.   Tobacco Institute documents uncovered as part of Minnesota's suit against the tobacco industry revealed the nature of this connection: Wes Lane, a prominent lobbyist for the Teamsters, received $2,500 a month as a consultant for the Tobacco Institute (Teamsters' officials claim they were unaware of this relationship). Lane lobbied against several tobacco control measures and regularly apprised a Tobacco Institute vice president of developments at the legislature (Hanners and Shaffer, 1998). In his words (quoted in ibid., 1998), "I am making a concerted effort during this [1989] session to develop a strong labor position. . . . on tobacco issues."

10.   Although they have not been a force in Minnesota (for obvious reasons), tobacco farmers, landowners, and quota owners have historically been allied with the cigarette companies, although schisms between the companies and the tobacco-growing sector have developed in the past few years (Altman et al.,1996b).

11.   To some extent, movements that have been depicted as "consensus movements" (McCarthy and Wolfson, 1992; Lofland, 1989) represent a departure from this generalization.

9

Arenas of Contention

The previous chapters discussed the actors—the advocates and their opponents—in the tobacco control movement. That discussion showed how the movement has built heavily on the infrastructure of health organizations and health professions, and how the movement and the state are in many ways intertwined. In this chapter, I examine how the actors come together in two important forums: the state legislature and local communities.[1] We will see that activists from movement organizations often worked very closely with state and local government officials in advocating for policy change. We will also see that movement actors have had to battle intense tobacco industry opposition in legislative battles that took place in the years subsequent to passage of the 1975 Minnesota Clean Indoor Air Act—especially in the late 1980s and the 1990s. As a result, the movement has had limited success at the state legislature, although the 1985 Omnibus Nonsmoking Act and a 1997 youth access law stand out as important exceptions. As discussed in the previous chapter, the political opportunity for the movement is often greater at the local level, and tobacco control activists in Minnesota in fact achieved important victories on youth access to tobacco in a number of local communities.

Since the Smoke-Free Coalition's founding in 1984, the movement's legislative effort has been led by the coalition's Public Policy Committee. Members of the committee—which have usually included representatives from ANSR, MDH, the voluntaries, and the Minnesota Medical Association Auxiliary—meet on a regular basis prior to and during the legislative session. The committee develops the legislative agenda, and carries out much of the lobbying effort. At times, members of the committee mobilize members or volunteers of their own organizations to take part in lobbying efforts. ANSR works mainly as a member of the coalition, but sometimes takes the lead responsibility for lobbying under its own banner. For example, ANSR has often taken the lead on clean indoor air legislation. ANSR also works separately from the coalition at times because it wishes to take a more aggressive position or use more aggressive tactics on a legislative issue.

Beginning in 1991, the coalition sponsored an annual Day at the Capitol. This was an effort to engage volunteers (or, in the case of ANSR, members) from coalition organizations—especially the voluntaries and ANSR—in the coalition's lobbying effort. Training was provided in the morning, including background on the coalition's issues that session, which legislators were being targeted, and how to go about educating the legislators on the bills. There was an effort to demystify lobbying, and to overcome the normal fears and apprehensions of people who have not lobbied before.[2] After the training session, which in 1991 was held In the Minnesota ALA headquarters, just a couple of minutes from the capitol in St. Paul, car pools took the volunteers, together with the more seasoned organizational representatives, to the capitol. Teams, usually consisting of a more experienced lobbyist (staff and leaders involved in the coalition's legislative committee) and a volunteer new to the process, were sent to meet with key legislators. This mechanism has succeeded, to a degree, in increasing the "grassroots" presence of the tobacco control forces at the legislature in the 1990s.[3]

STATE LEGISLATION

Since passage of the Minnesota Clean Indoor Air Act in 1975 (see Chapter 3), the movement has experienced a few victories and a number of defeats at the state legislature. One of the most significant victories was the 1985 passage of the Omnibus Nonsmoking and Disease Prevention Act as part of a large, consolidated tax cut bill (Shultz et al., 1986). This was truly a shining hour for proponents of tobacco control in Minnesota—both with respect to the process and the outcome. The Minnesota Plan for Nonsmoking and Health had been published the year before, and the Omnibus Act represented an attempt to put key features of the plan into law. The Smoke-Free Coalition had begun, and there was active support for the bill on the part of the member organizations of the coalition. As we saw in Chapter 3, ANSR worked extremely closely with MDH staff in support of the proposed legislation. The bill had the strong support of Governor Rudy Perpich. Surgeon General Koop came to Saint Paul to testify in favor of the bill before the House of Representatives. And the tobacco industry mobilized: its lobbyists were in force at the capitol, along with expert witnesses from Minnesota and other states. The industry embarked on a grassroots lobbying effort, mailing postcard response forms in opposition to the bill to smokers throughout the state. Finally, in a special session in June, the main provisions of the bill passed as part of a consolidated bill (ibid.).

ANSR and its members were happy, because, in the words of ANSR President, Jeanne Weigum, "There was money for a real staff person to enforce the Clean Indoor Act for the first time ever." In addition, the bill provided for an increase in the state cigarette tax from eighteen to twenty-three cents per pack.[4] Of this five cents per pack increase, one-third of a cent was earmarked for tobacco use prevention programs to be conducted by MDH and MDE—the Minnesota Nonsmoking Initiative (later to be renamed the Minnesota Tobacco-Use Prevention Initiative; see Chapter 7). In a model that would be replicated on a grander scale in California, Massachusetts, Arizona, and other states, this was the first time a portion of a tobacco excise tax increase was earmarked to support a state tobacco education and prevention effort. Clearly, this helped lay the groundwork for increasing state involvement in tobacco control efforts.

The Omnibus bill included a provision that would ban distribution of free cigarettes for promotional purposes, which didn't pass in 1985 (but did pass in 1986—see below). This provision was of keen importance to the tobacco industry, according to one participant in the legislative effort:

> It became apparent that that was one of the things they couldn't lose. I mean that they absolutely were not willing to give that up. . . . It interfered in a major way with their promotional plans. . . . A couple of times after major defeats on their part, we found [an unnamed tobacco industry lobbyist] on the phone just desperately talking to somebody about what to do next. That was obviously something that was real important . . . this was obviously really, really big for those people. So we thought it was pretty big, too.

The issue of free distribution of tobacco products was to resurface in the 1986 legislative session. ANSR was concerned about free distribution of tobacco products. Minneapolis and Saint Paul had each passed ordinances banning free distribution a few years before.

> Free distribution was really rampant. . . . I mean they were handing cigarettes—free cigarettes—out on street corners. Near rock concerts. And that country music festival that they had up in Northern Minnesota—they put the thing on. They'd practically . . . I mean a girlfriend went up there. She said they would practically tackle you and get you to take the free cigarettes. She said they were just . . . they were just everywhere, giving out free cigarettes. And we just felt this was real inappropriate. It was not an appropriate way of dealing with a controlled substance.

In an early illustration of joint advocacy, the AG's office approached ANSR. Jeanne Weigum:

> An interesting thing happened the next year after the Omnibus bill, and I'm not sure what instigated this, but Humphrey's office contacted us [ANSR] and said they wanted to do a tobacco bill. And what they wanted to do was

require warning labels on smokeless tobacco. And we convinced them that they also wanted to get rid of free distribution of smokeless. And although, there are some . . . some problems related to federal preemption on cigarettes, none of those things exist for smokeless. . . . At that time, there were no national warning labels on smokeless. So we worked with Humphrey's office . . . and this was basically an Attorney General's bill. And we had good fun because we had in mind something a whole lot more extensive than Humphrey's office had in mind . . . in terms of how far it was going to go. Like we intended to include a few things other than smokeless, like free distribution of other tobacco products. And basically, the attorney general's office lost control of the bill. But it didn't do anything they didn't want it to do. It just went further than they ever intended. And it was really pretty funny because . . . the lady I was working with from the Attorney General's office really wanted to be a little more bold than . . . than the other people in the office were ready for it to go. So I think she sort of sensed that there were plans afoot to help this go along. . . . We used that as a vehicle for getting our first initial ban on free distribution and then the following year it was improved.

So, in 1986, a prohibition on free distribution of smokeless tobacco and distribution of cigarettes to persons under the age of eighteen was achieved—another victory for the movement. It was the first state law of its kind:

It was considered pretty revolutionary in its time. After that [the 1986 bill] passed, then there were a lot of things that, you know, came across that you could send for free samples and so we sent for all we could. And had them sent to legislators and stuff. They were getting free samples in the mail, and one of them stood up and waved around the next session . . . waved around the free sample that had come to his house. Said obviously this isn't working. . . . And at that point they got rid of the free samples.

It is noteworthy that the free sampling issue marks the first time in the modern period (since the 1910s and 1920s) that Minnesota tobacco control advocates and legislators devoted their attentions to what was to come to be called "youth access to tobacco."[5] Moreover, this occurred before researchers and activists had really developed the concept, in the late 1980s, that a "supply side" approach of limiting the availability of cigarettes to youth had promise for reducing rates of tobacco use by youth (see Chapter 2). Thus, the focus on sampling was a sort of precursor to the conceptualization of the importance of limiting youth access to tobacco, and its application in efforts to restrict availability through changes in federal, state, and local laws and enforcement patterns. It appears from the quotations provided above that what motivated the activists (and, for that matter, legislators) at this time was not an explicit concept of the importance of limiting youth access, but outrage at the egregious disregard on the part of the tobacco industry for the state laws and prevailing norms on providing tobacco products to children.

Since that time, the movements' state legislative agenda has focused on three issues: youth access to tobacco, restrictions on where smoking is allowed, and increases in the state tobacco tax. In 1992, opposition to an industry-sponsored "smokers' rights bill" also made its way onto the legislative agenda of the movement.

Youth Access to Tobacco

In 1989, the coalition went into the legislative session with a goal of achieving a statewide ban on vending machine sales of cigarettes (Wymore, 1991). A strong ally, Senator John Marty (a DFL legislator from St. Paul),[6] had authored the bill (Senate File 276), but it went down to defeat in what was to become a continuing hurdle for youth access measures—the Senate Commerce Committee. Meanwhile, the movement had an ideological ally in the chairman of the Senate Judiciary Committee, Senator Allan Spear (a DFL legislator from Minneapolis). Spear came up with a strategy that involved a youth access bill going through his committee, rather than Commerce (ibid.). Spear wanted the penalties for tobacco sales to minors increased from a misdemeanor carrying a maximum fine of $700 and 90 days in jail to a felony. This was widely considered to be too draconian, so he altered the bill so that it would treat the offense as a gross misdemeanor, with a maximum fine of $3,000 and a year in jail. Surprisingly, opposition to the bill from retailers and the tobacco industry never materialized, and the bill passed and was signed into law by Governor Rudy Perpich (ibid.).

The issue of youth access was to resurface in 1990 in a way that changed the landscape of tobacco control efforts by drawing widespread public attention, in Minnesota and the other states, to the issue. As described below, a Saint Paul suburb, White Bear Lake, passed an ordinance banning vending machine sales of cigarettes in 1989. This event drew enormous attention to the issue, both in Minnesota and nationwide. There was a surge in local-level activity on the issue of youth access to tobacco in 1990, with a particular emphasis on vending machines.[7]

And the industry responded. As many analysts have noted (e.g., Sylvester, 1989; Skolnick, 1995; also see Chapter 8), the tobacco industry has much greater capacity to influence federal and state legislatures than local lawmakers. One way to take the wind out of the growing movement at the local level would be to pass a weak state law that preempted stronger local action. This was emerging as a critical tobacco industry response to growing local-level activism in several states (see Bearman, Goldstein and Bryan, 1995; Siegel et al., 1997). The Minnesota Coalition for Responsible

Vending Sales, which worked closely with the Tobacco Institute (Forster et al., 1990:13), found authors for a bill that would exempt vending machines located in places not open to the general public from any restrictions, require machines in bars and liquor stores to be located within view of an employee, and require all other machines to be fitted with locking devices (which, in theory, require an employee to "unlock" to allow sales). In addition, the bill would preempt stronger local ordinances, which were already in place in White Bear Lake and twenty or so other local communities in Minnesota (ibid.).

Movement activists understood well the threat of preemption for the growing movement to restrict youth access to cigarettes at the local level. In the words of one person closely involved in the legislative effort, "I'd heard about it happening in other states and several of us from the very beginning took it as deadly serious. That this was something that they could win. And they did in the House." ANSR, the Smoke-Free Coalition and its constituent organizations, researchers from the University of Minnesota School of Public Health, and others mobilized to defeat the legislation. A decision was made on the part of the Public Policy and Legislation Committee of the SFC to make opposition to the bill their sole issue for the 1990 state legislative agenda (ibid.).[8]

The opposition to preemption was strongly framed as a community issue and a youth issue, rather then just the health lobbyists with their ax to grind: "That was the message that we were trying to get out—that this was a youth bill. A youth health bill. And that it was coming from communities, not from health organizations, which was really good."

The opposition came to have a strong grassroots flavor:

> They [legislators] knew that there was a huge community movement happening and they wanted their votes for the upcoming year. So by the time that it got to the capitol and it was in committee, then Jeanne, Jean, and Mary kept bringing in community members instead of having us testify. We had a few doctors, but Stuart Hanson, I mean, it seemed to me that everybody over there knew Stuart Hanson and his issues. What they really were interested in hearing were what the other people were thinking. . . . They'd been bombarded enough by the experts. They knew the issues like the back of their hand and that's in general what I find. A lot of times they don't want to, they want to learn about the issue and then they want to hear what the constituents want.

And, in an example of the mobilization by activists of representatives of units of local government to lobby state government, local officials were engaged (ibid.:17):

> Probably the group most influential against preemption were the city council members, mayors, and community activists from the cities where restric-

tive ordinances or total bans had already been passed or were under consideration. Led by the mayor of White Bear Lake, these individuals participated in a press conference at the legislature the week of the House Commerce Committee hearings and lobbied their legislators, many of whom they knew personally. They very articulately relayed the level of thought and study that had gone into adopting these local ordinances, their sincere concern for children which had motivated their actions, and their outrage that the legislature might presume to know better than they what was good for their communities. They were a group of individuals totally activated on this issue, and they were the chief spokespeople against preemption at the hearings. Signs were made from each community which had passed an ordinance and representatives from those communities were very visible in the audience during the hearings.

The supporters of the legislation were vocal about the putative impact of the legislation on jobs: "There was one guy from the vending machine association that would come and testify all the time and would talk about how many jobs would be lost. It was a jobs issue that they were trying to play off of."

ANSR and the SFC had lined up a supporter on the House committee to which the bill had been assigned. However, the vote in the committee went in favor of the preemption bill, and the legislator felt the consequences of bucking the leadership:

I think it cost her a lot. She didn't go along with the chair of the committee. She didn't go along with other powerful people on the committee, and in a way they wanted her to. She really felt she was falling on her sword. She really did.

However, the opponents of preemption—the tobacco control advocates—prevailed in the House. According to one of the leaders of the effort, the decisive factor in defeating the bill in the House was

The media. No question about it. We had tried to stir up attention. I knew we were going to lose the vote in the House, and I tried to get media interest. And Klobachar [Jim Klobachar, a long-time columnist for the Star Tribune] said, look, when they pass a bill, tell me about it. That's news. The fact that they might pass a bill—that is not news. When they pass a bill, call me. And that's really what happened. . . . When the House committee did it, suddenly the media just came on like gang-busters. It was just amazing. There were editorials in the Minneapolis and St. Paul papers. The day we had the hearing in the Senate, there were two editorial cartoons—one in both the St. Paul and Minneapolis papers. . . . One of the cartoons is a picture of a cigarette . . . a cigarette box opening the lid of the capitol and smiling and blowing smoke in—powerful stuff.

In addition to the media, local officials from communities that had passed restrictions were powerful allies at the legislature:

> You know, we had city managers, we had mayors present, we had council members . . . of communities that had passed. Yeah. We had them there. And then we had the kids with the cigarettes. And you know, the evening news had a picture of two little boys dumping boxes of cigarettes on the table, saying "I bought these." You know, that was what—they spilled all over the table and down on the floor and . . . how do you follow that? That was our hearing. Incredible. We got that one, but . . . without the media, we had no chance.

After this victory—or, more precisely, a successful defense against a measure that would have represented a significant defeat—efforts to increase restrictions on youth access to tobacco through state legislative action have faltered. In 1992, a bill passed that increased the penalties for tobacco retailers who sold to minors—but also penalized youth for purchase or possession of tobacco products by minors, a provision that was opposed by most in the tobacco control movement (McGrath, 1992).

There were repeated efforts to enact a licensing bill, which would require local governments to license tobacco retailers, provide for civil penalties for violations on the part of merchants, and devote a portion of the funds from these penalties to enforcement activities.[9] The effort to push a licensing bill through the state legislative process encountered roadblock after roadblock:

> Licensing never got any attention but then it didn't get a hearing, either. You know, people give attention to bills that get hearings. They don't give attention to bills that are dead on arrival.

The chairman of the Senate Commerce Committee—which had been for sometime a Bermuda Triangle for youth access bills—represented the Northern Minnesota city of Duluth, where there was a strong contingent of activists affiliated with ALA and ANSR. They lobbied their legislator heavily, and he promised a hearing. He never came through with the hearing—he claimed, "We're out of time." One key leader from ANSR expressed her frustration with this experience: "And you know, I think that . . . that has just been done repeatedly with our kind of bill, with our bills."[10]

In the 1996 session, the only victory that was achieved on youth access was not in gaining passage of a movement-supported bill, but in narrowly blocking passage of a industry bill with weak statewide restrictions that would preempt stronger local actions. The House Commerce Committee had taken a Senate bill on youth access that the coalition supported, weakened it substantially, and added a preemption clause. This bill, which in its new form was sponsored by industry allies in the state (the Minnesota Grocers Association and the Minnesota Retail Merchants Association), was the cause for worry on the part of the tobacco control forces. In the words of one "action alert" (Hennepin County Community Prevention Coalition, 1996):

> The bill is fatally flawed. It establishes a ceiling on tobacco control for all cities in Minnesota. If this bill passes and becomes law, any stronger ordinance law that a city tries to pass to protect children from tobacco will be pre-empted by the state law. Cities will lose the ability to determine what is best for their community.

With the next step a vote on the floor of the House, the coalition, ANSR, and other tobacco control advocates mobilized to oppose the measure. As in the 1990 fight against preemption, there was an attempt to rally local governments to voice their opposition to state preemption of their local authority. When the bill came up on the floor of the House, an amendment removing the preemption clause was passed, and the author pulled the bill. So, the tobacco control forces had prevented an industry preemption bill from passing, but did not succeed in their original goal of obtaining passage of a strong youth access bill.

Finally, in 1997, the movement forces achieved a major victory in the area of youth access. By now, with the FDA regulations in place, the founding of the National Center for Tobacco-Free Kids, and law suits filed by Minnesota and seventeen other states (Kelder, 1999a), there was growing momentum nationwide to reduce youth access to tobacco. Documents revealing industry wrongdoing—including evidence of deliberate marketing to children—had been uncovered through litigation and other means and had been widely publicized (e.g., Glantz et al., 1996), further eroding the image of the tobacco industry.

Given the favorable national developments on youth access, and the string of defeats on the issue at the Minnesota legislature, there was a strong feeling among the Minnesota tobacco control forces that they needed a "win" in the 1997 session. At the beginning of the session, the Smoke- Free Coalition held a press conference, at which the House author (Ann Rest) introduced a bill that would require licensing of retail tobacco outlets, annual compliance checks of outlets, and a ban on self-service sales of cigarettes. Local government officials from cities that had strong local youth access restrictions, including city council members and a police chief, spoke in favor of the bill. Attorney General Humphrey also spoke in favor of the bill, and a considerable amount of media coverage was generated. The Speaker of the House was listed as a coauthor on the bill, signaling that it had a good chance of receiving a hearing (deFiebre, 1997a). As in past years, the tobacco industry and retail industry vigorously opposed the bill. A version of the bill passed the House, but not before it had been stripped of two of its strongest provisions—a requirement for annual compliance checks and a ban on self-service sales of cigarettes (Whereatt, 1997). The bill also passed the Senate, which had reinserted provisions requiring compliance checks and banning self-service sales of single packs of cigarettes. This time, the tobacco control forces, usually at the receiving end of behind-the-scenes maneuvering at the capital, also succeeded in tacking an ingredient disclosure provision—anathema to the industry—onto the bill. Senator John Marty, a longtime supporter of tobacco control measures and movement ally, introduced the ingredient amendment—modeled after a 1996 Massachusetts law (Porfiri, 1996)—on the floor of the Senate, where it passed on a voice vote (deFiebre, 1997b). In the words of Senate sponsor Ember Reichgott Junge, "It was put in the bill without notice. . . . The tobacco industry had not had a chance to visit with the members about it" (quoted in deFiebre, 1997c:A10). Thus, the conference committee was presented with a very strong Senate bill and a rather weak House bill (deFiebre, 1997d). The conference committee reported a fairly strong bill, which included a ban on self-service sales of single packs of cigarettes, and a requirement that the presence of five hazardous ingredients in tobacco products be disclosed (ibid.). Again, the tobacco control forces mobilized to ensure that the House would approve the bill reported out by the conference committee. According to a media account, "Everywhere a legislator turned, he or she was button-holed by representatives of health or education groups or their rivals from the retail and cigarette industries" (deFiebre, 1997e:B3). The bill barely survived (for want of one vote) a House motion to return it to the conference committee, after which it was approved by the House and, four days later, on the last day of the session, by the Senate (deFiebre, 1997f; Rosencrans, 1997).

Once the law had been passed by the legislature, concerns turned to the governor. The media had reported that Governor Carlson was considering a veto of the bill because of concerns that the ingredient disclosure requirement might lead the state into an expensive court battle (ibid.). The tobacco control forces launched a major effort to mobilize their networks to contact the governor to urge him to sign the bill into law. On May 30, after a long and convoluted legislative battle, the governor signed the Reducing Youth Access to Tobacco bill into law (deFiebre, 1997g).[11]

The new law required licensing of all retail outlets selling tobacco products, with provisions for fines for license-holders that sell tobacco products to minors and mandatory once-a-year compliance checks by local authorities. The legislation also included a ban on self-service sales of single packs of cigarettes—the first such state law in the country to do so (Forster and

Wolfson, 1998:211).[12] In an ironic twist that illustrates the industry's ability to quickly adapt to many of the restrictions supported by the movement, "two-packs" (the minimum number now allowable for self-service sales), in which two separate packs were packaged together in cellophane, were being sold at local outlets the day that the new law took effect (de-Fiebre, 1997h). Nevertheless, the law was regarded as a major victory—in fact, it was characterized as "the greatest tobacco control policy success in Minnesota in over a decade" (Minnesota Coalition for a Smoke-Free Society 2000, 1997).

In addition to the restrictions on youth access to tobacco, the new law included new penalties—suspension of driver's license—for minors who purchase or attempt to purchase tobacco products and for adults who lend their identification to minors to enable them to purchase tobacco products. In addition, the legislation included a requirement that manufacturers of cigarettes and smokeless tobacco submit an annual report to MDH disclosing the presence of ammonia, arsenic, cadmium, formaldehyde, and lead in their products.

Clean Indoor Air

In 1987, a prohibition on smoking in licensed day-care and health care facilities was passed. In 1988, legislation was passed requiring state agencies to implement restrictive indoor smoking policies. However, bills that would advance the core areas of interest of the tobacco control movement (especially ANSR)—protecting people who work in factories and warehouses, and people who live in apartments, condominiums, and other aggregate housing from exposure to secondhand smoke—have not fared well.

In 1989, a bill introduced by Representative Phyllis Kahn (the champion of the MCIAA of 1975) to strengthen the clean indoor act (by, among other things, restricting smoking in common areas of apartment buildings and condominiums) did not receive a hearing in the House Health and Human Services Committee.[13] The Senate bill, sponsored by John Brandl, was also killed (Wymore, 1991). Minnesota smokers' rights groups—which are generally considered to be front groups for the industry (see Chapter 8)—were active in opposing the bill (ibid.).

It has been difficult to engage media interest in clean indoor air legislation in Minnesota in the 1990s. According to Jeanne Weigum of ANSR:

> We never got the media interested. They're not . . . and they're not going to be interested this year [1991]. It's not the kind of issue they're going to get excited about. . . . And we've been unsuccessful at turning the media on to the tobacco industry tactics—the only reporter who is the least bit interested is based in California.

ANSR members testified on proposed Clean Indoor Air legislation in 1991:

> We wanted somebody to cover the public housing piece, and [name deleted] had actually testified without being asked a couple of years ago and had done a really nice job. And so we thought that since she had done such a nice job, we would like to use her again. We picked [name deleted] because we felt that he really was representative of a group of people, . . . that have that kind of problem. . . . He's going to spend the rest of his life in a factory polluted with smoke and other chemicals. And those are the people we're talking about protecting. You know, we're not talking about college-educated people in high-rises, big fancy office buildings where they've got a lot of choices in their life. We very carefully chose him because we felt he was representative of a real class of people.

But Phyllis Kahn couldn't get a hearing in the House.[14]

The following year (1992), a bill that would have strengthened MCIAA measures on smoking in apartments and workplaces passed the Senate but was defeated in the House (ANSR, 1992). However, by the 1993 session, it appeared that tobacco control forces had a number of factors in their favor. The EPA report on the health effects of secondhand smoke had been released in December 1992. Moreover, an experienced lobbyist from the law firm of Opperman, Heins and Paquin was providing pro bono consultation services to the legislative effort. In fact, a minor victory on indoor smoking restrictions—a ban on smoking in licensed family day-care facilities—was achieved this year. Initially, the coalition of organizations involved in state legislative advocacy was somewhat ambivalent about the issue. According to one participant,

> It's funny now that bill has changed completely in two years because the first year I remember nobody wanted to touch it because we were all fearful that that subset of people who do family day care by and large are lower-income young women, you know, and that's the group we're really trying to reach out to them with the no-smoking message. . . . You know, we're trying to build trust with a lot of communities and so I thought, "Is this something that's going to get us into trouble?"

However, efforts to tighten up the Minnesota Clean Indoor Act—for example, to extend the coverage to factories, warehouses, and common areas of apartment buildings and condominiums—have encountered considerable tobacco industry opposition, and have not been successful. In 1993, one of the legislative agenda items was enhancements to the MCIAA that would prohibit smoking in common areas of apartments and condominiums. The bill was opposed by the tobacco industry and by the owners of condominiums and apartment buildings, and was not given a hearing in the House (Chanen, 1993; ANSR, 1993b). Similarly, an effort was mounted during the 1993 session to tighten up restrictions on smoking in workplaces. This bill was vigorously opposed by the tobacco industry and the Teamsters (see Chapter 8 on the Teamsters' role in opposing tobacco control efforts) and was defeated in the House Health and Human Services Committee (ANSR, 1993c).

Finally, in 1994, a bill that extended the protections of the MCIAA to common areas of apartment buildings became law. Provisions covering condominiums had been dropped, and the bill allowed building managers to designate smoking areas. Despite these concessions, after years of struggle, this was recognized as a major victory, especially for ANSR, with its strong focus on protection of the rights and health of nonsmokers (ANSR, 1994).

In 1996 a law was passed that banned smoking in Minnesota prisons effective in August 1997 (Associated Press, 1997b). This was not a movement bill—it was largely motivated by concerns about health care costs borne by the state. In the words of the Senate sponsor, Senator Dave Kleis (a Republican from St. Cloud), "Since we pay 100 percent of inmates' health-care costs, if they choose to smoke, we pay a higher premium" (ibid.: B-3). In fact, the law was part of a national trend of trying to reduce the health care costs associated with imprisonment borne by the federal, state, and local governments (Robertson, 1997). The bill was opposed by many long-term supporters of the movement, such as Senator Sandy Pappas (a DFL legislator from St. Paul): "So much of our society is addicted to smoking, and it's not illegal. Let's look at breaking illegal addiction. I never heard that smoking led to someone robbing a grocery store" (ibid.:A10).

Tax

With the passage of the Omnibus Nonsmoking and Disease Prevention Act in 1985, Minnesota—for a time—had the highest state cigarette excise tax in the country ($0.23)[15]. A second increase, in 1987, increased the tax to $0.38 (Tobacco Institute, 1996:226). In 1991, the excise tax was increased for the third time in six years, from $0.38 to $0.43 a pack. Finally, in 1992, the tax was raised by a nickel, to $0.48.

However, Minnesota has not maintained the leadership position with respect to taxation of tobacco products that it enjoyed in 1985. In 1995, Minnesota's excise tax on cigarettes of $0.48 ranked ninth in the nation (Shelton et al., 1995). By September 1998, Minnesota had fallen to sixteenth among the states, with the same rate of $0.48 (one-half of the highest rate of $1.00 in Alaska and Hawaii, and less than ten cents over the average rate of $0.39; Fishman et al., 1999).[16] Beyond the frustration and embarrassment of los-ing its leadership position, the more important issue was that taxes, which had been identified as one of the most effective vehicles for reducing smoking—especially youth smoking—had not kept pace with the retail price of cigarettes (Tobacco Institute, 1996). Including 1985, the tax had been raised four times. However, each of these changes involved an increase of all of five cents (in 1985, 1991, and 1992) or, at most, fifteen cents (in 1987). Throughout this period, state and federal taxes as a percentage of the retail price of a pack of cigarettes in Minnesota remained virtually unchanged—hovering between $0.31 and $0.37 (ibid.). So these tax increases may have provided some revenue for tobacco control efforts (the Omnibus Act of 1985), and may have had some symbolic value as small victories, but are unlikely to have increased the economic disincentives for smoking in the state.[17] Moreover, they represent a marked decline in taxes as a percentage of retail price compared to earlier years (for example, in 1972 this figure was 57.5%) (ibid.:226).

These small increases, which were largely government-supported revenue measures, provided strategic dilemmas for movement activists. According to one longtime activist, it is difficult for the health advocates to promote increases where revenue is the goal:

> Excise tax actually got a fair amount of press, but none of it was very supportive . . . because it was such an obvious revenue-rasing thing. You know, it was real hard for us to show that as a health issue. You know, because the reason they . . . were wanting to raise it really . . . had nothing to do with health.

Another person involved in the legislative effort put a more favorable spin on the tax measures:

> I don't know, it's kind of nice that he [Governor Arne Carlson] did it, and that it takes the heat off of the coalition. I mean the coalition talked about proposing it and having funds be allocated to health issues, health promotion, prevention stuff, but people didn't think that was the route to go. So when the government did, as it did, that kind of took the heat off of us and we can support it, of course, so we'll support it.

Even in 1993, when the advocacy effort was broadened to include a wide variety of groups that would benefit from earmarking of revenues from a $0.33 increase in the tax (the Tobacco Tax Coalition for a Health Minnesota, described in Chapter 6), the tax went down to defeat. Thus, the movement in Minnesota—despite a long history, an active coalition, at least one organization with a true grassroots component (ANSR), the multimillion dollar investment of ASSIST (which, at the national level, had tax increases as one of its four specified strategies), and, in recent years, a Tobacco Tax

Coalition sponsored by Blue Cross/Blue Shield—was not able to overcome the industry opposition to increased taxes, and their influence in the state legislature.

"Smokers' Rights"

In the 1992 legislative session, a "smokers' bill of rights law" was introduced in the Minnesota legislature. This bill reflected a national effort by the tobacco industry in the late 1980s and early 1990s to support smokers' rights laws. By the end of 1992, over half the states had passed laws that prohibited employment discrimination against tobacco users (Malouff et al., 1993).[18]

The movement's legislative forces opposed the bill. Nevertheless, in April, 1992, a "Smokers' Bill of Rights" passed, and went into effect August 1 of that year. The legislation made it illegal for an employer to discipline an employee, or refuse to hire a prospective employee, because the worker smokes while off-duty.

LOCAL ORDINANCES

In contrast to its uneven record at the state level, the movement has achieved a string of significant victories at the local level, where the industry often lacks the manpower and the legitimacy to prevail. In addition, campaign contributions, which are coveted in national and state legislative races, are only critical factors in local races in the largest communities in Minnesota. Thus, this source of financial leverage of the industry is often absent—or greatly attenuated—in local politics in the state.

Starting in the late 1970s, local tobacco control ordinances have passed in many Minnesota communities. For example, Minneapolis passed one of the first ordinances in the country restricting free distribution of cigarettes in 1979. In 1989, White Bear Lake, a Saint Paul suburb, became the first city in the nation to ban the sale of cigarettes through vending machines.

> Jean [Forster] started the vending machine thing. . . . That was her little project. And it started out in White Bear and it just . . . it went like topsy. It was a really neat time because we were all working together and we were kind of feeding and watering what was happening naturally in the community. It was naturally occurring stuff that we just supplied . . . supplied the stuff for.

More generally, ANSR's involvement in local issues evolved out of the University of Minnesota effort to study and promote restrictions on youth access to tobacco in local communities:

Jean [Forster of the University of Minnesota School of Public Health] started that. No question. Jean's trying to focus on communities. And it wasn't that we hadn't talked about that, because they'd been doing this in California forever. California gave up on state legislation long ago, but we hadn't done any of it. It was a whole new place for us. . . . And we talked about maybe that's what we needed to start doing but we didn't do it until Jean got the ball rolling in White Bear. And that demonstrated fairly graphically that this was a new place we could do something. And we developed some real friends in the local communities, and I think that those are things that will play for state legislation, too. Owatonna was a good example. . . . We got to know a lot of people in Owatonna when they did their vending machine [ordinance]. And those were people that when [a state legislator from Owatonna] was waffling, I was able to call those people. And they knew who I was and it was not starting from ground zero trying to explain things. They made phone calls. You know, they just said give me the background on the issues. Send me a piece of paper and I'll take care of it. And they did.

Thus, working with local communities helped ANSR and other build a base of support that could subsequently be used in state legislative efforts.

Local communities were activating themselves on the issue of youth access—especially vending machines—and would often contact ANSR as a resource:

Things were happening we knew nothing about. We'd find out. Somebody would call and say this happened in our community. . . . Once it occurred in White Bear, it just grew. And in Bloomington, the tobacco people cornered Chris Olson [an ANSR board member, and council member in Chanhassen, active in the Republican party] and said you think you're smart now lady, but we're going to get you at the legislature. You won today. We'll win next time, and we're taking this one away from you [a reference to the proposed preemptive state legislation that would be introduced in 1990], is basically what they said.

Following White Bear Lake, ANSR, working with the University of Minnesota research group, organized workshops for both community activists and local government officials on methods for restricting youth access to tobacco at the local level (Forster et al., 1990).

What is the relationship between local communities and ANSR on youth access restrictions? Typically, it builds on existing networks of relationships. In some cases, an "insider" strategy is used, in which ANSR works directly with members of city councils or mayors. In other cases, there is an effort to use the membership as a catalyst in grassroots efforts. As Jeanne Weigum explains:

[A local mayor—name deleted] is kind of a classic, because he's really interested in this issue, and he seems to kind of like us. And he's been calling us off and on every once and a while, he'd give me a call and say, "Hey, what's up, what's up?" And I told him that something big was going to happen in Roseville and told him what it kind of involved. He wanted some copies of some stuff. I sent him some information. And he said, "We'll do it, we'll do it, we'll be ready." And we're going to create a little momentum here. And Roseville will go first and then we'll get Falcon Heights or Shoreview will go and then we'll have . . . a sense that things are really happening faster. And that was kind of staged. And he kind of engineered that. He supplied information. I know two of the other people on the council, one fairly well. I sent information to that person, I know that person from my involvement in the park [council person is on the Ramsey County Parks Board]. And I know the other council person because her husband was from the fire-safe cigarette committee. . . . So I know those two people. So I was kind of sending information periodically. I think the first stuff I sent [name deleted] was probably the week after she was named to the council. I sent her a bunch of stuff and said, "Hey, let's get some stuff going here." And it didn't bear fruit for six months or a year. You know, it just takes time. Now [name deleted] thinks that New Brighton's a possibility so I contacted a couple of ANSR members in New Brighton and said, "Would you write a letter to your mayor, saying look what Roseville's done, why don't we do this." So I know they've done it because I've gotten copies of those letters and I've got a note pasted to the side of my computer that says, "Call New Brighton mayor." So one of these days I'm going to call and say, "Hey, are you interested in this stuff?" Now he's got copies of stuff, I know that, and it's been in the newspapers. We've done some letters to the editor and things like that in *New Brighton Focus*. So I'm hopeful that we'll get something going. Edina is a real possibility. They have done vending machine stuff. We've got a lot of members in Edina, lots of members, including Arlene Wilson. . . . So we're trying to get something going there. And we're going to get something going in Bloomington, but we now have to wait until the election's over.

ANSR has played the primary role in working with local communities. One knowledgeable participant comments on the role of the coalition:

> The coalition doesn't seem to do any stirring up of things. You know, like I'm unaware of the coalition trying to get something going in Edina or anyplace that I'm aware of.

Early on, passage of local ordinances was often the result of local advocacy, carried out largely by ANSR, the University of Minnesota School of Public Health, and, in recent years, local ASSIST coalitions. However, a natural diffusion process appears to have taken hold for at least some of these local policies. By 1993, 94% of Minnesota cities with populations greater than 2,000 required licenses for tobacco retailers and 25% restricted vending machine sales in some way. However, levels of enforcement of these ordinances were low, and many other provisions sought by activists—such as bans on self-service sales of cigarettes—had not diffused widely.

In general, though, activism and innovation at the local level has drawn the attention of movement and government organizations throughout the nation.

In this chapter, we have seen how movement actors have pursued policy changes at the state and local level. Political opportunity is considerably greater at the local than the state level, because of the advantages that movement actors have over the industry with respect to credibility in local communities and because the financial leverage of the industry is considerably diminished at the local level—especially in smaller cities and towns—than at the state level. However, building relationships in the course of local-level initiatives helps build a base of support for state legislative efforts. Finally, we have also seen how movement actors often work closely with government officials and staff, both at the state and local level. This pattern lends credence to the description of tobacco control as an example of state/movement interpenetration.

NOTES

1. In addition to changes in public policies, movement actors have pursued changes in institutional polices. One example of a significant victory in this area is helping convince the Target discount chain (which is part of the Dayton Hudson Corporation, based in Minneapolis) to stop selling cigarettes in all of 714 stores in 1996 (Hodges, 1996; Kahn, 1996).

2. For example, the confirmation letter and schedule that went to ANSR members on ANSR's letterhead began with the following: "Thank you for volunteering to participate in our Day at the Capitol. It will be good fun and will help to educate our legislators about the various tobacco bills before the legislator."

3. The Day at the Capitol seemed to be a response to past difficulties in activating the putative "networks" of the organizational members of the Smoke-Free Coalition—especially those of the voluntaries. These difficulties are evident in this statement by the ALA legislative liaison in the early 1990s, describing the 1990 session and the effort to mobilize against the industry's preemption bill: "[Mary Hourigan and Jean Forster of the University of Minnesota] helped activate the communities and the city council members and what not to move their communities. They would call me [an ALA legislative liaison] to activate people in those communities, but I had nobody to activate. So it was a very, very frustrating situation."

4. The last excise tax increase had passed in 1971, increasing the rate from $0.13 to $0.18, effective in 1972 (Tobacco Institute, 1996:226).

5. The first Minnesota state law on tobacco sales to and use by minors was enacted in 1913 (Minnesota General Laws of 1913, Chapter 580, H.F. No. 866). The act prohibited both the use of cigarettes by minors as well as the supply of cigarettes and cigarette paper to minors. It also created provisions for the licensing of manufacture and sale of tobacco products. In 1917, a law was passed that decreased the penalty for furnishing cigarettes to minors from a fine, imprisonment, or both to a

fine or imprisonment (Minnesota General Laws of 1917, Chapter 245, No. 916). In 1919, a law was passed that provided a definition of a minor (a person under the age of eighteen), changed the penalty for furnishing tobacco to minors from a fine of $50 to $100 or 15 to 60 days of imprisonment to $25 to $100 or 15 to 90 days of imprisonment, transferred authority for licensing from counties to the state dairy and food commissioner (but allowing for local control, in that granting of licenses was prohibited in cities, villages, and counties that had an ordinance or resolution prohibiting the sale of tobacco; Minnesota General Laws of 1919, Chapter 348, No. 108).

6. Marty was not only a supporter of youth access restrictions, but also efforts to restrict the advertising of tobacco products. He introduced a bill, also in 1991, that would have banned billboard advertising of tobacco products. It, like his vending machine bill, was defeated (i.e., it did not get a hearing) in the Senate Commerce Committee (Wymore, 1991).

7. Between October 1989 and May 1990, thirty-six Minnesota communities passed ordinances restricting sales of cigarettes from vending machines (Forster et al., 1990).

8. ANSR emerged as a key leader of the legislative effort. In the words of one participant, "The actual orchestration of it was housed over at Jeanne [Weigum's] place. . . . So we'd have these meetings, but the housing of it was at another place. And then they'd call everyone to do what they were supposed to do."

9. Some of the advocates expressed ambivalence about this approach: "I have a little bit of a concern in that leaving control at the local level with it sometimes fizzles out so then you have a law that might not work. In a way, see, that might be happening with the vending machine law."

10. This same individual expressed her theory as to why that particular committee, and its chair, had been a continual roadblock for youth access and clean indoor air bills: "[Name deleted] is real tight with the tobacco people. That's as far as my theory goes. . . . And he doesn't like John Marty [the legislator who had sponsored many of these bills, and who had also worked to raise ethical standards for legislators]."

11. In addition to the ingredient disclosure provisions, Governor Carlson criticized the requirement for mandatory compliance checks and the "uneven regulatory environment" created by exempting "smoke shops" from the ban on self-service sales of single cigarette packs (deFiebre, 1997f).

12. Restrictions on self-service sales are based on evidence that youth are reluctant to ask to buy tobacco products that are kept behind a counter, that the more extended interaction between the clerk and the youth results in fewer sales on the part of the clerk (than if the youth simply presents the cigarettes or smokeless tobacco for purchase), and that there is a considerable amount of shoplifting by youth of tobacco on display for self-service (see Forster and Wolfson, 1998:211 for a review).

13. In my fieldwork, I often heard tobacco control advocates mention whether or not a legislator was a smoker. There was not a simple-minded belief that all smokers opposed tobacco control legislation; rather, that smoking status was a factor that could affect a legislator's perspective on the issue. According to Wymore (1991:17), "Public health lobbyists believed that [the chair of the House Health and

Human Services Committee] status as a smoker himself was a chief reason for their lack of success before that committee."

14.   Some participants in the legislative efforts of the movement had come to believe that Phyllis Kahn, the author of the 1975 MCIA, had come to be seen as a one-issue person: "I think she is strong, and I think she's respected, and I think that she's good for us to be using. She's known as tobacco, but that is not bad."

15.   The fact that $0.23 was the highest state excise tax in the nation in 1985 vividly demonstrates how far the movement has come. The highest rate as of December 31, 1998, was $1.00—the rate in both Alaska and Hawaii. Minnesota's rate at that time was $0.48, and the average rate was $0.39 (Fishman et al., 1999).

16.   Ranking the states on their excise taxes on smokeless tobacco is complicated by the fact that states use a number of different bases for calculating these taxes [e.g., a percentage of the wholesale sales price, a percentage of the manufacturer's list price, a percentage of costs, a percentage of factor list price, and an absolute charge (from a fraction of a cent to several cents) per ounce]. In 1998, half the states based their smokeless taxes on a percentage of the wholesale price or wholesale sales price; among these, Minnesota, with a rate of 35% of the wholesale sales price, ranked behind nine states (Washington, Massachusetts, and Alaska with a 75% rate, Oregon with a 65% rate, Maine with a 62% rate, New Jersey with a 48% rate, Vermont with a 41% rate, and Hawaii and Idaho with a 40% rate). Eight states (Georgia, Kentucky, Louisiana, Maryland, Pennsylvania, Virginia, West Virginia, and Wyoming) and the District of Columbia levied no state excise tax on smokeless tobacco in 1998 (Fishman et al., 1999).

17.   Of course, one could argue that in the absence of these increases, the cost of smoking would have dropped rather than remaining essentially the same.

18.   As Malouff and colleagues (1993:132) explain, there are a number of reasons why some employers might have a preference or a policy for hiring nonsmokers. These include evidence that smokers are more prone than nonsmokers to work injuries and disciplinary problems; concern about possible worker compensation claims for lung damage for which smokers would be at greater risk (e.g., fire fighters); a need for physically fit employees in such jobs as police officer and firefighter; concerns about smokers working in positions involving the treatment of addiction, including nicotine addiction; higher health care costs of smokers; a higher rate of using sick leave among smokers; concerns that exposure to toxins, such as asbestos, in the workplace may interact with smoking; and the preferences of some religious groups to hire nonsmokers.

10

Conclusion

This chapter summarizes the findings and arguments of the book and discusses their implications for understanding the tobacco control movement and other social movements. It begins by taking stock of the impact of the movement, including both intended and unintended consequences. It then summarize the findings of the book, including the ways in which the movement has built on the social infrastructure of health professionals and organizations, and the interpenetration of the movement and the state. I argue that the pattern of state-movement interpenetration has some generalizability beyond the tobacco control movement, and that it calls for an new or expanded model of the relationship between states and movements. This relationship suggests some important questions for social movement theory and research, which I categorize as strategic questions (e.g., What are the trade-offs inherent in state-movement interpenetration? How do social movement organizations and state agencies negotiate the constraints associated with such relationships?) and questions asking how and why interpenetration occurs. Finally, I offer some comments on the future of the tobacco control movement, with special reference to the explosion of litigation in recent years, the development and growth of state tobacco control programs, and the issue of tobacco control in developing nations.

THE CONSEQUENCES OF THE MOVEMENT

What can be said about the effects of the tobacco control movement—both in Minnesota and in the nation as a whole?[1] The movement has experienced considerable success in several states, such as Minnesota, California, and Massachusetts. Activist organizations such as ANSR and the Smoke-Free Coalition, the health voluntaries, and health care organizations, often working in concert with the staff of federal, state, and local government agencies, have achieved many of the policy changes they have sought: changes in state laws, local ordinances, law enforcement practices, voluntary merchant compliance, and changes in public opinion and norms. The movement has achieved a number of significant shifts in the policies and practices of nongovernmental organizations. These include voluntary changes in the practices of tobacco merchants, designed to discourage sales of tobacco to underage people. Many business smoke-free policies are implemented on a voluntary basis (Lewit, Botsko, and Shapiro, 1993). In addition, many private-sector organizations with authority over a particular sector have adopted tobacco use policies. For example, adoption of strong standards concerning tobacco use by the Joint Commission on Accreditation of Healthcare Organizations has resulted in almost universal compliance on the part of hospitals in the United States (96% of hospitals in a nationwide survey were in compliance with the Joint Commission's ban on smoking—see Longo, Brownson, and Kruse, 1995).

In addition, a number of the more distal goals of the movement have been achieved. The most notable of these is large reductions in the number of adults who smoke. There has been a marked decline in the overall smoking rate in the United States dating back to the widespread dissemination of scientific evidence on the health effects of smoking through the first Surgeon General Report on Smoking and Health in 1964, followed by a stream of advocacy, policy, and education efforts by the U.S. government, researchers, and nonprofit organizations (see Figure 10.1). Per capita ciga-

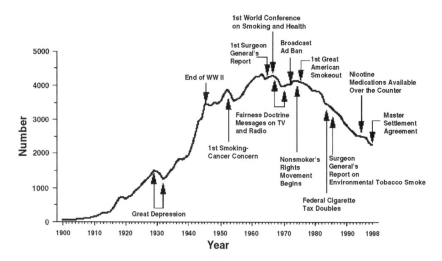

Figure 1.   Annual adult per capita cigarette comsumption and major smoking
     health events — United States, 1900–1998.
Sources: Centers for Disease Control and Prevention, 1999a.

rette consumption in the United States, which had climbed from very low levels at the beginning of the twentieth century—54 cigarettes per capita in 1900—to 4,345 in 1963, began to decline in 1964, the year the Surgeon General's report was released (Giovino et al., 1994). Between 1963 and 1970, per capita consumption dropped 8.3% (from 4,345 to 3,985), followed by a decline of 3.4% between 1970 and 1980 (falling to 3,849), 26.8% between 1980 and 1990 (falling to 2,817), and 19.7% between 1990 and 1998 (to 2,261) (Giovino et al., 1994; CDC, 1999a).[2]

The declines in per capita consumption described above are mirrored in data on the prevalence of tobacco use among adults. In 1965, 42.4% of adults (18 or older) were current smokers, compared to 24.7% in 1997, which represents a 41.7% reduction (Giovino et al., 1994; CDC, 1999a). In addition, cigar smoking and pipe smoking fell dramatically between 1970 and 1991 (national data on cigar and pipe smoking were not collected prior to 1970), although rates of smokeless tobacco use among males actually increased slightly between 1970 and 1991 (Giovino et al., 1994).

By most accounts, the reductions in tobacco use that have coincided with the rise of the modern tobacco control movement beginning in the 1960s have had a dramatic impact on morbidity and mortality associated with tobacco use. Warner (1989) estimated that in the absence of the contemporary antismoking campaign, 91 million Americans would have been smokers in 1985, compared to 56 million who actually were smokers. As a result, an estimated 789,200 smoking-related deaths were prevented or postponed, adding an additional 21 years of life expectancy among this group of people. Warner (1989) further estimated that between 1986 and 2000, decisions not to smoke resulting from tobacco control efforts would result in the avoidance or postponement of 2.1 million deaths.

While the overall trends in tobacco use over the past 35 years have been positive, there are a number of areas of concern. Much to the frustration of tobacco control advocates, there have been minimal declines in adolescent smoking in recent years. According to the Monitoring the Future Study, 36.7% of high school seniors reported smoking in the past 30 days in 1975, dropping to 30.5% in 1980 (Johnston, O'Malley, and Bachman, 1999). However, the prevalence of current smoking by high school seniors hovered around 30% throughout the 1980s, and was 29.4% in 1990. In the early and mid-1990s, the prevalence of smoking in this group *increased,* peaking at 36.5% in 1997. This number has diminished slightly, to 34.6%, in 1999. The prevalence of current smoking also increased among eighth-graders and tenth-graders during the 1990s.[3] Finally, the prevalence of smoking by African-American high school seniors in 1998 and 1999 (14.9%) was at the highest level since 1986, and the prevalence among Hispanic high school seniors in 1999 (27.3%) was at the highest level since 1978 (ibid.).

With respect to smoking by adults, there is continuing frustration about continuing disparities by SES in smoking rates (Escobedo and Peddicord, 1996). While smoking rates declined among adults at all educational levels between 1965 and 1997, the declines were markedly greater among adults (age 25 and older) who had more years of education. Thus, the disparities in smoking rates by education level, which were pronounced in 1966, are even greater in 1997.[4] Moreover, adults at poverty level or below are far more likely to smoke than adults who are not in poverty (CDC, 1999b).

Disparities in smoking rates by racial and ethnic categories have not been eliminated (USDHHS, 1998b). In the late 1970s, American Indians and Alaska Natives had the highest smoking rates of any of the five major race/ethnicity groupings used by the United States government (African-Americans, American Indians/Alaska Natives, Asian Americans/Pacific Islanders, Hispanics, and whites) (ibid.). In the mid-1990s, this was still the case (ibid.). Similarly, African-American adult smoking rates in 1965 slightly exceeded rates of smoking by whites (45.8 and 42.1%, respectively; CDC, 1994d); this was still true in 1997 (26.7% and 25.3%; CDC, 1999b). Finally, as mentioned above, smoking among African-American youth increased dramatically during the 1990s, although 30-day prevalence of smoking in this group remains substantially lower than among white youth (Johnston et al., 1999).

Because national data collection on exposure to secondhand smoke has only taken place during recent years, it is difficult to gauge whether the tobacco control movement over the past 35 years has been accompanied by significant reductions in exposure at the national level. Many evaluations of state and local laws and worksite nonsmoking policies suggest that these polices have been accompanied by reductions in exposure in work settings (Hammond, Sorensen, Youngstrom, and Ockene, 1995; Pierce et al., 1994; Borland et al., 1992). There have been dramatic increases in the number of workers who work in settings covered by smoking restrictions. In 1985, an estimated 38% of workers were employed by firms that had some restriction and 25% were in firms that restricted smoking in all work areas, allowing smoking only in common areas. By 1993, this had increased to 82% of workers being subject to some type of restriction and 67% being subject to immediate work area smoking restrictions (Farrelly, Evans, and Andrew Sfekas, 1999). Thus, it seems likely that there have been dramatic reductions in exposure to secondhand smoke in work settings. However, exposure in the home, among both adults and children, is still common (Mannino et al., 1996; CDC, 1997a; Pirkle et al., 1996).

There are some encouraging results from the national evaluation of the largest-ever federal initiative focused on discouraging tobacco use—ASSIST (discussed in Chapter 7). Per capita cigarette consumption was at equivalent levels within the seventeen ASSIST states (as a group) and in the thirty-two states that were not part of the project from 1989 through 1992 (Manley et al., 1997b).[5] Beginning in 1993 (the year in which the implementation phase of the project began, following a planning/developmental period in 1991 and 1992), the ASSIST states, as a group, began to show lower per capita consumption levels, so that by the beginning of 1996, per capita consumption was about 7% lower in the ASSIST states than in the comparison states (Manley et al., 1997b).

Moreover, there is evidence that the large tobacco control programs funded (in major part) by state excise taxes in California and Massachusetts—in conjunction with the large tax increases by which they are funded—have achieved substantial decreases in tobacco use in these states. For example, in California, initiation of the California Tobacco Control Program in 1989, along with a $0.25 tax increase, dramatically accelerated the rate of decline in per capita cigarette consumption and in the prevalence of smoking (Pierce et al., 1998). An econometric analysis of the reductions in cigarette sales between 1990 and 1992 attributed 22% of the drop to the state's media campaign and 78% to the $0.25 tax increase (Hu et al., 1995). However, after 1993, the declines in per capita consumption slowed dramatically and declines in the prevalence of smoking stopped entirely (Pierce et al., 1998).[6]

In Massachusetts, the downward trend in per capita consumption of cigarettes accelerated after implementation of its excise tax–funded tobacco control program in 1993. Between 1992 and 1997, the state experienced a 31% decline in per capita consumption, compared to a decline of 8% in the other states (excluding California; Abt Associates, 1998).

What about the unintended consequences of the movement? Movement leaders argue that the enemy is "Big Tobacco," not the smoker. They argue that to demonize the smoker is a mistake, both strategically and ethically. However, many of the policies that have resulted from tobacco control advocacy result in stigmatization, if not outright criminalization, of smokers and smoking.

One example is the volume of research that has been produced that seeks to identify the undesirable characteristics and behaviors of smokers (see Chapter 2). For example, published research has reported that smokers, as a group, are in some ways less responsible as parents. One study found that parents who smoke are less likely than nonsmoking parents to attend HMO-sponsored classes for parents of asthmatic children. Moreover, smoking parents were more likely to deny that their child was asthmatic (Fish, Wilson, Latini, and Starr, 1996).

There is a strong movement toward issuing citations to underage persons for possessing or attempting to purchase tobacco products (Wolfson and Hourigan, 1997). While many (but not all) in the movement oppose these practices (see Carol, 1992; Talbot, 1992), they may prove to be a major unintended consequence of the movement (Wolfson and Hourigan, 1997; Forster and Wolfson, 1998). For example, Cismoski and Sheridan (1997) examined youth access enforcement efforts in all Wisconsin cities with populations of 10,000 or greater and a random sample of smaller cities and villages. They found that one or more citations had been issued to businesses for selling tobacco to minors in only 17% of the cities surveyed, while youth had been cited for purchase or possession in 87% of the cities. A similar pattern—relatively low levels of enforcement aimed at merchants, and somewhat higher levels of enforcement aimed at youth—was apparent in most of the fifty states included in a 1997 national survey of enforcement of laws related to youth access to tobacco in over 1,000 cities throughout the United States (Wolfson et al., 1997). Compliance checks had been conducted in a median of 22% of cities in each state; in-store observations in 28%; actions against clerks for selling to minors occurred in 17% and actions against businesses in 10%. Again, actions against youth were more common—youth had been cited minors for purchase, use of false identification to purchase, or possession of tobacco in a median of 38% of cities within each state.

Tobacco control advocates and analysts are divided on the issue of criminalization of tobacco purchase and possession by youth. Some argue that criminalization of possession is a necessary part of any effective strategy to reduce demand (Talbot, 1992). Others argue that criminalization will not be an effective deterrent, will divert resources away from enforcement focused on merchants, will further stigmatize youth who are already at risk, and will have a chilling effect on the use of tobacco purchase attempts ("stings") using youthful confederates by activists or even (in some cases) by law enforcement agencies (Carol, 1992; Mosher, 1995; DiFranza and Godshall, 1996; Wolfson and Hourigan, 1997). In a number of states, it appears that the tobacco industry lobby has actively promoted enforcement aimed at youth (Carol, 1992; Working Group of State Attorneys General, 1994). It is possible that increased attention to youth access to tobacco may inadvertently result in dramatic increases in enforcement against minors for purchase and/or possession of tobacco products.

Public opinion studies and experimental studies indicate that people who smoke are viewed unfavorably in a number of respects (Goldstein, 1991; Malouff and Kenyon, 1991). Nonsmokers have a marked preference for other nonsmokers in work, friendship, and marital relationships (Goldstein, 1991). Many tobacco control strategies are likely to increase the stigma experienced by smokers and smokeless tobacco users—in some cases intentionally, and in others not. Educational efforts targeting children that portray initiation of tobacco use as a foolish and self-destructive choice are an example of a deliberate attempt to stigmatize tobacco use by youth. Clean indoor air rules result in the spatial segregation of smokers (while they are smoking) in airport smoking "lounges" and outside the doors to office buildings, where they are often readily observed and are often the object of pity (especially in Minnesota's frigid winter months) or scorn (see Williams, 1996; Haga, 1996; Winegar, 1993; Sicherman, 1997).

In fact, despite efforts on the part of many in the tobacco control movement to shift blame from people who use tobacco to the tobacco industry, smokers (and smokeless tobacco users) are widely considered to be responsible for their own present and future health problems. In a 1999 Gallup poll of a random sample of United States adults age 18 and older, 24% said that smokers are completely to blame and 31% said that smokers are mostly to blame for "the health problems faced by smokers in this country," compared to 9% who responded that tobacco companies are completely to blame, 21% who said that tobacco companies are mostly to blame, and 13% who said that smokers and tobacco companies are equally to blame (Moore, 1999).[7]

SUMMARY OF FINDINGS

The Social-Infrastructural Base of the Movement

I found that the movement built heavily on a social infrastructure of health organizations and professionals in Minnesota. Like other recent work on social movements, the findings presented in this book underscore the importance of the social "infrastructure" on which movements are built. Building on particular infrastructures—whether communities, organizations, professions, or other collectivities—is both an important strength and a significant weakness of the movement.

As we saw in earlier chapters, the tobacco control movement in Minnesota has benefited greatly from building on the existing infrastructure of health organizations and professionals. The single-issue organizations grew out of existing health organizations with broader purposes: ANSR emerged out of the American Lung Association and the Smoke-Free Coalition grew out of efforts of the state medical society and pulled together many health organizations into a coordinated effort. The health voluntaries—the American Cancer Society, the American Lung Association, and the American Heart Association, have played important roles, although several factors—their dependence on contributions from the public and their tax-exempt, tax-deductible]501(c)(3)] status—have tended to have a conservatizing influence, although this began to change in the latter part of the 1990s. The movement has drawn heavily on health care professionals, and their professional associations—especially physicians—have played an important role. The health care organizations—BCBS, and to a lesser extent Allina and HealthPartners, initially played a backstage role in the movement, but have increasingly come to prominence, as evidenced by the landmark suit against the tobacco industry undertaken jointly by BCBS and the Minnesota Attorney GeneralAG. The growing involvement of these organizations is important, in that they have a substantial presence at the state capitol and they appear to be less constrained then the voluntaries in their willingness to lobby.

Thus, building on the "infrastructure" of health organizations and health professionals has enabled the tobacco control movement to obtain the resources needed to carry out collective action, including labor, money, organization, and expertise. As we have seen in earlier chapters, there are some important trade-offs associated with the use of this infrastructure—such as limiting the range and scope of strategies and tactics. Moreover, it is possible to imagine—or in some cases, observe—situations in which there are direct contradictions in the interests of tobacco control advocates and health organizations. Looking at tobacco control efforts in other states, there are examples of splits between elements of the health system—such as organized medicine and health insurance—and tobacco control. In the 1988 campaign to pass the California tobacco tax initiative (Proposition 99) in California, differences in the interests and priorities of the health care industry—the California Association of Hospital and Health Systems (CAHHS) and the California Medical Association (CMA) in particular—and public health and tobacco control groups were apparent (Traynor and Glantz, 1996). The CAHHS and the CMA were primarily interested in generating funds for medical care, while the public health and tobacco control groups were concerned with the deterrent effect of the tax increase on smoking and generating revenues for tobacco education and prevention programs (ibid.). The CMA, which had provided some financial resources for the campaign, backed off in its support, in part because of concern about the potential political fallout from taking on a political battle with the tobacco industry (ibid.).[8] Moreover, the CMA, CAHHS, and the tobacco industry have successfully advocated to redirect funds generated by Proposition 99 from tobacco use prevention and education efforts to support for the delivery of medical services (Begay, Traynor, and Glantz, 1993; Traynor and Glantz, 1996). Finally, as we saw in Chapter 6, health insurers in some states have had close financial ties with the tobacco industry, as well as sharing lobbyists in some cases (Boyd et al., 1995; Goldstein and Bearman, 1996; Pallarito, 1993).

Despite these caveats, building on the health infrastructure, as well as collaborating with elements of government, has enabled the movement to grow rapidly and achieve a number of significant successes. My analysis suggests that the infrastructure of health organizations and professions is a fertile ground for the growth of movements that are consistent with the self definitions, economic interests, and ideologies of these groups. For example, health organizations and professionals are increasingly claiming the antiviolence movement as their "turf" (e.g., Winnett, 1998; Koop and Lundberg, 1992; American Medical Association, 1989).[9] For example, a 1998 national survey of local organizations involved in gun control issues at the state and local level found that over half (56%) of the 256 organizations could be classified as health organizations (e.g., firearm violence prevention groups, local chapters of the American Academy of Pediatrics, and state medical societies);[10] the remaining groups were classified as social action organizations (21%), law enforcement organizations (12%), and education organizations (11%) (calculated from Zakocs, Earp, and Runyan, 2000:Table 1).

Based on my analysis of the tobacco control movement, this would probably lead to rapid growth of a credible, expert, professionalized movement. But it would lack a true grassroots component, and would be limited in its definition of the problem and solutions. [The 2000 Million Mom march on Washington suggests that this movement is developing a potentially strong and active grassroots component.]

State-Movement Interpenetration

As we have seen, subdivisions of the state—federal agencies like NCI and the CDC, state health departments, some state attorneys general, as well as selected legislators and local officials—have played central roles in the movement. Federal and state agencies have engaged in a number of efforts to promote tobacco control efforts, including funding and disseminating scientific research; providing training and technical assistance in how to conduct tobacco control advocacy efforts; and providing direct funding of such efforts, such as in the NCI ASSIST program. Moreover, we have seen that government organizations and officials often have a close, collaborative relationship with activists from tobacco control social movement organizations. Examples include the collaboration between a state legislator and ANSR in promoting passage of the Minnesota Clean Indoor Air Act in the early 1970s, the collaboration between MDH and ANSR in promoting passage of the Omnibus Nonsmoking and Disease Prevention Act of 1985; the role of MDH in the Smoke-Free Coalition-2000, and MDH's work with ACS, ANSR, and the coalition to promote community action on tobacco control (particularly youth access to tobacco) as part of the ASSIST project.

As I will argue below, the case materials presented in this book suggest a new model of social movements and the state: state/movement interpenetration. As I will discuss, this characterization has some generalizability to tobacco control efforts in other states and nations, and to other social movements.

SOCIAL MOVEMENTS AND THE STATE: A NEW MODEL?

I have argued that three images of the state dominate analyses of social movements: (1) the state as a target, (2) the state as a provider of constraints and opportunities, and (3) the state as a facilitator or sponsor. At least in the case of the tobacco control movement, as represented in this case study of the movement in Minnesota, these images are incomplete at best.

The first image—state as target—obviously captures an aspect of the state-movement relationship in tobacco control. We have seen that the movement in Minnesota has targeted the state legislature, city councils, and state bureaucracies to achieve changes in policy, and the enforcement of policy, in such areas as tobacco taxes, clean indoor air, and youth access to tobacco. But, we have also seen that the state is not just a target, but also a key actor in the movement. Subdivisions of the state are often active participants—even collaborators, and sometimes instigators—in the movement's efforts to obtain desired changes in public policy. In the early 1970s, a maverick state legislator with an interest in clean indoor air enlisted the assistance of the fledgling grassroots organization ANSR to work together in pursuing the landmark Minnesota Clean Indoor Air Act of 1975 (see Chapter 3). In the mid-1980s, officials at the Minnesota Department of Health (MDH) enlisted the help of—again—ANSR in gaining passage of the Omnibus Nonsmoking and Disease Prevention Act of 1985 (see Chapters 3 and 9). MDH has for years been represented on the board of the Minnesota Smoke-Free Coalition-2000 (see Chapter 4), and has consistently been involved in planning the legislative strategy of the coalition (see Chapters 4 and 9). And, with the onset of ASSIST, MDH worked closely with ACS, ANSR, and the coalition to galvanize community action on tobacco control (particularly youth access to tobacco) throughout the ASSIST intervention region of the state (see Chapter 7). The depiction of "the state" as a passive target, separate from the movement, is misleading.

The state as a system or systems of constraints and opportunities faced by the movement is certainly an important element in thinking about the state-movement relationship we have seen in this account of tobacco control in Minnesota. The ways in which the federal and state governments regulate nonprofit organizations has an important bearing on the strategic and tactical choices by organizations such as ACS, AHA, ALA, the Smoke-Free Coalition, and ANSR, all of which need to be concerned about not violating restrictions on lobbying that would jeopardize their ability to receive tax deductible contributions [i.e., their 501 (c)(3) status] and complying with state lobbying regulations (e.g., rules covering registration of lobbyists and reporting of lobbying activity). The degree of openness of the U.S. political system in general, and Minnesota state government in particular, is obviously a key element in the shape and trajectory of the movement in Minnesota. But, again, the image is incomplete, in that it does not capture the active, integral role of elements of the state in the movement.

Finally, the image of the state as a facilitator or repressor of movements is probably the closest to the concept of interpenetration that I am proposing. It accurately reflects—in this case—the manifold indirect and direct efforts of federal and state agencies to promote tobacco control efforts, including funding, publication, and dissemination of scientific research; training and technical assistance in how to conduct tobacco control advocacy efforts; and direct funding of such efforts (see Chapter 7). My objection, however, is that it is an incomplete, and in some ways misleading, image of the state-movement relationship, at least as observed in this movement (the generalizability of the Minnesota case study of tobacco control will be discussed below). "Facilitation"[11] inaccurately connotes both unidirectionality and a fairly narrowly defined role, neither of which is reflected in the case materials presented in this book.

Thus, I have chosen the term "interpenetration" to label the state-movement relationship described in this book (below I will explore the extent to which this conceptualization is applicable to other movements as well). The term "interpenetration" is bidirectional, reflecting my observation that the state and movement organizations have a symbiotic relationship that involves both mutual influence and mutual benefit. As explained above, accounts that focus on state "facilitation" of movements stress the way that state support affects the movement (with some authors emphasizing the positive and some emphasizing the negative sequelae of state support—see McCarthy and Zald, 1973, 1977; McAdam, 1982; Jenkins and Eckert, 1986; Helfgot, 1974; Piven and Cloward, 1977). On the other hand, McCarthy and Wolfson (1992) introduce the concept of movement "co-optation" of elements of the state. The idea of co-optation, which they define as "using group resources for purposes *other than those for which they were originally created*" [ibid.:282 (emphasis in the original)], also suggests unidirectionality—focusing on the movement acting upon the state. Moreover, the idea of co-optation suggests that the goals of movement organizations and state agencies are necessarily disparate. In fact, as I will argue below, an important part of the basis of state-movement interpenetration is overlapping interests of movement and state organizations.

In addition to being bidirectional, the term "interpenetration" encompasses the range of interactions between the state and movement organizations we have observed in the tobacco control movement in Minnesota. These include close collaboration in planning and implementing efforts to influence state legislation (e.g., the Minnesota Clean Indoor Air Act of 1975, the Omnibus Nonsmoking and Disease Prevention Act of 1985, and a variety of tobacco control bills—some of which passed, and some of which did not—aimed at reducing youth access to tobacco, reducing exposure to secondhand smoke, and increasing the state excise tax on tobacco products). They also include many local efforts, in which supportive local officials (sometimes mayors, sometimes council persons) worked closely with movement organizations (such as ANSR) toward passage of local youth access ordinances. In the ASSIST project, MDH worked closely with state-level movement organizations, and funded regional and local units of government to foster local-level tobacco control advocacy efforts (see Chapters 7 and 9). Finally, they include joint efforts to enforce existing laws and regulations, such as the division of labor between ANSR and MDH in enforcing the Minnesota Clean Indoor Air Act (described in Chapter 3).

The phenomenon of state-movement interpenetration—which has been underconceptualized in the social movements literature[12]—has been considered more extensively in theory and research on nonprofit organizations.[13] In fact, analysts of the "third" (nonprofit) sector have coined a variety of terms to characterize the extensive (and increasing) ties between government and the nonprofit sector, including "The Shadow State" (Wolch, 1990), "Third Party Federalism" and "Nonprofit Federalism" (Anton, 1989), and "Nonprofits for Hire" (Smith and Lipsky, 1993). As explained below, this literature offers some important insights that may help us begin to unravel the causes and consequences of state-movement interpenetration.

The origins, extent, and consequences of the ties between governments and nonprofits have been discussed in the nonprofits literature. Historically, government agencies have enlisted nonprofits as a means of extending the reach of government (Anton, 1989; Smith and Lipsky, 1993; Salamon, 1995; Wolch, 1990).[14] This has been especially important in historical periods in which government services are rapidly expanding in size and scope (Anton, 1989). In addition, analysts have argued that government often turns to nonprofits because these organizations are in some instances better suited then government agencies to provide services, depending on the service in question and the characteristics of the consumers or clients to whom it is being delivered (Kramer, 1987). Finally, the move toward privatizing services (by contracting with both nonprofits and businesses) over the past twenty or so years is rooted in the desire to reduce costs and reduce the size and scope of government (Rekart, 1993; Smith and Lipsky, 1993).

Many authors have noted the long-term historical trend of increasing levels of government funding of the nonprofit sector in the United States and other countries (Salamon and Anheier, 1996; Rekart, 1993). A number of significant concerns have been raised about this trend—concerns that in many instances mirror issues I raise concerning state-movement interpenetration in this book. The unifying theme of this literature is that there are significant costs—for individual nonprofits, the nonprofit sector, and society as a whole—associated with increasing reliance of nonprofits on government funding. For example, Wolch and Rocha argue that:

> Government penetration into the planning practices of state-supported voluntary groups via grant funding and contracting ties, oversight requirements, and political pressure appears to have deepened and could impair the sector's ability to plan for an autonomous future (Dawes and Saidel, 1988; Lipsky and Smith, 1989; Stone, 1989; Gray, 1991). There are several possible dimensions of this scenario of reduced autonomy. First, the state is forcing voluntary groups to plan reactively in response to government policies and priorities, which may create incentives and pressures for groups to be conservative and cautious rather than innovative and system challenging (Helfgot, 1981; Wolch, 1990). Second, contracts and grants increasingly come with requirements for stringent, rigid, and quantitatively oriented approaches to evaluation and monitoring, which may discount the value-orientation of voluntary recipients and undervalue their qualitative achievements (Lipsky and Smith, 1989; Gronbjerg, 1990). Third, those organizations unable to meet the expanding demands for planning may become increasingly marginalized and unable to secure public funding, thus curbing the rise of antiestablishment social movements (Leat, 1990). Fourth, newly formed groups may be jeopardized by new government funding programs as they are lured into whatever program is offered even if it is not in accord with group goals (Dawes and Saidel, 1988). Fifth, there may be little room for voluntary sector development and new initiatives, leading to voluntary sector stagnation and loss of innovatory capacities (Powell and Friedkin, 1987; Jackson, 1983). (1993:389–90)

Many of the themes raised in the literature on the nonprofit-government relationship are relevant to theory and research on state-movement interpenetration. However, before examining this further, it is important to assess the generalizability of the pattern of state-movement interaction documented in this book.

Generalizability: Is State-Movement Interpenetration Atypical?

How generalizable is the pattern of state-movement portrayed in this book? Within the tobacco control movement, does it fit other states besides Minnesota? What about the tobacco control movement in other nation-states? Finally, is the tobacco control movement idiosyncratic with respect to state/movement interpenetration, or are there other movements that fit the description of interpenetration? If so, how common is state-movement interpenetration? And, how do the extent and form of interpenetration vary across historical periods, nation-states and their subdivisions, and movements? Obviously, these questions are important avenues for future research, and a detailed treatment is beyond the scope of the current volume. However, I offer a few examples of such movements to provide tentative support for the claim that state-movement interpenetration is a phenomenon of some generality.

First, to what extent is state–tobacco control movement interpenetration a national phenomenon? As argued in Chapter 7 and elsewhere in this book, federal agencies, including NCI and CDC, have been extremely active players in the movement, by sponsoring and disseminating research and providing funding for state and local tobacco control advocacy efforts. Moreover, the national ASSIST program can be seen as a vehicle for interjecting state health departments in the ASSIST states into a central role in state tobacco control networks.[15]

Finally, Table 10.1 presents data from my 1996 survey of 641 nonprofit and governmental organizations involved in tobacco control efforts in all 50 states [see Wolfson (1997) for details on how organizations were identified and survey procedures]. The responses of the organizations in each state were aggregated to create measures of the size of the network of organizations and level of government-movement interpenetration within the network of organizations involved in tobacco control efforts in the state. Table 10.1 presents descriptive statistics on the size and extent of government penetration of state tobacco control networks. The state organizational networks vary dramatically in size and resources. The distribution, however, is quite skewed: while a handful of states have very large and resource-intense networks, most states have a small number of organizations (the median is five[16]), paid staff (median of twelve full-time employees), and tobacco control budget (median of about $342,000).[17]

Turning to the measures of state-movement interpenetration, we again see considerable variation across the states, as indexed by the range and standard deviation. However, most of the networks were composed primarily of nonprofit organizations (median of 85%), with tobacco control volunteers and budgets largely concentrated in these organizations (medians of 82.5 and 78%, respectively). Consistent with this pattern, a median of 18% of organizations reported reliance on government funds for their tobacco control budgets (i.e., over 75% of funds used to support tobacco control efforts). The proportion engaging in joint advocacy with the health department showed the highest values (mean and median of about 78%) and the smallest amount of variation of any of the measures of interpenetration (s.d. = .188), with at least one-third of the surveyed organizations in each state reported doing so. Thus, joint advocacy between movement organizations and government agencies on tobacco control issues is a common occurrence in the states, suggesting that the pattern observed in Minnesota has some generalizability.[18]

To what extent does the pattern of state-movement interpenetration with respect to tobacco control efforts observed in the United States hold across nations? Comparative analyses are needed to address this question.

Table 10.1 **Measures of the Size and Extent of Interpenetration of State Tobacco Control Networks**

Variable	Range	Mean	Median	Standard Deviation
Measures of Network Size				
Number of organizations	2–93	12.26	5	17.30
FTEs	1–820	77.74	12	162.25
Tobacco control expenditures (in dollars)	500–11.16M	843,570	341,961	1.81M
Measures of Interpenetration				
Proportion nonprofits	0–1	.778	.847	.259
Proportion of volunteers in nonprofits	0–1	.825	.990	.294
Proportion of tobacco control budget in nonprofits	0–1	.778	.989	.324
Proportion relying on government funds	0–.860	.253	.183	.280
Proportion relying on state health department information	.200–1	.643	.623	.242
Proportion engaging in joint advocacy with state health department	.333–1	.775	.785	.188

It is probably helpful to decompose the question into three separate questions: (1) How involved is the state in tobacco control efforts? (2) To what extent are private-sector social movement organizations involved in tobacco control efforts? (3) To what extent do state agencies and these private sector organizations collaborate in these efforts?

In most industrialized countries, the national government appears to have a strong interest in tobacco control efforts as a result of the economic burden stemming from tobacco use (Jha and Chaloupka, 1999). As a group, the developed countries have much higher rates of cigarette consumption per capita than developing countries (WHO, 1997).[19] Moreover, these countries—including the United States—are experiencing the burden of death and disability from increases in smoking that took place many years ago, since there is a long "latency" period between the onset of smoking and development of life-threatening diseases, such as heart disease and lung cancer (Jha and Chaloupka, 1999:23–24). The developed countries have experienced the "epidemiologic transition"—so the majority of the population lives long enough to experience chronic diseases, including those caused by smoking, such as emphysema, lung cancer, and heart disease (Marshall, 1991). Finally, government covers a far greater share of health care costs in industrialized, high-income countries than in countries in the developing world (Frenk and Donabedian, 1987; World Health Organization, 2000a). Thus, these countries have clear economic and public health interests in controlling levels of smoking and other tobacco use.

Of course, there is variation even among this group of nations. Six of the OECD high-income countries (the United States, Greece, Italy, Canada, Japan, and Spain) are among the top thirty raw-tobacco-producing countries in the world (Jha and Chaloupka, 1999:Table 5.1).[20] Thus, it might be expected that organized tobacco farming interests may be a countervailing force that serves to limit the degree to which the state pursues strong controls on tobacco use. As discussed in Chapter 8, this has often been the case in the United States However, several factors may limit the degree to which tobacco production impinges on these states' interests in tobacco control. First, tobacco export revenues represent only a small share of total exports in these countries.[21] Second, tobacco control efforts affecting domestic consumption will have relatively little impact on tobacco growing economies that are based largely on exports, as is the case in Italy (which exports 79% of its crop), Greece (75%), and, to a lesser extent, Spain (54%) (ibid.).[22]

Manufacturing of cigarettes and other tobacco products, as well as wholesaling and retailing, also contribute to the economies of many of the wealthy nations (Warner, 1993; Warner and Fulton, 1995). For example, three of the top five countries in cigarette manufacturing (measured by number of cigarettes produced) in 1994 were OECD countries: the United States, Japan, and Germany (WHO, 1997). The United Kingdom, Korea, The Netherlands, Spain, Canada, and Italy, and several other OECD countries also have sizable cigarette manufacturing industries (ibid.).[23] Because cigarette manufacturing is highly mechanized in these countries, it contributes a relatively small number of jobs (Jha and Chaloupka, 1999; WHO, 1997).[24] In fact, in the United States and other OECD countries, there are typically more jobs in retailing than in manufacture of tobacco products (Warner, 1993).

Warner (Warner et al., 1996; Warner and Fulton, 1995) and others (Jha and Chaloupka, 1999) have documented the tobacco industry's strategy, both in the United States and abroad, of arguing that controls on tobacco, by reducing consumption, would adversely affect the national economy by adversely affecting the number of jobs and tax revenues. As these analysts have pointed out, the arguments made by the tobacco industry are based on the flawed premise that money not spent on tobacco will not be spent on other goods and services (Warner et al., 1996; Warner and Fulton, 1995; Jha and Chaloupka, 1999). Analyses that assume that money not spent on tobacco products will be spent on other goods and services lead to dramatically different results than the tobacco industry–sponsored studies. For example, Warner and colleagues (1996) estimated that "intensified tobacco control activities" leading to a doubling of the historical 2.06% average rate of decline in purchases in tobacco products beginning in 1993 would result in loss of 222,248 jobs in the "Southeast Tobacco region" (North Carolina, Kentucky, South Carolina, Virginia, Tennessee, and Georgia) by the year 2000. However, they estimate that the other regions of the United States would see an increase of 355,248 jobs during this period. Thus, they estimate a net increase of 133,000 jobs for the United States as a whole, as resources are shifted from the tobacco industry to other industries with greater labor intensity (Warner et al., 1996).[25]

Governments depend on revenues from taxes on tobacco products, which may also constrain the willingness of policymakers to actively pursue tobacco control (as we saw in Chapter 1, this phenomenon can be dated back at least as far as King James I of England). However, two factors may help alleviate concerns about loss of tobacco tax revenues. First, recent estimates from the United States and elsewhere indicate that the tobacco-related health care costs borne by government exceed by a considerable margin revenues from tobacco taxes.[26] In addition, evidence from the United Kingdom and Canada, as well as several U.S. states, suggests that one of the key tobacco control strategies available to governments— increases in tax rates—results, in the short to medium term, in both increases in revenues and reductions in tobacco use (because the demand for tobacco products is relatively inelastic, the amount realized from increased taxes exceeds the amount lost because of reduced consumption; Jha and Chaloupka, 1999).

Of course, there are a number of factors that complicate any analysis of the interests of nation-states in tobacco control. For example, the relationship between government and the tobacco manufacturing industry varies among the OECD nations. In Portugal and Spain, the state owns the major cigarette manufacturer (WHO, 1997). In Japan, the finance ministry owns all of the stock of a private, international tobacco company. In other countries, the tobacco manufacturers are private companies, although the political power of these companies, as well as the receptivity of nation-states to corporate interests, varies widely.

The definition of government interests in tobacco control is being actively contested. The tobacco industry, as described above, marshals its considerable resources to convince the public and policymakers that a healthy tobacco industry is in the best interest of the state. Health advocates argue, with increasing success in recent years, that tobacco use imposes a huge economic and public health burden on government and on the public as a whole. As noted by political sociologists and others, states vary in their capacity to recognize and act on their interests.

There has not been a great deal of research on the extent to which the tobacco control efforts of governments and social movement actors are intertwined in the developed nations. An analysis by Kagan and Vogel (1993) suggests that tobacco control efforts in France are largely the province of the state, while a movement located in civil society plays a more balanced role in Canada.[27]

Interestingly, accounts of state/movement interaction in other Western countries often raise the issue of constraints that we have seen in the Minnesota movement. For example, in Sweden in 1988:

> [A] governmental Committee—the third of its kind—was again appointed. It was instructed to look closely into the issue of tobacco control legislation. The tobacco industry was very disturbed over this new Committee and tried to influence its work. For example, an attempt was made to get rid of two civil servants whom the industry knew to be committed tobacco control advocates, from the Committee. The attempt failed, but it taught us that civil servants cannot personally campaign as actively as others (e.g. doctors). This influenced our future strategy. (Nordgren and Haglund, 1995:973)

The picture in developing countries is likely to be quite different, because of different state interests and a different role of civil societies. In a handful of these countries, tobacco growing and/or cigarette production is a major contributor to the overall economy. For example, China—by a considerable margin—grows more tobacco, makes more cigarettes, and consumes more tobacco than any other country in the world (WHO, 1997). The state monopoly, the China National Tobacco Corporation, provides employment for 10 million farmers, 3 million retailers, and over 500,000 workers in manufacturing. Tobacco taxes in 1992 represented about 10% of China's annual tax income (ibid.). After China and the United States, the top tobacco-growing countries are India, Brazil, Turkey, and Zimbabwe (ibid.). Tobacco growing represents a significant segment of these countries' economies.[28] Moreover, tobacco manufacturing contributes from 2.5 to 8% of jobs in several low- and middle-income countries, including Indonesia, Turkey, Bangladesh, Egypt, the Philippines, and Thailand (Jha and Chaloupka, 1999). The *kretek* (cigarettes made of a clove/tobacco mixture) industry is the second leading employer in Indonesia, after the Indonesian government (WHO, 1997).

Even in countries that lack a major domestic tobacco farming or manufacturing industry, retail sales of cigarettes may be viewed as making an important contribution to the economy and to tax revenues. Developing countries are viewed as major untapped markets by the transnational tobacco companies, especially as smoking declines in the United States and other developed countries (Mackay, 1994a). The transnationals exert considerable pressure on developing countries to open up their markets, allow aggressive marketing campaigns, and minimize regulation of cigarette sales and marketing (Warner and Fulton, 1995; Mackay, 1994a).[29] The dilemmas faced by developing countries with respect to tobacco control have been noted by several authors. The threat of epidemic levels of to-bacco-related diseases several decades in the future often is less compelling than the immediate revenues from taxes, generation of jobs, and more pressing public health problems, such as infant mortality and infectious disease (including, in many countries, epidemic levels of AIDS; Stebbins, 1991; Chapman, Yach, Aloojee, and Simpson, 1994; Mackay, 1994a, Warner and Fulton, 1995; Jha and Chaloupka, 1999). In recent years, there have been efforts on the part of the international public health community to influence developing countries to adopt a strong posture on tobacco control issues. In particular, there have been efforts to (1) demonstrate the fallacies and exaggerations inherent in tobacco industry arguments concerning the domestic economic benefits of tobacco farming, production, and marketing (Warner and Fulton, 1995); (2) publicize the magnitude of the health care costs that these countries can expect to experience if levels of tobacco use increase sharply (Warner et al., 1999);[30] and (3) identify more immediate benefits of tobacco control efforts, such as generation of tax revenues and preventing deforestation, which is associated with flue curing of tobacco in tobacco-growing countries (Chapman et al., 1994; Mackay, 1994a; Geist, 1999).

As a consequence of heavy dependence on the economic contribution of tobacco in some developing countries, the national government is often loathe to take a strong stand in favor of tobacco control efforts. For example, in Indonesia, in which the tobacco industry is (as noted above) the second largest employer, the health minister in 1996 indicated that "the government had no intention of trying to regulate smoking through legislation" [Anonymous, 1996c (quoted in Reynolds, 1999)]. As a result, the national governments in these countries are more likely to actively repress social movements aimed at tobacco control, or at most tolerate them, rather than engage in active, collaborative efforts with tobacco control advocacy organizations. For example, in Indonesia, "If NGO's [nongovernmental organizations] get too verbal, they get warned that tobacco industries are vital to the nation's development" [Schwarz, 1990 (quoted in Reynolds, 1999)].

In developing countries in which tobacco growing and manufacturing play a relatively minor role in the economy, the state may be much more likely to actively pursue tobacco control efforts. Moreover, there is some evidence that a kind of state-movement interpenetration may come into being. Marshall (1991) documents the interplay in Papua New Guinea (PNG) of government agencies (the Institute of Medical Research, the Ministry of Health, and University of Papua New Guinea) and the PNG Medical Society and its National Anti-Smoking Committee in advocating over a number of years for tobacco control measures. After a number of twists and turns, the Tobacco Products (Health Control) Act of 1987 was passed, which provided the state with authority to regulate tobacco marketing and use.

Research is needed to determine how typical this pattern is. Of course, the nonprofit sector is underdeveloped, and often severely constrained by the state, in many developing countries (Wuthnow, 1991). Writing in the early 1990s, Marshall argues that "[a]nti-smoking groups have only gained significant political clout in developed countries during the 1980s, and there is still a woeful lack of such groups in most of the Third World, including Oceania" (1991:1337). Similarly, Mackay described the situation in Laos in the early 1990s as follows: "As in many developing countries, awareness of the harmfulness of tobacco has evolved very recently, and up to now there has been no national policy on tobacco" (1994b:10). Nevertheless, accounts have emerged of private-sector tobacco control organizations in developing countries ranging from Senegal [the Federation of NGOs and CBOs (community-based organizations) Fighting Against Tobacco (White, 1999)], to Ladakh [Ladakh Action on Smoking and Health (Ball, 1995)],[31] to Peru [Comision Nacional Permanente de Lucha Antitabaquica (Ashton, 1997)].

Looking beyond the tobacco control movement, are there other social movements in which the relationship between the movement and the state may be accurately characterized as interpenetration? In fact, it appears that a number of movements related to public health reflect this pattern, at least in part. Examples include movements focusing on drinking and driving (McCarthy and Wolfson, 1992) and alcohol control more generally (Bandow, 1995), traffic safety, and violence. For example, McCarthy and Wolfson (1992) and others have noted the close relationship between the National Highway Traffic Safety Administration (NHTSA; part of the U.S. Department of Transportation) and the movement against drinking and driving. In the late 1970s, NHTSA provided seed money to replicate the original California chapters of Mothers Against Drunk Driving (MADD; nee Mothers Against Drunk Drivers) in other states (ibid.). In addition, state and local police departments often formed alliances with state and local MADD and RID (Remove Intoxicated Drivers) chapters (ibid.). As in the tobacco control movement, these collaborations were based on overlapping interests of state and movement actors. NHTSA and many state and local law enforcement agencies had a strong interest in generating community support for policy and enforcement efforts to counter drinking and driving in states and local communities. However, government agencies such as these have limited means of generating community support for such efforts. Thus, citizens' organizations, such as MADD and RID, could be enlisted as key allies to build community support for stepped-up enforcement efforts and a more focused prosecutorial and judicial response to the problem of drinking and driving. Similarly, the citizens' organizations could benefit from a close relationship with law enforcement agencies, which were empowered to carry out law enforcement efforts and could be important allies in advocating for policies and practices demonstrating a more consistent criminal justice system response to the problem of drinking and driving.

More generally, it could be argued that alcohol control may be characterized as a state-penetrated movement. As in the case of tobacco control, advocacy efforts to reduce the harm associated with alcohol use in the United States flow from interconnecting networks of government agencies, health organizations, advocacy organizations, and researchers (Lewis, 1982; Gusfield, 1982; Mott, 1991; Bandow, 1995; Jernigan and Wright, 1996). Mirroring the experience of the tobacco control movement, state involvement in this movement has drawn the fire of the targeted industry (Mott, 1991; Bandow, 1995).

In addition, community crime prevention appears to represent an arena in which there are manifold interconnections between federal, state, and local government agencies and organized groups of citizens advocating for change (U.S. Department of Justice, 1996). In the late 1990s, the Bureau of Justice Assistance (part of the U.S. Department of Justice) funded a number of "community mobilization" efforts under its Edward Byrne Memorial State and Local Law Enforcement Assistance Discretionary Grant Program. These included a $3 million award to the National Crime Prevention Council to conduct "technical assistance and training workshops that reach thousands of local activists" and to produce and disseminate "an array of crime and drug abuse prevention support materials, including publications, action kits, and videos" (U.S. Department of Justice, 1997:3).

Finally, the contemporary violence prevention movement has many of the hallmarks of state-movement interpenetration. At the federal level, the Centers for Disease Control and Prevention play a central role in these efforts (although a role that is constrained in important ways, as we shall see shortly). At the state and local level, a number of government agencies play a prominent role—and one that frequently involves close collaboration with nongovernmental activist organizations. As in the tobacco control movement, some state attorneys general have emerged as prominent leaders in efforts to regulate firearms as consumer products (Anonymous, 1996b). In addition, some local health departments have gotten actively involved in violence prevention activities, including, in some cases, advocacy for changes in public policy to help prevent firearm injuries (Price and Oden, 1999).[32]

It is clear that government agencies have found it useful to sponsor and collaborate in advocacy by citizens and by nongovernmental organizations in a variety of programmatic areas, including amelioration of social problems associated with poverty, mistreatment of youth by educational, criminal justice, and social service agencies; and prevention of alcohol, tobacco, and drug abuse.[33] Moreover, movement actors have found these alliances useful as well. Consistent with my case study of tobacco control, a number of these accounts reveal the double-edged nature of state involvement in movements: access to a wide variety of resources (including expertise, money, legitimacy, and influence) is counterbalanced by constraints on the selection of goals, strategies, and tactics (Morgen, 1986; Cain, 1995; Epstein, 1996; Crumpton, 1997; Morrill and McKee, 1993).

QUESTIONS FOR SOCIAL MOVEMENT THEORY AND RESEARCH

Finally, the analysis presented here raises a number of questions for social movement theory and research.

Political/Strategic Questions

A critical examination of interpenetration from a strategic perspective is called for. The intertwining of movement and government actors may provide substantial benefits to movements, especially with respect to resource acquisition. However, government financial, political, and technical support may impose a number of important constraints on advocacy organizations and networks.

The foremost of these constraints is formal restrictions on lobbying. The ability of public agencies to lobby is severely circumscribed. And, as mentioned earlier, nonprofits are prohibited from federal-and state-level lobbying using federal funds. Although organizations with ASSIST funds are permitted to engage in local-level lobbying, the passage of the Federal Acquisition Streamlining Act of 1994 (which is further discussed below) means that future efforts to use federal funds to catalyze local activism will be severely hampered by a prohibition against local-level lobbying by federal contractors.

Other constraints apply mainly to units of government that are involved in tobacco control advocacy efforts. One example is vulnerability to information requests under the federal Freedom of Information Act (FOIA) and state public records acts. Tobacco industry representatives have extensively used these laws to request information on the tobacco control activities of state and local government units. We saw one of example of this in Chapter 7, where retailers and grocers allied with the tobacco industry submitted extensive, time-consuming requests for information from MDH and ASSIST contractors. Another example is provided by Aguinaga and Glantz's (1995) analysis of the tobacco industry's use of this tactic in California. Between January 1991 and December 1993, the tobacco control section of the California Department of Health Services was subjected to 59 requests, for a total of 371 documents. Similarly, local health departments in California, which receive funding under California's state-funded (Proposition 99) tobacco control program, received requests for hundreds of documents under the California Public Records Act. In addition, CDC's Office on Smoking and Health, the National Cancer Institute, and several of the seventeen state health departments that received federal funding under the ASSIST program were the targets of industry requests for information under FOIA or state data practices acts (ibid.). According to Aguinaga and Glantz, these requests are used to create an environment in which staff have to worry about industry lawsuits, to divert resources from carrying out programs to responding to these requests, and to provide ammunition for industry efforts to discredit government-funded tobacco control activities. A movement in which a significant fraction of organizations is subject to such disclosure requirements—as well as the burden in time and effort to respond to such requests—may be handicapped in significant ways.

The central role of the state in the tobacco control movement also raises questions about the breadth of the tactical repertoire. A number of authors have noted the importance of tactical diversity in movements (Tilly, 1978; McAdam, 1983; Morris, 1993). A high level of state-movement interpenetration may narrow the range of tactics in use in a couple of ways.

First, it may discourage the use of "radical" or "unruly" tactics, such as protest and boycotts (Jenkins and Eckert, 1986). As we have seen in previous chapters, such tactics did not play a central role in tobacco control efforts in Minnesota. Similarly, my 1996 survey of nonprofit and government organizations involved in tobacco control efforts in all fifty states (Wolfson, 1997) found that protest only 21% of responding organizations reported involvement in a protest related to their tobacco control efforts in the year preceding the survey. Research on a variety of social movements suggests that, under some circumstances, protest and similar tactics can be quite effective, either in obtaining "concessions" from authorities (Gamson, 1990; Schumaker, 1978; Piven and Cloward, 1977; McAdam, 1983; Morris, 1993) or in legitimating more "mainstream" organizations in the movement (Gamson, 1990; Jenkins and Eckert, 1986; Haines, 1988).

Second, a high level of state-movement interpenetration may facilitate the institutionalization of a limited number of approaches to collective action. For example, government agencies have played a significant role in the diffusion of "compliance checks" (tobacco purchase attempts by youth working in concert with activists or authorities to document the ready availability of tobacco products to minors through commercial sources in some political unit, such as a city or state, or to enforce tobacco age-of-sale laws; Forster and Wolfson, 1998).[34] Because opponents or targets of social movements are often able to develop ways to counteract the previously successful tactics of advocacy organizations, it is important for these organizations to continually develop new tactics as old tactics become obsolete (McAdam, 1983).[35]

Beyond the question of the narrowed range, some of these approaches may have questionable value. For example, the use of "coalitions" is widespread [see Rogers et al. (1993); also see Butterfoss, Goodman, and Wandersman, (1995) on government and foundation support for advocacy by coalitions aimed at a variety of community health problems], and promoted by the NCI ASSIST program and other authorities (Stillman et al., 1999). Some authors—including some academics closely involved in tobacco control advocacy efforts—have begun to question the strength of a model that focuses on engaging key "stakeholders" or "movers and shakers" in a community, representing their organization's interest in the topic at hand—whether it be tobacco control, infant mortality, or exposure to lead. The criticisms of standard coalition models can be grouped into two categories. First, it is argued that coalitions, as typically implemented with support from government agencies and/or foundations, tend to exclude or restrict the role of ordinary citizens (especially nonprofessionals, ethnic and racial minorities, and low-income individuals) in decision-making by the coalition (Helfgot, 1974; Hatch and Eng, 1984; Goodman, Steckler, Hoover, and Schwartz, 1993; Poland, Taylor, Eyles, and White, 1995). Second, these coalitions tend to be conservative in their choice of goals and tactics (Poland et al., 1995; Blaine et al., 1997; Helfgot, 1974). These and other critics have suggested that grassroots approaches that use community organizing methods to mobilize citizens, and a willingness to use "direct action" tactics, can be a more effective strategy, or at least a useful complement to the efforts of coalitions comprised of representatives of organizations with a stake in the issue (Blaine et. al., 1997; Poland et al., 1995).

Intensive state involvement in movements may also constrain the array of goals that are pursued (see McCarthy and Wolfson, 1992; Jenkins and Eckert, 1986). For example, there is a scientific consensus that large tax increases on cigarettes would reduce the prevalence of smoking, especially among adolescents (Grossman et al., 1993). However, ASSIST staff in Minnesota (see Chapter 7) and other states have often been unable to advocate for state tax increases because of the antitax posture of their governors. And local ASSIST contractors—both nonprofit and government organizations—are prohibited from lobbying for a state increase, whether by voter initiative or legislation. Thus, organizational advocacy networks may have difficulty in mounting intensive, coordinated lobbying campaigns for policies known to be effective in situations where there is widespread reliance on government resources.[36]

Finally, a number of authors have argued that government agencies tend to frame social and health problems in fairly narrow ways (Beckett, 1995). For example, for many years government data collection efforts related to health and health care neglected to collect systematic data on social class. As a consequence, the role of social class is often neglected in government-sponsored analyses of and responses to health problems in the United States (Terris, 1999; Krieger, Williams, and Moss, 1997). State-movement interpenetration may be associated with the dominance of narrow "framings" of problems and solutions.

The central role of the state in this movement also raises questions about movement continuity. Reliance on state structures may imply a high degree of vulnerability to shifts in political leadership. For example, where would local tobacco control efforts be if former Senator Robert Dole had won the 1996 presidential election? Dole, of course, had been the beneficiary of large tobacco industry contributions, and made criticism of tobacco control efforts (including raising questions about the addictiveness of cigarettes, long a matter of mainstream scientific consensus) a campaign issue (Will, 1996). It is easy to imagine a scenario in which a president at odds ideologically and politically with the movement is elected, and pushes for reductions in funding and greater restrictions on the use of federal funds for tobacco control efforts. In fact, the shift to a Republican-controlled Congress in 1994 precipitated several legislative efforts to impose additional limits on the advocacy activities of nonprofits, as we shall see below.

Government-sponsored advocacy has not gone unnoticed by critics. Critics of interpenetration have raised a number of normative issues. These issues have frequently been voiced by critics of the tobacco control movement and other movements to which they are ideologically opposed (e.g., Bandow, 1995; Bennett and DiLorenzo, 1994, 1998). One key issue is the absence of direct accountability for government actions carried out by nongovernment agents.[37] Another charge made by critics is that programs such as the NCI's Project ASSIST "politicize" federal scientific efforts, undermining the credibility of actual scientific work (Bennett and DiLorenzo, 1998).[38] In addition, these critics have raised questions about the "propriety and legality of tax-funded politics—the use of tax revenues by special-interest groups to promote one side of a political issue" (ibid.:5). Finally, criticism of state-movement interpenetration is consistent with a more general critique of the excessive and/or expanding reach of the state into civil society (Habermas, 1976, 1985; Berger and Neuhaus, 1977; Evans and Boyte, 1986; Putnam, 2000).

In fact, waves of efforts to channel, control, constrain, or repress government-sponsored advocacy have occurred periodically over the past twenty years. One such wave took place in the early 1980s, amid calls by the newly elected Reagan administration to "de-fund the left" (Greve, 1987). In 1982 the Office of Management and Budget sent a memorandum to the heads of federal departments and agencies reminding them of the prohibition against federal grantees and contractors using federal funds "to influence legislation or appropriations" or for "partisan or political advocacy purposes." Agencies could continue to provide funds to "political advocacy groups" so long as "meticulous attention [is] paid to ensure that . . . Federal funds are only used to fulfill specific grant and contract purposes" (United States General Accounting Office, 1982). Also in the early 1980s, many federal programs that had been criticized for sponsoring advocacy activities were converted into block grants, which left many funding and programmatic decisions to the states. For example, the Consumer Education Program and the Environmental Education Program of the Department of Education were rolled into the Educational Consolidation and Improvement Act Block Grant as of Fiscal Year 1982 (ibid.). This "new federalism" represented, to some degree, a reaction to both the programmatic emphases and the advocacy tactics embraced by these and other federal programs (Conlan, 1998).

In the mid-1990s, another wave of attempts to restrict advocacy efforts of federal contractors and grantees took place. Nonprofits and government organizations were already subject to a number of restrictions on their advocacy efforts. Nonprofit organizations eligible to receive tax-deductible donations [known as 501(c)(3) organizations]—including ANSR, the Smoke-Free Coalition, and the voluntaries—had to comply with limitations on the amount of lobbying in which they could engage (Moody, 1996; USDHHS, 1993c; McCarthy et al., 1991). In addition, acceptance of federal funds already carried additional limitations on political activity. Nonprofits receiving federal funds were prohibited from using these funds to support attempts to influence federal or state legislation, whether directly—by lobbying government officials—or indirectly—by trying to influence members of the general public (grassroots lobbying; USDHHS, 1993c). State agencies were prohibited by federal law from using federal funds to lobby Congress, but could use these funds to support efforts to influence state legislatures, city and county councils, and ballot initiatives (ibid.).

As we have seen, in the case of the tobacco control movement, these restrictions imposed some constraints on organizations involved in the movement, but these constraints were not overly severe. Nonprofits had to watch their lobbying expenditures, but for organizations like the health voluntaries, which engage in substantial service efforts, there was little danger of exceeding spending limitations on lobbying (see Chapter 5). The constraints were perhaps trickier for the single-issue groups. The Smoke-Free Coalition devoted considerable effort to educational efforts (such as Smoke-Free Class 2000), and much of its lobbying effort was conducted by volunteers from member organizations. And most of ANSR's lobbying was conducted by its president, who drew no salary from the organization. Restrictions on the use of federal funds meant that these funds could not be used by ASSIST contractors—including the Smoke-Free Coalition, ANSR, and local governments—to lobby the state legislature on tobacco control measures, but people were able to do so on their own time. And MDH could use ASSIST funds to support changes in local ordinances.

However, a series of measures were instituted at the federal level that whittled away at the ability of ASSIST and similar programs to support policy advocacy efforts at the state and local level in the mid-1990s. The first such measure was the Federal Acquisition Streamling Act (P.L. 103-355) of 1994. This law—known as FASA—prohibits federal contractors from lobbying local legislative bodies, such as city and county councils (Gallagher, 1995). As we saw in Chapter 7, it turned out—after a several-month moratorium on local lobbying by local ASSIST projects in Minnesota—that these projects were not subject to the ban on local lobbying, since the ASSIST contract with MDH predated FASA. Nevertheless, future efforts to use federal funds to catalyze local activism will be severely hampered by a prohibition against local-level lobbying by federal contractors.

A sweeping effort to constrain the advocacy efforts of nonprofits was launched in Congress the following year. Congressional critics of "tax-subsidized advocacy" efforts, with the vocal support of industries that had been targeted by such efforts, introduced two pieces of legislation that went well beyond existing restrictions in that they would restrict the political activities of federal grantees and contractors using *nonfederal* funds. The first of these measures—known as the Simpson Amendment—passed and was signed into law. The Simpson Amendment targets nonprofits whose tax status allows them to lobby [501(c)(4) "social welfare" organizations; Moody, 1996]. The law prohibits all lobbying activities—including activities completely funded by nonfederal sources—on the part of 501(c)(4) organizations that receive federal funds (ibid.).

The Istook Amendment—which surfaced in three forms over the course of the 1995 congressional session—was far more sweeping than Simpson. If enacted, it would have restricted political advocacy by all organizations that receive federal funds, including 501(c)(3) and 501(c)(4) nonprofits. Specifically, it would have prohibited federal grants and contracts from being awarded to organizations that engage in lobbying—again, even using their own funds—over a "political advocacy threshold" (ibid.). The nonprofit community rallied in opposition to the bill, labelling it a nonprofit "gag law," and, after a heated battle and several attempts to float less draconian versions of the bill, it went down to defeat.

Since the skirmishes of 1994 and 1995, proposed restrictions on advocacy efforts have continued to emerge. The fiscal year 1998 appropriations act for the Departments of Labor, Health and Human Services, Education, and related agencies [Section 503 (a) and (b)] prohibited the use of any part of the appropriation for

> publicity or propaganda purposes, for the preparation, distribution, or use of any kit, pamphlet, booklet, publication, radio, television, or video presentation designed to support or defeat legislation pending before the Congress or any State legislature, except in presentation to the Congress or any State legislature itself. No part of any appropriation contained in this Act shall be used to pay the salary or expenses of any grant or contract recipient, or agent acting for such recipient, related to any activity designed to influence legislation or appropriations pending before the Congress or any State legislature.

Thus, a state health department can not use federal funds to engage in legislative or grassroots lobbying to pass a bill increasing the state excise tax on cigarettes or restricting smoking in workplaces.

In addition to blanket prohibitions on advocacy aimed at Congress, state legislatures, and (in some cases) local government, restrictions on the *content* of advocacy efforts have recently been enacted. For example, the Departments of Labor, Health and Human Services, and Education, and Related Agencies Appropriations Act of 1998 stated that "none of the funds made available for injury prevention and control at the Centers for Disease Control and Prevention may be used to advocate or promote gun control."

Clearly, organizations in a state-penetrated movement—including both government agencies and nonprofits—are subject to a host of significant constraints. Moreover, the history of the past twenty years suggests that these constraints will continue to grow. An important topic for students of social movements is the way that movement organizations adapt to these constraints, and the impact of the constraints on the viability and impact of state-penetrated movements.

Explanation: Why Does Interpenetration Occur?

How can the pattern of interpenetration of the tobacco control movement and the state reported in this book be explained? Why has the state laid the groundwork for, encouraged, and worked hand-and-hand with a social movement to promote controls on tobacco use? And why have movement organizations entered into alliances with government organizations to mutually pursue their goals? To some extent, interpenetration is likely to reflect the state's interests in and capacity surrounding strong tobacco control measures, as discussed earlier. Federal and state governments have a strong interest in tobacco control because these units of government carry a significant part of the burden of economic costs related to morbidity and mortality stemming from tobacco use. Obviously, there are countervailing interests and pressures in states with a large tobacco-growing and / or cigarette manufacturing economy. And revenues from tobacco taxes also complicate the calculation of the interests of the federal and state governments in tobacco control measures. Nevertheless, the CDC has estimated that the medical costs associated with smoking amount to about $2 a pack in 1993, 43% of which ($0.89 per pack) is borne by government (CDC, 1994a).

However, the translation of objective interests into subjective interests, and subjective interests into collective action, is problematic. Recognizing and acting on interests is not automatic, but contingent. In the case of the tobacco control movement, two factors are likely to have played an important role in motivating state governments' involvement in tobacco control efforts. The first factor is external pressures brought to bear by two groups of actors: (1) nonprofit organizations involved in tobacco control (especially in the early years of the movement, before government involvement attained its current levels), and (2) elements of the business community interested in lowering health care costs (see Bergthold, 1991; Mintz, 1995). As mentioned above, there are important countervailing forces as well, especially in states with substantial economic interests in tobacco production.

A second factor that is likely to have set the stage for state government involvement in tobacco control is suggested by organizational analyses of the state (e.g., Laumann and Knoke, 1987; Lehman, 1988; McCarthy and Wolfson, 1992). These accounts reject monolithic images of the state, and attempt to understand the distribution of common and divergent interests across state agencies and the implications of this distribution for agency responsiveness to outside forces and agency behavior. A number of government agencies—NCI and CDC at the federal level, and state health departments—have organizational interests in tobacco control because of their responsibilities for reducing morbidity and mortality and containing health care costs. The existence of an agency or subdivision of an agency charged with public health in each state, along with an assemblage of federal agencies supporting this system, is a critical factor that has facilitated state government involvement in tobacco control efforts.[39]

However, government has limited options at its disposal for promoting policy changes that would achieve tobacco control. For example, the ability of state government to promote strong local ordinances restricting youth access to tobacco is somewhat limited. Moreover, both government and public health had increasing levels of experience with activism as a means of achieving particular policy ends. Advocacy was becoming part of the known repertoire for achieving these ends. Thus, government actors have turned to active initiation of activities and sponsorship of and collaboration with advocacy organizations in order to pursue their interests in tobacco control.

Analyses are needed of the historical process by which sponsorship of and collaboration in activism come to be discovered and institutionalized in government circles (and, for that matter, in foundation circles) as a strategy for addressing social and health problems. A number of factors, some specific to the health arena and others not, are likely to have influenced this development: a growing interest in public policy as a vehicle for health promotion efforts; the emphasis of international agencies (such as WHO) and, more recently, the United States and Canadian governments, in popular "participation" in government health care and health promotion initiatives (Hardiman, 1986); and a history of community-organizing approaches in such professional arenas as health education and health promotion (APHA, 1941; Bracht, 1990; Minkler, 1997) and social work (Rothman, 1970).

A number of programs have come to embrace a more pointed form of citizen participation. These programs provide R&D services, dissemination of information, technical assistance, and, in some cases, direct funding to promote political activism in furtherance of the goals of the program. In many cases, they reflect an ideology that holds that changes in the social environment—importantly including state and local public policy— are needed to prevent public health and social problems (Schmid, Pratt, and Howze, 1995).

The Volunteers in Service to America (VISTA) program, which began in 1965, is an early example of this phenomenon. This program has employed a community-organizing approach in using VISTA volunteers to work with and address the needs of low-income communities. In the late 1970s and early 1980s, the Midwest Academy, among other organizer training programs, was used to provide training in community organizing methods to VISTA volunteers (United States General Accounting Office, 1982).

A second example, which was launched in 1979, was the Youth Advocacy Program of the U.S. Office of Juvenile Justice and Delinquency Prevention, an agency of the U.S. Department of Justice (U.S. Department of Justice, 1979). The program targeted "statutes, regulations, policies and practices of the juvenile justice system, education system and the social services system which are insensitive or detrimental to the needs and best interests of youth" (ibid.:2). Changes were to be effected using such "youth advocacy" approaches as "(1) effective coalition building among public and private groups and organizations to impact the needs of youth; (2) meaningful youth participation in policy decisions affecting youth for the purpose of better defining youth needs and impacting on the policies, practices and utilization of funds in youth servicing institutions; and, (3) effective legal advocacy in support of the above two approaches for the purpose of protecting the interests and rights of children and youth" (ibid.:1).

THE FUTURE OF THE TOBACCO CONTROL MOVEMENT

Prognostication is a risky undertaking. Rather than make predictions, I will point to three critical issues that will shape the future of tobacco control efforts. The first is the explosion of lawsuits against the tobacco industry. The second is the institutionalization of state-run tobacco control programs. The third issue is the future of tobacco control efforts in developing nations.

The Litigation Explosion

As discussed in Chapter 2, lawsuits against the tobacco companies, like other product liability suits, have tremendous potential to impact the public's health. Successful suits have the potential to force increases in the prices of tobacco products stemming from damages awarded or the financial terms of settlements. If these price increases are large, they will lead to significant declines in smoking rates and initiation of smoking by youth. The publicity surrounding suits can have the dual functions of educating potential and actual tobacco users about the negative health consequences of tobacco use; moreover, information revealed in the discovery process concerning tobacco company disinformation campaigns could embarrass the companies and reduce their political clout in Congress, state legislatures, and town halls, and among regulatory bodies (Daynard, 1988; Jacobson and Warner, 1999). Finally, successful suits can have a kind of regulatory function, by forcing the industry to curtail deceptive advertising and promotion practices.

During what analysts of tobacco litigation have come to call the "first wave" (from about 1954 to 1973) and the "second wave" (from 1983 to 1992) of litigation (Daynard, 1988; Kelder and Daynard, 1996), tobacco companies won every case (Annas, 1997). However, the record in the "third wave"—which began with the *Castano* class action suit, filed in 1994 in Louisiana—is looking much more promising (Annas, 1997; Kelder and Daynard, 1996; Jacobson and Warner, 1999). Third-wave suits, as opposed to earlier suits brought by individual smokers, involve class actions by past and present smokers, class actions by people exposed to secondhand smoke, suits brought by state attorneys general, as well as other innovative legal strategies that previously had not been used against the tobacco industry (Jacobson and Warner, 1999; Kelder and Daynard, 1996). The third wave of tobacco litigation has benefited from pooling of resources and information on the part of attorneys representing the plaintiffs in these cases, as well as extensive documentation of misbehavior by the tobacco industry made public in earlier suits or by industry whistleblowers (Kelder and Daynard, 1996).

These developments have been reflected in staggering settlements and awards over the last few years. In 1997, the Mississippi and Florida suits to recover the state's share of Medicaid costs for the treatment of smoking-related illnesses were settled for $3.4 billion and $11 billion, respectively. The flight attendants' class action suit was settled in the same year (for $300 million). In 1998, the Texas and Minnesota Medicaid suits were settled (for $6 billion and $14 billion, respectively). Also in 1998, the forty-six-state, $206-billion-dollar Master Settlement Agreement was reached. Finally, in July 2000, a Florida jury awarded $144 billion in punitive damages to the plaintiffs in the *Engle* case, the first class action lawsuit by smokers to go to trial (Tobacco Products Liability Project, 2000).[40]

How far will a litigation strategy take tobacco control efforts? As mentioned above, one key factor is whether or not judgments or the financial terms of settlements are sufficiently large so as to require large price increases on the part of cigarette manufacturers. According to the National Center for Tobacco-Free Kids, the cigarette companies have raised prices by $0.94/pack since they began to make tobacco settlement payments to the states in 1998 (Campaign for Tobacco-Free Kids, 2000a). However, they have also engaged in aggressive discounting at the retail level through the use of coupons and three packs for the price of two promotions, which blunts the effects of the price increases on demand (Jacobson and Warner, 1999; Campaign for Tobacco-Free Kids, 2000a).[41] Moreover, average prices of cigarettes in the United States remain low by international standards (compared to other industrialized nations; Scollo and Sweanor, 1999) and when compared with the recommendations of the National Academy of Sciences and the Advisory Committee on Tobacco Policy and Public Health (the "Koop-Kessler Committee") on the magnitude of increases—at least $2 a pack—needed to achieve substantial reductions in smoking by teenagers (Advisory Committee on Tobacco Policy and Public Health, 1997; Institute of Medicine, 1998).

Moreover, some analysts have argued that the financial settlements between the tobacco industry and the state attorneys general may undermine attempts to persuade Congress and state legislatures to raise tobacco taxes, since these bodies may believe that sufficient price increases have been obtained as a result of the financial terms of the Master Settlement Agreement and the individual settlements with four states (Mississippi, Florida, Texas, and Minnesota; Jacobson and Warner, 1999).

There are serious questions about the adequacy of the public health measures that have resulted from litigation to date. For example, a number of critics have argued that the primary attraction of lawsuits against the tobacco industry on the part of most state attorneys general was reimbursement for the costs borne by states for treatment of tobacco-related illnesses suffered by Medicaid patients (and any political benefits associated with obtaining such reimbursement). Obtaining stronger public health measures was of less importance to the AGs, as a group (Jacobson and Warner, 1999; see also Lima and Siegel, 1999).[42] In the end, the strength of the public health provisions included in the settlements of the four states that negotiated independent settlements varied. Mississippi, for example, is said to have "essentially abdicated its broader public health objectives" in its settlement (Jacobson and Warner, 1999:797); Minnesota's settlement, on the other hand, included strong restrictions on industry behavior.

The Master Settlement Agreement included a number of public health provisions, including restrictions on youth access to tobacco, marketing, lobbying, and outdoor advertising (USDHHS, 2000).[43] Critics, however, have argued that the tobacco control provisions contained in the MSA are "modest" at best (Jacobson and Warner, 1999; Kelder and Davidson, 1999). For example, many important restrictions on youth access to tobacco—including restrictions on self-service sales of tobacco products, point-of-sale advertising, and vending machines sales of tobacco products—are not addressed by the MSA (Hermer and Kelder, 1999). Moreover, the MSA contains no "lookback" provisions, which would levy financial penalties on tobacco companies if specified reductions in underage tobacco use are not met (ibid.).[44] Critics have also noted omissions or shortfalls in the MSA's restrictions on state and local lobbying (Kelder, 1999b) and advertising (Kline and Davidson, 1999). The provisions of the MSA apply only to cigarettes and smokeless tobacco products, and do not include cigars (Davidson, 1999). Finally, the MSA includes important restrictions on funds to be allocated by the National Foundation (which has been named the American Legacy Foundation). Specifically, these funds are to be "used only for public education and advertising regarding the addictiveness, health effects, and social costs related to tobacco product" (Multistate Master Settlement Agreement of November 23, 1998 [quoted in ibid.]). Moreover, the National Public Education Fund cannot be used for "any personal attack on or vilification of, any person (by name or business affiliation), company, or governmental agency, whether individually or collectively" (Multistate Master Settlement Agreement of November 23, 1998 [quoted in ibid.]). Thus, the foundation may be prohibited from supporting counteradvertising campaigns that focus on specific misdeeds and manipulation on the part of the tobacco industry (ibid.). The limitations inherent in the public health provisions of the MSA led to the following conclusion in a comprehensive analysis of the MSA conducted by the Tobacco Control Resource Center of the Northeastern University School of Law: "The best way to effectuate the public health purposes of the Tobacco Settlement—to modify patterns of tobacco use so as to protect the health of the United States' citizens and their children and to reduce or eliminate the future costs attributable to tobacco use—would be to dedicate a substantial portion of the funds generated by the Tobacco Settlement to tobacco control in each Settling State" (Hermer, 1999: 15; Kelder and Davidson, 1999:18). As we shall see below, getting states to dedicate a significant portion of these funds to tobacco control efforts has been, and is likely to continue to be, a difficult undertaking.

Thus, a litigation strategy—while clearly an important component of the tobacco control movement—may have some significant limitations. As discussed above, the public policy measures that result from litigation may be less than optimal. Measures resulting from litigation may not be self-enforcing. Recent research indicates that following implementation of the MSA, advertising of tobacco products in magazines with large numbers of teen readers increased dramatically (Turner-Bowker and Hamilton, 2000). In response to this development, a top official at the American Heart Association stated, "The tobacco companies apparently feel free to violate the spirit, if not the letter, of the Master Settlement Agreement at will. Perhaps it's time to turn to other solutions to end the tobacco companies' continuing assault on the health and well-being of our children" (quoted in Collins, 2000).

In addition, monetary judgments from litigation, such as the money awarded to the states as a result of the multistate suit against the tobacco industry—are not necessarily spent on tobacco control programs, as I will discuss in the following section. From a social movements perspective, one can ask whether a litigation strategy supports, undermines, or has no net effect on the extent of grass-roots mobilization. On the one hand, litigation can be seen as a highly professionalized strategy, which usually does not involve grassroots mobilization. On the other hand, litigation—such as class action suits—may be a way to educate a large class of people about a shared grievance. It is possible to imagine a strategy whereby systematic attempts are made to recruit and mobilize a class of litigants to take collective action in support of tobacco control measures.

According to Jacobson and Warner:

> From an institutional perspective . . . litigation may be a second-best solution; but as a component of a broader, comprehensive approach to tobacco control policy making, litigation has a distinct role given the lackluster performance of the political institutions. Litigation can be viewed as a necessary but not sufficient component, with its necessity dictated by the failure of the conventional policy system to represent the will of the citizenry. Minnesota's recent settlement with the tobacco industry, replete with public health policy measures supported by the public but never adopted by its elected representatives, serves as a vivid illustration of the practical role that can be played by litigation. (1999:798)[45]

State Tobacco Control Programs

In the years ahead, we can expect to see continued growth in state government–led tobacco control programs. As we saw in Chapter 7, the Omnibus Nonsmoking and Disease Prevention Act of 1985 established an important excise tax–funded program in Minnesota. Following this, ballot initiatives were used to establish larger tobacco control programs in California (in 1998), Massachusetts (in 1992), Arizona (in 1994), and Oregon (in 1996) (Pierce and Geller, 1998). Other states may continue to follow this model—whether by ballot initiative or state legislation[46]—although the influx of settlement funds from the MSA (see below) and the new, fifty-state CDC tobacco control program (also see below) may make it harder to obtain legislative or popular approval of programs based on state excise taxes.

In addition to excise tax–funded programs, some states—including Minnesota[47]—have used funds from individual state settlements or the MSA to establish or enhance existing tobacco control programs. However, according to a mid-2000 analysis by the Campaign for Tobacco-Free Kids, only eight states—Hawaii, Maryland, Massachusetts, Minnesota, New Jersey, Vermont, Wisconsin, and Washington—made "substantial, new commitments in 1999 to fund tobacco prevention and cessation" (Campaign for Tobacco-Free Kids, 2000b:2). According to this analysis, an additional six states (Alaska, Montana, Nevada, New York, Virginia, and New Hampshire) allocated "modest amounts" to tobacco prevention and cessation programs, and another five states (Alabama, Connecticut, Louisiana, Rhode Island, and Texas) made a "minimal financial commitment" to such efforts (ibid.).[48] The remaining thirty-one states and the District of Columbia either decided to allocate all settlement funds to other purposes (including general budget deficit reduction, water projects, education, and capital construction) or had not yet made a decision about how to spend the funds at the time of the report (ibid.).

The federal government's primary efforts to catalyze state and local tobacco control efforts continue to operate through the "infrastructure" of state health departments. Federal funding for state tobacco control activities, which had been provided to seventeen states by the NCI ASSIST program and in thirty-two of the thirty-three remaining states by the CDC's IMPACT program (see Chapter 7), has been consolidated into the CDC's National Tobacco Control Program (NTCP), which began in Fiscal Year 1999 with a $50 million budget for grants to all fifty states, the District of Columbia, and seven territories (USDHHS, 2000).

Tobacco control programs managed by the states are vulnerable to tobacco industry attempts to undermine them and to restructure or constrain them in such as way as to minimize their effectiveness. For example, tobacco control programs funded by state excise taxes in Arizona, California, and Massachusetts have been weakened by a number of successful attempts to divert funds earmarked for tobacco control to other purposes, to soften the messages included in mass media campaigns, and to limit the scope of the program to such areas as smoking by pregnant women and tobacco use by youth (Aguinaga and Glantz, 1999; Begay et al., 1993; Begay and Glantz, 1997; Bialous and Glantz, 1999; Traynor and Glantz, 1996). The experiences in these states led Bialous and Glantz to conclude:

> It is not enough for health advocates to campaign for an increase in tobacco tax and to protect the funds at the legislature. Tobacco control advocates must closely monitor the development and implementation of tax-funded tobacco education programmes at the administrative level and be willing to press the executive to implement effective programmes. (1999:141)

The same caution applies to government-managed tobacco control programs funded from other sources, such as settlement funds. In Florida, a successful pilot program aimed at youth smoking was funded as an outgrowth of the Florida settlement with the tobacco industry. However, after showing effectiveness in its first year, its budget was cut almost by half and the program's administrative structure was dismantled (Givel and Glantz, 2000).

Clearly, establishing major state tobacco control programs may not be a sufficient means for achieving strong tobacco control measures and reducing tobacco use. There is a need for continuing scrutiny to ensure that implementation of these programs is done in such a way as to maximize the impact on tobacco use and exposure to secondhand smoke. Moreover, there is a need for continuing activism by nongovernmental groups. More generally, the development and growth of state tobacco control programs underscores the importance, for social movement theory and tobacco control strategy, of understanding the causes and consequences of state/movement interpenetration.

Tobacco Control in Developing Nations

In the economically developed countries as a group, tobacco control efforts continue to proliferate and tobacco use continues its downward trend. Clearly, developing nations will be the tobacco control battleground of the future. It is estimated that 70% of a projected 10 million annual deaths resulting from tobacco use will occur in developing nations by the year 2030 (Peto et al., 1994). As discussed above, the future of tobacco control efforts in and aimed at developing nations will be conditioned by the interests and capacity of states and NGOs in developing countries, international organizations (e.g., WHO), the industry, and the major producing countries (such as the United States). Although tobacco control advocates in the United States have condemned the industry for aggressive marketing in developing countries, few inroads have been made on achieving policies that would rein in the industry. While the ill-fated McCain Committee bill[49] contained restrictions on United States government support for overseas marketing of tobacco products and on the international marketing practices of the industry (Mackay, 1999). The Master Settlement Agreement with the states did not include any restrictions on the behavior of the tobacco industry outside the United States. International organizations, such as WHO, have been stymied by industry efforts to subvert their tobacco control efforts (World Health Organization, 2000b).[50] Consequently, the industry is able to aggressively market its products in developing countries unfettered by restrictions it increasingly faces in the West, such as warning label requirements, television and radio advertising bans, and restrictions on marketing to youth (Aftab, Kolben, and Lurie, 1999; Makary and Kawachi, 1998). These trends are exacerbated by the worldwide movement toward globalization and liberalization of trade (Baris and McLeod, 2000; Yach and Bettcher, 2000). It remains to be seen whether international tobacco control efforts are able to halt, and even reverse, the global epidemic of tobacco use.

The theme of state/movement interpenetration, which played prominently in the Minnesota case study and in the United States as a whole, is echoed in discussions about international tobacco control efforts. One of the common features of the various plans that were proposed to settle the state AGs' lawsuit against the tobacco industry (except the plan that was ultimately approved—the Master Settlement Agreement) was that the settlement should include funding for a new organization which would lead international tobacco control efforts (Bloom, 1998). This organization was to be an NGO modeled after the National Endowment for Democracy, and, if it had been approved, would have been called the American Center on Global Health and Tobacco (ACT) (ibid.).[51] According to one analyst,

> U.S. NGOs receive significant government support for their work addressing HIV/AIDS and other public health issues, international development, emergency relief and democracy-building. . . . NGOs tend to be more entrepreneurial, less bureaucratic, and less subject to political interference than most governmental bodies. . . . [They] should play an equal if not greater role in international tobacco control, complementing the equally important work of federal and multilateral government agencies. (ibid.)

Thus, as in the case of domestic tobacco control efforts, we see recognition on the part of state actors (i.e., legislators and others who supported legislation that would have established ACT) of the need for advocacy efforts that require state support and would involve close collaboration with government bodies in the United States and elsewhere. The NGO carrying out these efforts would be less constrained in its framing of the problem and the strategies and tactics it employed than would a U.S. government body or a multilateral organization, such as WHO. However, the case study of the tobacco control movement in Minnesota suggests that such an approach would bring substantial resources to bear on the problem, and would in fact be subject to fewer and less severe constraints than a unit of government would face. But this case underscores the importance of assessing the ways in which the interpenetration of state and movement limits the scope and intensity of advocacy efforts. The literature on international NGOs is replete with examples of the vulnerability of advocacy efforts that ultimately depend on the support of nation-states or multilateral organizations, such as WHO, UNICEF, the Food and Agriculture Organization (FAO), and the World Bank (Fisher, 1997; Keck and Sikkink, 1998; Risse-Kappen, 1995; Smith, Chatfield, and Pagnucco, 1997; Jalali, 1998; OMB Watch, 1998).[52]

Each of the three issues facing tobacco control efforts—the litigation explosion, the rise of state tobacco control programs, and tobacco control efforts in developing nations—involves, in part, questions about the size, scope, and influence of social movements. Moreover, the relationship between the state and the movement is an important element in how each of these issues plays out.

CONCLUSION

I hope to have shed some light on the tobacco control movement in this book. I have argued that the movement has built heavily on the "infrastructure" of health, which has resulted in access to important resources, but has also imposed some significant constraints on the form and scope of collective action. In addition, I have argued that conventional images of the relationship between the state and social movements provide a picture that is incomplete at best. I put forward the concept of state-movement interpenetration to describe the relationship in the tobacco control arena.

While I have focused primarily on the movement in Minnesota, I believe that the themes that emerged in the case study have some generality: to tobacco control efforts in other states and nationally, to tobacco control in developed and developing nations, and to other social movements. The analysis I have put forward suggests future avenues of social movements theory and research, and has important implications for the future of tobacco control both in the United States and around the world.

NOTES

1.   After years of neglect, there is now a growing literature on the effects of social movements (Amenta et al., 1994; Gamson, 1990; Burstein, 1985; Freeman, 1975; Broadbent, 1989; Wolfson, 1995a; see Giugni, 1998 for a recent review).

2.   Over the past twenty-five years, researchers have attempted to understand the links between particular components of the movement—research and dissemination of research on health effects of tobacco use; public education campaigns; federal, state, and local policy; and advocacy efforts—and declines in tobacco use. For example, Nelson and colleagues (1995) examined declines in smoking prevalence between 1974 and 1985, and identified the 1971 federal radio and television advertising ban, a growing cultural emphasis on healthier lifestyles and physical fitness, and decreased social acceptability of smoking as factors that may underlie these declines. Other examples of this research include Warner (1977, 1981, 1989) and Lewit, Coate, and Grossman (1981). Also see the research literature reviewed in Chapter 2 of this book.

3.   There has been a lively debate among tobacco control advocates and researchers about the factors underlying increases in adolescent smoking rates. Possible reasons that have been cited include a response by adolescents to the characterization of cigarettes as a "forbidden fruit"; decreases in the real price of cigarettes; increased cigarette advertising and promotion, targeted toward youth; emergence of a group of high-risk adolescents who are more likely to experiment with cigarette smoking and who may have resisted school, parental, and media efforts to discourage smoking; and the fact that 1980s media and school-based education campaigns focused largely on illicit drugs, such as marijuana and cocaine (Nelson et al., 1995; Glantz, 1996).

4.   In 1966, 35.3% of adults (age 25 and up) with 16 or more years of schooling, 44.8% of adults with 13-15 years of schooling, 44.7% of adults with 12 years of schooling, and 41.7% with less than 12 years of schooling were current smokers (Giovino et al., 1994). In 1997, only 11.6% of adults with 16 or more years of schooling smoked, compared to 25.1% of adults with 13-15 years of schooling, 28.4% of adults with 12 years of schooling, 35.4% of adults with 9-11 years of schooling, and 22.5% of adults with eight or fewer years of schooling (CDC, 1999b).

5.   California was excluded from the group of comparison states because it had "implemented a large and ongoing tobacco control programme funded by a substantial increase in its cigarette tax in 1989" (Manley et al.,1997b:S13).

6.   Pierce and colleagues (1998) speculate that the positive effects of the California program may have tapered off as a result of the tobacco industry lowering the prices of cigarettes in 1993, cutbacks in the California Tobacco Control Program (which are discussed later in this chapter), political action on the part of the industry to water down state government's commitment to the program, or increases in tobacco industry expenditures for advertising and promotion.

7.   In fact, this poll compared with a 1994 poll does "suggest that the public may be shifting the blame somewhat toward tobacco companies" (Moore, 1999:2). For example, 64% of respondents in the earlier (1994) poll indicated that smokers were mostly or completely to blame for tobacco-related health problems in the United States, compared to 55% in the 1999 poll.

8.   According to a 1988 CMA memorandum (quoted in Traynor and Glantz, 1996:564–65), "The CMA believes it is not in the best interest of physicians to battle the tobacco industry, which has pledged to defeat the November ballot measure with a multi-million dollar campaign that is likely to single out physicians as personal beneficiaries of the revenues generated."

9.   See Nathanson (1999) for an account of claims-making on the violence issue by public health and medical organizations.

10.   If local chapters of Physicians for Social Responsibility had been classified as a health rather than a social action organization, health organizations would represent 64% of the overall sample of organizations involved in gun control efforts; calculated from Zakocs et al., 2000:Table 1).

11.   I choose to focus on the example of facilitation, rather than repression, for this discussion because it better fits the case of tobacco control in Minnesota. However, I believe the argument applies equally to state repression of movements.

12.   I would suggest two factors that have contributed to the relative neglect of state-movement interpenetration in the social movements literature. First, a monolithic image of "the state," which directs attention away from the multiplicity of state subdivisions and interests, has tended to prevail in the literature on social movements. Second, the traditional image of social movements as collectivities of the oppressed and dispossessed rising up against the state makes it hard to conceive of ongoing, collaborative, and mutually beneficial relationships between state and movement actors. [In contrast, the phenomenon of professionalized social movement organizations, noted by McCarthy and Zald (1973, 1977) and others, makes it much easier to imagine state-movement interpenetration.]

13.   The close relationship between the state and movement organizations has also been noted by conservative critics of federal support for organizations involved in advocacy efforts (Bennett and DiLorenzo, 1985). These critics popularized the cry of "defunding the left" when the political opportunity to accomplish this arose with the beginning of the Reagan administration in the early 1980s [see Greve (1987) for an account of why this effort did not, in the main, succeed]. More recently, some of the same critics have leveled their sights on NCI and ACS support for tobacco control advocacy in connection with the ASSIST project (Bennett and DiLorenzo, 1994, 1998). Work in political science on the interest group/government agency relationship (such as the "iron triangle" concept) also may be useful in developing the concept of state/movement interpenetration (e.g., Gais, Peterson, and Walker, 1984; Lowi, 1969). (This point was made previously by McCarthy and Wolfson, 1992:290).

14.   Of course, there has been a parallel movement over the years to contract with private firms for the delivery of government-sponsored goods and services (Smith and Lipsky, 1993; Anton, 1989).

15.   This is especially important in states in which state health departments had not been playing an active role in tobacco control prior to ASSIST. According to a former staffer of the North Carolina ASSIST project, prior to ASSIST, "Government was not interested in working with them [tobacco control advocates]. Until the money for ASSIST came, to a state like North Carolina, where there are very strong economic interests in tobacco, and influence in state agencies and the legislature, there wouldn't have been anybody. . . . The prenatal care people wouldn't mention

it [the relationship between smoking by pregnant women and unfavorable birth outcomes, such as low birth weight]." Thus, the national ASSIST project was, in many ways, a vehicle for creating political opportunities for tobacco control efforts at the state and local level. As noted by Gamson and Meyer (1996), "Opportunities open the way for political action, but movements also make opportunities."

16.   Variables that are based on sums (such as these three) rather than proportions may be especially affected by the number and characteristics of nonresponding organizations in the state. However, even if we use the number of organizations enumerated in the census (deducting those that were known to meet the exclusion criteria) the descriptive statistics for the number of organizations variable are quite comparable to those reported in Table 10.1.

17.   It is important to keep in mind that all of these measures are based on the reports of organizations we defined as being part of a state advocacy network. Thus, these statistics exclude budgets, full-time employees, and volunteers located in entities that were not surveyed, such as state health departments and local health departments that did not receive ASSIST or state tax-funded tobacco control funding.

18.   Published accounts of tobacco control efforts in other states (e.g., Jacobson et al., 1992) suggest that collaboration between state agencies—particularly state health departments—and tobacco control movement organizations occurs in many states, although the depth and extent of this collaboration vary considerably across the states.

19.   As discussed in Chapter 2 and later in this chapter, cigarette consumption is declining in most developed countries and growing dramatically in the developing world (also see WHO, 1997). Moreover, over 80% of smokers live in low- and middle-income countries (Jha and Chaloupka, 1999:Table 1.1).

20.   In 1997, the United States ranked second (746.4 metric tons), Greece ninth (132.5 metric tons), Italy tenth (131.4 metric tons), Canada fourteenth (71.1 metric tons), Japan sixteenth (68.5 metric tons), and Spain twenty-first (42.3 metric tons), representing about 15% of production worldwide (calculated from Jha and Chaloupka, 1999:Table 5.1).

21.   Tobacco export revenues represented 2.05% of 1995 total revenues from exports in Greece, 0.55% in the United States, 0.06% in Spain, and 0.04% in Italy, Canada, and Japan (Jha and Chaloupka, 1999:Table 5.1).

22.   On the other hand, the state's efforts to reduce consumption are likely to significantly affect, and therefore to be vigorously opposed by, tobacco growing interests in countries that use most of their crop for the domestic market, such as Japan (which exported only 0.5% of its crop in 1997), Canada (24%), and the United States (35.5%) (Jha and Chaloupka, 1999:Table 5.1).

23.   In 1994, estimates of cigarettes produced, in millions, were: 725,600 in the United States, 268,900 in Japan, 220,000 in Germany, 122,000 in the United Kingdom, 90,679 in Korea, 88,000 in The Netherlands, 84,000 in Spain, 55,475 in Canada, and 55,000 in Italy.

24.   For example, among the top ten OECD nations with respect to cigarette manufacturing, early to mid-1990s estimates of the number of jobs in cigarette manufacturing ranged from 49,000 in the United States (representing about 0.4 of the total labor force) to 5,000 in Canada (WHO, 1997).

25.   Of course, these transitions would involve social costs, as workers move out of declining tobacco-related jobs into other areas of the economy (Warner et al., 1996; Jha and Chaloupka, 1999).

26.   For example, the Tobacco Institute estimated that in 1994, tobacco core and supplier industries contributed $20.6 billion and retail sales contributed $15 billion in federal, state, and local taxes (Tobacco Institute, 1997). While earlier estimates of smoking-related medical expenditures fell below this figure (ranging from $8.2 billion to $23.3 billion), more recent estimates (from the 1990s) exceed it (ranging from $50 billion to $72.7 billion) (see Warner, Hodgson, and Carroll, 1999). It should be noted that these estimates do not include the medical costs associated with smokeless tobacco use, which would increase the estimate of medical costs.

27.   In the United States, according to this analysis, "antismoking advocates more often . . . pursued an 'outside' strategy, seeking to persuade governments to act by first influencing public opinion" (Kagan and Vogel, 1993:25).

28.   For example, tobacco exports represented almost one-quarter of all export earnings for Zimbabwe in 1993; by contrast, they represented only about 2% of exports in Brazil (WHO, 1997).

29.   Marketing campaigns in developing countries can substantially enhance the allure of manufactured cigarettes. According to Marshall, "Through clever advertising the tobacco transnationals have created and manipulated an image of manufactured cigarettes that associates them with a sophisticated, modern, urban lifestyle. In Tonga, for example, alcohol and tobacco use are seen as symbols of westernization (along with western-style dwellings, foods, and vehicles) that give status deriving from familiarity and `seasoned acquaintance' with a prestigious lifestyle" (1991:1329).

30.   Warner and colleagues, in a recent review (1999:297), lament the fact that cost-of-smoking studies have been limited almost exclusively to Western developed nations, with the exception of recent studies on China.

31.   Ladakh is a "remote and beautiful mountain kingdom . . . north of India" (Ball, 1995:19).

32.   It should be noted that a criticism of the public health response to firearm injuries is that a minority of these agencies have become actively involved in firearm injury prevention efforts (Price and Oden, 1999; Zakocs et al., 2000).

33.   Other potential examples of state-movement interpenetration include the rape crisis centers/antirape movement (Matthews, 1994), the women's health movement (Morgen, 1986), the "Free Cuba" movement (Smith, 2000), AIDS/HIV activism (Epstein, 1996; Cain, 1995); the environmental justice movement (Crumpton, 1997), and alternative dispute resolution (Morrill and McKee, 1993).

34.   In connection with ASSIST, both NCI and state health departments have developed handbooks on changing local policy, which typically recommend the use of compliance checks, both by community organizations to demonstrate the availability of tobacco to youth, and by enforcement authorities. Both NCI and state health departments often contract with activist organizations to prepare these handbooks (e.g., Americans for Nonsmokers' Rights, no date; Association for Nonsmokers-Minnesota, 1993). In my fifty-state survey of organizations involved in tobacco control efforts, 68% of the respondents reported involvement in compliance

checks in the year preceding the survey. The percentage among organizations with ASSIST funding was even greater (75%).

35. McAdam provides several examples of authorities developing successful counters to the tactics of the civil rights movement. For example, after initial successes, bus boycotts were effectively countered with "legal obstruction and extralegal harassment" (1983:741), and sit-ins were effectively countered with "mass arrests by the police, the passage of state or local anti-trespassing ordinances, the permanent closure of the lunch counters, and the establishment of various biracial negotiating bodies to contain or routinize the conflict" (ibid.:744).

36. Only 22% of the respondents to our survey reported heavy involvement in tobacco tax issues, compared to 54% reporting such involvement in secondhand smoke issues and 79% in youth access.

37. This issue has been raised more generally with respect to recent dramatic growth in government contracting out for services (Kettl, 1994).

38. Of course, the belief that "normal science" is apolitical has been widely criticized by both academics and advocacy groups (Merton, 1970; Proctor, 1995; Epstein, 1996; Baird, 1999).

39. In the late 1990s, there were over 2,800 local health departments in the United States, with median expenditures of $689,457 (National Association of County and City Health Officials unpublished data, cited in Rawding and Brown, 2000). The "infrastructure" of public health at the local level may include a variety of other organizations, including nonprofits, managed care organizations, hospitals, and universities (Mays et al., 2000: Chapter 3). At the state level, a state health agency in each state, often in combination with other agencies (e.g., substance abuse, mental health, and environmental health), carries out the "core public health functions" of surveillance, preventive services, outreach, quality assurance, training, and planning (CDC, 1995). Although public health officials and advocates argue that the resources allocated to public health are inadequate (e.g., Institute of Medicine, 1988; Bowser and Gostin, 1999), it nevertheless represents a substantial infrastructure on which health movements, such as the tobacco control movement, can build.

40. As this is being written, the jury's decision in the *Engle* case is being appealed.

41. The Center for Tobacco-Free Kids has also argued that the cigarette companies raised prices to a level about twice as high as that needed to cover payments to the states and other parties (i.e., support for the American Legacy Foundation, private law firms that represented the states in their suits, and tobacco growers), thus realizing an estimated increase in net revenues (after these payments are deducted) of over $18 billion a year (Campaign for Tobacco-Free Kids, 2000a).

42. Of course, there were divisions in the ranks on the issue of the importance of public health measures. As discussed in Chapter 7, Attorney General Humphrey of Minnesota was among the most outspoken advocates of strong public health measures (see Humphrey, 1997a, 1997b).

43. The restrictions on youth access included a ban on free samples except in enclosed areas where the operator ensures that no underage persons are present, a ban on gifts to youth in exchange for buying tobacco products, a ban on gifts

through the mail without proof of age, and a ban on production, distribution, and sale of cigarettes in packs of less than twenty until December 31, 2001 (USDHHS, 2000). The restrictions on marketing include bans on brand-name sponsorships of concerts, team sporting events, or events with significant youth audiences; a ban on sponsorship of events involving paid underage participants; a ban on the use of tobacco brand-names in stadiums and arenas; a ban on the use of cartoon characters in advertising, packaging, and promotions; a ban on payments for promotion of tobacco products in movies and other entertainment settings; and a ban on the distribution and sale of merchandise with tobacco brand-name logos (USDHHS, 2000). The restrictions on lobbying include a ban on industry efforts to support the use of settlement funds for purposes other than health, a ban on industry lobbying against restrictions on advertising in or around schools, and a ban on new industry challenges to state and local tobacco control laws enacted prior to June 1, 1998 (USDHHS, 2000). Restrictions on outdoor advertising include a ban on transit and outdoor advertising, and a requirement that existing tobacco billboards and transit ads be removed.

44.   Lookback provisions were included in the 1997 tobacco settlement proposal that a group of state AGs presented to Congress and the American public ("the June 20th agreement"); however, Congress never approved this agreement (Hermer and Kelder, 1999).

45.   See Rosenberg (1991) and McCann (1994) for more general discussions of whether litigation can be an effective strategy for achieving social change.

46.   Strategic choices about whether to use referenda or legislation to establish such programs depend in part on state laws that regulate the referendum process. Although Minnesota tobacco control advocates considered the referendum option over the years, it is very difficult to achieve policy change by referendum because of a requirement that it be approved by a majority of those voting in a given election—not just those voting on the referendum itself (see Schmidt, 1989).

47.   A major portion of Minnesota's settlement has been set aside to establish a tobacco prevention and public health endowment. Interest from the endowment is being used, in part, to fund an ambitious Youth Tobacco Prevention Initiative, which includes grants to local communities, development of statewide tobacco control programs, youth advocacy, countermarketing, and grants to help enforce laws regulating youth access to tobacco (Minnesota Prevention Resource Center, 2000).

48.   For the purposes of the Campaign for Tobacco-Free Kid's analysis, a "modest" financial commitment was defined as less than one-third of the minimum amount recommended by CDC, while a "minimal" financial commitment was defined as less than 25% of the minimum amount recommended by the CDC (Centers for Disease Control and Prevention, 1999e).

49.   S 1415, known as the "National Tobacco Policy and Youth Smoking Reduction Act" (Kelder, 1999). This bill, which was widely regarded as a stronger tobacco control bill than the initial "June 20th" agreement presented by the state attorneys general (and stronger than the MSA), was scuttled following a $40 million industry advertising and lobbying campaign opposing the bill (Kelder, 1999; Blendon and Young, 1998).

50.   According to a report by the WHO Committee of Experts on Tobacco In-

dustry Documents (WHO, 2000b), evidence from industry documents released as a result of the suits by the state attorneys general and others against the tobacco industry points to "elaborate, well financed, sophisticated, and usually invisible" attempts to undermine WHO tobacco control efforts (WHO, 2000b:iii). According to this report, strategies used by the industry have included "establishing inappropriate relationships with WHO staff to influence policy," "wielding financial power to influence WHO policy," "using other UN agencies to influence or resist WHO tobacco control," "discrediting WHO or WHO officials to undermine WHO's effectiveness," "influencing WHO decision making through surrogates," "distorting WHO research," "media events," and "surveillance of WHO activities" (WHO, 2000b:2-4).

51. Language creating such an organization was included in four of the proposed settlement bills, including the McCain Committee bill (Bloom, 1998).

52. A recent illustration of this vulnerability is provided by congressional proposals to prohibit award of federal family planning funds to foreign NGOs that have used their own funds to support advocacy on abortion policy within their own country (OMB Watch, 1998).

References

Aamot, G. (1997). "Humphrey Explains Objections to Tobacco Pact to Senate Panel." *Star Tribune*, July 17, p. A12.

Abt Associates, Inc. (1998). *Independent Evaluation of the Massachusetts Tobacco Control Program, 4th Annual Report, January 1994–June 1997*. Cambridge: Author.

Advisory Committee on Tobacco Policy and Public Health (1997). *Final Report*. (No address given.)

Aftab, M., D. Kolben, and P. Lurie (1999). "International Cigarette Labelling Practices." *Tobacco Control* 8:368–72.

Aguinaga, S. and S. A. Glantz (1995). "The Use of Public Records Acts to Interfere with Tobacco Control." *Tobacco Control* 4:222–30.

Aguinaga, S. and S. A. Glantz (1999). "Arizona's Tobacco Control Initiative Illustrates the Need for Continuing Oversight by Tobacco Control Advocates." *Tobacco Control* 8:141–51.

Alcaraz, R., E. A. Klonoff, and H. Landrine (1997). "The Effects on Children of Participating in Studies of Minors' Access to Tobacco." *Preventive Medicine* 26:236–40.

Allen, K., A. Moss, G. A. Giovino, D. R. Shopland, and J. P. Pierce (1993). "Teenage Tobacco Use Data. Estimates from the Teenage Attitudes and Practices Survey, United States, 1989." Advance Data. Atlanta: Centers for Disease Control and Prevention.

Altman, D. G., V. Foster, L. Rasenick-Douss, and J. B. Tye (1989). "Reducing the Illegal Sale of Cigarettes to Minors." *JAMA* 261:80–83.

Altman, D. G., D. W. Levine, R. Coeytaux, J. Slade, and R. Jaffe (1996a). "Tobacco Promotion and Susceptibility to Tobacco Use among Adolescents Aged 12 through 17 Years in a Nationally Representative Sample." *American Journal of Public Health* 86:1590–93.

Altman, D. G., D. W. Levine, G. Howard, and H. Hamilton (1996b). "Tobacco Farmers and Diversification: Opportunities and Barriers." *Tobacco Control* 5:192–98.

Altman, D. G., C. Schooler, and M. D. Basil (1991). "Alcohol and Cigarette Advertising on Billboards." *Health Education Research* 6:487–90.

Ambrosone, C. B, J. L. Freudenheim, S. Graham, J. R. Marshall, J. E. Vena, J. R. Brasure, A. M. Michalek, R. Laughlin, T. Nemoto, K. A. Gillenwater, and P. G. Shields (1996). "Cigarette Smoking, N-Acetyltransferase 2 Genetic Polymorphisms and Breast Cancer Risk." *JAMA* 276:1494–1501.

Amenta, E., K. Dunleavy, and M. Bernstein (1994). "Stolen Thunder? Huey Long's 'Share Our Wealth,' Political Mediation, and the Second New Deal." *American Sociological Review* 59:678–702.

American Cancer Society (1990a). *Annual Report 1989*. Atlanta: Author.
American Cancer Society (1990b). *Minnesota Division, Inc. 1990 Annual Report*. Minneapolis: ACS Minnesota Division, Inc.
American Cancer Society (1991a). *Cancer Facts and Figures 1991*. Atlanta: Author.
American Cancer Society (1991b). *Minnesota Division, Inc. 1990–1991 Annual Report*. Minneapolis: ACS Minnesota Division, Inc.
American Cancer Society (1994). *World Smoking & Health* 19(1).
American Cancer Society (1997). *Stop Illegal Tobacco Sales: A Manual for Community Action*. Atlanta: Author.
American Cancer Society (no date). *Public Issues in the American Cancer Society: A Guide for Minnesota Division Public Issues/Quick Response Team Volunteers*. Minneapolis: ACS Minnesota Division, Inc.
American Heart Association (1989). *1990 Research Facts*. Dallas: Author.
American Heart Association (1992). *American Heart Association History 1992*. Dallas: Author.
American Heart Association Minnesota Affiliate (1991). *Annual Report 1991*. Minneapolis: Author.
American Lung Association (no date). *The Story of Christmas Seals*. New York: Author.
American Lung Association of Minnesota (1990). *Annual Report, 1989–1990*. St. Paul: Author.
American Lung Association of Ramsey County (1990). *Annual Report, 1990*. St. Paul: Author.
American Medical Association (1989). "Firearm Injuries and Deaths: A Critical Public Health Issue." *Public Health Reports* 104:114–20.
American Medical Association (2000). "Five Years of Making a Difference: The SmokeLess States National Tobacco Prevention and Control Program." Chicago: SmokeLess States National Tobacco Prevention and Control Program, AMA. Available on-line at http://www.ama-assn.org/special/aos/tobacco/history.htm.
American Public Health Association (1941). *Community Organizing for Health Education*. Cambridge: Technology Press.
American Public Health Association (1997). "APHA Joins Lung Association in 'Breaking the Chain.'" *Nation's Health*, August, p. 14.
American Society of Clinical Oncology (1996). "Tobacco Control: Reducing Cancer Incidence and Saving Lives." *Journal of Clinical Oncology* 14:1961–63.
Americans for Nonsmokers' Rights (no date). *Youth Access to Tobacco: A Guide to Developing Policy*. Berkeley: Author.
Annas, G. J. (1997). "Tobacco Litigation as Cancer Prevention: Dealing with the Devil." *New England Journal of Medicine* 336:304–8.
Anonymous (1974). "Minnesota Doctors Ask for Smoking Ban in Hospitals." *St. Paul Pioneer Press*, May 18, Section 3, p. 2.
Anonymous (1996a). "Urge Your Elected Officials to Protect Kids from Tobacco." *Discover* (Spring):3. Minneapolis: HealthPartners, Inc.
Anonymous (1996b). "Massachusetts Takes a New Aim at Gun Safety." *Nation's Health*, December 8.

Anonymous (1996c). "Where There's Smoke There's Money." *Economic and Business Review Indonesia On-line,* June 19.

Anton, T. J. (1989). *American Federalism and Public Policy.* Philadelphia: Temple University Press.

Ashley, M. J., S. B. Bull, and L. L. Pederson (1995). "Support Among Smokers and Nonsmokers for Restrictions on Smoking." *American Journal of Preventive Medicine* 11:283–87.

Ashton, L. P. (1997). "Peru: Carpet Power." *Tobacco Control* 6:173.

Aspen Systems Corporation (1996). *A Report to the Governor on State Regulation of Health Maintenance Organizations.* Rockville: Author.

Associated Press (1995). "MCLU Backs Tobacco Interests Against Town's Advertising Ban." *Minneapolis Star Tribune,* August 18, p. B3.

Associated Press (1996a). "Cancer Society Trades Product Endorsements for Cash." *Star Tribune,* August 17, A1.

Associated Press (1996b). "Minnesota Leads 33-State Call for FDA to Regulate Tobacco." *Star Tribune,* November 28, B2.

Associated Press (1997a). "Fortune 500 Companies' Profits Soar 23.3 Percent." *Star Tribune,* April 8, p. D–1.

Associated Press (1997b). "Smoke-Free Rule Kicks in at State Prisons on Friday." *Star Tribune,* July 28, p. B–3.

Association for Nonsmokers-Minnesota (1991). "Return of Organization Exempt from Income Tax (IRS form 990, 1990)." St Paul: Author.

Association for Nonsmokers-Minnesota (1992). "Tobacco Interests Score Near Perfect Record in Legislature." *ANSR* 6(2, May). St. Paul: Author.

Association for Nonsmokers-Minnesota (1993a). *ASSIST Community Action Book: A Handbook for Community Tobacco Control Activists.* Saint Paul: Author.

Association for Nonsmokers-Minnesota (1993b). "Common Areas Bill Stalls." *ANSR* 7(1, April). St. Paul: Author.

Association for Nonsmokers-Minnesota (1993c). "Workplace Amendments to MCIAAA Fail . . . Again." *ANSR* 7(1, April). St. Paul: Author.

Association for Nonsmokers-Minnesota (1994a). *ANSR* 8(3, September). St. Paul: Author.

Association for Nonsmokers-Minnesota (1994b). *Community Tobacco Control: A Handbook for Community Action.* Saint Paul: Author.

Association for Nonsmokers-Minnesota (1994c). "Nonsmokers Score Two— Maybe." *ANSR* 8(2, May). St. Paul: Author.

Association for Nonsmokers-Minnesota (1997). "Allina Provides Grant to Assist Community Coalitions." *ANSR* 11(April). St. Paul: Author.

Association of State and Territorial Health Officials (1994). *State Tobacco Use Prevention and Control Activities: Progress Report 1990 to 1992.* Washington: Author.

Baden, P. L. (1995). "Anti-Tobacco Organizations Challenged." *Minneapolis Star Tribune,* November 9, p. B1.

Bailey, W. J. and J. W. Crowe (1994). "A National Survey of Public Support for Restrictions on Youth Access to Tobacco." *Journal of School Health* 64:314–17.

Baird, K. L. (1999). "The New NIH and FDA Medical Research Policies: Targeting Gender, Promoting Justice." *Journal of Health Politics, Policy, and Law* 24:531–65.

Ball, K. 1995. "LASH for Health." *Tobacco Control* 4:19–20.

Ballard, J. E., T. D. Koepsell, and F. Rivara (1992). "Association of Smoking and Alcohol Drinking with Residential Fire Injuries." *American Journal of Epidemiology* 135:26–34.

Bandow, D. (1995). "The Politics of Science: The Federal Bureaucracy's War on Social Drinking." Policy Report No. 13-June. Raleigh, NC: John Locke Foundation.

Baris, E. and K. McLeod (2000). "Globalization and International Trade in the Twenty-First Century: Opportunities for and Threats to the Health Sector in the South." *International Journal of Health Services* 30:187–210.

Barkan, S. E. (1984). "Legal Control of the Southern Civil Rights Movement." *American Sociological Review* 49:552–65.

Bearman, N. S., A. O. Goldstein, and D. C. Bryan (1995). "Legislating Clean Air: Politics, Preemption and the Health of the Public." *NCMJ* 56:14–19.

Beckett, K. (1994). "Setting the Public Agenda: 'Street Crime' and Drug Use in American Politics." *Social Problems* 41:425–47.

Beckett, K. (1995). "Media Depictions of Drug Abuse: The Impact of Official Sources." *Research in Political Sociology* 7:161–82.

Begay, M. E. and S. A. Glantz (1997). "Question 1: Tobacco Education Expenditures in Massachusetts, USA." *Tobacco Control* 6:213–18.

Begay, M. E., M. Traynor, and S. A. Glantz (1993). "The Tobacco Industry, State Politics and Tobacco Education in California." *American Journal of Public Health* 83:1214–21.

Benford, R. D. and D. A. Snow (2000). "Framing Processes and Social Movements: An Overview and Assessment." *Annual Review of Sociology* 26:611–39.

Bennett, J. T. and T. J. DiLorenzo (1994). *Unhealthy Charities: Hazardous to Your Health and Wealth.* New York: Basic Books.

Bennett, J. T. and T. J. DiLorenzo (1998). *CancerScam: Diversion of Federal Cancer Funds to Politics.* New Brunswick, NJ: Transaction.

Berger, P. L. (1986). "A Sociological View of the Antismoking Phenomenon." Pp. 225–40 in *Smoking and Society: Toward a More Balanced Assessment*, edited by Robert D. Tollison. Lexington, MA: Lexington.

Berger, P. L. and R. J. Neuhaus (1977). *To Empower People: The Role of Mediating Structures in Public Policy.* Washington, DC: American Enterprise Institute.

Bergthold, L. (1991). "The Fat Kid on the Seesaw: American Business and Health Care Cost Containment, 1970–1990." *Annual Review of Public Health* 12:157–75.

Bero, L. A. and S. A. Glantz (1993). "Tobacco Industry Response to a Risk Assessment of Environmental Tobacco Smoke." *Tobacco Control* 2:103–13.

Best, J. (1979). "Economic Interests and the Vindication of Deviance: Tobacco in Seventeenth Century Europe." *Sociological Quarterly* 20:171–82.

Bialous, S. A. and S. A. Glantz (1999). "Arizona's Tobacco Control Initiative Illustrates the Need for Continuing Oversight by Tobacco Control Advocates." *Tobacco Control* 8:141–51.

Blackburn, H. (1983). "Research and Demonstration Projects in Community Cardiovascular Disease Prevention." *Journal of Public Health Policy* 4:398–421.

Blaine, T., D. Hennrikus, J. L. Forster, S. O'Neil, M. Wolfson, and H. Pham (1997).

"Creating Tobacco Control Policy at the Local Level: Implementation of a Direct Action Organizing Approach." *Health Education and Behavior* 24:640–51.

Blendon, R. J. and J. T. Young (1998). "The Public and the Comprehensive Tobacco Bill" *JAMA* 280:1279–84.

Blewett, L. A. (1994). "Reforms in Minnesota: Forging the Path." *Health Affairs* 13:200–9.

Blewett, L. A. and S. K. Hofrenning (1997). "Minnesota: The Land of Nonprofit HMOs." *Minnesota Medicine* 80:21–24.

Bloch, M. (1994). "Tobacco Industry Funding of Biomedical Research." *Tobacco Control* 3:297–98.

Bloom, J. L. (1998). "International Interests in U.S. Tobacco Legislation." Health Science Analysis Project, Policy Analysis No. 3, April 14. Washington, DC: Advocacy Institute.

Blum, A. (1992). "Ethics of Tobacco-Funded Research in U.S. Medical Schools." *Tobacco Control* 1:244–45.

Blum, A. (1994). "Paid Counter-Advertising—Proven Strategy to Combat Tobacco Use and Promotion." *American Journal of Preventive Medicine* 10:8–10.

Blum, A. (1995). "DOC's Deck-O-Butts Trading Cards: Using Humour to Change Youth Attitudes about Tobacco." *Tobacco Control* 4:219–21.

Blum, A. and R. Daynard (1995). "A Review of Divestment by Medical Organizations and Academic Institutions of Shareholdings in Tobacco Companies." Pp. 1005–6 *Tobacco and Health*, edited by in Karen Slama. New York: Plenum.

Blum, A., E. Vidstrand, and E. Solberg (1995). "Counteracting Marlboro Promotions in the United States." Pp. 655–56 in *Tobacco and Health*, edited by Karen Slama. New York: Plenum Press.

Borland, R., J. P. Pierce, D. M. Burns, E. Gilpin, M. Johnson, and D. Bal (1992). "Protection from Environmental Tobacco Smoke in California: The Case for a Smoke-Free Workplace." *JAMA* 268:749–52.

Bowser, R. and L. O. Gostin (1999). "Managed Care and the Health of a Nation." *Southern California Law Review* 72:1209–95.

Boyd, J., D. Wesley, U. Himmelstein, and S. Woolhandler (1995). "The Tobacco / Health-Insurance Connection." *Lancet* 346:64.

Boyle, R. G., J. Stedman, and J. L. Forster (1995). "Availability of Smokeless Tobacco to Underage Youth in Two Minnesota Communities." *Health Values* 19:10–16.

Bracht, N. (Ed.) (1990). *Health Promotion at the Community Level.* Newbury Park, CA: Sage.

Brandt, A. M. (1990). "The Cigarette, Risk, and American Culture." *Daedalus* 19:155–76.

Breslau, N. M., M. Kilbey, and P. Andreski (1993). "Nicotine Dependence and Major Depression: New Evidence from a Prospective Investigation." *Archives of General Psychiatry* 50:31–35.

Breslau, N. and E. L. Peterson (1996). "Smoking Cessation in Young Adults: Age at Initiation of Cigarette Smoking and Other Suspected Influences." *American Journal of Public Health* 86:214–20.

Broadbent, J. (1989). "Strategies and Structural Contradictions: Growth Coalition Politics in Japan." *American Sociological Review* 54:707–21.

Brown, L. D. (1991). "Capture and Culture: Organizational Identity in New York Blue Cross." *Journal of Health Politics, Policy, and Law* 16:651–70.

Brownson, R. C., J. Jackson-Thompson, J. C. Wilkerson, J. R. Davis, N. W. Owens, and E. B. Fisher, Jr. (1992). "Demographic and Socioeconomic Differences in Beliefs about the Health Effects of Smoking." *American Journal of Public Health* 82:99–103.

Buechler, S. M. (1995). "New Social Movement Theories." *Sociological Quarterly* 36:441–64.

Burstein, P. (1985). *Discrimination, Jobs, and Politics.* Chicago: University of Chicago Press.

Butterfoss, F. D., R. M. Goodman, and A. Wandersman (1995). "Community Coalitions for Prevention and Health Promotion." *Health Education Research* 8:315–30.

Cain, R. (1995). "Community-Based AIDS Organizations and the State: Dilemmas of Dependence." *AIDS and Public Policy Journal* 10:83–93.

Campaign for Tobacco-Free Kids (1996). "Public Strongly Supports New FDA Rule to Reduce Tobacco Use by Youth According to National Poll." Press Release, Washington, DC: Author.

Campaign for Tobacco-Free Kids (2000a). "U.S. Cigarette Companies' Settlement-Related Price Hikes Excessive." Washington, DC: Author, May 24. Available on-line at http://tobaccofreekids.org/research/factsheets/pdf/0071.pdf.

Campaign for Tobacco-Free Kids (2000b). "Special Reports: State Tobacco Settlement." Washington, DC: Author, August 17. Available on-line at http://tobaccofreekids.org/reports/settlements/.

Cardador, M. T., A. R. Hazan, and S. A. Glantz (1995). "Tobacco Industry Smokers' Rights Publications: A Content Analysis." *American Journal of Public Health* 85:1212–17.

Carol, J. (1992). "It's a Good Idea to Criminalize Purchase and Possession of Tobacco by Minors—NOT!" *Tobacco Control* 1:296–97.

Center for Substance Abuse Prevention (1996). *Synar regulation: Sample design guidance.* Rockville, MD: Department of Health and Human Services.

Center for Substance Abuse Prevention (no date). *Implementing the Synar Regulation: Strategies for Reducing Sales of Tobacco Products to Minors,* Workshop Edition. Rockville, MD: Department of Health and Human Services.

Centers for Disease Control (1991a). "Public Attitudes Regarding Limits on Public Smoking and Regulation of Tobacco Sales and Advertising—10 U.S. Communities, 1989." *Morbidity and Mortality Weekly Report* 40:344–45, 351–53.

Centers for Disease Control (1991b). *State Tobacco Prevention and Control Activities: Results of the 1989–1990 Association of State and Territorial Health Officials (ASTHO) Survey. Final Report.* Atlanta: Office on Smoking and Health.

Centers for Disease Control and Prevention (1993a). "Cigarette Smoking—Attributable Mortality and Years of Potential Life Lost—United States, 1990." *Morbidity and Mortality Weekly Report* 42:645–49.

Centers for Disease Control and Prevention (1993b). "Years of Potential Life Lost Before Age 65—United States, 1990 and 1991." *Morbidity and Mortality Weekly Report* 42:251–53.

Centers for Disease Control and Prevention (1994a). "Medical-Care Expenditures

Attributable to Cigarette Smoking—United States, 1993." *Morbidity and Mortality Weekly Report* 43:469–71.

Centers for Disease Control and Prevention (1994b). "Attitudes Toward Smoking Policies in Eight States—United States, 1993." *Morbidity and Mortality Weekly Report* 43:786–89.

Centers for Disease Control and Prevention (1994c). "Guidelines for School Health Programs to Prevent Tobacco Use and Addiction." *Morbidity and Mortality Weekly Report* 43:1–18.

Centers for Disease Control and Prevention (1994d). "Surveillance for Selected Tobacco-Use Behaviors—United States, 1900–1994." *Morbidity and Mortality Weekly Report* 43 (SS-3):1–43.

Centers for Disease Control and Prevention (1995). "Estimated Expenditures for Core Public Health Functions—Selected States, October 1992–September 1993" *Morbidity and Mortality Weekly Report* 44(22):427–29.

Centers for Disease Control and Prevention (1996). "Tobacco Use and Usual Source of Cigarettes among High School Students—United States, 1995." *Morbidity and Mortality Weekly Report* 45(20):413–18.

Centers for Disease Control and Prevention (1997a). "State-Specific Prevalence of Cigarette Smoking Among Adults and Children's and Adolescents' Exposure to Environmental Tobacco Smoke—United States, 1996." *Morbidity and Mortality Weekly Report* 46(44):1038–43.

Centers for Disease Control and Prevention (1997b). "Cigarette Smoking Among Adults—United States, 1995." *Morbidity and Mortality Weekly Report* 46:1217–20.

Centers for Disease Control and Prevention (1997c). "Illegal Sales of Cigarettes to Minors—Mexico City, Mexico, 1997" *Morbidity and Mortality Weekly Report* 46:440–44.

Centers for Disease Control and Prevention (1998). "State-Specific Prevalence Among Adults of Current Cigarette Smoking and Smokeless Tobacco Use, and Per Capita Tax-Paid Sales of Cigarettes—United States, 1997" *Morbidity and Mortality Weekly Report* 47:922–26.

Centers for Disease Control and Prevention (1999a). "Achievements in Public Health, 1900–1999: Tobacco Use—United States, 1900–1999." *Morbidity and Mortality Weekly Report* 48(43):986–93.

Centers for Disease Control and Prevention (1999b). "Cigarette Smoking Among Adults—United States, 1997." *Morbidity and Mortality Weekly Report* 48:993–96.

Centers for Disease Control and Prevention (1999c). "State-Specific Prevalence of Current Cigarette and Cigar Smoking Among Adults—United States, 1998." *Morbidity and Mortality Weekly Report* 48(45):1034–39.

Centers for Disease Control and Prevention (1999d). "Bidi Use Among Urban Youth—Massachusetts, March-April 1999." *Morbidity and Mortality Weekly Report* 48:796–99.

Centers for Disease Control and Prevention (1999e). *Best Practices for Comprehensive Tobacco Control Programs—August 1999*. Atlanta, GA: Office on Smoking and Health.

Centers for Disease Control and Prevention (2000). "Tobacco Use Among Middle and High School Students—United States, 1999." *Morbidity and Mortality Weekly Report* 49:49–53.

Chanen, D. (1993.) "Smoking Rules: Amendment Would Add Apartment Common Areas to Clean-Air Act." *Star Tribune,* March 5, p. 2-B.

Chapman, S. (1996). "Civil Disobedience and Tobacco Control: the Case of BUGA UP." *Tobacco Control* 5:179–85.

Chapman, S., D. Yach, Y. S. Aloojee, and D. Simpson (1994). "All Africa Conference on Tobacco Control." *British Medical Journal* 308:189–91.

Chapman, S., W.L. Wong, and W. Smith. "Self-exempting Beliefs about Smoking and Health: Differences Between Smokers and Ex-smokers." *American Journal of Public Health* 83 (2): 215–219.

Chen, Y., W. X. Li, S. Yu, and W. Qian (1988). "Chang-Ning Epidemiological Study of Children's Health: I: Passive Smoking and Children's Respiratory Diseases." *International Journal of Epidemiology* 17:348–55.

Christianson, J., B. Dowd, J. Kralewski, S. Hayes, and C. Wisner (1995). "Managed Care in the Twin Cities: What Can We Learn?" *Health Affairs* 14:114–30.

Chun, R. and T. R. Pender (1994). The Basics of MinnesotaCare: A Guide for Legislators. St Paul: Research Department, Minnesota House of Representatives.

Cismoski, J. and M. Sheridan (1993). "Availability of Cigarettes to Under-Age Youth in Fond du Lac, Wisconsin." *Wisconsin Medical Journal* November:626–30.

Cismoski, J. and M. Sheridan (1997). "Enforcement of Minor Tobacco Laws: Wisconsin, 1996." *Wisconsin Medical Journal* (November): 35–38.

Coalition on Smoking OR Health (1993). "Saving Lives and Raising Revenue: Reasons for Major Increases in State and Federal Tobacco Taxes." Washington, DC: Author.

Coeytaux, R. R., D. G. Altman, and J. Slade (1995). "Tobacco Promotions in the Hands of Youth." *Tobacco Control* 4(3):253–57.

Coffman, J. B. and T. J. Collins (1992). "How the Hired Guns Work." *Saint Paul Pioneer Press,* Special Reprint Section (*Bankrolling the Legislature*), April, p. 22–23.

Cohn, V. (1965). "Former 'U' Doctor Leads Crusade Against Smoking." *Minneapolis Tribune,* April 4, p. 18B.

Coleman, B. C. (1997). "The AMA at 150: Whom Is It Looking Out For?" *Star Tribune,* June 27, p. 15.

Collins, A. (2000). "Targeting Youth? Study: Big Tobacco Spending More on Ads in Magazines with Teen Readers." ABC News.com, May 17, http://abcnews.go.com/sections/us/DailyNews/tobaccoads000517.html.

COMMIT Research Group (1995). "Community Intervention Trial for Smoking Cessation (COMMIT): I. Cohort Results from a Four-Year Community Intervention." *American Journal of Public Health* 85(2):183–92.

Conlan, T. J. (1998). *From New Federalism to Devolution: Twenty-Five Years of Intergovernmental Reform.* Washington: Brookings Institution Press.

Correa, P., L. W. Pickle, E. Fontham, Y. Lin, and W. Haenszel (1983). "Passive Smoking and Lung Cancer." *Lancet* 2:595–97.

Crumpton, A. C. (1997). "Environmental Justice, Expertise, and the EPA: Institutionalizing a People's Epidemiology?" Paper presented at the annual meeting of the American Sociological Association, Toronto, Canada, August.

Cummings, K. M. (1993). "An Obituary: Complacency Claims the Life of a Model Tobacco Control Programme." *Tobacco Control* 2:270.

Cummings, K. M., T. Saunders-Martin, H. Clarke, and J. Perla (1996). "Monitoring Vendor Compliance with Tobacco Sales Laws: Payment vs. No Payment Approaches" (Letter to the editor). *American Journal of Public Health* 86:750–51.

Cummings, K. M., E. Sciandra, T. F. Pechacek, M. Orlandi, and W. R. Lynn (1992). "Where Teenagers Get Their Cigarettes: A Survey of the Purchasing Habits of 13–16-Year-Olds in 12 U.S. Communities." *Tobacco Control* 1:264–67.

Cummings, K. M., T. Pechacek, and D. Shopland (1994). "The Illegal Sale of Cigarettes to U.S. Minors: Estimates by State." *American Journal of Public Health* 84:300–2.

Daynard, R.A. 1988. "Tobacco Liability Litigation as a Cancer Control Strategy." *Journal of the National Cancer Institute* 80(1):9–13.

Davidson, P. (1999). "The National Foundation." Pp. 78–84 in *The Multistate Master Settlement Agreement and the Future of State and Local Tobacco Control: An Analysis of Selected Topics and Provisions of the Multistate Master Settlement Agreement of November 23, 1998*, edited by Graham Kelder and Patricia Davidson. Boston: Tobacco Control Resource Center, Northeastern University School of Law.

Davies, J. C. (1962). "Toward a Theory of Revolution." *American Sociological Review* 6:5–19.

Davis, R. M. (1992). "Is There a Role for Health-Effects Research?" *Tobacco Control* 1:241–43.

Davis, R. M. (1995). "In Reply." *Tobacco Control* 4:195–96.

Dawes, S. and J. Saidel (1988). *The State and the Voluntary Sector*. New York: Foundation Center / Nelson A. Rockefeller Institute of Government.

Dawson, J. (1995). "State Agency Accused of Misusing Funds." *Star Tribune*, October 19, p. B3.

Dean, A. G., J. M. Shultz, S. W. Gust, K. C. Harty, and M. E. Moen (1986). "The Minnesota Plan for Nonsmoking and Health: A Multidisciplinary Approach to Risk Factor Control." *Public Health Reports* 101:270–77.

Dean, A. G., J. M. Shultz, T. E. Kottke, S. W. Gust, and K. C. Harty (1985). "The Minnesota Plan for Nonsmoking and Health: Ideas for Statewide Action." *Minnesota Medicine* 68:371–77.

deFiebre, C. (1996). "Ethics Board Clears Antismoking Groups." *Star Tribune*, January 27, p. A8.

deFiebre, C. (1997a). "Tobacco-Regulation Bill Makes Return Appearance." *Star Tribune*, January 17, p. B–3.

defiebre, C. (1997b). "Where There's Smoke, There's a Lobby." *Star Tribune*, May 12, p. B–3.

defiebre, C. (1997c). "Sweeping Tobacco-Control Bill Sent to Governor." *Star Tribune*, May 20, p. A10.

defiebre, C. (1997d). "Tobacco-Access Bill Faces Uncertain Future in House." *Star Tribune*, May 14, p. B3.

defiebre, C. (1997e). "Tobacco Lobbying Lights Up at Capitol." *Star Tribune*, May 15, p. B1.

defiebre, C. (1997f). "House Oks Major Anti-Tobacco Bill." *Star Tribune*, May 16, p. B1.

defiebre, C. (1997g). "Carlson Flays Tobacco-Control Bill, But Signs It Anyway." *Star Tribune,* May 31, p. B2.

defiebre, C. (1997h). "Cigarette Firms Skirt Law with 2-Packs." *Star Tribune,* August 2, p. B1.

DeJong, W. (1996). "When the Tobacco Industry Controls the News: KKR, RJR Nabisco, and the Weekly Reader Corporation." *Tobacco Control* 5:142–48.

della Porta, D. (1995). *Social Movements, Political Violence, and the State.* New York: Cambridge University Press.

della Porta, D. (1996). "Social Movements and the State: Thoughts on the Policing of Protest." Pp. 62–92 in *Comparative Perspectives on Social Movements,* edited by Doug McAdam, John D. McCarthy, and Mayer N. Zald. New York: Cambridge University Press.

Delvecchio, R. (1991). "Smokers Speak Up for Right to Light Up." *Star Tribune,* August 12, 3E. [Originally published in *San Francisco Chronicle.*]

DiFranza, J. R. and L. Brown (1992). "The Tobacco Institute's 'It's the Law' Campaign: Has It Halted Illegal Sales of Tobacco to Children." *American Journal of Public Health* 82: 1271–73.

DiFranza, J. R. and W. T. Godshall (1996). "Tobacco Industry Efforts Hindering Enforcement of the Ban on Tobacco Sales to Minors: Actions Speak Louder Than Words." *Tobacco Control* 5:127–31.

DiFranza, J. R. and R. A. Lew (1995). "Effect of Maternal Cigarette Smoking on Pregnancy Complications and Sudden Infant Death Syndrome." *Journal of Family Practice* 40:385–94.

DiFranza, J. R., B. D. Norwood, D. W. Garner, and J. B. Tye (1987). "Legislative Efforts to Protect Children from Tobacco." *JAMA* 257:3387–89.

DiFranza, J. R., J. W. Richards, Jr., P. M. Paulman, N. Wolf-Gillespie, C. Fletcher, R. D. Jaffe, and D. Murray (1991). "RJR Nabisco's Cartoon Camel Promotes Camel Cigarettes to Children." *JAMA* 266(22):3149–53.

DiFranza, J. R., J. A. Savageau, and B. F. Aisquith (1996). "Youth Access to Tobacco: The Effects of Age, Gender, Vending Machine Locks, and 'It's the Law' Programs." *American Journal of Public Health* 86:221–24.

DiFranza, J. R. and J. B. Tye (1990). "Who Profits from Tobacco Sales to Children?" *JAMA* 263:2784–87.

DiMaggio, P. J. and W. W. Powell (1983). "The Iron Cage Revisited: Institutional Isomorphism and Collective Rationality in Organizational Fields." *American Sociological Review* 48:147–60.

Dolan, T. A., S. P. McGorray, C. L. Grinstead-Skiger, and R. Mecklenburg (1997). "Tobacco Control Activities in U.S. Dental Practices." *Journal of the American Dental Association* 128:1669–79.

Doll, R. (1998). "Uncovering the Effects of Smoking: Historical Perspective." *Statistical Methods in Medical Research* 7:87–117.

Doll, R. and A. B. Hill (1950). "Smoking and Carcinoma of the Lung." *British Medical Journal* 1950:740–48.

Doll, R. and A. B. Hill (1956). "Lung Cancer and Other Causes of Death in Relation to Smoking." *British Medical Journal* 1956:1071–81.

Durbin, R. J. (1993). "The Tobacco Industry Strategy: New Subject, Same Tactics." *Tobacco Control* 2:93–94.

Edwards, B. S. and B. Burfeind (1997). "Campaign Aims to Get Tobacco's Money out of Politics." *Star Tribune*, August 16, p. A19.

Ehlert, B. (1991). "Bill of Rights Tour Called Philip Morris Puffery." *Star Tribune*, September 12, p. 5E.

Eisinger, P. (1973). "The Conditions of Protest Behavior in American Cities." *American Political Science Review* 67:11–28.

Elnicki, J. (1992). "Evaluation of Membership Involvement in the Association for Nonsmokers-Minnesota." Unpublished MPH thesis, Division of Epidemiology, School of Public Health, University of Minnesota.

Elzay, R. and P. Swanson (1996). "Cancer Society's Partnerships Do Not Constitute Endorsements." *Star Tribune*, September 6, p. A–20.

Emont, S. L., W. S. Choi, T. E. Novotny, and G. A. Giovino (1993). "Clean Indoor Air Legislation, Taxation, and Smoking Behaviour in the United States: an Ecological Analysis." *Tobacco Control* 2:13–17.

Environmental Protection Agency (1993). Respiratory Health Effects of Passive Smoking: Lung Cancer and Other Disorders. Washington, DC: National Institutes of Health.

Epstein, S. (1996). *Impure Science; Aids, Activism and the Politics of Knowledge.* Berkeley: University of California Press.

Ernster, V. L., D. Grady, R. Miike, D. Black, J. Selby, and K. Kerlikowske (1995). "Facial Wrinkling in Men and Women, by Smoking Status." *American Journal of Public Health* 85:78–82.

Escobedo, L. G. and J. P. Peddicord (1996). "Smoking Prevalence in U.S. Birth Cohorts: The Influence of Gender and Education." *American Journal of Public Health* 86:231–36.

Evans, N., A. Farkas, E. Gilpin, C. Berry, and J. P. Pierce (1995). "Influence of Tobacco Marketing and Exposure to Smokers on Adolescent Susceptibility to Smoking." *Journal of the National Cancer Institute* 87:1538–45.

Evans, S. M. and H. C. Boyte (1986). *Free Spaces: The Sources of Democratic Change in America.* New York: Harper & Row.

Farrelly, M. C., W. N. Evans, and E. S. Sfekas (1999). "The Impact of Workplace Smoking Bans: Results from a National Survey." *Tobacco Control* 8:272–77.

Feighery, E., D. G. Altman, and G. Shaffer (1991). "The Effects of Combining Education and Enforcement to Reduce Tobacco Sales to Minors. A Study of Four Northern California Communities." *JAMA* 266:3168–71.

Ferris, B. G., Jr., J. H. Ware, C. S. Berkey, D. W. Dockery, A. Spiro III, and F. E. Speizer (1985). "Effects of Passive Smoking on Health of Children." *Environmental Health Perspectives* 62:289–95.

Fiore, M. C., W. C. Bailey, S. J. Cohen, et al. (1996). *Smoking Cessation. Clinical Practice Guideline No. 18.* Rockville, MD: Agency for Health Care Policy and Research.

Fish, L., S. R. Wilson, D. M. Latini, and N. J. Starr (1996). "An Education Program for Parents of Children with Asthma: Differences in Attendance between Smoking and Nonsmoking Parents." *American Journal of Public Health* 86:246–48.

Fisher, W. F. (1997). "Doing Good? The Politics and Antipolitics of NGO Practices." *Annual Review of Anthropology* 26:439–64.

Fishman, J. A., S. B. Knowles, T. A. Woolery, D. M. Shelton, and M. P. Eriksen (1999). "State Laws on Tobacco Control—United States, 1998." *Morbidity and Mortality Weekly Report* 48:(SS03):21–62.

Fleming, D. W., S. L. Cochi, A. W. Hightower, and C. V. Broome (1987). "Childhood Upper Respiratory Tract Infections: To What Degree Is Incidence Affected by Day-Care Attendance?" *Pediatrics* 79:55–60.

Folsom, A. R, T. F. Pechacek, R. de Gaudemaris, R. V. Luepker, D. R. Jacobs, Jr., and R. F. Gillum (1984). "Consumption of 'Low-Yield' Cigarettes: Its Frequency and Relationship to Serum Thiocyanate." *American Journal of Public Health* 74:564–68.

Ford, D., R. Scragg, and J. Weir (1997). "Sale of Cigarettes to School Children Aged 14 and 15 Years in New Zealand." *New Zealand Medical Journal* 110:225–27.

Forster, J. L. and M. Wolfson (1998). "Youth Access to Tobacco: Policies and Politics." *Annual Review of Public Health* 19:203–35.

Forster, J. L. and M. E. Hourigan (1994). "Regulation of Cigarette Sales to Youth." Pp. 249–55 in *Prevention of Atherosclerosis and Hypertension Beginning in Youth,* edited by Lloyd J. Filer, Jr., Ronald M. Lauer, and Russell V. Luepker. Philadelphia and Baltimore: Lea & Febiger.

Forster, J. L., M. Hourigan, and P. McGovern (1992). "Availability of Cigarettes to Youth in Three Communities." *Preventive Medicine* 21:320–28.

Forster, J. L., M. Hourigan, and J. Weigum (1990). "The Movement to Restrict Children's Access to Tobacco in Minnesota." Paper presented at the Surgeon General's Interagency Committee on Smoking and Health, May 31.

Forster, J. L., Knut-Inge Klepp, and R. W. Jeffrey (1989). "Sources of Cigarettes to Tenth Graders in Two Minnesota Cities." *Health Education Research* 4:45–50.

Forster, J. L., K. Komro, and M. Wolfson (1996). "Survey of City Ordinances and Local Enforcement Regarding Commercial Availability of Tobacco to Minors in Minnesota (USA)." *Tobacco Control* 5:46–51.

Forster, J. L., C. McBride, R. Jeffrey, T. L. Schmid, and P. L. Pirie. 1991. "Support for Restrictive Tobacco Policies among Residents of Selected Minnesota Communities." *American Journal of Health Promotion* 6:99–104.

Forster, J. L. and M. Wolfson (1998). "Youth Access to Tobacco: Policies and Politics." *Annual Review of Public Health* 19:203–35.

Fortune 500 (2000). Fortune 5 Hundred 2000: Philip Morris. Available on-line at http://cgi.fortune.com/.

Freedman, A. and L. P. Cohen. (1993). "Smoke and Mirrors: How Cigarette Makers Keep Health Question 'Open' Year after Year." *Wall Street Journal,* February 11, p. A1.

Freeman, J. (1975). *The Politics of Women's Liberation.* New York: McKay.

Frenk, J. and A. Donabedian (1987). "State Intervention in Medical Care: Types, Trends, and Variables." *Health Policy and Planning* 2:17–31.

Fritschler, A. L. (1989). *Smoking and Politics: Policy Making and the Federal Bureaucracy,* 4th ed. Englewood Cliffs, NJ: Prentice Hall.

Gais, T. L., M. A. Peterson, and J. L. Walker (1984). "Interest Groups, Iron Triangles, and Representative Institutions in American National Government." *British Journal of Political Science* 14:161–85.

Gallagher, J. G. 1995. "Lobbying and Political Activity Restrictions for Federal Grantees and Contractors." Washington, DC: OMB Watch. Available on-line at http://www.ombwatch.org/las/galrpt.html.

Gamson, W. A. (1990). *The Strategy of Social Protest*, 2nd ed. Belmont, CA: Wadsworth.

Gamson, W. A. and D. S. Meyer (1996). "Framing Political Opportunity." Pp. 275–290 in *Comparative Perspectives on Social Movements*. New York: Cambridge University Press.

Garner, D. W. (1996). "Banning Tobacco Billboards: The Case for Municipal Action." *JAMA* 275:1263–69.

Geist, H. J. (1999). "Global Assessment of Deforestation Related to Tobacco Farming." *Tobacco Control* 8:18–28.

Giovino, G. A., M. W. Schooley, Bao-Ping Zhu, J. H. Chrismon, S. L. Tomar, J. P. Peddicord, R. K. Merritt, C. G. Husten, and M. P. Eriksen (1994). "Surveillance for Selected Tobacco-Use Behaviors—United States, 1900–1994." *Morbidity and Mortality Weekly Report* 43(SS–3):1–43.

Giugni, M. G. (1998). "Was It Worth the Effort? The Outcomes and Consequences of Social Movements." *Annual Review of Sociology* 24: 371–93.

Givel, M. S. and S. A. Glantz (2000). "Failure to Defend a Successful State Tobacco Control Program: Policy Lessons from Florida." *American Journal of Public Health* 90(5):762–67.

Glantz, S. A. (1987). "Achieving a Smokefree Society." *Circulation* 76(4):746–52.

Glantz, S. A. (1996). "Editorial: Preventing Tobacco Use—The Youth Access Trap." *American Journal of Public Health* 86(2):156–58.

Glantz, S. A. and E. D. Balbach (2000). *Tobacco War: Inside the California Battles*. Berkeley and Los Angeles: University of California Press.

Glantz, S. A. and W. W. Parmley (1991). "Passive Smoking and Heart Disease: Epidemiology, Physiology, and Biochemistry." *Circulation* 83 (1):1–12.

Glantz, S. A., J. Slade, L. A. Bero, P. Hanauer, and D. E. Barnes (1996). *The Cigarette Papers*. Berkeley and Los Angeles: University of California Press.

Glynn, T. J., M. W. Manley, and T. F. Pechacek (1990). "Physician-Initiated Smoking Cessation Program: The National Cancer Institute Trials." Pp. 11–25 in *Advances in Cancer Control: Screening and Prevention Research*, edited by P. Engstrom, B. Bimea, and B. Rimer. New York: Alan R. Liss.

Gold, D. R., X. Wang, D. Wypij, F. E. Speizer, J. H. Ware, and D. W. Dockery (1996). "Effects of Cigarette Smoking on Lung Function in Adolescent Boys and Girls." *New England Journal of Medicine* 335(13):931–37.

Golding, J., M. Paterson, and L. Kinlen (1990). "Factors Associated with Cancer in a National Cohort Study." *British Journal of Cancer* 62:304–8.

Goldsmith, J. C., M. J. Goran, and J. G. Nackel (1995). "Managed Care Comes of Age." *Healthcare Forum Journal* (September/October):14–24.

Goldstein, A. O. and N. S. Bearman (1996). "State Tobacco Lobbyists and Organizations in the United States: Crossed Lines" *American Journal of Public Health* 86(8):1137–42.

Goldstein, A. O., R. A. Sobel, J. D. Martin, S. D. Crocker, and S. H. Malek (1998). "How Does North Carolina Law Enforcement Limit Youth Access to Tobacco Products? A Study of Officers' Attitudes and Behaviors." *North Carolina Medical Journal* 59(2):90–94.

Goldstein, J. (1991). "The Stigmatization of Smokers: An Empirical Investigation." *Journal of Drug Education* 21(2):167–82.

Goodman, E. (1995). "Tobacco's Lame Hunt for a New Bad Guy." *Star Tribune*, October 18, p. A17.

Goodman, R. M., A. Steckler, S. Hoover, and R. Schwartz (1993). "A Critique of Contemporary Health Promotion Approaches: Based on a Qualitative Review of Six Programs in Maine." *American Journal of Health Promotion* 7(3):208–20.

Gordon, E. P. (1924). *Women Torch-Bearers: The Story of the Woman's Christian Temperance Union*. Evanston, IL: National Woman's Christian Temperance Union Publishing House.

Gordon, G. (1997). "Humphrey Advises: Wait for Tobacco Documents." *Star Tribune*, August 16, p. A15.

Gortmaker, S. L., D. K. Walker, F. H. Jacobs, and H. Ruch-Ross (1982). "Parental Smoking and the Risk of Childhood Asthma." *American Journal of Public Health* 72:574–79.

Gottlieb, S. (2000). "Supreme Court Rules That FDA Cannot Regulate Tobacco Industry." *British Medical Journal* 320(7239):894.

Gottsegen, J. J. (1940). *Tobacco: A Study of Its Consumption in the United States*. New York: Pitman.

Gould, R. V. (1993). "Trade Cohesion, Class Unity, and Urban Insurrection: Artisanal Activism in the Paris Commune." *American Journal of Sociology* 98(4):721–54.

Graves, A. B., C. M. Van Duijn, V. Chandra, et al. (1991). "Alcohol and Tobacco Consumption as Risk Factors for Alzheimer's Disease: a Collaborative Re-Analysis of Case-Control Studies." International Journal of Epidemiology 20(suppl. 2):48–57.

Gray, B. (1991). "Trusteeship in Nonprofit Hospitals: Change and Its Consequences." Independent Sector Research Forum Working Paper. Washington, DC: Independent Sector.

Gray, V. (1973). "Innovation in the States: A Diffusion Study." *American Political Science Review* 67(4):1174–85.

Green, L. W. and M. W. Kreuter (1990). "Health Promotion as a Public Health Strategy for the 1990s." *Annual Review of Public Health* 11:319–34.

Gregorio, D. I. (1994). "Counseling Adolescents for Smoking Prevention: A Survey of Primary Care Physicians and Dentists." *American Journal of Public Health* 84(7):1151–53.

Greve, M. S. (1987). "Why 'Defunding the Left' Failed." *Public Interest* 89(Fall):91–106.

Griffin, G. (1990). "Tobacco Use Prevention in Minnesota Schools: A Case Study." *American Journal of Health Promotion* 5(2):122–31.

Griffin, G. A., H. J. Loeffler, and P. Kasell (1988). "Tobacco-Free Schools in Minnesota." *Journal of School Health* 58(6):236–39.

Grodstein, F., F. E. Speizer, and D. J. Hunter (1995). "A Prospective Study of Incident Squamous Cell Carcinoma of the Skin in the Nurses' Health Study." *Journal of the National Cancer Institute* 87(14):1061–66.

Groeneveld, B. (1998). "Settlement Reached in Minnesota Trial." Reuters, May 8

(Fox Market Wire, available on-line at http://www.foxmarketwire.com/050898/tobacco.sml).

Gronbjerg, K. (1990). "Managing Nonprofit Funding Relations: Case Studies of Six Human Services Organizations." Working paper No. 156, Program on Non-Profit Organizations. New Haven, CT: Yale University.

Grossman, M., J. L. Sindelar, J. Mullahy, and R. Anderson (1993). "Policy Watch: Alcohol and Cigarette Taxes." *Journal of Economic Perspectives* 7(4):211–22.

Group Health Association of America (1994). *1994 National Directory of HMOs.* Washington, DC: Author.

Guinta, M. A. and J. P. Allegrante (1992). "The President's Committee on Health Education: A 20-Year Retrospective on Its Politics and Policy Impact." *American Journal of Public Health* 82(7):1033–41.

Gurr, T. R. (1970). *Why Men Rebel.* Princeton, NJ: Princeton University Press.

Gusfield, J. R. (1982). "Prevention: Rise, Decline, and Renaissance." Pp. 402–25 in *Alcohol, Science, and Society Revisited,* edited by Edith S. Gomberg, Helene Raskin White, and John A. Carpenter. Ann Arbor: The University of Michigan Press.

Gusfield, J. R. (1993). "The Social Symbolism of Smoking and Health." Pp. 49–68 in *Smoking Policy: Law, Politics, and Culture,* edited by Robert L. Rabin and Stephen D. Sugarman. New York: Oxford University Press.

Haber, J. (1994). "Smoking Is a Major Risk Factor for Periodontitis." *Current Opinion in Periodontology*:12–18.

Habermas, J. (1976). *Legitimation Crisis.* Boston: Beacon.

Habermas, J. (1985). *The Theory of Communicative Action.* Boston: Beacon.

Haga, C. (1996). "Chilling Out with a Smoke." *Star Tribune,* February 3, p. A–8.

Haines, H. H. (1988). *Black Radicals and the Civil Rights Mainstream, 1954–1970.* Knoxville: University of Tennessee Press.

Hammond, E. C. and D. Horn (1958). "Smoking and Death Rates—Report on Fifty-Four Months of Follow-Up on 187,783 Men." *JAMA* 166:1159–72.

Hammond, S. K., G. Sorensen, R. Youngstrom, and J. K. Ockene (1995). "Occupational Exposure to Environmental Tobacco Smoke." *JAMA* 274(12):956–60.

Hanners, D. and D. Shaffer (1998). "Documents Say State Teamsters Official Lobbied for Tobacco." *St. Paul Pioneer Press,* May 17.

Hardiman, M. (1986). "People's Involvement in Health and Medical Care." Pp. 45–69 in *Community Participation, Social Development, and the State,* edited by J. Midgely (with A. Hall, M. Hardiman, and D. Narine). New York: Methuen.

Harish, K. and R. Ravi (1995). "The Role of Tobacco in Penile Carcinoma." *British Journal of Urology* 75(3):375–77.

Harris, J. E. (1997). "Prepared Remarks at the American Cancer Society's Press Conference on the Proposed Tobacco Industry-Wide Resolution, Washington DC, July 24, 1997." Washington, DC: National Public Affairs Office, American Cancer Society.

Harrison, L. (1986). "Tobacco Battered and the Pipes Shattered: A Note on the Fate of the First British Campaign Against Tobacco Smoking." *British Journal of Addiction* 81:553–58.

Harty, K. C. (1993). "Animals and Butts: Minnesota's Media Campaign Against Tobacco." *Tobacco Control* 2:271–74.

Hatch, J. W. and E. Eng (1984). "Community Participation and Control: Or Control of Community Participation." Pp. 223–244 in *Reforming Medicine: Lessons of the Last Quarter Century*, edited by Victor W. Sidel and Ruth Sidel. New York: Pantheon.

Helfgot, J. H. (1974). "Professional Reform Organizations and the Symbolic Representation of the Poor." *American Sociological Review* 39(4):475–91.

Helfgot, J. H. (1981). *Professional Reforming: Mobilization for Youth and the Failures of Social Science*. New York: Lexington.

Hennepin County Community Prevention Coalition (1996). "Urgent Action Necessary!!!" Action alert (no date), Hennepin County Prevention Center, Hennepin County Community Health Department, Minneapolis, MN.

Herdman, R, M. Hewitt, and M. Laschover (1993). "Smoking-Related Deaths and Financial Costs: Office of Technology Assessment Estimates for 1990." U.S. Congress, Office of Technology Assessment testimony before the Senate Special Committee on Aging, Amy 6, Washington, DC.

Hermer, L. (1999). "Executive Summary." Pp. 5–15 in *The Multistate Master Settlement Agreement and the Future of State and Local Tobacco Control: An Analysis of Selected Topics and Provisions of the Multistate Master Settlement Agreement of November 23, 1998*, edited by Graham Kelder and Patricia Davidson. Boston, MA: Tobacco Control Resource Center, Northeastern University School of Law.

Hermer, L. and G. Kelder (1999). "Youth Access Provisions." Pp. 53–60 in *The Multistate Master Settlement Agreement and the Future of State and Local Tobacco Control: An Analysis of Selected Topics and Provisions of the Multistate Master Settlement Agreement of November 23, 1998*, edited by Graham Kelder and Patricia Davidson. Boston, MA: Tobacco Control Resource Center, Northeastern University School of Law.

Hilton, M. (1995). "'Tabs,' 'Fags,' and the 'Boy Labour Problem' in Late Victorian and Edwardian Britain." *Journal of Social History* 28 (Spring):587–607.

Hirsch, E. (1990). "Sacrifice for the Cause: Group Processes, Recruitment, and Commitment in a Student Social Movement." *American Sociological Review* 55:243–54.

Hodges, J. (1996). "Target Alone in No-Cigarette Stand." *Star Tribune*, August 29, p. A–1.

Holm, B. (1993). "Just Say No to the Reformers." *Minnesota Monthly* (November):55.

Hoppock, K. C. and T. P. Houston (1990). "Availability of Tobacco Products to Minors." *Journal of Family Practice* 30(2):174–76.

Houston, T. P. (Ed.) (1993). *Tobacco Use: An American Crisis. Final Conference Report and Recommendations from America's Health Community*. Washington, DC: American Medical Association.

Hovell, M. F., S. Russos, M. K. Beckhelm, J. A. Jones, S. M. Burkham-Kreitner, D. J. Slymen, C. R. Hofstetter, and B. Rubin (1995). "Compliance with Primary Prevention in Private Practice: Creating a Tobacco-Free Environment." *American Journal of Preventive Medicine* 11(5):288–93.

Howatt, G. (1997). "96 Hard on Health Plan Industry." *Minneapolis Star-Tribune* April 1, p. D2.

Howe, I. (1985). *Socialism in America*. New York: Harcourt Brace Jovanovich.

Hu, Teh-wei, Hai-Yen Sung, and T. E. Keeler (1995). "Reducing Cigarette Consumption in California: Tobacco Taxes vs. an Anti-Smoking Media Campaign." *American Journal of Public Health* 85(9):1218–22.

Humphrey, H. H., III (1994). "Remarks of Hubert Humphrey III, Attorney General re: Tobacco Lawsuit." August 17, 1994. St. Paul, MN: Office of the Attorney General

Humphrey, H. H., III (1997a). "Winning Against Big Tobacco: Let's Take the Time to Get it Right." *Public Health Reports* 112(5):378–85.

Humphrey, H. H., III (1997b). "'Holding Tobacco's Feet to the Fire." *Star Tribune,* April 24, p. A23.

Hurt, R. D., D. P. L. Sachs,E. D. E. D. Glover, K. P. Offord, J. Johnston, D. Andrew, C. Lowell, M. A. Khayrallah, D. R. Schroeder, P. N. Glover, C. R. Sullivan, I. T. Croghan, and P. M. Sullivan (1997). "A Comparison of Sustained-Release Bupropion and Placebo for Smoking Cessation." *New England Journal of Medicine* 337(17):1195–1202.

Hyman, G. S. (1997). *Descriptive Case Series of Three Highly Effective Grassroots Tobacco Control Groups.* Fieldwork Project Report, Family Health Track, New Jersey Graduate Program of Public Health, University of Medicine and Dentistry of New Jersey-Robert Wood Johnson Medical School, Piscataway, New Jersey.

Institute of Medicine (1988). *The Future of Public Health.* Washington, DC: National Academy Press.

Institute of Medicine (1998). *Taking Action to Reduce Tobacco Use.* Washington, DC: National Academy Press.

Jackson, H. (1983). "Developing Local Voluntary Action: Four Experimental Small Grants Schemes." *Home Office Research Bulletin* 16:51–53.

Jacobson, P. D. and K. E. Warner (1999). "Litigation and Public Health Policy Making: The Case of Tobacco Control." *Journal of Health Politics, Policy, and Law* 24(4):769–804.

Jacobson, P. D. and J. Wasserman (1997). "Tobacco Control Laws: Implementation and Enforcement." Santa Monica, CA: RAND.

Jacobson, P. D., J. Wasserman, and K. Raube (1992). "The Political Evolution of Anti-Smoking Legislation." Santa Monica, CA: RAND (R-4152-UCOP).

Jalali, R. (1998). "Channeling Social Activism? International Funding of NGOs and Social Movements in Developing Countries." Paper presented at the Annual Meeting of the American Sociological Association, San Francisco, August.

Jeddeloh, R. and J. Roski (1998). "Tobacco Control at Allina Health System: Intramural Strategies." *Medical Journal of Allina* 7(4). [Minnetonka, Minnesota: Allina Health System.]

Jenkins, J. C. (1983). "Resource Mobilization Theory and the Study of Social Movements." *Annual Review of Sociology* 9:527–53.

Jenkins, J. C. and C. M. Eckert (1986). "Channeling Black Insurgency: Elite Patronage and Professional Social Movement Organizations in the Development of the Black Movement." *American Sociological Review* 51(December):812–29.

Jenkins, J. C. and B. Klandermans (Eds.) (1995). *The Politics of Social Protest: Comparative Perspectives on States and Social Movements.* Minneapolis: University of Minnesota Press.

Jenkins, J. C. and C. Perrow (1977). "Insurgency of the Powerless: Farm Worker Movements (1946–72)." *American Sociological Review* 42:249–68.

Jenkins, J. C. and M. Wallace (1996). "The Generalized Action Potential of Protest Movements: The New Class, Social Trends, and Political Exclusion Explanations." *Sociological Forum* 11(2):183–207.

Jernigan, D. H. and P. A. Wright (1996). "Media Advocacy: Lessons from Community Experiences." *Journal of Public Health Policy* 17(3):306–30.

Jha, P. and J. F. Chaloupka (1999). "Curbing the Epidemic: Governments and the Economics of Tobacco Control." Washington, DC: International Bank for Reconstruction and Development/World Bank.

Johns, M. B., M. F. Hovell, C. A. Drastal, C. Lamke, and K. Patrick (1992). "Promoting Prevention Services in Primary Care: A Controlled Trial." *American Journal of Preventive Medicine* 8(3):135–39.

Johnston, L. D., P. M. O'Malley, and J. G. Bachman (1992). *Smoking, Drinking, and Illicit Drug Use Among American Secondary School Students, College Students, and Young Adults.* Vol. 1: *Secondary School Students.* Rockville, MD: U.S. Department of Health and Human Services, National Institute on Drug Abuse.

Johnston, L. D., P. M. O'Malley, and J. G Bachman (1999). "Cigarette Smoking among American Teens Continues Gradual Decline." Ann Arbor, MI: University of Michigan News and Information Services. Available on-line at www.monitoringthefuture.org.

Jones, D, B., T. H. Dunayer, C. Hill, and L. Oatman (2000). "Where There's Smoke, There's Disease. The Dangers of Environmental Tobacco Smoke." *Minnesota Medicine* 83(3):29–32.

Kagan, R. A. and D. Vogel (1993). "The Politics of Smoking Regulation: Canada, France, the United States." Pp. 22–48 in *Smoking Policy: Law, Politics, and Culture,* edited by Robert L. Rabin and Stephen D. Sugarman. New York: Oxford University Press.

Kahn, A. (1996). "Target Stores Stamp Out Cigarettes." *Saint Paul Pioneer Press,* August 28, p. 1A.

Kahn, P. L. (1983). "The Minnesota Clean Indoor Air Act." *New York State Journal of Medicine* 83:1300–1.

Källén, K. (1997). "Maternal Smoking during Pregnancy and Limb Reduction Malformations in Sweden." *American Journal of Public Health* 87(1):29–32.

Kandel, D. B., P. Wu, and M. Davie (1994). "Maternal Smoking during Pregnancy and Smoking by Adolescent Daughters." *American Journal of Public Health* 84(9):1407–13.

Kauffmann, F, I. B. Tager, A. Munoz, and F. E. Speizer (1989). "Familial Factors Related to Lung Function in Children Aged 6–10 Years: Results from the PAARC Epidemiologic Study." *American Journal of Epidemiology* 129:1289–99.

Keck, M. E. and K. Sikkink (1998). *Activists Beyond Borders: Advocacy Networks in International Politics.* Ithaca, NY: Cornell University Press.

Kelder, G. (1999a). "Historical Background." Pp. 20–24 in *The Multistate Master Settlement Agreement and the Future of State and Local Tobacco Control: An Analysis of Selected Topics and Provisions of the Multistate Master Settlement Agreement of November 23, 1998.* Boston, MA: Tobacco Control Resource Center, Northeastern University School of Law.

Kelder, G. (1999b). "State and Local Lobbying Restrictions." Pp. 61–77 in *The Multistate Master Settlement Agreement and the Future of State and Local Tobacco Control: An Analysis of Selected Topics and Provisions of the Multistate Master Settlement Agreement of November 23, 1998*. Boston, MA: Tobacco Control Resource Center, Northeastern University School of Law.

Kelder, G. and P. Davidson (Eds.) (1999). *The Multistate Master Settlement Agreement and the Future of State and Local Tobacco Control: An Analysis of Selected Topics and Provisions of the Multistate Master Settlement Agreement of November 23, 1998*. Boston, MA: Tobacco Control Resource Center, Northeastern University School of Law.

Kelder, G. E., Jr., and R. A. Daynard (1996). "Tobacco Litigation as a Public Health and Cancer Control Strategy." *JAMWA* 51(1–2):57–62.

Kettl, Donald F. (1994). "Deregulating at the Boundaries of Government: Would It Help?" Pp. 175–97 in *Deregulating the Public Service*, edited by J. J. DiIulio, Jr. Washington, DC: Brookings Institution.

Kiernan, V. (1998). "Tobacco Industry Paid Letter-Writing Scientists." *Chronicle of Higher Education*, August 14, p. A–16.

Kitschelt, H. P. (1986). "Political Opportunity Structures and Political Protest: Anti-Nuclear Movements in Four Democracies." *British Journal of Political Science* 16:57–85.

Klandermans, B. and D. Oegema (1987). "Potentials, Networks, Motivations, and Barriers: Steps towards Participation in Social Movements." *American Sociological Review* 52:519–31.

Kline, R. and P. Davidson (1999). "Advertising Restrictions." Pp. 42–52 in *The Multistate Master Settlement Agreement and the Future of State and Local Tobacco Control: An Analysis of Selected Topics and Provisions of the Multistate Master Settlement Agreement of November 23, 1998*, edited by Graham Kelder and Patricia Davidson. Boston, MA: Tobacco Control Resource Center, Northeastern University School of Law.

Klobuchar, J. (1994). "Marlboro Man Lights Up a Controversy . . ." *Star Tribune*, May 4, p. 3B.

Kluger, R. (1996). *Ashes to Ashes: America's Hundred-Year Cigarette War, the Public Health, and the Unabashed Triumph of Philip Morris*. New York: Alfred A. Knopf.

Knight, E. C., A. Patricia, and G. Mayer (1998). *The U.S. Tobacco Industry in Domestic and World Markets. Report for Congress* (Report No. 98–506 E), June 9. Washington, DC: Congressional Research Service.

Koh, H. K. (1996). "An Analysis of the Successful 1992 Massachusetts Tobacco Tax Initiative." *Tobacco Control* 5:220–25.

Koop, C. E. (1989). "A Parting Shot at Tobacco." *JAMA* 262(20):2894–95.

Koop, C. E., and G. D. Lundberg (1992). "Violence in America: A Public Health Emergency." *JAMA* 267:3075–76.

Kornhauser, W. (1959). *The Politics of Mass Society*. New York: Free Press.

Kramer, R. M. (1987). "Voluntary Agencies and the Personal Social Services." Pp. 240–257 in *The Nonprofit Sector: A Research Handbook*, edited by Walter W. Powell. New Haven, CT: Yale University Press.

Krieger, N., D. R. Williams, and N. E. Moss (1997). "Measuring Social Class in U.S.

Public Health Research: Concepts, Methodologies, and Guidelines." *Annual Review of Public Health* 18:341–78.

Kriesi, H., R. Koopmans, J. W. Dyvendak, and M. G. Giugni (1995). *New Social Movements in Western Europe: A Comparative Analysis.* Minneapolis: University of Minnesota Press.

Kuntz, P. (1995). "Alcoholic Beverage Industry Lobbies for Bill to Gut Substance Abuse Agency Seen as Threat." *Wall Street Journal,* August 14, p. A12.

Lando, H. A., J. L. Forster, M. Hourigan, and J. Weigum (1990a). "The Movement to Restrict Cigarette Vending Machines in Minnesota: The Fight Against Pre-Emption." Paper presented at the Seventh World Conference on Tobacco & Health, Perth Western Australia, April 1–5.

Lando, H. A., P. G. McGovern, F. X. Barrios, and B. D. Etringer (1990b). "Comparative Evaluation of American Cancer Society and American Lung Association Smoking Cessation Clinics." *American Journal of Public Health.* 80(5):554–59.

Lando, H. A., T. F. Pechacek, P. L. Pirie, D. M. Murray, M. B. Mittelmark, E. Lichtenstein, F. Nothwehr, and C. Gray (1995). "Changes in Adult Cigarette Smoking in the Minnesota Heart Health Program." *American Journal of Public Health* 85(2):201–8.

Laraña, E., H. Johnston, and J. R. Gusfield (Eds.) (1994). *New Social Movements: From Ideology to Identity.* Philadelphia, PA: Temple University Press.

Laumann, E. O. and D. Knoke (1987). *The Organizational State.* Madison: University of Wisconsin Press.

Launer, L. J., E. J. M. Feskens, S. Kalmijn, and D. Kromhout (1996). "Smoking, Drinking, and Thinking." *American Journal of Epidemiology* 143(3):219–27.

Leat, D. (1990). "Voluntary Organizations and Accountability." In *The Third Sector: Comparative Studies of Nonprofit Organizations,* edited by H. K. Anheier and W. Seibel. Hawthorne, NY: Aldine de Gruyter.

Lehman, E. W. (1988). "The Theory of the State Versus the State of Theory." *American Sociological Review* 53:807–23.

Leichter, H. M. (1991). *Free to Be Foolish: Politics and Health Promotion in the United States and Great Britain.* Princeton, NJ: Princeton University Press.

Levin, E. D. (1992). "Nicotinic Systems and Cognitive Function." *Psycho-pharmacology* 108:417–31.

Levin, M. (1993). "Who's Behind the Building Doctor?" *Nation* 257(5):168–71.

Levin, M. L., H. Goldstein, and B. R. Gerhardt (1950). "Cancer and Tobacco Smoking." *JAMA* 143:336–38.

Lewis, J. (1982). "The Federal Role in Alcoholism Research, Treatment, and Prevention." Pp. 385–401 in *Alcohol, Science, and Society Revisited,* edited by Edith S. Gomberg, Helene Raskin White, and John A. Carpenter. Ann Arbor: University of Michigan Press.

Lewit, E. M., M. Botsko, and S. Shapiro (1993). "Workplace Smoking Policies in New Jersey Businesses." *American Journal of Public Health* 83(2):254–56.

Lewit, E. M., D. Coate, and M. Grossman (1981). "The Effects of Government Regulation on Teenage Smoking." *Journal of Law and Economics* 24:545–69.

Li, De-Kun, B. A. Mueller, D. E. Hickok, J. R. Daling, A. G. Fantel, H. Checkoway, and N. S. Weiss (1996). "Maternal Smoking during Pregnancy and the Risk of Congenital Urinary Tract Anomalies." *American Journal of Public Health* 86(2):249–53.

Lichtenstein, E., L. Wallack, and T. Pechacek (1991). "Introduction to the Community Intervention Trial for Smoking Cessation." *International Journal of Community Health Education* 11(3):173–85.

Lightwood, J. M., C. S. Phibbs, and S. A. Glantz (1999). "Short-Term Health and Economic Benefits of Smoking Cessation: Low Birth Weight." *Pediatrics* 104(6): 1312–20.

Lima, J. C. and M. Siegel (1999). "The Tobacco Settlement: An Analysis of Newspaper Coverage of a National Policy Debate, 1997–1998." *Tobacco Control* 8(3):247–53.

Lineberry, R. and E. Fowler (1967). "Reformism and Public Policies in American Cities." *American Political Science Review* 61(3):701–16.

Lipset, S. M. (1950). *Agrarian Socialism.* Berkeley: University of California Press.

Lipsky, M. (1968). "Protest as a Political Resource." *American Political Science Review* 62(4):1144–58.

Lipsky, M. and S. R. Smith (1989). "Nonprofit Organizations, Government, and the Welfare State." *Political Science Quarterly* 104(4):625–49.

Lofland, J. (1989). "Consensus Movements: City Twinning and Derailed Dissent in the American Eighties." *Research in Social Movements, Conflict, and Change* 11:163–96.

Longo, D. R., R. C. Brownson, and R. L. Kruse (1995). "Smoking Bans in U.S. Hospitals: Results of a National Survey." *JAMA* 274(6):488–91.

Lowi, T. J. (1969). *The End of Liberalism.* New York: W. W. Norton.

Luepker, R. V., C. A. Johnson, D. M. Murray, and T. F. Pechacek (1983). "Prevention of Cigarette Smoking: Three-Year Follow-Up of an Education Program for Youth." *Journal of Behavioral Medicine* 6(1):53–62.

Luft, H. S. and M. R. Greenlick (1996). "The Contribution of Group- and Staff-Model HMOs to American Medicine." *The Milbank Quarterly* 74(4):445–67.

Lynch, B. S. and R. J. Bonnie (1994). *Growing Up Tobacco Free: Preventing Nicotine Addiction in Children and Youths.* Washington, DC: National Academy Press.

Lynch, T. A. and R. S. Hopkins (1996). "Estimating Tobacco-Related Health-Care and Mortality Costs in Florida." *Journal of the Florida Medical Association* 83(2):128–33.

Mackay, J. (1994a). "The Tobacco Problem—Commercial Profit versus Health: The Conflict of Interests in Developing Countries." *Preventive Medicine* 23(4):535–38.

Mackay, J. (1994b). "Laos—'The Land of Smiles' (and Smokes)." *Tobacco Control* 3(1):10–11.

Mackay, J. (1999). "International Aspects of U.S. Government Tobacco Bills." *JAMA* 281(19):1849–50.

Madigan, J. H. and K. B. Wilson (Eds.) (1990). *American Cancer Society Public Affairs/ Public Issues Handbook.* Washington, DC: National Public Affairs Office, American Cancer Society.

Makary, M. A. and I. Kawachi (1998). "The International Tobacco Strategy." *JAMA* 280(13):1194–95.

Malarcher, A. M., J. H. Chrisman, G. A. Giovino, and M. P. Eriksen (1997). "Editorial Note—1997." *Morbidity and Mortality Weekly Report* 46(20):448–50.

Malouff, J. S. and N. S. A. Kenyon (1991). "Negative Social Effects of Being a Smoker." *Journal of Drug Education* 21(4):293–302.

Malouff, J., J. Slade, C. Nielsen, N. Schutte, and E. Lawson (1993). "U.S. Laws that Protect Tobacco Users from Employment Discrimination." *Tobacco Control* 2:132–38.

Manley, M., W. Lynn, R. Payne Epps, D. Grande, T. Glynn, and D. Shopland (1997a). "The American Stop Smoking Intervention Study for Cancer Prevention: An Overview." *Tobacco Control* 6(suppl. 2):S5–S11.

Manley, M. W., J. P. Pierce, E. A. Gilpin, B. Rosbrook, C. Berry, and Lap-Ming Wun (1997b). "Impact of the American Stop Smoking Intervention Study on Cigarette Consumption." *Tobacco Control* 6(suppl. 2):S12–S16.

Mannino, D. M., M. Siegel, C. Husten, D. Rose, and R. Etzel (1996). "Environmental Tobacco Smoke Exposure and Health Effects in Children: Results from the 1991 National Health Interview Survey." *Tobacco Control* 5:13–18

Marcus, S. E., S. L. Emont, R. D. Corcoran, G. A. Giovino, J. P. Pierce, M. N. Waller, and R. M. Davis (1994). "Public Attitudes about Cigarette Smoking: Results from the 1990 Smoking Activity Volunteer Executed Survey." *Public Health Reports* 109(1):125–34.

Marmor, T. R. (1991). "New York's Blue Cross and Blue Shield, 1934–1990: The Complicated Politics of Nonprofit Regulation." *Journal of Health Politics, Policy, and Law* 16(4):761–92.

Marmor, T. R., M. Schlesinger, and R. W. Smithey (1987). "Nonprofit Organizations and Health Care." Pp. 221–39 in *The Nonprofit Sector: A Research Handbook,* edited by Walter W. Powell. New Haven, CT: Yale University Press.

Marshall, M. (1991). "The Second Fatal Impact: Cigarette Smoking, Chronic Disease, and the Epidemiological Transition in Oceania." *Social Science and Medicine* 33(12):1327–42.

Martinez, F. D., A. L. Wright, L. M. Taussig, and the Group Health Medical Associates (1994). "The Effect of Paternal Smoking on the Birthweight of Newborns Whose Mothers Did Not Smoke." *American Journal of Public Health* 84(9):1489–91.

Marwick, C. (1997). "Timetable Set for Reducing Use of Tobacco by Children and Adolescents." *JAMA* 277(1):778.

Marx, G. T. (1979). "External Efforts to Damage or Facilitate Social Movements: Some Patterns, Explanations, Outcomes, and Complications." Pp. 94–125 in *The Dynamics of Social Movements,* edited by M. N. Zald, and J. D. McCarthy. Cambridge, MA: Winthrop.

Matthews, N. A. (1994). *Confronting Rape: The Feminist Anti-Rape Movement and the State.* New York: Routledge.

Mays, G. P., C. A. Miller, and P. K. Halverson (2000). *Local Public Health Practice: Trends & Models.* Washington, DC: American Public Health Association.

McAdam, D. (1982). *Political Process and the Development of Black Insurgency.* Chicago, IL: University of Chicago Press.

McAdam, D. (1983). "Tactical Innovation and the Pace of Insurgency." *American Sociological Review* 48(6):735–53.

McAdam, D. (1986). "Recruitment to High-Risk Activism: The Case of Freedom Summer." *American Journal of Sociology* 92(1):64–90.

McAdam, D. (1996). "Conceptual Origins, Current Problems, Future Directions." Pp. 23–40 in *Comparative Perspectives on Social Movements,* edited by Doug

McAdam, John D. McCarthy, and Mayer N. Zald. New York: Cambridge University Press.

McAdam, D. and R. Paulsen (1993). "Specifying the Relationship between Social Ties and Activism." *American Journal of Sociology* 99:640–67.

McAdam, D., J. D. McCarthy, and M. N. Zald (1996). "Introduction: Opportunities, Mobilizing Structures and Framing Processes—Toward a Synthetic, Comparative Perspective on Social Movements." Pp. 1–20 in *Comparative Perspectives on Social Movements*, edited by Doug McAdam, John D. McCarthy, and Mayer N. Zald. New York: Cambridge University Press.

McCallum, L. (1998). "Blue Cross and Blue Shield Is Tobacco Case's Other Plaintiff." Transcript of radio broadcast, January 21, Minnesota Public Radio, St. Paul. Available on-line at http://news.mpr.org/features/199801/21_mccalluml_blues/.

McCann, M. W. (1994). *Rights at Work: Pay Equity Reform and the Politics of Legal Mobilization.* Chicago, IL: University of Chicago Press.

McCarthy, J. D. (1987). "Pro-Life and Pro-Choice Mobilization: Infrastructure Deficits and New Technologies." Pp. 49–66 in *Social Movements in an Organizational Society*, edited by Mayer N. Zald and John D. McCarthy. New Brunswick, NJ: Transaction.

McCarthy, J. D. (1996). "Constraints and Opportunities in Adopting, Adapting, and Inventing." Pp. 141–51 in *Comparative Perspectives on Social Movements*, edited by Doug McAdam, John D. McCarthy, and Mayer N. Zald. New York: Cambridge University Press.

McCarthy, J. D., D. W. Britt, and M. Wolfson (1991). "The Institutional Channeling of Social Movements in the Contemporary United States." *Research in Social Movements, Conflict, and Change* 13:45–76.

McCarthy, J. D. and M. Wolfson (1992). "Consensus Movements, Conflict Movements, and the Cooptation of Civic and State Infrastructures." Pp. 273–97 in *Frontiers in Social Movement Theory*, edited by Aldon D. Morris and Carol McClurg Mueller. New Haven, CT: Yale University Press.

McCarthy, J. D. and M. N. Zald (1973). *The Trend of Social Movements in America: Professionalization and Resource Mobilization.* Morristown, NJ: General Learning Press.

McCarthy, J. D. and M. N. Zald (1977). "Resource Mobilization and Social Movements: A Partial Theory." *American Journal of Sociology* 82(6):1212–41.

McGinnis, J. M. and W. H. Foege. 1993. "Actual Causes of Death in the United States." *JAMA* 270(18):2207–12.

McGrath, D. J. (1991). "Lobbyists' Spending Rises 86% in 2 Years." *Star Tribune*, September 28, p. 1B.

McGrath, D. J. (1992). "Bill Would Make It Illegal for Kids to Buy Tobacco." *Star Tribune*, March 13, p. 2B.

Melucci, A. (1980). "The New Social Movements: A Theoretical Approach." *Social Science Information* 19:199–226.

Merton, R. K. ([1938] 1970). *Science, Technology, and Society in Seventeenth-Century England.* New York: Howard Fertig.

Meyer, D. S. and S. Staggenborg (1996). "Movements, Countermovements, and the Structure of Political Opportunity." *American Journal of Sociology* 101(6):1628–60.

Miles, S. H., D. Haugen, and N. Lurie (1992a). "Minnesota Physicians and Health Care Reform. After 'Health Right.'" *Minnesota Medicine* 75(10):13–16.

Miles, S. H., N. Lurie, L. Quam, and A. Caplan (1992b). "Health Care Reform in Minnesota." *New England Journal of Medicine* 327(15):1092–95.

Minkler, M. (Ed.). (1997). *Community Organizing and Community Building for Health.* New Brunswick, NJ: Rutgers University Press.

Minkoff, D. C. (1994). "From Service Provision to Institutional Advocacy: The Shifting Legitimacy of Organizational Forms." *Social Forces* 72(4):943–69.

Minnesota Coalition for a Smoke-Free Society 2000 (1990). *It's Time We Clear the Air: The 1990 Program of Work.* Minneapolis: Author.

Minnesota Coalition for a Smoke-Free Society 2000 (1993). "1993 Members." Unpublished document, Minneapolis: Author.

Minnesota Coalition for a Smoke-Free Society 2000 (1997). "Public Policy Committee Meeting Announcement." Unpublished document, Minneapolis: Author.

Minnesota D-Day Steering Committee (no date). "Celebrate D-Day: Minnesota's 'Don't Smoke' Day." Information packet. St. Paul: American Lung Association of Minnesota; Minneapolis: American Cancer Society, Minnesota Division, Inc.

Minnesota Department of Health (1984). *The Minnesota Plan for Nonsmoking and Health: Report and Recommendations of the Technical Advisory Committee on Nonsmoking and Health.* Minneapolis: Author.

Minnesota Department of Health (1987). *The Minnesota Nonsmoking Initiative, June, 1985–December, 1986. A Report to the 1987 Legislature.* Minneapolis: Author.

Minnesota Department of Health (1991). *Minnesota Tobacco-Use Prevention Initiative 1989–1990: A Report to the 1991 Legislature.* Minneapolis: Author.

Minnesota Department of Health (1993). "Minnesota ASSIST: Community Action for a Tobacco-Free Environment." Minneapolis: Author.

Minnesota Department of Health (1996a). "ASSIST Project Subcontractor Awards." *Minnesota ASSIST Quarterly,* October, p. 10.

Minnesota Department of Health (1996b). "Smoke-Free Apartment Project." *Minnesota ASSIST Quarterly,* October, p. 2.

Minnesota Department of Health (1997). "ASSIST Project Strategic Planning Summary: Impacting the Future of Tobacco Control Policy in Minnesota." Draft document, June. Minneapolis: Author.

Minnesota Department of Health (no date). "Budget History of the MDH Nonsmoking Program." Unpublished document. Minneapolis: Author.

Minnesota Health Care Commission (1994). *Consumer Incentives and Prevention Report.* St. Paul, MN: Health Technology Advisory Committee.

Minnesota Prevention Resource Center (2000). "What Has Happened with the Tobacco Endowments?" *Impact* 19(October):6–7. [Anoka, MN: MPRC.]

Mintz, B. (1995). "Business Participation in Health Care Policy Reform: Factors Contributing to Collective Action within the Business Community." *Social Problems* 42(3):408–28.

Mitchell, Robert Cameron (1979). "Public Opinion and Environmental Politics in the 1970s and 1980s." In *Environmental Policy in the 1980s: The Impact of the Reagan Administration,* edited by Norman J. Vig and Micahael E. Kraft. Washington, DC: Congressional Quarterly Press.

Mittelmark, M. B., D. M. Murray, R. V. Luepker, and T. F. Pechacek (1982). "Cigarette Smoking among Adolescents: Is the Rate Declining?" *Preventive Medicine* 11(6):708–12.

Mizoue, T, T., N., K. Nishisaka, S. Nishisaka, I. Ogimoto, M. Ikeda, and T. Yoshimura (2000). "Prospective Study on the Relation of Cigarette Smoking with Cancer of the Liver and Stomach in an Endemic Region." *International Journal of Epidemiology* 29(2):232–37.

Moody, A. E. (1996). "Conditional Federal Grants: Can the Government Undercut Lobbying by Nonprofits through Conditions Placed on Federal Grants?" *Boston College Environmental Law Review* 24:113–58.

Moore, D. W. (1999). "Nine of Ten Americans View Smoking as Harmful." Poll Releases, October 7, 1999. Princeton, NJ: Gallup Organization. Available on-line at http://www.gallup.com/poll/releases/pr991007.asp.

Morain, C. (1993). "Mission Possible." *American Medical News,* August 9, p. 11.

Morgen, S. (1986). "The Dynamics of Cooptation in a Feminist Health Clinic." *Social Science and Medicine* 23(2):201–10.

Morrill, C. and C. McKee (1993). "Institutional Isomorphism and Informal Social Control: Evidence from a Community Mediation Center." *Social Problems* 40(4):445–63.

Morris, A. D. (1984). *The Origins of the Civil Rights Movement: Black Communities Organizing for Change.* New York: Free Press.

Morris, A. D. (1993). "Birmingham Confrontation Reconsidered: An Analysis of the Dynamics and Tactics of Mobilization." *American Sociological Review* 58(5):621–36.

Mosher, J. F. (1995). "The Merchants, Not the Customers: Resisting the Alcohol and Tobacco Industries' Strategy to Blame Young People for Illegal Alcohol Sales." *Journal of Public Health Policy* 16(4):412–31.

Mott, G. (1991). "Anti-Alcohol Network." *Market Watch* 10(6; May). New York: M. Shanken Communications, Inc.

Murray, C. J. L. and A. D. Lopez (Eds.) (1996). *The Global Burden of Disease: Summary.* Boston, MA: Harvard School of Public Health.

Nathanson, C. A. (1999). "Social Movements as Catalysts for Policy Change: The Case of Smoking and Guns." *Journal of Health Politics, Policy, and Law* 24(3):421–88.

National Research Council (1986). *Environmental Tobacco Smoke: Measuring Exposures and Assessing Health Effects.* Washington, DC: National Academy Press.

Nelson, D. E., G. A. Giovino, D. R. Shopland, P. D. Mowery, S. L. Mills, and M. P. Eriksen (1995). "Trends in Cigarette Smoking among U.S. Adolescents, 1974 through 1991." *American Journal of Public Health* 85(1):34–40.

Nelson, J. M., P. Q. Marson, and R. M. Roby (1989). "Mini-Study on the Availability of Cigarettes to Minors." *South Dakota Nurse* 32(2):17–18.

Neutel, C. I. and C. Buck (1971). "Effect of Smoking During Pregnancy on the Risk of Cancer in Children." *Journal of the National Cancer Institute* 47:59–63.

New York Times (1997). "A Top Health Group calls for Overhaul of Tobacco Settlement." *Star Tribune,* July 25, p. A4.

Nguyen, M. N., L. Potvin, L. Philibert, J. Oloughlin, J. Moisan, and G. Paradis (1995). "The Sale of Cigarettes to Miners and the Availability of Health Food in Rural, Urban, and Suburban Grocery Stores of Quebec" [in French]. *Canadian Journal of Public Health (Revue Canadienne de Sante Publique)* 86(6):377–79.

Nordgren, P. and M. Haglund (1995). "Introducing the Swedish Tobacco Control Act." Pp. 973–977 in *Tobacco and Health,* edited by Karen Slama. New York: Plenum.

Novotny, T. E. and M. B. Siegel (1996). "California's Tobacco Control Saga." *Health Affairs* 15(1):58–72.

Oberschall, A. (1973). *Social Conflicts and Social Movements.* Englewood Cliffs, NJ: Prentice Hall.

Ockene, J. K. (1987). "Smoking Intervention: The Expanding Role of the Physician." *American Journal of Public Health* 77(7):782–83.

Oegma, D. and B. Klandermans (1994). "Why Social Movement Sympathizers Don't Participate: Erosion and Nonconversion of Support." *American Sociological Review* 59:703–22.

Oliver, P. E. (1984). "'If You Don't Do It, Nobody Else Will': Active and Token Contributors to Local Collective Action." *American Sociological Review* 49:601–10.

OMB Watch (1998). *Nonprofit Advocacy Year in Review.* Washington, DC: OMB Watch. Available on-line at http://www.ombwatch.org/npadv/1998/1998-review.html.

Omram, A. R. (1971). "The Epidemiologic Transition: A Theory of the Epidemiology of Population Change." *Milbank Memorial Fund* 49:509–38.

Opp, K. Dieter and C. Ger (1993). "Dissident Groups, Personal Networks, and Spontaneous Cooperation: The East German Revolution of 1989." *American Sociological Review* 58:659–80.

Pallarito, K. (1993). "Can Lobbyists Represent Tobacco and Health?" *Modern Healthcare* (March):20.

Pawluch, D. (1983). Transitions in Pediatrics: A Segmental Analysis." *Social Problems* 30(4):448.

Pechacek, T. F., D. M. Murray, R. V. Luepker, M. B. Mittelmark, C. A. Johnson, and J. M. Shultz (1984). "Measurement of Adolescent Smoking Behavior: Rationale and Methods." *Journal of Behavioral Medicine* 7(1):123–40.

Perry, C. L., K. I. Klepp, A. Halper, K. G. Hawkins, and D. M. Murray (1986). "A Process Evaluation Study of Peer Leaders in Health Education." *Journal of School Health* 56(2):62–67.

Pertschuk, M. and A. Erickson (1987). *Smoke Fighting: A Smoking Control Movement Building Guide.* Atlanta, GA: American Cancer Society.

Pertschuk, M. and D. R. Shopland (Eds.) (1989). *Major Local Smoking Ordinances in the United States.* Bethesda, MD: National Cancer Institute, USDHHS.

Peterson, D. E., S. L. Zeger, P. L. Remington, and H. A. Anderson (1992). "The Effects of State Cigarette Tax Increases on Cigarette Sales, 1955 to 1988." *American Journal of Public Health* 82(1):94–96.

Peto, R., et al. (1994). *Mortality from Smoking in Developed Countries, 1950–2000: Indirect Estimates from National Vital Statistics.* New York: Oxford University Press.

Pham, H. (1996). "Policy Advocacy for Tobacco Control in Minnesota ASSIST Communities: A Survey of City Council Members." Unpublished MPH thesis, Community Health Education Program, Division of Epidemiology, School of Public Health, University of Minnesota, Minneapolis.

Phelps, D. (1996a). "Did Big Tobacco Target State?" *Star Tribune,* October 23, p. D1.

Phelps, D. (1996b). "State Files Memos Outlining Industry's Concern about State" *Star Tribune*, November 9, p. D1.

Phelps, D. (1996c). "Tobacco Depository." *Minneapolis Star-Tribune*, July 18, p. D1.

Pichardo, N. A. (1997). "New Social Movements: A Critical Review." *Annual Review of Sociology* 23:411–30.

Pierce, J. P., W. S. Choi, E. A. Gilpin, A. J. Farkas, and C. C. Berry (1998). "Tobacco Industry Promotion of Cigarettes and Adolescent Smoking." *JAMA* 279(7): 511–15.

Pierce, L., C. and A. C. Geller (1998). "Creating Statewide Tobacco Control Programs after Passage of a Tobacco Tax: Executive Summary." *CANCER* (suppl.) 83(12):2659–65.

Pierce, J. P. and E. Gilpin (1996). "How Long Will Today's New Adolescent Smoker Be Addicted to Cigarettes?" *American Journal of Public Health* 86(2):253–56.

Pierce, J. P., E. A. Gilpin, S. L. Emery, M. M. White, B. Rosbrook, C. C. Berry, and A. J. Farkas (1998). "Has the California Tobacco Control Program Reduced Smoking?" *JAMA* 280(10):893–99.

Pierce, J. P., T. G. Shanks, M. Pertschuk, E. Gilpin, D. Shopland, M. Johnson, and D. Bal. (1994). "Do Smoking Ordinances Protect Non-Smokers from Environmental Tobacco Smoke at Work?" *Tobacco Control* 3(1):15–20.

Pirkle, J. L., K. M. Flegal, J. T. Bernert, D. J. Brody, R. A. Etzel, and K. R. Maurer (1996). "Exposure of the U. S. Population to Environmental Tobacco Smoke: The Third National Health and Nutrition Examination Survey, 1988 to 1991." *JAMA* 275(16):1233–40.

Piven, F., F. and R. A. Cloward (1977). *Poor People's Movements: Why They Succeed, How They Fail*. New York: Pantheon.

Poland, B. D., S. M. Taylor, J. D. Eyles, and N. F. White (1995). "Qualitative Evaluation of Community Mobilization for Smoking Cessation: The Brantford COMMIT Intervention Trial." Pp. 843–847 in *Tobacco and Health*, edited by Karen Slama. New York: Plenum.

Political Communications, Inc. (1996). *Politics in Minnesota* 15 (March 26):5.

Porfiri, R. (1996). "No Butts about It—Massachusetts Enacts Cigarette Ingredients Disclosure Bill." *Tobacco on Trial* (September). Tobacco Products Liability Project, Northeastern University, Boston, MA. Available on-line at http://www.tobacco.neu.edu/tot/sept96/toc.htm.

Potter, J. D. (1999). "Colorectal Cancer: Molecules and Populations." *Journal of the National Cancer Institute* 91(11):916–32.

Potter, M. A. and B. B. Longest, Jr. (1994). "The Divergence of Federal and State Polices on the Charitable Tax Exemption of Nonprofit Hospitals." *Journal of Health Politics, Policy, and Law* 19(2):393–419.

Powell, W. W. and R. Friedkin (1987). "Organizational Change in Nonprofit Organizations." In W. W. Powell (ed.), *The Nonprofit Sector: A Research Handbook*. New Haven: Yale University Press.

Price, J. H. and L. Oden (1999). "Reducing Firearm Injuries: the Role of Local Public Health Departments." *Public Health Reports* 114(6):533–39.

Proctor, R. N. (1995). *Cancer Wars*. New York: Basic Books.

Proctor, R. N. (1996). "The Anti-Tobacco Campaign of the Nazis: A Little Known

Aspect of Public Health in Germany, 1933–45." *British Medical Journal* 313: 1450–53.

Prummel, M.F. and Wiersinga, W.M. "Smoking and Risk of Graves' Disease." *JAMA* 269(4):479–82.

Putnam, R.D. (2000). *Bowling Alone: the Collapse and Revival of American Community.* New York: Simon and Schuster, 2000.

Rawding, N. and C. Brown (2000). "An Overview of the Nation's Health Departments." Pp. 13–22 in *Local Public Health Practice: Trends & Models,* edited by Glen P. Mays, C. Arden Miller, and Paul K. Halverson. Washington, DC: American Public Health Association.

Raza, M. W., S. D. Essery, R. A. Elton, D. M. Weir, A. Busuttil, and C. Blackwell (1999). "Exposure to Cigarette Smoke, a Major Risk Factor for Sudden Infant Death Syndrome: Effects of Cigarette Smoke on Inflammatory Responses to Viral Infection and Bacterial Toxins." *FEMS Immunology & Medical Microbiology* 25(1–2):145–54.

Rekart, J. (1993). *Public Funds, Private Provision: The Role of the Voluntary Sector.* Vancouver, British Columbia: University of British Columbia Press.

Reynolds, C. (1999). "The Fourth Largest Market in the World." *Tobacco Control* 8(1):89–91.

Richards, J. W., J. R. DiFranza, C. Fletcher, and P. M. Fischer (1995). "RJ Reynolds' 'Camel Cash': Another Way to Reach Kids." *Tobacco Control* 4(3):258–60.

Rimm, E. B., J. E. Manson, M. J. Stampfer, G. A. Colditz, W. C. Willett, B. Rosner, C. H. Hennekens, and F. E. Speizer (1993). "Cigarette Smoking and the Risk of Diabetes in Women." *American Journal of Public Health* 83(2):211–14.

Risse-Kappen, T. (Ed.) (1995). *Bringing Transnational Relations Back In: Non-State Actors, Domestic Structures, and International Institutions.* New York: Cambridge University Press.

Robert Wood Johnson Foundation (1993). *Smokeless States: Statewide Tobacco Prevention and Control Initiatives.* Princeton, NJ

Robert Wood Johnson Foundation (1996). *Media Resource Guide on Tobacco.* Princeton, NJ: Author.

Robertson, Tatsha (1997). "State Will Stomp Out Cigarettes Inside and Outside Prison Walls." *Star Tribune,* February 6, p. A1.

Roeseler, A., A. Capra, and V. Quinn (1994). "A Special Campaign to Generate Support for State Legislation to Decrease Youth Access to Tobacco." Paper presented at the Annual Meeting of the American Public Health Association, Washington, DC, November 2.

Rogers, T., B. Howard-Pitney, E. D. Feighery, D. G. Altman, J. M. Endres, and A. G. Roeseler (1993). "Characteristics and Participant Perceptions of Tobacco Control Coalitions in California." *Health Education Research* 8(3):345–57.

Rosen, M. P., A. J. Greenfield, T. G. Walker, P. Grant, J. Dubrow, M. A. Bettmann, L. E. Fried, and I. Goldstein (1991). "Cigarette Smoking: an Independent Risk Factor for Atherosclerosis in the Hypogastric-Cavernous Arterial Bed of Men with Arteriogenic Impotence." *Journal of Urology* 145(4):759–63.

Rosenberg, G. N. (1991). *The Hollow Hope: Can Courts Bring About Social Change?* Chicago, IL: University of Chicago Press.

Rosencrans, K. (1997). "Carlson Cool to Anti-Tobacco Bill, Aides Say." *Saint Paul Pioneer Press,* May 22, p. 3D.

Rosenthal, N., M. Fingrutd, M. Ethier, R. Karant, and D. McDonald (1985). "Social Movements and Network Analysis: A Case Study of Nineteenth Century Women's Reform in New York State." *American Journal of Sociology* 90(5):1022–55.

Roski, J. and R. Jeddeloh (1997). "Tobacco Use Control: An Example of Community Health Improvement in Action." *Medical Journal of Allina* 6(1). [Minnetonka, Minnesota: Allina Health System.]

Roski, J. and R. Jeddeloh (1999). "Tobacco Control at Allina Health System: Extramural Strategies." *Medical Journal of Allina* 8(1). [Minnetonka, Minnesota: Allina Health System.]

Ross, W. S. (1987). *Crusade: The Official History of the American Cancer Society.* New York: Arbor House.

Rothman, J. (1970). "Three Models of Community Organization Practice." In *Strategies of Community Organization,* edited by F. M. Cox, J. L. Erlich, J. Rothman, and J. E. Tropman. Itasca: Peacock.

Ryan, J., C. Zwerling, and E. J. Orav (1992). "Occupational Risks Associated with Cigarette Smoking: A Prospective Study." *American Journal of Public Health* 82(1):29–32.

Rybak, D. C. and D. Phelps (1998). *Smoked: The Inside Story of the Minnesota Tobacco Trial.* Minneapolis, MN: MSP Books.

Salamon, L. M. (1995). *Partners in Public Service: Government-Nonprofit Relations in the Modern Welfare State.* Baltimore, MD: Johns Hopkins University Press.

Salamon, L. M. and H. K. Anheier (1996). *The Emerging Nonprofit Sector: An Overview.* Manchester, UK: Manchester University Press.

Samuels, B. E. and S. A. Glantz (1991). "The Politics of Local Tobacco Control." *JAMA* 266:2110–17.

Sandborn, W. J., W. J. Tremaine, K. P. Offord, G. M. Lawson, B. T. Petersen, K. P. Batts, I. T. Croghan, L. C. Dale, D. R. Schroeder, and R. D. Hurt (1997). "Transdermal Nicotine for Mildly to Moderately Active Ulcerative Colitis: A Randomized, Double-Blind, Placebo-Controlled Trial." *Annals of Internal Medicine* 126(5):364–71.

Sandell, S. D. (1996). "'Garbage Face': A Managed Care Organisation's Response to Tobacco Use." *Tobacco Control* 5(4):259–61.

Sandell, S. D. (1998). "Using Multiple Interventions to Make an Impact in the Community" *Tobacco Control* 7(suppl.):S31.

Sanders, D., R. Peveler, D. Mant, and G. Fowler (1993). "Predictors of successful smoking cessation following advice from nurses in general practice." *Addiction* 88(12):1699–705.

Sandok, M. K. (1992). "Lobbyists' Spending Is Up 36.2 Percent in Minnesota." *Star Tribune,* October 2, p. 5B.

Schauffler, H. H. and T. Rodriguez (1994). "Availability and Utilization of Health Promotion Programs and Satisfaction with Health Plan." *Medical Care* 32(12): 1182–96.

Schauffler, H. H. and T. Rodriguez (1996). "Exercising Purchasing Power for Preventive Care." *Health Affairs* 15(1):73–85.

Schelling, T. C. (1992). "Addictive Drugs: The Cigarette Experience." *Science* 255(January 24):430–33.

Schlesinger, M. and B. Gray (1998). "A Broader Vision for Managed Care. Part 1: Measuring the Benefit to Communities." *Health Affairs* 17(3):152–67.

Schlesinger, M., B. Gray, and E. Bradley (1996). "Charity and Community: the Role of Nonprofit Ownership in a Managed Health Care System." *Journal of Health Politics, Policy, and Law* 21(4):697–751.

Schmid, T. L., M. Pratt, and E. Howze (1995). "Policy as Intervention: Environmental and Policy Approaches to the Prevention of Cardiovascular Disease." *American Journal of Public Health* 85(9):1207–11.

Schoenbaum, M. (1997). "Do Smokers Understand the Mortality Effects of Smoking? Evidence from the Health and Retirement Survey." *American Journal of Public Health* 87(5):755–59.

Schooler, C., E. Feighery, and J. A. Flora (1996). "Seventh Graders' Self-Reported Exposure to Cigarette Marketing and Its Relationship to Their Smoking Behavior." *American Journal of Public Health* 86(9):1216–21.

Schreck, R., L. A. Baker, G. Ballad, et al. (1950). "Tobacco Smoking as an Etiological Factor of Cancer." *Cancer Research* 1950(10):49–58.

Schumaker, P. D. (1978). "The Scope of Political Conflict and the Effectiveness of Constraints in Contemporary Urban Protest." *Sociological Quarterly* 19:168–84.

Schwartz, J. (1994). "Smoking Recast: From Sophistication to Sin." *Washington Post,* May 29, A1.

Schwarz, A. (1990). "Battle of the Brands: Kretek's Tar and Nicotine Levels Create a Clove Scented Controversy." *Far Eastern Economic Review* 19(April):32–33.

Scollo, M. and D. Sweanor (1999). "Cigarette Taxes." Letter to the editor, *Tobacco Control* 8(1):110–11.

Scovell, B. L. (1939). *A Brief History of the Minnesota Woman's Christian Temperance Union from its Organization, September 6, 1877 to 1939.* Saint Paul / Minneapolis: Bruce.

Secker-Walker, R. H., L. J. Solomon, B. S. Flynn, J. M. Skelly, S. S. Lepage, G. D. Goodwin, and P. B. Mead (1995). "Smoking Relapse Prevention Counseling During Prenatal and Early Postnatal Care." *American Journal of Preventive Medicine* 11(2):86–93.

Seddon, J. M., W. C. Willett, F. E. Speizer, and S. E. Hankinson (1996). "A Prospective Study of Cigarette Smoking and Age-Related Macular Degeneration in Women." *JAMA* 276(14):1141–46.

Sharfstein, J. M. and S. S. Sharfstein (1994). "Campaign Contributions from the American Medical Political Action Committee to Members of Congress—For or Against the Public Health." *New England Journal of Medicine* 330(1):32–37.

Shelton, D. M., M. H. Alciati, M. M. Chang, J. A. Fishman, L. A. Fues, J. Michaels, R. J. Bazile, J. C. Bridgers, Jr., J. L. Rosenthal, L. Kutty, and M. P. Eriksen (1995). "State Laws on Tobacco Control—United States, 1995." *Morbidity and Mortality Weekly Report* 44(SS-6):1–28.

Shiffman, S. M., K. M. Mason, and J. E. Henningfield (1998). "Tobacco Dependence Treatments: Review and Prospectus." *Annual Review of Public Health* 19:335–58.

Shopland, D. R. (1993). "Smoking Control in the 1990s: A National Cancer Institute Model for Change." *American Journal of Public Health* 83(9):1208–10.

Shultz, J. M. (1985). *Smoking-Attributable Mortality, Morbidity, and Economic Costs:*

Methodology and Guide to Computer Software, Version 1. Minneapolis: Center for Nonsmoking and Health, Minnesota Department of Health.

Shultz, J. M., M. E. Moen, T. F. Pechacek, K. C. Harty, M. A. Skubic, S. W. Gust, and A. G. Dean (1986). "The Minnesota Plan for Nonsmoking and Health: The Legislative Experience." *Journal of Public Health Policy* 7(3):300–13.

Sicherman, A. L. (1997). "Beleaguered Smokers' Habitat Vanishing." *Star Tribune,* January 6, p. E-1.

Siegel, M., J. Carol, J. Jordan, R. Hobart, S. Schoenmarklin, F. DuMelle, and P. Fisher (1997). "Preemption in Tobacco Control: Review of an Emerging Public Health Problem." *JAMA* 278(10):858–63.

Silva Goldfarb, L. M. d. C. e., T. M. Cavalcante, T. P. Feitosa, and V. d. C.e . Silva (1995). "Network Information on Tobacco Control Actions." Pp. 875–78 in Karen Slama (ed.), *Tobacco and Health.* New York: Plenum.

Simpson, D. (1995). "North Carolina: Trojan Horse Defends Health." *Tobacco Control* 4(2):122–23.

Skolnick, A. A. (1995). "Cancer Converts Tobacco Lobbyist: Victor L. Crawford Goes On the Record." *JAMA* 274(3):199–202.

Slovut, G. (1991). "Minnesota Wins Grant to Lower Smoking Rate for Women, Minorities." *Minneapolis Star Tribune,* October 5, p. 1B.

Slovut, G. (1997). "Doctors Group Asks That State Ban Smoking at Day-Care Centers." *Star Tribune,* September 17, p. 3B.

Smith, J. G., C. Chatfield, and R. Pagnucco (1997). *Transnational Social Movements and Global Politics: Solidarity Beyond the State.* Syracuse, NY: Syracuse University Press.

Smith, M. D., W. F. McGhan, and G. Lauger (1995). "Pharmacist Counseling and Outcomes of Smoking Cessation." *American Pharmacy* NS35(8):20–32.

Smith, S., R. and M. Lipsky (1993). *Nonprofits for Hire: the Welfare State in the Age of Contracting.* Cambridge, MA: Harvard University Press.

Smith, W. S. (2000). "Washington's Costly Cuba Policy." *Nation,* July 3, 19–21.

Snow, D. A. and R. D. Benford (1992). "Master Frames and Cycles of Protest." Pp. 133–55 in *Frontiers in Social Movement Theory,* edited by Aldon D. Morris and Carol McClurg Mueller. New Haven, CT: Yale University Press.

Snow, D. A., E. B. Rochford, Jr., S. K. Worden, and R. D. Benford (1986). "Frame Alignment Processes, Micromobilization, and Movement Participation." *American Sociological Review* 45(5):787–801.

Snow, D. A., L. A. Zurcher, Jr., and S. Ekland-Olson (1980). "Social Networks and Social Movements: A Microstructural Approach to Differential Recruitment." *American Sociological Review* 45:787–801.

Sobel, R. (1978). *They Satisfy: The Cigarette in American Life.* Garden City, NY: Anchor.

Staggenborg, S. (1986). "Coalition Work in the Pro-Choice Movement: Organizational and Environmental Opportunities and Obstacles." *Social Problems* 33(5):374–90.

Starr, P. (1976). "The Undelivered Health System." *Public Interest* 42(Winter):66–85.

Starr, P. and E. Immergut (1987). "Health Care and the Boundaries of Politics." Pp. 221–54 in *Changing Boundaries of the Political: Essays on the Evolving Balance between the State and Society, Public and Private in Europe,* edited by Charles S. Maier. New York: Cambridge University Press.

State of Minnesota Office of the Secretary of State. 1991. *The Minnesota Legislative Manual 1991–1992.* Saint Paul, MN: Office of the Secretary of State.

Stebbins, K. R. (1991). "Tobacco, Politics, and Economics: Implications for Global Health." *Social Science and Medicine* 33(12):1317–26.

Steenland, K. 1992. "Passive Smoking and the Risk of Heart Disease." *Journal of the American Medical Association* 267(1):94–99.

Stillman, F., A. Hartman, B. Graubard, E. Gilpin, D. Chavis, J. Garcia, L. Ming Wun, W. Lynn, and M. Manley (1999). "The American Stop Smoking Intervention Study: Conceptual Framework and Evaluation Design." *Evaluation Review* 23(3):259–80.

Stjernfeldt, M., K. Berglund, J. Lindsten, and J. Ludvigsson (1986). "Maternal Smoking During Pregnancy and Risk of Childhood Cancer." *Lancet* 1:1350–52.

Stodghill, R., II (1996). "What's a Ton of Prevention Worth?" *Business Week,* October 18, Pp. 162–163.

Stone, M. M. (1989). "Planning as Strategy in Nonprofit Organizations: An Exploratory Study." *Nonprofit and Voluntary Sector Quarterly* 18:297–318.

Strachan, D. P, M. J. Jarvis, and C. Feyerabend (1989). "Passive Smoking, Salivary Cotinine Concentrations, and Middle Ear Effusion in 7 Year Old Children." *British Medical Journal* 298:1549–52.

Strang, D. (1995). "Health Maintenance Organizations." Pp. 163–182 in *Organizations in Industry: Strategy, Structure, and Selection,* edited by Glenn R. Carroll, and Michael T. Hannan. New York: Oxford University Press.

Sumner, W., II, and D. G. Dillman II (1995). "A Fist Full of Coupons: Cigarette Continuity Programmes." *Tobacco Control* 4(3):245–52.

Susser, M. (1985). "Epidemiology in the United States after World War II: The Evolution of Technique." *Epidemiologic Reviews* 7:147–77.

Sylvester, K. (1989). "The Tobacco Industry Will Walk a Mile to Stop an Anti-Smoking Law." *Governing* (May):34–40.

Tager, I. B., M. R. Segal, A. Munoz, S. T. Weiss, and F. E. Speizer (1987). "The Effect of Maternal Cigarette Smoking on the Pulmonary Function of Children and Adolescents." *American Review of Respiratory Disease* 136:1366–70.

Talbot, B. (1992). "Adolescent Smokers' Rights Laws." *Tobacco Control* 1:294–95.

Tarrow, S. (1994). *Power in Movement: Social Movements, Collective Action, and Mass Politics in the Modern State.* New York: Cambridge University Press.

Tate, C. 1999. *Cigarette Wars: The Triumph of "the Little White Slaver".* New York: Oxford University Press.

"Teens Buy Cigarettes Easiest in Discount Stores, Sting Finds" (1996). *Star Tribune,* October 25, p. A-4.

Terris, M. 1999. "The Development and Prevention of Cardiovascular Disease Risk Factors: Socioenvironmental Influences." *Preventive Medicine* 29(6 pt 2):S11-17.

Thompson, B., L. Wallack, E. Lichtenstein, and T. Pechacek (1991). "Principles of Community Organization and Partnership for Smoking Cessation in the Community Intervention Trial for Smoking Cessation (COMMIT)." *International Quarterly of Community Health Education* 11(3):187–203.

Thompson, R. S., S. H. Taplin, T. A. McAfee, M. T. Mandelson, and A. E. Smith (1995). "Primary and Secondary Prevention Services in Clinical Practice:

Twenty Years' Experience in Development, Implementation, and Evaluation." *JAMA* 273(14):1130–35.

Thomson, B. and W. L. Toffler (1990). "The Illegal Sale of Cigarettes to Minors in Oregon." *Journal of Family Practice* 31(2):206–2.

Tilly, C. (1978). *From Mobilization to Revolution.* Reading, PA: Addison Wesley.

Tobacco Institute (1996). *The Tax Burden on Tobacco—Historical Compilation,* Volume 31. Washington, DC: Author.

Tobacco Institute (1997). *Tobacco Industry Profile 1997.* Washington, DC: Author.

Tobacco Products Liability Project (2000). "Engle Verdict Unlikely to Be Reversed on Appeal." Engle Press Release, July 14, Tobacco Products Liability Project, Northeastern University. Available on-line at http://www.tobacco.neu.edu/PR/ENGLEVICTORY2000.htm.

Tobacco Working Group of the National Association of Attorneys General (1993). *Fast Food, Growing Children, and Passive Smoke: A Dangerous Menu.* Saint Paul: Minnesota Attorney General's Office.

Touraine, A. (1981). *The Voice and the Eye: An Analysis of Social Movements.* Cambridge, MA: Cambridge University Press.

Traynor, M. P. and S. A. Glantz (1996). "California's Tobacco Tax Initiative: The Development, and Passage of Proposition 99." *Journal of Health Politics, Policy, and Law* 21(3):543–85.

Troyer, R. J. (1989). "The Surprising Resurgence of the Smoking Problem." Pp. 159–176 in *Images of Issues: Typifying Contemporary Social Problems,* edited by Joel Best. Hawthorne, NY: Aldine de Gruyter.

Troyer, R. J. and G. E. Markle (1983). *Cigarettes: The Battle Over Smoking.* New Brunswick, NJ: Rutgers University Press.

Turner, R. and L. Killian (1972). *Collective Behavior.* Englewood Cliffs, NJ: Prentice Hall.

Turner-Bowker, D. and W. L. Hamilton. 2000. "Cigarette Advertising Expenditures Before and After the Master Settlement Agreement: Preliminary Findings." Boston: Massachusetts Department of Public Health. Available on-line at: http://www.state.ma.us/dph/mtcp/report/mag.htm.

U.S. Department of Agriculture (1998). *Farm Cash Receipts Data.* Washington, DC: Economic Research Service, USDA.

U.S. Department of Commerce (1998). *Regional Accounts Data, Gross State Product by Industry 1977–1996.* Washington, DC: Bureau of Economic Analysis, U.S. Department of Commerce.

U.S. Department of Justice (1979). *Youth Advocacy.* Program Announcement, October. Washington, DC: Office of Juvenile Justice and Delinquency Prevention, Law Enforcement Assistance Administration.

U.S. Department of Justice. 1996. *National Institute of Justice Journal* (No. 231, August). Washington, DC: National Institute of Justice.

U.S. Department of Justice. 1997. "FY 1996 Discretionary Grant Program Awards." NCJ163919. Washington, DC: Bureau of Justice Assistance.

U.S. General Accounting Office. 1982. *Summary of Survey on the Federal Sources of Funding for Nine Nonprofit Organizations* (GAO/AFMD-83-9). Washington, DC: Author.

United States Fire Administration (1999). *Fire in the United States: 1987–1996* (11th edition). Emmitsburg, MD: Federal Emergency Management Agency.

USDHEW (1964). *Smoking and Health: Report of the Advisory Committee of the Surgeon General of the Public Health Service.* Princeton, NJ: Von Nostrand.

USDHHS (1983). *The Health Consequences of Smoking—Cardiovascular Disease: A Report of the Surgeon General.* Washington, DC: US Government Printing Office.

USDHHS (1984). *The Health Consequences of Smoking—Chronic Obstructive Lung Disease: A Report of the Surgeon General.* Washington, DC: U.S. Government Printing Office.

USDHHS (1986). *The Health Consequences of Involuntary Smoking: A Report of the Surgeon General.* Washington, DC: US Government Printing Office.

USDHHS (1989). *Reducing the Health Consequences of Smoking: 25 Years of Progress.* Washington, DC: Author.

USDHHS (1990). *The Health Benefits of Smoking Cessation.* Washington, DC: Author.

USDHHS (1991). *Strategies to Control Tobacco Use in the United States.* Bethesda, MD: National Cancer Institute.

USDHHS (1992). *Smokeless Tobacco or Health: an International Perspective.* Bethesda, MD: National Cancer Institute.

USDHHS (1993a). "Substance Abuse Prevention and Treatment Block Grants: Sale or Distribution of Tobacco Products to Individuals Under 18 Years of Age" (45 CFR Pt. 96) *Federal Register* 58(164):45156–74.

USDHHS (1993b). "Second Report of the Expert Panel on Detection, Evaluation, and Treatment of High Blood Cholesterol in Adults" (NIH publication no. 93–3095). Rockville, MD: National Institutes of Health.

USDHHS (1993c). *Restrictions on Lobbying and Public Policy Advocacy by Government Contractors: The ASSIST Contract.* Bethesda, MD: Division of Cancer Prevention and Control, National Cancer Institute.

USDHHS (1994). *Preventing Tobacco Use Among Young People: A Report of the Surgeon General.* Atlanta, GA: Public Health Service, CDC, National Center for Chronic Disease Prevention and Health Promotion, Office on Smoking and Health.

USDHHS (1996). "Regulations Restricting the Sale and Distribution of Cigarettes and Smokeless Tobacco to Protect Children and Adolescents; Final Rule." Food and Drug Administration, 21 CFR Parts 801, et al.

USDHHS (1998a). *Tobacco Use Among U.S. Racial/Ethnic Minority Groups—African Americans, American Indians, and Alaska Natives, Asian Americans, and Pacific Islanders, and Hispanics: A Report of the Surgeon General.* Atlanta, GA: CDC, Office on Smoking and Health.

USDHHS (1998b). *Health, United States, 1998 with Socioeconomic Status and Health Chartbook.* Hyattsville, MD: National Center for Health Statistics.

USDHHS (1999). " Summary of Findings from the 1998 National Household Survey on Drug Abuse." Rockville, MD: Office of Applied Studies, Substance Abuse, and Mental Health Services Administration.

USDHHS (2000). *Reducing Tobacco Use: A Report of the Surgeon General.* Atlanta, GA: Centers for Disease Control and Prevention, National Center for Chronic Disease Prevention and Health Promotion, Office on Smoking and Health.

Veal, Y. S. (1996). "The NMA's Advocacy Against Smoking." *Journal of the National Medical Association* 88(2):75–76.

Viscusi, W. K. (1992). *Smoking: Making the Risky Decision.* New York: Oxford University Press.

Wagner, S. (1971). *Cigarette Country: Tobacco in American History and Politics.* New York: Praeger.

Wakefield, M., J. Carrangis, D. Wilson, and C. Reynolds (1992). "Illegal Cigarette Sales to Children in South Australia." *Tobacco Control* 1:114–17.

Walker, J. (1983). "The Origins and Maintenance of Interest Groups in America." *American Political Science Review* 77:390–406.

Walker, J. L. (1991). *Mobilizing Interest Groups in America: Patrons, Professions, and Social Movements.* Ann Arbor: University of Michigan Press.

Walker, R. B. (1980). "Medical Aspects of Tobacco Smoking and the Anti-Tobacco Movement in Britain in the Nineteenth Century." *Medical History* 24:391–402.

Wallack, L. and R. Sciandra (1991). "Media Advocacy and Public Education in the Community Intervention Trial to Reduce Heavy Smoking (COMMIT)." *International Quarterly of Community Health Education* 11(3):205–22.

Ware, J. H. and T. Fischer (1984). "Passive Smoking, Gas Cooking, and Respiratory Health of Children Living in Six Cities." *American Review of Respiratory Disease* 129:366–74.

Warner, K. E. (1977). "The Effects of the Anti-Smoking Campaign on Cigarette Consumption." *American Journal of Public Health* 67:645–50.

Warner, K. E. (1981). "Cigarette Smoking in the 1970's: The Impact of the Anti-smoking Campaign on Consumption." *Science* 211:729–31.

Warner, K. E. (1989). "Effects of the Antismoking Campaign: An Update." *American Journal of Public Health* 79:144–51.

Warner, K. E. (1993). "The Economics of Tobacco." Pp. 46–58 in *Nicotine Addiction: Principles and Management,* edited by C. Tracy Orleans and John Slade. New York and Oxford: Oxford University Press.

Warner, K. E. (1998). "Smoking Out the Incentives for Tobacco Control in Managed Care Settings." *Tobacco Control* 7(suppl):S50–S54.

Warner, K. E. and G. A. Fulton (1995). "Importance of Tobacco to a Country's Economy: An Appraisal of the Tobacco Industry's Economic Argument." *Tobacco Control* 4:180–83.

Warner, K. E., G. A. Fulton, P. Nicolas, and D. R. Grimes (1996). "Employment Implications of Declining Tobacco Product Sales for the Regional Economies of the United States." *JAMA* 275(16):1241–46.

Warner, K. E., T. A. Hodgson, and C. E. Carroll (1999). "Medical Costs of Smoking in the United States: Estimates, their Validity, and their Implications." *Tobacco Control* 8(3):290–300.

Wasserman, J. (1992). "How Effective Are Excise Tax Increases in Reducing Cigarette Smoking?" *American Journal of Public Health* 82(1):19–20.

Wasserman, J., W. G. Manning, J. P. Newhouse, and J. D. Winkler (1991). "The Effects of Excise Taxes and Regulations on Cigarette Smoking." *Journal of Health Economics* 10:43–64.

Weinstein, N. D. (1998). "Accuracy of Smokers' Risk Perceptions." *Annals of Behavioral Medicine* 20(2):135–40.

Welch, C. E. (Ed.) (1996). *State Legislated Actions on Tobacco Issues.* Washington, DC:

American Lung Association, American Heart Association, American Cancer Society.

Wells, A. J. (1988). "An Estimate of Adult Mortality in the United States from Passive Smoking." *Environment International* 14(3):249–65.

Wells, A. J. (1994). "Passive Smoking as a Cause of Heart Disease." *Journal of the American College of Cardiology* 24(2):546–54.

Wetter, D. W. and T. B. Young (1994). "The Relation between Cigarette Smoking and Sleep Disturbance." *Preventive Medicine* 23(3):328–34.

Whereatt, R. (1997). "Tobacco Regulations Clear Hurdles They Haven't Before." *Star Tribune*, February 9, p. B-3.

White, A. (1999). "Senegal: Birth of a New Tobacco Control Group." *Tobacco Control* 8(1):16–17.

Will, G. F. (1996). "Dole Bit Off More Than He Could Chew on Tobacco." *Minneapolis Star Tribune*, July 10, p. A-11.

Willatt, D. J. (1986). "Children's Sore Throats Related to Parental Smoking." *Clinical Otolaryngology* 11:317–21.

Williams, J. (1996). "Smokers Are Now a Fixture in the Urban Streetscape." *Star Tribune*, February 15, p. A-27.

Winegar, K. (1993). "Smoke-Free Office Buildings Force Smokers to Take Their Habits to Sidewalks, Doorways." *Star Tribune*, June 24, p. 1-E.

Winnett, L. B. (1998). "Constructing Violence as a Public Health Problem." *Public Health Reports* 113:498–507.

Wolch, J. R. (1990). *The Shadow State: Government and Voluntary Sector in Transition*. New York: Foundation Center.

Wolch, J. R. and E. M. Rocha (1993). "Planning Responses to Voluntary Sector Crises." *Nonprofit Management and Leadership* 3(4):377–95.

Wolfson, M. (1995a). "The Legislative Impact of Social Movement Organizations: The Anti-Drunken Driving Movement and the 21-Year-Old Drinking Age." *Social Science Quarterly* 76(2):311–27.

Wolfson, M. (1995b). "Organization, Grievances, Professional Identity, and Social Movement Participation: Tobacco Control in Minnesota." Paper presented at the Annual Meeting of the American Sociological Association, Washington, DC, August.

Wolfson, M. (1997). "Nonprofit Advocacy Organizations and the State: Tobacco Control in the United States." Final Report to the Nonprofit Sector Research Fund of the Aspen Institute, July.

Wolfson, M. and M. Hourigan (1997). "Unintended Consequences and Professional Ethics: Criminalization of Alcohol and Tobacco Use by Youth and Young Adults." *Addiction* 92(9):1159–64.

Wolfson, M., M. Hourigan, and T. Johnson (1998). "Managed Care, Population Health, and Public Health." *Research in the Sociology of Health Care* 15:217–31.

Wolfson, M., J. Forster, A. Sidebottom, P. Hannan, D. Stewart, and L. Brodsky. "Local Ordinances Regulating Youth Access to Tobacco: Results of a National Survey." Presented at the Annual Meeting of the American Public Health Association, Indianapolis, IN, November 1997.

Wolinsky, H. and T. Brune (1994). *The Serpent on the Staff: The Unhealthy Politics of the American Medical Association*. New York: G. P. Putnam's Sons.

Working Group of State Attorneys General (1994). *No Sale: Youth, Tobacco, and Responsible Retailing*.

World Health Organization (1997). "Tobacco or Health: a Global Status Report." Geneva: Author.

World Health Organization (2000a). *The World Health Report 2000: Health Systems: Improving Performance*. Geneva: Office of Publications, World Health Organization.

World Health Organization (2000b). *Tobacco Company Strategies to Undermine Tobacco Control Activities at the World Health Organization*. Report of the Committee of Experts on Tobacco Industry Documents. Geneva: Author.

Wuthnow, R. (Ed.) (1991). *Between States and Markets: The Voluntary Sector in Comparative Perspective*. Princeton, NJ: Princeton University Press.

Wymore, K. S. (1991). "Supply Restriction Approaches to Cigarette Smoking among Minors in Minnesota." Unpublished master's thesis, Hubert H. Humphrey Institute of Public Affairs, University of Minnesota, Minneapolis.

Wynder, E. L. and E. A. Graham (1950). "Tobacco Smoking as a Possible Etiological Factor in Bronchogenic Carcinoma." *JAMA* 143:329–36.

Yach, D. and D. Bettcher (2000). "Globalisation of Tobacco Industry Influence and New Global Responses." *Tobacco Control* 9(2):206–16.

Zakocs, R. C., J. L. Earp, and C. W. Runyan (2000). "U.S. Gun Control Movement at the State Level." Unpublished paper, Department of Health Behavior and Health Education, School of Public Health, University of North Carolina at Chapel Hill.

Zald, M. N. and R. Ash (1966). "Social Movement Organizations: Growth, Decay, and Change." *Social Forces* 44:327–41.

Zenzes, M. T., P. Wang, and R. F. Casper (1995). "Cigarette Smoking May Affect Meiotic Maturation of Human Oocytes." *Human Reproduction* 10(12):3213–17.

Zieve, A. M. and A. B. Morrison (1996). *Comments of Public Citizen, Inc. Regarding the FDA's Proposal to Regulate the Sale and Promotion of Tobacco Products to Minors*. Washington, DC: Public Citizen.

Index

Access to tobacco, children's, 33–36,
    143, 159, 162–169
Accommodation of smokers theme,
    152
ACLU, 157
ACS (*see* American Cancer Society)
ACT, 215
Action on Smoking and Health (ASH),
    1, 22, 32, 45–46
Advertising (*see* Marketing of tobacco)
Advisory Committee on Tobacco Pol-
    icy and Public Health, 210
Advocacy Institute, 48, 86
Aguinaga, S., 200–201
AHA (*see* American Heart Association)
ALA (*see* American Lung Association)
Allina (HMO), 113, 117, 185–186
AMA, 1, 85–86, 103–104
American Cancer Society (ACS)
   ASSIST program and, 84–87
   founding of, 85
   Kennedy administration and, 22, 84
   Minnesota, 86–92
   Public Issues Committee of, 87–89
   publications by, 86
   Quick Response Team and, 87–89
   role of, in Tobacco Control Move-
     ment, 85–92, 185
   Smoke-Free Coalition and, 87–88, 91
American Center on Global Health
    and Tobacco (ACT), 215
American Civil Liberties Union
    (ACLU), 157
American Heart Association (AHA)
   Kennedy administration and, 22, 84
   publication of, 97
   role of, in Tobacco Control Move-
     ment, 97–98, 185

American Lung Association (ALA)
   emergence of Association of Non-
     smokers-Minnesota and, 185
   Kennedy administration and, 22, 84
   Minnesota, 93–96
   role of, in Tobacco Control Move-
     ment, 92–96, 185
American Medical Association (AMA),
    1, 85–86, 103–104
American Public Health Association
    (APHA), 22, 84, 104
American Stop Smoking Intervention
    Study (*see* ASSIST program)
American Tuberculosis Association (*see*
    American Lung Association
    [ALA])
Americans for Nonsmokers Rights
    (ANR), 1, 46–47
ANSR (*see* Association of Nonsmokers-
    Minnesota)
Antinuclear power movements, 8
APHA, 22, 84, 104
ASH, 1, 22, 32, 45–46
Ash, R., 3
ASSIST program
   American Cancer Society and, 84–87
   Community Action Book (handbook),
     134
   contract awards by, 123–124, 128–
     130, 202
   federal funding through, 123–124,
     128–130, 187, 213
   federal involvement in tobacco con-
     trol and, 123–124
   goals of, 98
   Minnesota Department of Health
     and, 13, 87, 131–139, 141, 190,
     205